Violence

Against Women and Children

Violence

Against Women and Children

MAPPING THE TERRAIN

Edited by
Jacquelyn W. White,
Mary P. Koss, and
Alan E. Kazdin

Volume 1

American Psychological Association • Washington, DC

Published by
American Psychological Association
750 First Street, NE
Washington, DC 20002
www.apa.org

To order
APA Order Department
P.O. Box 92984
Washington, DC 20090-2984
Tel: (800) 374-2721; Direct: (202) 336-5510
Fax: (202) 336-5502; TDD/TTY: (202) 336-6123
Online: www.apa.org/pubs/books
E-mail: order@apa.org

In the U.K., Europe, Africa, and the Middle East, copies may be ordered from
American Psychological Association
3 Henrietta Street
Covent Garden, London
WC2E 8LU England

Typeset in Goudy by Circle Graphics, Inc., Columbia, MD

Printer: Maple-Vail Book Manufacturing Group, York, PA
Cover Designer: Naylor Design, Washington, DC
Cover Art: *All the Little Children*, 1990, oil paints and Cray-Pas, by Dori Jalazo

The opinions and statements published are the responsibility of the authors, and such opinions and statements do not necessarily represent the policies of the American Psychological Association.

Library of Congress Cataloging-in-Publication Data

Violence against women and children / edited by Jacquelyn W. White, Mary P. Koss, and Alan E. Kazdin. — 1st ed.
    p. cm.
Includes bibliographical references and index.
ISBN-13: 978-1-4338-0912-5
ISBN-10: 1-4338-0912-5
ISBN-13: 978-1-4338-0913-2 (e-book)
ISBN-10: 1-4338-0913-3 (e-book)
  1. Women—Violence against—United States. 2. Women—Violence against—United States—Prevention. 3. Children—Violence against—United States. 4. Children—Violence against—United States—Prevention. I. White, Jacquelyn W. II. Koss, Mary P. III. Kazdin, Alan E.

HV6250.4.W65V5216 2010
362.82'920973—dc22

2010023861

British Library Cataloguing-in-Publication Data

A CIP record is available from the British Library.

Printed in the United States of America
First Edition

CONTENTS

CONTRIBUTORS

Etiony Aldarondo, PhD, Dunspaugh-Dalton Community and Educational Well-Being Research Center, School of Education, University of Miami, Coral Gables, FL

Jeanne Alhusen, PhD candidate, CRNP, Johns Hopkins University School of Nursing, Baltimore, MD

Ileana Arias, PhD, Principal Deputy Director, Centers for Disease Control and Prevention, Atlanta, GA

Gia Barboza, PhD, JD, Assistant Professor, Department of African American Studies, Northwestern University, Boston, MA

Brian J. Biroscak, MS, MA, Yale University School of Medicine, New Haven, CT

Ernestine C. Briggs, PhD, Duke University School of Medicine, Durham, NC

Jacquelyn C. Campbell, PhD, RN, FAAN, Johns Hopkins University School of Nursing, Baltimore, MD

Michelle Castro-Fernandez, MSEd, PhD candidate, School of Education, University of Miami, Coral Gables, FL

Ann T. Chu, PhD, Department of Psychology, University of Denver, Denver, CO

Ann L. Coker, PhD, MPH, Center for Research on Violence Against Women and Department of Obstetrics and Gynecology, College of Medicine, University of Kentucky, Lexington

Anne P. DePrince, PhD, Department of Psychology, University of Denver, Denver, CO

Jessica Draughon, MSN, RN, Johns Hopkins University School of Nursing, Baltimore, MD

David Finkelhor, PhD, Crimes Against Children Research Center, University of New Hampshire, Durham

Diane R. Follingstad, PhD, Center for Research on Violence Against Women and Department of Psychiatry, College of Medicine, University of Kentucky, Lexington

Jennifer J. Freyd, PhD, Department of Psychology, University of Oregon, Eugene

Carol E. Jordan, MS, Center for Research on Violence Against Women, University of Kentucky, Lexington

Alan E. Kazdin, PhD, Yale University, New Haven, CT

Raymond A. Knight, PhD, Department of Psychology, Brandeis University, Waltham, MA

Mary P. Koss, PhD, University of Arizona, Tucson

Joan Kub, PhD, RN, Johns Hopkins University School of Nursing, Baltimore, MD

Ruby Lekwauwa, BS, Duke University School of Medicine, Durham, NC

Caroline Lippy, PhD candidate, Department of Psychology, Georgia State University, Atlanta

Rebecca J. Macy, PhD, School of Social Work, University of North Carolina at Chapel Hill

Sandra L. Martin, PhD, Department of Maternal and Child Health, Gillings School of Global Public Health, University of North Carolina at Chapel Hill

Cynthia J. Najdowski, MA, Department of Psychology, University of Illinois at Chicago

Sarah Ostrowski, PhD, Department of Psychology, Western Kentucky University, Bowling Green

Julia L. Perilla, PhD, Department of Psychology, Georgia State University, Atlanta

Annarheen S. Pineda, MA, Department of Psychology, University of Denver, Denver, CO

Lori Ann Post, PhD, Yale University School of Medicine, New Haven, CT

Alvina Rosales, MA, Department of Psychology, Georgia State University, Atlanta

Josephine V. Serrata, PhD candidate, Department of Psychology, Georgia State University, Atlanta

Judith Sims-Knight, PhD, Department of Psychology, University of Massachusetts–Dartmouth

Richard Thompson, PhD, Juvenile Protective Association, Chicago, IL

Sarah E. Ullman, PhD, Department of Criminology, Law, and Justice, University of Illinois at Chicago

Benita Walton-Moss, DNS, FNP-BC, Johns Hopkins University School of Nursing, Baltimore, MD

Jacquelyn W. White, PhD, University of North Carolina, Greensboro

Corrine M. Williams, ScD, Department of Obstetrics and Gynecology, College of Medicine, University of Kentucky, Lexington

David A. Wolfe, PhD, ABPP, Professor and RBC Chair in Children's Mental Health, CAMH Centre for Prevention Science and the University of Toronto, London, Ontario, Canada

Siobhan K. Young, MPH, Department of Maternal and Child Health, Gillings School of Global Public Health, University of North Carolina at Chapel Hill

FOREWORD

ILEANA ARIAS

Violence against women and children is a prevalent and costly public health problem in the United States. However, medical and social sciences have been able to garner unprecedented levels of the social and political will necessary to support research on the etiology and maintenance of violence against women and children to guide development of prevention and treatment programs and strategies. *Violence Against Women and Children* presents state-of-the-art theoretical and empirical perspectives on the response to violence against women and children. The two volumes, *Violence Against Women and Children, Volume 1: Mapping the Terrain* and *Violence Against Women and Children, Volume 2: Navigating Solutions*, document the tremendous health and economic burden to individuals, families, communities, and society, highlighting the huge disparities related to race, class, and other marginalized dimensions. Empirically based responses of various sectors—criminal justice, health care, mental health—are represented in this book, but, most important, *Violence Against Women and Children* issues a strong call for innovative, interdisciplinary approaches that aim for the primary prevention of violence against women and children, adopting the public health perspective.

Identifying and controlling factors that affect morbidity and mortality across the life span are the objectives of public health. Traditionally, public health practitioners and researchers have focused on infectious diseases in controlling morbidity and mortality. However, the relevance of infectious diseases has decreased over time while the relevance of chronic diseases has increased. Although not considered a traditional public health problem in the past, violence is a priority among public health problems because of its impact on morbidity and mortality, and because like smallpox and many other infectious diseases, it is a problem that can be understood and prevented through the application of epidemiological methods.

Traditionally, the functions of public health in the United States have included assessment of morbidity and mortality trends, causes, and prevention needs; assurance of implementation of legislative mandates and statutory responsibilities; policy development to support individual and community health efforts; and evaluation of effectiveness, accessibility, and quality of population-based health services. In the United States, federal, state, and local governments have had the lead responsibility for these functions because many public health functions require the exercise of authority and because the government is obligated to ensure that the public interest is served by any policy decisions. More recently, a "public health model" that moves beyond the traditional notion of public health as a function of government agencies has focused on assuring and providing individual-level services. This model describes a comprehensive approach to address significant public health problems, placing an increased emphasis on the development and dissemination of interventions at the community level and explicitly encouraging input from others outside the public sector and from multiple disciplines. Specifically, the public health approach begins with the definition and description of the problem and the determination of its scope. Empirical research is supported to identify risk and protective factors. These empirical data guide the development of prevention strategies and interventions. Finally, the public health model disseminates effective prevention strategies and interventions and supports widespread adoption and implementation.

Critical to the success of the public health approach is the inclusion of the various spheres of influence and control of the problem and responses to it. As documented by the work in these volumes, the socioecological model is key to developing and implementing what to do. Violence is a complex issue, and no single variable or sector alone is adequate to explain and prevent it. The socioecological model allows the integration of risk and protective factors from multiple domains of factors that influence violence. It includes and directs attention to variables at the individual, relationship, community, and societal levels, such as individual attitudes about violence, family environment, economic situation, and social policies. The model accommodates the complex interplay among the different levels of risk and protective factors and offers the possibility of a more robust and appropriate approach to prevention. Complexity is not limited to considerations of *what* to do to prevent; it is also central to considerations of *how* to effectively prevent. Traditionally, the focus of violence has been on changing individuals or individual attitudes and behavior through the use of individually focused interventions, such as psychological interventions, arrest and prosecution, or media campaigns. However, the socioecological model points to a wide spectrum of prevention ranging from personal-level change to policy-level change. Attempts to change individual attitudes and behavior may not aggregate to true population change. Likewise, broad contextual changes (e.g., policy change, systems change) are indispensible to support and sustain an individual behavioral change. In addition to changing and strengthening individual knowledge and skills to prevent violence against women and children, we need to create contextual changes by promoting community education, educating providers, fostering coalitions and networks to support change, changing organizational practices, and influencing policy and legislation.

We know through our experience in addressing other public health issues that prevention is possible. Violence prevention is broad and multifaceted, and it requires skills and approaches from many disciplines and areas of expertise. Capitalizing on the strengths of public health, we can prevent violence by promoting efforts to modify or eliminate the individual, relationship, community, and societal influences that result in perpetration, victimization, and bystander attitudes that allow violence to occur. Our efforts need to increasingly target general populations (universal efforts) and those at heightened risk (selected efforts) to ensure that the greatest number of people benefit from the prevention of violence. Advances in our science and attitudes about women, children, and violence suggest that it is time for ending violence against women and children to become a public health priority.

PREFACE

Less violence tops most lists of what would make a better world. Violence-related problems are preeminent on today's health and development agenda. Among the acknowledged realities about violence is the disproportionate amount experienced by women and children in their day-to-day lives at the hands of those who are expected to love and nurture them (Krug, Dahlberg, Mercy, Zwi, & Lozano, 2002).

Violence against women and children is an all-too-frequent outgrowth of historical patterns. Even today, most cultures, despite varying practices, embrace patterns of courtship, marriage, and child rearing that reinforce deeply entrenched traditions that support female and child deference to men and adults, respectively (Henson & Wilson, 2008).

Reducing violence against women and children has been a long-sought goal. Many agendas for reducing violence exist that were formulated on the basis of reviews of empirical research, such as the American Psychological Association report *No Safe Haven: Male Violence Against Women at Home, at Work, and in the Community* (Koss et al., 1994); the National Academy of Sciences volume *Understanding Violence Against Women* (Crowell & Burgess, 1996); the Centers for Disease Control and Prevention's *Injury Research*

Agenda, 2009–2018 (National Center for Injury Prevention and Control, 2009); and the World Health Organization's (2009) *Violence Prevention: The Evidence* (see also Burchart, Phinney, Check, & Villavecces, 2004; Krug et al., 2002; National Scientific Council on the Developing Child, 2007; Whitaker, Lutzker, & Shelley, 2005). Universally, these documents conclude that experiencing violence and abuse can have lifelong negative consequences for individuals, communities, nations/states, and the world and that violence is broadly significant across public health, development, and security policy planning. However, Koss and White (2008) observed that these antiviolence agendas typically are expressed in broad language. Analysis of them across time may suggest to the casual reader that little progress has been made because the same items have been included for almost 20 years. The lack of concise summaries of current science and analysis of the gaps and deficits in the evidence constitutes a significant challenge in formulating strategic agendas to reflect the scope of knowledge and its increasing sophistication.

The two volumes *Violence Against Women and Children, Volume 1: Mapping the Terrain* and *Violence Against Women and Children, Volume 2: Navigating Solutions* are part of an ambitious initiative by the American Psychological Association (APA) begun under the leadership of then–APA President Alan E. Kazdin in 2008. Additional activities, described below, helped shape the development of these volumes, and they will in turn serve as a valuable resource as the initiative grows. To begin, the Presidential Summit on Violence and Abuse in Relationships: Connecting Agendas and Forging New Directions was convened. The meeting demonstrated clearly that advocacy groups, nongovernmental organizations, and governmental agencies both nationally and globally have prioritized changing violence-supportive genderized norms and reducing violence, among other goals. As laudatory as these efforts are, however, they are occurring piecemeal. Splintered and self-contained groups have formed within research, practice, and policy communities. And even within these fenced yards, still smaller play areas are delineated where those trained in a single discipline gather together. Although it is true that many do similar work that only superficially appears different due to definitional and methodological preferences, it is not well shared in print because of narrow publication indexing systems. It is also true that disciplines perform services, such as medical or justice, that must remain separate systems but could improve their response through coordination.

To counteract nonproductive duplication of effort, reduced voice, lost potential for innovations stemming from cross-fertilization, and inadequate dissemination of current scholarship in accessible formats, the field is challenged to develop a multifaceted and coordinated set of activities that would at once bring together individuals working on critical issues of interpersonal violence and identify advances, commonalities, and opportunities for synergies. Essential to this work is the recognition of the interconnectedness of various types of interpersonal violence (e.g., child maltreatment, elder abuse, intimate partner violence, sexual assault), disciplines (e.g., criminal justice, public health, medicine, psychology, social work, sociology), and areas of focus (e.g., research, practice, policy, advocacy, services, survivor voices). The presidential summit stimulated a series of meetings that revealed the hunger in the field for a forum to meet, share perspectives and knowledge, forge alliances, build workforce capacity, and plan advocacy and policy initiatives to realize a national, multidisciplinary commitment to end interpersonal violence across the life span. Hence, the National Partnership to End Interpersonal Violence was born.

To foster information exchange, APA launched a new journal, *Psychology of Violence*. This journal was conceived to reflect the goals of the initiative that led to its creation by, for example, having research, practice, and policy sections rather than focusing exclusively on knowledge as it is defined within academic, research-oriented disciplines. The present volumes were also commissioned under the presidential initiative with the goal of providing an updated and sound scientific foundation communicated in an accessible format that would interest a broad group of readers. We envisioned the potential readership to include advocates, practitioners, funders, policymakers, and academics trained in a variety of disciplines, such as anthropology, criminology, cultural studies, economics, family studies, gender studies, law, media studies, medicine, nursing, policy, psychology, public health, sociology, theology, and victimology.

The editors' intent with these volumes was to depart from the traditional review format and avoid as much jargon as possible within the overarching goal of communicating usable scientific knowledge. The study of violence against women and children has evolved as independent specialties that focus on one point in the life span, an organizational evolution that fails to capture the reality that multiple forms of violence happen to the same people. Our admittedly imperfect solution to avoid recreating the same problems we have critiqued was to invite diverse contributors who represent the fields of epidemiology; maternal and child health; clinical, social, and community psychology; sociology; social work; and law. These eminent scholars provide a statement of what is known about prevalence, impact, sector response, and prevention of child abuse, domestic violence, and sexual violence. The authors took on the challenge to condense into short formats topics that have been the subject of encyclopedic edited volumes and to nevertheless acknowledge nuances and alternative viewpoints. They direct a spotlight on the lack of clarity regarding definitions, theories, and appropriate methodologies that characterizes work on violence aimed at women and children (Jordan, 2009). The contributors were asked to answer three seemingly simple questions:

- What do we know?
- How do we know it?
- What are the next steps?

Each chapter follows that organization. The editors' intent was to capture the careful study and accumulated knowledge of the recent past and to prod our experts to acknowledge the distance already covered before charting future directions. Because these volumes are focused on communicating science, we recognize that there are other important perspectives that are not represented, most particularly those of the women and children who live surrounded by violence. It is from them that workers across all the fields of violence draw their inspiration and perseverance.

The present volumes serve as a significant feature of the initiative because they archive expertise from many different areas. The volumes convey what experts have learned, what the gaps are, and priority areas of work. As a first, the integration of multiple disciplines and the culling of commonalities represent an important step for moving forward. We are grateful to the many who contributed to the volumes as well as the thinking behind them. The contributors, all eminent in their areas, agreed to come together to bring diverse areas into a common format. The volume editors also appreciate the collaborative and collegial working relationships that we developed with each other and with all the contributors. As we mulled over difficult issues and came to consensus, we are all the more committed to the collaborative process, and we believe that it is the best approach for addressing the complex and important issue of interpersonal violence. Finally, we acknowledge the support of our home institutions, the University of Arizona, the University of North Carolina at Greensboro, and Yale University, for giving us the opportunity to collaborate on this project.

REFERENCES

Burchart, A., Phinney, A., Check, P., & Villavecces, A. (2004). *Preventing violence: A guide to implementing the recommendations of the world report on violence and health*. Geneva, Switzerland: World Health Organization.

Crowell, N. A., & Burgess, A. W. (Eds.). (1996). *Understanding violence against women*. Washington, DC: National Academy Press. doi:10.1037/10204-000

Henson, C. B., & Wilson, S. M. (2008). *Families in a global context*. New York, NY: Routledge.

Jordan, C. E. (2009). Advancing the study of violence against women: Evolving research agendas into science. *Violence Against Women, 15*, 393–419. doi:10.1177/1077801208330692

Koss, M. P., Goodman, L. A., Browne, A., Fitzgerald, L. F., Keita, G. P., & Russo, N. F. (1994). *No safe haven: Male violence against women at home, at work, and in the community*. Washington, DC: American Psychological Association.

Koss, M. P., & White, J. W. (2008). National and global agendas on violence against women: Historical perspective and consensus. *American Journal of Orthopsychiatry, 78*, 386–393. doi:10.1037/a0014347

Krug, E. G., Dahlberg, L. L., Mercy, J. A., Zwi, A. B., & Lozano, R. (Eds.). (2002). *The world report on violence and health*. Geneva, Switzerland: World Health Organization.

National Center for Injury Prevention and Control. (2009). *CDC injury research agenda, 2009–2018*. Atlanta, GA: U.S. Department of Health and Human Services, Centers for Disease Control and Prevention.

National Scientific Council on the Developing Child. (2007). *The science of early childhood development: Closing the gap between what we know and what we do*. Cambridge, MA: Harvard University, Center on the Developing Child. Retrieved from http://www.developingchild.net

Whitaker, D. J., Lutzker, J. R., & Shelley, G. A. (2005). Child maltreatment prevention priorities at the Centers for Disease Control and Prevention. *Child Maltreatment, 10*, 245–259. doi:10.1177/1077559505274674

World Health Organization. (2009). *Violence prevention: The evidence*. Geneva, Switzerland: Author.

Violence

Against Women and Children

INTRODUCTION

JACQUELYN W. WHITE, MARY P. KOSS, AND ALAN E. KAZDIN

The magnitude of violence against women and children is alarming, and awareness of the problem is the first step toward prevention. People cannot stop something they cannot see or name. Once named, violence against women and children, in its various forms, is no longer socially and culturally invisible. Furthermore, identification of key modifiable risk and protective factors builds the foundation for scientifically sound primary prevention. Simultaneously, description and quantification of psychological, health, behavioral, and economic consequences contribute to design and implementation of best practices in secondary and tertiary prevention. Therefore, this book focuses on prevalence, risk factors for perpetration, vulnerability and protective factors, and impact, including psychological, reproductive, maternal and child health, behavioral, and economic consequences. Eminent scholars representing several disciplines summarize what is currently known about child abuse, sexual violence, and domestic violence broadly conceptualized. They identify consensus in findings, and where it does not exist, they delineate competing positions. They also address the importance of understanding methods used in research, gaps in knowledge, and priorities that emerge from their analyses. The identification of current methods and their strengths and weaknesses provides insight into how to improve definitions, assessment methods, theoretical models, and research methods. The chapters are selective, not comprehensive, reviews. Furthermore, certain forms of violence against women and children, such as teen dating violence and elder abuse, are only touched upon in the context of broader analyses.

TERMINOLOGY

We as editors chose the terms *child abuse and maltreatment, sexual violence,* and *domestic violence* to title each section, with some reluctance. Some contributors preferred to use different terms such as *child victimization and violence, sexual assault,* and *intimate partner violence,* each of which indicates a shift in emphasis. For example, sexual assault includes a spectrum of unwanted sex acts beginning with those that may lack overt violence. Domestic violence, in our formulation, covers a variety of behaviors, including physical, sexual, psychological, and economic abuse. Clearly, this broad definition necessitates some overlap in content with chapters on sexual violence. Nevertheless, omitting forced sex acts from our discussion of domestic violence would be at variance with reality. Subsuming all unwanted sex acts under the heading of domestic violence, however, would be just as problematic. Based on a Google search, the term *domestic violence* is far more frequently used than the terms *intimate partner violence, woman abuse,* or *partner abuse.* Similarly, child maltreatment is extremely broad, yet *child abuse* is the most frequently searched phrase. The various terms capture different elements and nuances, but the lack of standard terminology is one of the most evident obstacles in the field of violence against women and children. Neither we as editors nor the individual contributors undertook to recommend the best terms to use.

ATTENTION TO DIVERSITY

Chapters vary in coverage of intersections of ethnicity with violence and with marginalized populations, including lesbian, gay, bisexual, or transgender individuals and individuals with disabilities. This variability reflects in part the extent to which these interactions have been ignored in research studies, an oversight noted by several authors.

OVERVIEW OF *VIOLENCE AGAINST WOMEN AND CHILDREN, VOLUME 1: MAPPING THE TERRAIN*

The chapters in this volume make it abundantly clear that huge numbers of people are likely affected by intergenerational violence, that there is significant overlap between child maltreatment and domestic violence in families, and that sexual violence co-occurs with other forms of maltreatment and within domestic violence. Likewise, authors document the large number of people suffering from rape, the number of assaults pedophiles commit in their career, the number of batterers who serially assault their partners, and child and woman fatalities in the context of child abuse and domestic violence.

Volume 1 is organized into four sections: Child Abuse and Maltreatment, Sexual Violence, and Domestic Violence, each containing four chapters, and a conclusion. The first chapter in each section focuses on incidence and prevalence, whereas the second and third chapters in each section focus on risk and protective factors for perpetration and victimization, respectively. The fourth chapter in each section focuses on psychological, health, behavioral, and economic consequences.

The incidence and prevalence of child abuse, sexual violence, and domestic violence are quite high. In Chapter 1, David Finkelhor documents the prevalence of child victimization. He notes a disturbing pattern: For youths ages 12 to 17 years, aggravated assault occurs at twice the rate of the general population, and the rate for rape is threefold the adult rate. Not only are these findings distressing because they are likely underestimates due to underreporting, but they are also distressing when considered in comparison with the staggering rates of sexual, physical, and psychological violence reported in the adult population, as reported by Lori Ann Post and colleagues in Chapter 5 on sexual violence (rates of 11% to 30% depending on definition) and Julia Perilla and colleagues in Chapter 9 on domestic violence (rates of 4% to 75% depending on definition). These authors in each of these chapters tackle the thorny problems of definitions and data collection techniques. They make it clear that surveillance techniques and survey methods, in combination with operational definitions, dramatically affect what we "see" and "do not see." The challenges for mental health professionals and law enforcement, as well as researchers, are far-reaching.

Similar challenges are noted by the authors who reviewed the state of our knowledge with regard to risk and protective factors for perpetration. David A. Wolfe in Chapter 2 on child abuse, Ray Knight and Judith Sims-Knight in Chapter 6 on sexual violence, and Etiony Aldarondo and Michelle Castro-Fernandez in Chapter 10 on domestic violence embrace a levels-of-analysis approach, identifying factors at the individual, interpersonal, and sociocultural levels. Their cogent analyses make it clear that there are likely to be multiple pathways to the perpetration of various forms of violence against women and children. It is important to note that these factors are often interdependent.

A similar conclusion emerges from the reviews of risk and protective factors for victimization. One message that is clear from the review by Ann T. Chu and colleagues in Chapter 3 on child abuse, Sarah E. Ullman and

Cynthia J. Najdowski in Chapter 7 on sexual violence, and Jacquelyn C. Campbell and colleagues in Chapter 11 on domestic violence is that victims are never responsible for their victimization. Rather, a number of factors coalesce to render some individuals more vulnerable than others, with the ultimate cause being the perpetrators' actions. Unique to issues of child abuse are the roles that parents play, both as perpetrators and as governors of the recovery environments for maltreated children. This volume concludes with a chapter by the editors that culls what we know, what gaps exist in our knowledge, and what steps are needed next. In addition to recognizing the scope of the problem, this chapter notes the need for further work on definitions, approaches to assessment, and advances in methodological and analytic techniques that reflect the multileveled and complex phenomena under investigation.

In sum, the scope and the costs of violence against women and children are almost incalculable and span the breadth of human experience in the short term as well as long term. Costs can be seen psychologically, cognitively, behaviorally, socially, and in individual and societal economic costs. The remarkable similarities across forms of victimization are noteworthy. Most important is the repeated finding of the profound effects of early victimization on subsequent victimization as well as perpetration, and the resultant cumulative negative outcomes. Childhood victimization increases the risk of numerous negative consequences in adolescence, including teen dating violence, and these consequences in turn increase the likelihood of continued experiences of domestic violence. The chapters that follow highlight advances in knowledge in the specific areas, and from that knowledge emerge many commonalities to which we return at the end of both volumes. Lest the reader be left with a sense of hopelessness from the overwhelming scope of the problems identified in this volume, rest assured that each expert offers carefully thought-out plans and concrete steps to move ahead. All of the authors, like the readers of this volume, take their inspiration from the fact that our work is not abstract. Violence directly affects women and children; we sit with them, are both saddened and inspired, and move forward knowing that this topic is of utmost relevance to building a stronger, safer, and more sustainable human civilization.

I

CHILD ABUSE
AND MALTREATMENT

1

PREVALENCE OF CHILD VICTIMIZATION, ABUSE, CRIME, AND VIOLENCE EXPOSURE

DAVID FINKELHOR

Although the literature about the scope and nature of the problem of child victimization, abuse, crime, and violence exposure is large and growing, it is still far from satisfying the needs of policymakers, practitioners, and researchers. In this chapter, I examine and document the prevalence of the problem.

DEFINITIONAL MATTERS

The epidemiology of child victimization, abuse, crime, and violence exposure is muddled by terminology, making an accurate counting of the problem harder. For example, take three of the key terms used to define this field: *exposure to violence*, *child abuse*, and *child maltreatment*. Unfortunately, none of these terms accurately and distinctively covers the domain that professionals are actually concerned about. For example, *violence* (as in exposure to violence) rigorously defined means acts of physical force intended to cause pain. Yet many people concerned about these issues are interested in inappropriate but nonviolent sex offenses against children that do not require actual force and are not intended to cause pain. This is not technically violence; so *violence* is not a fully accurate term.

The same can be said about the term *child abuse*, usually used as short-hand for *child abuse and neglect* or *child maltreatment*. Those terms have the advantage that they conventionally do encompass many nonviolent offenses against children, like neglect and emotional abuse and nonviolent sexual abuse. But *child abuse* and *child maltreatment* also have limitations as general terms for this field. These terms apply by statute in many states (and thus in many tabulations) only to acts committed by caregivers. This means that acts of violence against children by peers, like gang assaults, and crimes like abduction by strangers are not technically child abuse. Thus, none of the most frequently used terms in this area is accurate and comprehensive.

Childhood Victimization

My preferred solution is to call this field *childhood victimization* or *developmental victimology*, using the broader victimization concept instead of the terms *violence* or *abuse* (Finkelhor, 2008). *Victimization* refers to harms caused by human agents acting in violation of social norms. The human agency component excludes things like natural disasters and illnesses, even though these are sometimes referred to as having victims. The victimization term is broad enough to include most of what people are concerned about in this realm: child maltreatment, extrafamily violence, sex crimes, exposure to violence, and even bullying. It does not solve all the problems (for more details, see Finkelhor, 2008), but it is more comprehensive and does not exclude any of the major areas of concern.

From this starting point, childhood victimization can then also be subdivided into three broad subcategories that differentiate the social response to this broad spectrum of child victimization:

1. Conventional crimes against children (rape, robbery, assault), which can be called *criminal offenses against children*, or just *crimes*.
2. Acts that violate child welfare statutes, including abuse and neglect, but also some less frequently discussed topics like the exploitation of child labor; they can be called child maltreatment.
3. Other victimizations that would clearly be crimes if committed by adults against adults, but by convention are not generally of concern to either the official criminal justice or child welfare system when they occur among or against children; these include peer and sibling violence. They might be termed *noncriminal juvenile crime equivalents* but can be called *noncrime victimizations* for short.

Each of these three categories is a complex domain, but each has its stereotypical forms, which sometimes help and at other times hinder thinking about the category. When the public thinks of crimes against children, what stands out are stranger abductions and child molestations—situations of adults threatening children, in which the proper domain of protective and retributive action is clearly the police, courts, and criminal justice system. When the public thinks of child maltreatment, they tend to think of parents abusing or neglecting parental responsibilities, with the appropriate domain of intervention being family courts, social work, and mental health remedies. The public also is aware of noncriminal victimizations, such as bullying, that would be ordinarily handled by parents or school authorities.

Different as their stereotypes may be, however, these are not neat and distinct subcategories; there is substantial overlap. Child maltreatment is sometimes treated as criminal, sometimes not. Child molesting committed by a relative, for example, is often considered both as a crime and a child welfare violation, and can be dealt with through both criminal and child protective investigations. Noncrimes such as peer assault may actually result in an arrest in some jurisdictions but are delegated to parents or school authorities to sort out in other jurisdictions.

Indeed, this category of noncriminal juvenile crime equivalents is one that often creates confusion or draws objections. Many see its inclusion in discussions of crime, violence, and abuse as a watering down of the concept. Is it really violence, abuse, or victimization if a sibling hits another sibling or a sixth grader punches another sixth grader? But it is difficult to deny some behavioral equivalence, for example, between one adult hitting another, say, in a bar, and one child hitting another, say, on a playground. To study victimization in a developmental fashion, we must look at behaviorally equivalent acts across the life span, even if the social labels placed on the acts change as the participants get older.

The cultural assumption is that these acts are less serious or less criminal when they occur at earlier ages. Whether and how these acts are different should really, however, be a matter of empirical investigation. In research that my colleagues and I did previously, we did not, for example, find from the vantage point of the victim that violence between younger children is less physically or psychologically injurious (Finkelhor, Turner, & Ormrod, 2006). Understanding the basis for the social construction of victimization across the span of childhood should in fact be one of the key challenges for this field.

Corporal Punishment

An even more problematic type of juvenile crime equivalent, moreover, is spanking and corporal punishment, which certainly does fit the definition of violence if one defines violence as acts of physical force intended to cause physical pain. Some people may consider it prosocial violence and claim not much pain is involved. But certainly an equivalent act among adults (e.g., a supervisor striking his or her employee on the rear or on the hand as a sanction for a workplace infraction) would be considered an assault and thus violence. Nonetheless, corporal punishment is not just typically viewed as minor victimization; it is actually viewed as salutary and educational by many segments of society. Because the proposed definition of victimization requires the violation of social norms, forms of normatively accepted corporal punishment may not strictly qualify.

However, there are signs that a normative transformation is in progress regarding corporal punishment (Greven, 1990). A majority of states have banned all its forms in schools; some 26 countries, mostly European but including Costa Rica, have outlawed spanking even by parents; and the American Academy of Pediatrics has officially opposed its use as a disciplinary technique. Social scientists have begun to study it as a form of victimization with short- and long-term negative consequences (Strassberg, Dodge, Pettit, & Bates, 1994; Straus, 1994). Some have argued that it is the template on which other violent behavior gets built (Straus, 1994). Even if negative consequences are small and infrequent, because corporal punishment is so widespread, the total societal impact may be considerable compared with even more traumatic but much less frequent forms of violence. All this suggests that the field could benefit from a great deal of definitional refinement and organization.

Fragmentation

The terminological confusion is in part a reflection of a field that is highly fragmented. This fragmentation is in part the result of the fact that different institutional domains—including law enforcement and child protection—claim jurisdiction in this area. The fragmentation is also a product of the fact that many topics in child victimization have been targets of advocacy mobilizations, which have often chosen to highlight a particular subset of the child victimization spectrum. Examples are date rape, bullying, and children exposed to domestic violence. Generally, these specialty categories can be nested within or have many overlapping dimensions with other categories. Nonetheless, many studies have been done on these specialty categories without locating them within the context of other broad categories, for example, date rape within general sexual assault epidemiology or exposure to domestic violence within general child maltreatment epidemiology. There is a shortage of clearly delineated categories in this field that all researchers and practitioners make reference to.

This fragmentation creates problems for epidemiology because studies have often been done on differently defined or subdivided categories. For example, some studies on what is labeled *sexual abuse* often count sex offenses committed against a child by anyone—any adult or other child. However, some other studies of sexual abuse, if they are within the larger context of a study of child abuse and neglect, will typically only count sex offenses committed by caregivers. This makes the estimates difficult to compare. The fragmentation creates problems for institutions because they find themselves being asked to respond with limited resources to narrow segments of the child victimization problem. For example, should the school spend money on a date rape, a sexual harassment, a bullying, or a sexual abuse prevention curriculum?

I have argued that this field would benefit from a much more integrated approach that puts less emphasis on the subdivisions and more on the larger whole, in the way that the field of juvenile delinquency unifies the subcategories of youths who assault, steal, misuse drugs, commit sex crimes, and belong to gangs (Finkelhor, 2008). The subdivisions that should be emphasized most, if any, are the developmental ones: victimization patterns specific to infants, preschool, school age, or adolescent children. And approaches to identifying the causes and preventing occurrence of victimizations should be as unified and integrated as possible. These are the tasks I confer on the field of developmental victimology.

The discussion of how child victimization should be defined does highlight the fact that in some very important ways, child victimization differs from the victimization of adults. Children, of course, suffer from all the victimizations that adults experience—homicides, robberies, sexual assault, and even economic crimes like extortion and fraud. But one salient difference is that children also suffer from offenses that are particular to their status. The main status characteristic of childhood is its condition of dependency, which is a function, at least in part, of social and psychological immaturity. The violation of this dependency status results in forms of victimization, like physical neglect, that are not suffered by most adults (with the exception of those, such as older people and sick people, who also become dependent). Other aspects of childhood influence the dynamics of victimization, even in crimes that can occur to both children and adults. Inflicted blows that would not harm an adult can be lethal to a small child, which is one reason why the homicide rate is so high for infants. The differences between child and adult victimizations are an important reason why there needs to be a field of developmental victimology.

WHAT DO WE KNOW?

Not all of what is known about child victimization has been well publicized. Some has, but much has not. This section examines the scope of and trends in child victimization.

Scope of Child Victimization

Children are the most victimized segment of the population. It is interesting that this point has been so rarely made in the crime, violence, or maltreatment literatures. This is in part because data sources from which to make good age comparisons have not been that readily available. But some are available, and they point to children as having extremely high vulnerability.

The National Crime Victimization Survey (NCVS) is one of the most methodologically sound sources of information on crime and violence exposure. This survey, conducted annually by the U.S. Census Bureau, interviews tens of thousands of citizens about exposure to conventional crime, in particular, the more serious part of crime and violence spectrum.

The high vulnerability of children is clear-cut in the NCVS. For example, during the 1990s, the rate for aggravated assault against youths ages 12 to 17 was 15.5 per 1,000, more than twice the rate for the general population (i.e., 6.9 per 1,000). For rape, the comparison was 3.2 for youths to 1.3 for adults, almost 2.5 times higher. For violence overall, the ratio was 2.6 times higher for youths (Baum, 2005).

Unfortunately, the NCVS, which is the preferred source on crime victimization in general, has two deficiencies when it comes to child victimization. First, it does not gather information on victims younger than age 12. Second, it does not effectively encompass certain important forms of child victimization, such as child abuse, sexual abuse, and kidnapping, that preoccupy public policy regarding children. But national estimates that compensate for these deficiencies of the NCVS are available from other sources. Some of these various estimates are arrayed in Table 1.1.

Table 1.1 includes multiple estimates from different studies about some forms of victimization, and sometimes they show widely divergent rates. These differences stem from a variety of factors. Some of the studies listed base their rates on cases known to authorities (National Child Abuse and Neglect Data System) or professionals (Fourth National Incidence Study of Child Abuse and Neglect). Such studies are certain to count fewer cases than studies that obtain information directly from youths and their families. Although they miss many unreported cases, the advantage of studies based on authorities and professionals is that professional judgment is typically involved in assessing whether a real qualifying victimization (e.g., physical abuse) occurred.

Other discrepancies are more complicated to account for. For a variety of victimizations in Table 1.1, estimates are available both from the NCVS and the National Survey of Children Exposed to Violence (NatSCEV; Finkelhor, Turner, Ormrod, & Hamby, 2009), a study conducted by my colleagues and me. The NCVS is a survey conducted every year by the U.S. Census Bureau that interviews nearly 10,000 youths ages 12 to 17 years. The NatSCEV was

TABLE 1.1
One-Year Rate (per 1,000) and National Incidence Estimates for Various Childhood Victimizations

Type of victimization	Age	Rate/1,000[a]	No. victimized	Year	Source[b]	Report type	Notes
Physical assault	0–17	463	34,335,000	2008	NatSCEV	Self/caretaker report	
	12–17	(72.8)	(1,686,842)	1993–2003	NCVS	Self-report	
Robbery	0–17	48	3,549,000	2008	NatSCEV	Self/caretaker report	Nonsibling
	12–17	7.8	(180,733)	1993–2003	NCVS	Self-report	
Theft	0–17	69	5,102,000	2008	NatSCEV	Self/caretaker report	Nonsibling
	12–15	2.1	(35,874)	2004	NCVS 2003	Self-report	
Sexual assault/rape	0–17	18	1,331,000	2008	NatSCEV	Self/caretaker report	
	12–17	3.2	(74,147)	1993–2003	NCVS	Self-report	
	7th–12th grades	(22.9)	NA	1995–1996	Ad Health	Self-report	
Sexual abuse (sexual assault by known adult)	0–17	4.1	285,400	1999	NISMART-2	Self/caretaker report	
	0–17	3	222,000	2008	NatSCEV	Self/caretaker report	
	0–17	2.4	180,500	2005–2006	NIS-4	Agency reports	
	0–17	(1.12)	83,810	2005	NCANDS	Agency reports	
	0–17	10.5	NA	2002	NCANDS	Caretaker reports	North and South Carolina
Sexual harassment	0–17	26	1,922,000	2008	NatSCEV	Self/caretaker report	
	8th–11th grades	(810)	(13,006,580)	2000	Hostile Hallways	Self-report	
Physical abuse	0–17	44	3,253,000	2008	NatSCEV	Self/caretaker report	
	0–17	(2.3)	166,920	2002	NCANDS	Agency reports	
	0–17	6.5	476,000	2005–2006	NIS-4	Agency reports	
	0–17	49	(3,359,195)	1995	CTSPC-Gallup	Self-reports	
	0–17	4.95	311524	1986	SNIPSCDN	Agency reports	
	0–17	(2.00)	149,319	2005	NCANDS	Agency reports	
	0–17	43	NA	2002	NCANDS	Caretaker reports	North and South Carolina

(continues)

TABLE 1.1
One-Year Rate (per 1,000) and National Incidence Estimates for Various Childhood Victimizations (Continued)

Type of victimization	Age	Rate/ 1,000[a]	No. victimized	Year	Source[b]	Report type	Notes
Neglect	0–17	15	1,109,000	2008	NatSCEV	Self/caretaker report	
	0–17	16.2	1,192,200	2005–2006	NIS-4	Agency reports	
	0–17	270	(18,509,850)	1995	CTSPC-Gallup	Self-reports	
	0–17	(7.58)	564,765	2005	NCANDS	Agency reports	
Psychological/ emotional abuse	0–17	64	4,732,000	2008	NatSCEV	Self/caretaker report	
	0–17	(0.85)	63,497	2005	NCANDS	Agency reports	
Witnessing/domestic violence	0–17	64	4,584,000	2008	NatSCEV	Self/caretaker report	
Family abductions (or custodial interference)	0–17	(2.9)	203,900	1999	NISMART-2	Caretaker reports	
Nonfamily abductions	0–17	(0.8)	58,200	1999	NISMART-2	Caretaker reports	Legal definition, includes stereotypical kidnappings
	0–17	(0.0015)	115	1999	NISMART-2	Law enforcement	Stereotypical kidnapping
Homicide	0–17	(0.02)	1,571	2002	SHR	Agency reports	
	0–4	(0.024)	NA	2004	NVDRS	State-based surveillance system	Alaska, Maryland, Massachusetts, New Jersey, Oregon, South Carolina, Virginia
	<1	(0.071)	NA	1998	CDC	Vital statistics	

	6th–10th grades	(168.8)	(3,245,904)	1998	HBSC	Self-report
Bullying						
Teasing or emotional bullying	0–17	132	9,760,000	2008	NatSCEV	Self/caretaker report
	0–17	614	42,092,770	1995	CTSPC-Gallup	Caretaker reports
	0–17	197	14,567,000	2008	NatSCEV	Self/caretaker report
Online victimization						
Sexual solicitations and approaches	10–17	130	3,220,000	2005	YISS-2	Self-reports
Harassment	10–17	90	2,230,000	2005	YISS-2	Self-reports
Corporal punishment	0–17	(147.6)	(29,887,672)	1999	PCAA	Caretaker reports
	0–17	(171.7)	34,800,000	2002	ABC News Poll	Caretaker reports

[a]Numbers given in parentheses did not appear in original source but were derived from data presented therein.
[b]Source acronyms: NatSCEV = National Survey of Children Exposed to Violence (Finkelhor, Turner, Ormrod, & Hamby, 2009); NCVS = National Crime Victimization Survey (Baum, 2005); NCVS 2003 = National Crime Victimization Survey, 2003 (Catalano, 2004); NA = not applicable/not able to calculate; Ad Health (Raghavan, Bogart, Elliot, Vestal, & Schuster, 2004); NISMART-2 = Second National Incidence Study of Missing, Abducted, Runaway and Thrownaway Children, 1999 (Finkelhor, 2008; Hammer, Finkelhor, & Sedlak, 2002; Sedlak, Finkelhor, Hammer, & Schultz, 2002); NIS-4 = Fourth National Incidence Study of Child Abuse and Neglect, 1993 (Sedlak et al., 2010); NCANDS = National Child Abuse and Neglect Data System, 2002 (U.S. Department of Health and Human Services, Administration on Children Youth and Families, 2004); Hostile Hallways (Axelrod & Markow, 2001); CTSPC-Gallup = Parent–Child Conflict Tactics Scales (Straus, Hamby, Finkelhor, Moore, & Runyan, 1998); SNIPSCDN = Second National Incidence and Prevalence Study of Child Abuse and Neglect (Cappelleri, Eckenrode, & Powers, 1993); SHR = Supplemental Homicide Reports (Fox, 2005); NVDRS = National Violent Death Reporting System (Bennett et al., 2006); CDC = Centers for Disease and Control and Prevention (Tomashek, Hsia, & Iyasy, 2003); HBSC = Health Behaviour in School-Aged Children (Nansel et al., 2001); YISS-2 = Second Youth Internet Safety Survey (Wolak, Mitchell, & Finkelhor, 2007); PCAA = Prevent Child Abuse America (Daro, 1999); ABC News Poll (Crandall, 2002).

a survey of both youths and caretakers regarding the experiences of over 4,500 children from the ages of 0 to 17 years. The NCVS estimates are considerably lower than those from the NatSCEV for every crime and also lower than many other survey estimates of specific forms of juvenile victimization.

The lower estimates from the NCVS are generally attributed to several factors. First, the NCVS uses complex definitions for each crime it measures, and respondents need to endorse several sets of questions in specific ways to qualify. Second, the NCVS interviews respondents on several occasions at 6-month intervals over a period of 3 years to make sure that the incidents reported clearly fall within and not outside an exact 1-year time period. Third, the NCVS survey clearly orients respondents to the topic of conventional "crime," so incidents that respondents might not think of as crimes (e.g., forced sex by a dating partner or being beaten by a parent) are less likely to get reported. Fourth, the NCVS does not require that youths be interviewed confidentially, and young people may fail to disclose incidents they would not want their parents or family members to know about. What this means is that the NCVS estimates are very conservative and count primarily incidents that would be considered conventional crimes in the narrow sense. By contrast, the NatSCEV estimates are inflated with less serious incidents and incidents that some observers might dismiss as "not real crimes," such as sibling and peer assaults and disciplinary acts.

It is important to note that the estimates in Table 1.1 are all single-year estimates. For some kinds of victimization, so-called lifetime prevalence estimates (i.e., over the course of the full childhood) have also been made. Such estimates are particularly familiar with regard to sexual abuse and sexual assault, for which one meta-analysis of 22 American-based studies suggested that 30% to 40% of girls and 13% of boys experienced sexual abuse during childhood (Bolen & Scannapieco, 1999). A different international meta-analysis of 169 studies found that lifetime prevalence rates of sexual abuse for females was 25% and for males was 8%, with the range in North America for females from 15% to 22% (Andrews, Corry, Slade, Issakidis, & Swanston, 2004).

However, there are several disadvantages to lifetime prevalence estimates, which is why they are not summarized in Table 1.1. First, single-year estimates are the more common currency in crime and victimization epidemiology and exist for a wider range of victimizations. Second, single-year estimates provide a better contrast between methods and among victimization types, especially since the long span of lifetime prevalence estimates blurs the contrast between rare and more frequently occurring events. Third, many childhood lifetime estimates are collected from adults after a long hiatus, which is problematic for the validity and reliability of the reports. Finally, many lifetime estimates are no longer current and apply only to an earlier generation of children, a serious problem given the evidence of recent large changes in incidence rates (see below).

Even as single-year estimates, Table 1.1 reveals an enormous quantity and variety of victimization of children and youths. Based on the NatSCEV, almost half of all children experienced a physical assault in the course of the previous year, much of it by siblings and peers; 13.2% experienced physical bullying; 6.9% experienced a theft; and 4.8% experienced a robbery. The NCVS rates are typically only a fraction, in some cases a 10th or less of the NatSCEV estimates, which suggests how far we may still be from a consensus about the epidemiology of child victimization. But even the NCVS estimates suggest that conventional crime victimization rates for youths are at least 3 to 4 times larger than what is known to police (Finkelhor & Ormrod, 2001) and 2 to 3 times the victimization rate for adults (Finkelhor, 2008).

The scope and variety of victimization suggest some general comments rather than discussion of specific estimates. First, there is clearly a spectrum of victimization exposures, from the more serious to the less serious, from the less frequent to the more frequent. I have proposed dividing the spectrum into three groupings (Finkelhor, 2008). *Pandemic* victimizations, like peer assaults, occur to most or a large majority of children over the course of development. *Acute* victimizations, like child maltreatment by parents, occur to a minority but are generally considered to have quite lasting developmental consequences. *Extraordinary* victimizations refer to events like stranger abductions and homicides, which are rare but garner tremendous attention when they occur. Although the more serious victimizations receive the greatest attention, it is also important to recognize that relatively low-impact or low-risk events can have large public health and societal consequences when these events are widespread in the population. So it is important not to dismiss exposures to peer violence and other pandemic victimizations as of little consequence.

Second, the frequencies, particularly in comparison with adult frequencies, raise the question of why children are so intensively exposed to victimization, a question that has not received much theoretical or empirical attention. Elsewhere (Finkelhor, 2008), I have proposed four factors that help account for high levels of childhood violence and victimization exposure: (a) Children are smaller, weaker, and less experienced (and the younger more so than the older), which places them at disadvantage; (b) children have less behavioral self-control, which can entail at times provocative and risky behavior; (c) social norms are not as strong in the inhibition of violence against children as they are in violence against adults (e.g., it is a crime for a man to hit his wife but not his child); and (d) children have less choice over whom they associate with and are less able than adults to voluntarily leave dangerous families, neighborhoods, or schools.

Overall, the frequency of both acute and pandemic victimizations does suggest that childhood for ordinary American children runs a gauntlet of risky, unpleasant, and dangerous exposures. It violates our sense of what childhood should be and raises the question of whether society has been doing enough to promote the safety and security of children.

Poly-Victims

Because so many different victimizations occur to so many children, it is obvious that there must be considerable overlap. Ironically, though, the fragmentation of the field of child victimization has impeded inquiry into just how much overlap there is and why. Advocates and policymakers concerned about one form of child victimization or another, like dating violence, have tended to present estimates and studies about their victims as though this was the primary or only victimization that such children suffered from. They could do this because studies of one kind of victimization rarely asked about other kinds. Some studies might inquire about multiple forms of child maltreatment, such as physical and sexual abuse. Other studies, like the NCVS, inquire about multiple forms of conventional crime, like rape, robbery, and aggravated assault. But studies almost never asked about a very broad and comprehensive range of victimizations, including child maltreatment, conventional crime, and exposure to pure violence, for example.

It turns out that most juvenile victims do experience multiple victimizations. This was demonstrated in the Developmental Victimization Survey, which used a questionnaire (the Juvenile Victimization Questionnaire) that asked about 34 different kinds of child victimization in five broad domains: conventional crime, child maltreatment, peer and sibling, sexual victimization, and witnessing/indirect victimization.

Whereas 71% of the children and youths experienced at least one victimization in the past year, even more important was the percentage experiencing multiple victimizations (the Developmental Victimization Survey defined multiple victimizations as having a different kind of victimization in a different episode over the course of a year). This means that an assault and robbery on different occasions, even by the same perpetrator, would count as multiple victimizations, but two assaults by the same or even different perpetrators would not count as a multiple. This conservative way of defining multiple victimization was adopted in light of findings that different kinds of victimization seem to be more impactful than repeated episodes of the same type (see Finkelhor, Ormrod, & Turner, 2007; Finkelhor, Ormrod, Turner, & Hamby, 2005). Of the children with any victimization in the last year, two thirds had had two or more. The average number of victimizations for a victimized child was three in the past year, and the total ranged all the way up to 15.

One of the most important findings was the concentration of risk. Children who had had one kind of victimization were at increased likelihood of having other victimizations as well. For example, if you had been physically assaulted by a caretaker, you were 60% more likely than other children to also have been assaulted by a peer.

These children with multiple victimizations should be a particular policy concern. In other fields it has been widely recognized that multiple intersecting adversities frequently have impacts far beyond those of individual stressful events. For example, clients with several psychiatric diagnoses (comorbidity) or who abuse different kinds of drugs (polydrug users) have been found to pose particularly challenging problems. There is every reason to believe that this is also the case with children victimized in multiple ways.

My colleagues and I (Finkelhor, 2008) have proposed to call this group of multiply victimized children *poly-victims*. We prefer the term *poly-victim* over *multiple victim* because the term *multiple victim* can imply victimization in which there were several victims, a meaning that could be confused with what we were intending to designate: a victim who had several victimizations. We expected that the data would show them to be highly vulnerable and distressed young people, and that was the case.

We categorized as poly-victims the youths in our national survey who had experienced four or more victimizations over the course of the single year. Such youths represented 31% of all victims and 22% of the full sample. But they were the youths with the most serious kinds of victimization. Of the poly-victims, 40% had had a victimization injury, 42% had experienced a form of maltreatment, and 25% had been victimized by a weapon-toting assailant. They had considerably more other lifetime adversities, like major illnesses, accidents, or other family problems. They were also clearly the most distressed youths. They were 5.8 times more likely than other youths to be angry, 20.2 times more likely to be depressed, and 10.3 times more likely to be anxious. In fact, most of the clinically distressed kids were also poly-victims; 86% of the clinically depressed children also fit the criteria as poly-victims (Finkelhor et al., 2007).

The research concerning poly-victims has important implications. For one, it suggests that what professionals should be on the lookout for among children is poly-victimization, not just one individual type of victimization, even a serious one. Analyses have suggested that poly-victimization is the pattern most associated with mental health problems and bad outcomes, and that poly-victims are the kids harboring the greatest amount of distress. The associations between distress and individual victimizations disappear when poly-victimization is taken into account (Finkelhor et al., 2007). That is, children who experience a single kind of victimization, such as bullying or even child maltreatment, look like they are able to recover from it. But youths who experience victimization of multiple kinds from multiple sources are showing signs that they are locked in a pattern or trapped in a downward spiral that should be of the greatest concern to those trying to help.

The poly-victim idea has implications for theory as well. Victimizations have in the past mostly been conceptualized as stressful or traumatic *events*. This is in part a legacy of the child victimization field's close connection to the literature on posttraumatic stress. The earliest victimization experiences to be studied in detail were sexual assaults, which were considered to be highly threatening individual episodes, happening to otherwise ordinary victims who were overwhelmed by a short-term incident. But as victimization research has expanded, researchers have come to understand that many victims are subjected to repeated episodes over a period of time, as with the child who is bullied again and again on the playground or emotionally and physically abused again and again by a parent. The poly-victimization research highlights that many children are subjected to a variety of different kinds of victimization, like being beaten and sexually assaulted and robbed, over a relatively short period of time. This suggests that victimization for some children is more like a *condition* than an event. A condition is a much more stable and ongoing process, whereas an event is more time limited. It is like the difference between failing a test and failing a course, or the difference between an acute medical condition, such as appendicitis, and a chronic one, such as diabetes. One of the most important diagnostic challenges faced by professionals concerned about child victimization is discerning those children for whom victimization has become a condition rather than just an event. We should expect them to have different characteristics and a different prognosis.

In recent work (Finkelhor, Ormrod, Turner, & Holt, 2009), we found evidence to suggest at least four distinct pathways to this poly-victimization condition. The first pathway is through violent family environments, in which there may be exposure to domestic violence and direct maltreatment with such developmental experiences creating both cognitive sets and emotional deficits that make subsequent victimization outside the family more likely as well. There is a second pathway to poly-victimization through family disruption and adversity, including divorce and stepfamily environments, illnesses, accidents, homelessness, and the like. This pathway likely operates through mechanisms like poor supervision, emotional deprivation, and exposure to a lot of potentially predatory persons, deficits that lead to peer victimization, sexual victimization, and other victimizations.

The third pathway to poly-victimization has to do with living in dangerous neighborhoods and community environments. Children even without violent, disrupted, or disorganized families may become poly-victims in such environments, where there may be gangs, vandalism, and unsafe schools and where families may use coercive techniques for socializing children because they believe these are helping to "protect" children from the dangerous environment.

Then there is a fourth pathway or set of pathways to poly-victimization that operate through the personal characteristics of children. These include certain temperaments, disabilities, and being different in ways that may mobilize dislike because of sociocultural stigmas (e.g., the stigma of gender-atypical behavior). Children with certain kinds of trauma or mental health problems may actually seek out or trigger conflicts that they are unable to handle.

These pathways to poly-victimization highlight some of the features that have been shown in past research to be associated with higher rates of victimization. Urban, lower income, and minority neighborhoods do have higher rates of many kinds of child victimization, although Lauritsen (2003) showed that the excess is primarily explained by the density of the youth population and the proportion from single-parent families (suggesting inadequate supervision) in such areas. Family disruption has consistently been shown to be associated with a wide variety of childhood victimization exposures. Certain personal characteristics have also been shown to be associated with vulnerability to various kinds of victimization, including disabilities and mental health problems (Finkelhor, 2008). With regard to gender differences, girls experience more sexual offenses, and boys somewhat more physical assaults.

Trends

A chapter on scope would not be complete without some commentary on historical trends. Most authors believe that the long-term trend is for less violence, abuse, and child victimization. Several authors have speculated on the basis of historical documents, for example, that the use of severe forms of corporal punishment (e.g., whippings, beatings, hitting on the head) has declined (Greven, 1990). Data also show declines in corporal punishment and decreasingly favorable attitudes toward corporal punishment from the 1970s to the present (Straus, 2001).

The tracking of data sources for child victimization for recent periods also shows declines since the early 1990s in various types of child abuse and crimes against children, in some cases very dramatic declines. Here are some specific trend findings:

- Sexual abuse reported by state child welfare authorities started to decline in the early 1990s, after at least 15 years of steady increases. From 1990 to 2000, sexual abuse substantiations were down 53%.
- Physical abuse substantiations (also reported by state authorities) joined the downward trend starting in the mid-1990s, in a decline

that was most dramatic between 1997 and 2000. From 1992 to 2006, physical abuse substantiations declined 48%.

- Sexual assaults of teenagers dropped, according to the NCVS. From 1993 to 2004, overall sexual assaults decreased 67%. The subgroup of sexual assaults by known persons was down even more.

- Other crimes against teens ages 12 to 17 were also down dramatically as measured by the NCVS. Aggravated assault was down 74%, simple assault down 63%, robbery down 72%, and larceny down 55%. This has been in the context of a crime decline for victims of all ages.

- Juvenile victim homicides declined 50% from 1993 to 2004, a drop that was larger than the 42% drop in homicide for victims 18 and older. The drop was also more dramatic for youths ages 14 through 17 (down 62%) than for younger children (down 36%).

- Domestic violence also declined in recent years according to the NCVS, down 49% from 1993 to 2001, meaning that children were probably being exposed to fewer violent parents.

The converging evidence points to a real decline. The decline appears in both official and self-report sources during a similar time interval. The decline has a persistence and breadth across a wide variety of crime and abuse categories as well as different regions and residential environments. Analyses to look for signs of changes in standards or willingness to report could not find much evidence for such explanations (Finkelhor & Jones, 2004). Among published reports on recent crime trends, the vast majority of criminologists accept the reality of a large and broad decline in crime, and it would be surprising if child forms of victimization were not included in these overall trends.

The declines have also occurred across a broad range of victimization types. They include victimizations, such as homicides, that are rare, serious, regionally variable, and indicative of more pathological circumstances, but they also include victimizations that are fairly common, like simple assaults. This is important because some of the factors that affect homicide trends, such as gun availability and the quality of medical care, are not likely to be factors in explaining trends for simple assaults among youths.

This suggests that children are escaping some portion of the perils faced by earlier generations. One of the implications is that widely cited statistics about the lifetime prevalence of certain childhood victimizations may no longer represent the experience of the current generation. Meta-analyses of general population surveys of adults, for example, have suggested that a quarter or a fifth of women suffered sexual abuse in childhood. But if recent trends are down, then these estimates, based on adults growing up in earlier decades, may not be predictive of what will be the lifetime experience of childhood sexual abuse for the current cohort of children. This highlights one of the limitations of using adult retrospective surveys to develop policy for current child victimization.

The Context for Declines

It is interesting to note that as juvenile victimization has declined, other related social problems affecting youth have improved. Teen suicide fell 41% from 1994 to 2003. Births to teens fell 40% from 1994 to 2003. The number of children living in poverty declined 24% starting in 1994 until 1999, when it leveled off. Running away declined, both in police statistics and in reports from children and families. The decade of the 1990s also saw an improvement in child behavior problem and competence scores on the Child Behavior Checklist, reversing an earlier period of significant deterioration in this widely used child assessment measure.

There are conflicting opinions among scholars about what lies behind the crime decline and relatively little discussion among child victimization experts about the specific improvement in child victimization or child welfare indicators. One review highlighted some factors that were powerful enough to effect broad changes and temporally situated properly with respect to the onset of the recent declines in child victimization (Finkelhor & Jones, 2006). First, a large and sustained economic prosperity in the United States began in the early 1990s. Second, a new class of psychiatric medications to treat depression and anxiety became available in the late 1980s, and prescription trends show a huge boom in the numbers of children and adults taking psychiatric drugs (including the behavioral control drug Ritalin), which were being widely disseminated by primary care physicians. Third, there was a large deployment of police and child protection workers, many of whom were equipped with better training and a specific orientation to child victimization and family violence. It was during this period that many new shelter programs and children's advocacy programs were established, and aggressive new case finding and prosecution efforts were undertaken. Finally, there had been a considerable increase in the 1980s, continuing throughout the 1990s, in offenders incarcerated for crimes against children and other family-related offenders.

The declines in childhood victimization are certainly good news for those concerned about child well-being and the future quality of childhood. It is curious that they have not been publicized extensively by practitioners and advocates, in part because of questions about their validity, concern about whether they would persist, and fear that the improvements might be taken by funders as an opportunity to turn their attention elsewhere. They do pose a tremendous opportunity for policy if the declines can be analyzed in ways that uncover the sources of success. Unfortunately, the existing data systems may be sufficiently limited to make these analyses impossible or inconclusive. But the potential learning opportunity of dramatic trends should be a lesson about the utility of rigorous, detailed, and repeated epidemiology, a lesson it is hoped will inspire future improvements.

HOW WE KNOW IT: THE BASIS FOR EPIDEMIOLOGY ON CHILDHOOD VICTIMIZATION

Epidemiological information on child victimization comes from two broadly defined sources: community surveys and agency tabulations. The main community survey source is the NCVS, which in recent years has been supplemented by topical studies such as the Developmental Victimization Survey. The main agency tabulations come from the Federal Bureau of Investigation in its national tabulations on reported crime and the U.S. Children's Bureau with the tabulation on child maltreatment, the National Child Abuse and Neglect Data System.

WHERE DO WE GO FROM HERE? GAPS AND RECOMMENDATIONS

The research needs for epidemiology about child victimization are vast and urgent, given the size of the problem and the seriousness of its impact. Ultimately, comprehensive yearly national and state figures are needed on all officially reported crimes and forms of child abuse committed against children of all ages. These need to be supplemented by regular national studies to assess the vast quantity of unreported victimization, including family violence, child-to-child, and indirect victimization such as exposure to domestic violence. Although such efforts pose methodological challenges, studies demonstrate that they are feasible. In addition, long-term longitudinal studies are needed to document the sequence of child victimizations and child victimization risk factors over the course of a full childhood.

It is not hard to imagine what an effective system for tracking the epidemiology of childhood violence exposure would look like. One only has to look at the public health system for tracking diseases and other health-related threats. Systems exist for gathering and reporting on a wide range of infectious diseases, illnesses, and accidental injuries and for providing national, regional, and local rate calculations with only a brief time lag. National health epidemiological surveys on the general population are also a feature of the comprehensive health assessment system. It is disappointing that similarly comprehensive, detailed, and prompt systems do not exist for tracking childhood violence exposure, which arguably is every bit as much a threat to public health and certainly a major topic of public and policy concern. Such systems could be valuable resources in efforts to reduce the toll of exposure. Those concerned about such exposure should mobilize to make such systems a reality.

REFERENCES

Andrews, G., Corry, J., Slade, T., Issakidis, C., & Swanston, H. (2004). Child sexual abuse. In M. Ezzati, A. D. Lopez, A. Rodgers, & C. J. L. Murray (Eds.), *Comparative quantification of health risks* (Vol. 2, pp. 1850–1940). Geneva, Switzerland: World Health Organization.

Axelrod, A., & Markow, D. (2001). *Hostile hallways: Bullying, teasing, and sexual harassment in school.* Washington, DC: American Association of University Women Educational Foundation.

Baum, K. (2005). *Juvenile victimization and offending, 1993–2003* (Bureau of Justice Statistics Special Report No. NCJ209468). Washington, DC: Office of Justice Programs, U.S. Department of Justice.

Bennett, M. D., Jr., Hall, J., Frazier, L., Jr., Patel, N., Barker, L., & Shaw, K. (2006). Homicide of children aged 0–4 years, 2003–04: Results from the National Violence Death Reporting System. *Injury Prevention, 12*(Suppl. 2), ii39–ii43. doi:10.1136/ip.2006.012658

Bolen, R. M., & Scannapieco, M. (1999). Prevalence of child sexual abuse: A corrective meta-analysis. *Social Service Review, 73,* 281–313. doi:10.1086/514425

Cappelleri, J. C., Eckenrode, J., & Powers, J. L. (1993). The epidemiology of child abuse: Findings from the Second National Incidence and Prevalence Study of Child Abuse and Neglect. *American Journal of Public Health, 83,* 1622–1624. doi:10.2105/AJPH.83.11.1622

Catalano, S. M. (2004). *Criminal victimization, 2003* (BJS/NCVS Report No. NCJ 205455). Washington, DC: U.S. Department of Justice.

Crandall, J. (2002). *Most say spanking's OK by parents but not by grade-school teachers.* Retrieved from http://abcnews.go.com/sections/us/DailyNews/spanking_poll 021108.html

Daro, D. (1999). *Public opinion and behaviors regarding child abuse prevention: 1999 survey.* Chicago, IL: Prevent Child Abuse America.

Finkelhor, D. (2008). *Childhood victimization: Violence, crime, and abuse in the lives of young people.* New York, NY: Oxford University Press.

Finkelhor, D., & Jones, L. M. (2004). *Explanations for the decline in child sexual abuse cases* (Juvenile Justice Bulletin No. NC199298). Washington, DC: Office of Juvenile Justice and Delinquency Prevention.

Finkelhor, D., & Jones, L. M. (2006). Why have child maltreatment and child victimization declined? *Journal of Social Issues, 62*, 685–716. doi:10.1111/j.1540-4560.2006.00483.x

Finkelhor, D., & Ormrod, R. K. (2001). *Child abuse reported to the police* (Juvenile Justice Bulletin No. NCJ187238). Washington, DC: Office of Juvenile Justice and Delinquency Prevention.

Finkelhor, D., Ormrod, R. K., & Turner, H. A. (2007). Poly-victimization: A neglected component in child victimization trauma. *Child Abuse & Neglect, 31*, 7–26. doi:10.1016/j.chiabu.2006.06.008

Finkelhor, D., Ormrod, R. K., Turner, H. A., & Hamby, S. L. (2005). Measuring poly-victimization using the JVQ. *Child Abuse & Neglect, 29*, 1297–1312. doi:10.1016/j.chiabu.2005.06.005

Finkelhor, D., Ormrod, R. K., Turner, H. A., & Holt, M. A. (2009). Pathways to poly-victimization. *Child Maltreatment, 14*, 316–329. doi:10.1177/1077559509347012

Finkelhor, D., Turner, H. A., & Ormrod, R. K. (2006). Kid's stuff: The nature and impact of peer and sibling violence. *Child Abuse & Neglect, 30*, 1401–1421. doi:10.1016/j.chiabu.2006.06.006

Finkelhor, D., Turner, H. A., Ormrod, R., & Hamby, S. L. (2009). Violence, abuse, and crime exposure in a national sample of children and youth. *Pediatrics, 124*, 1411–1423. doi:10.1542/peds.2009-0467

Fox, J. A. (2005). *Uniform crime reports, United States: Supplementary homicide reports, 1976–2003* (computer file ICPSR04351-v1). Ann Arbor, MI: Inter-University Consortium for Political and Social Research.

Greven, P. (1990). *Spare the child: The religious roots of punishment and the psychological impact of physical abuse*. New York, NY: Alfred A. Knopf.

Hammer, H., Finkelhor, D., & Sedlak, A. J. (2002). *Children abducted by family members: National estimates and characteristics* (Juvenile Justice Bulletin No. NCJ196466). Washington, DC: Office of Juvenile Justice and Delinquency Prevention.

Lauritsen, J. L. (2003). *How families and communities influence youth victimization* (Juvenile Justice Bulletin No. NCJ201629). Washington, DC: Office of Juvenile Justice and Delinquency Prevention.

Nansel, T. R., Overpeck, M., Pilla, R. S., Ruan, W. J., Simons-Morton, B., & Scheidt, P. C. (2001). Bullying behaviors among US youth: Prevalence and association with psychosocial adjustment. *JAMA, 285*, 2094–2100. doi:10.1001/jama.285.16.2094

Raghavan, R., Bogart, L. M., Elliot, M. N., Vestal, K. D., & Schuster, M. A. (2004). Sexual victimization among a national probability sample of adolescent women. *Perspectives on Sexual and Reproductive Health, 36*, 225–232. doi:10.1363/3622504

Sedlak, A. J., Finkelhor, D., Hammer, H., & Schultz, D. J. (2002). *National estimates of missing children: An overview* (Juvenile Justice Bulletin No. NCJ196466). Washington, DC: Office of Juvenile Justice and Delinquency Prevention.

Sedlak, A. J., Mettenburg, J., Basena, M., Petta, I., McPherson, K., Greene, A., & Li, S. (2010). *Fourth National Incidence Study of Child Abuse and Neglect (NIS-4): Report to Congress*. Washington, DC: U.S. Department of Health and Human Services, Administration for Children and Families.

Strassberg, Z., Dodge, K. A., Pettit, G. S., & Bates, J. E. (1994). Spanking in the home and children's subsequent aggression toward kindergarten peers. *Development and Psychopathology, 6*, 445–461. doi:10.1017/S0954579400006040

Straus, M. A. (1994). *Beating the devil out of them: Corporal punishment in American families*. New York, NY: Lexington Books.

Straus, M. A. (2001). *Beating the devil out of them: Corporal punishment in American families and its effects on children* (2nd ed.). New Brunswick, NJ: Transaction.

Straus, M. A., Hamby, S. L., Finkelhor, D., Moore, D., & Runyan, D. K. (1998). Identification of children maltreatment with the Parent–Child Conflict Tactics Scales: Development and psychometric properties data for a national sample of American parents. *Child Abuse & Neglect, 22*, 249–270. doi:10.1016/S0145-2134(97)00174-9

Tomashek, K. M., Hsia, J., & Iyasy, S. (2003). Trends in postneonatal mortality attributable to injury, United States, 1988–1998. *Pediatrics, 111*, 1219–1225.

U.S. Department of Health and Human Services, Administration on Children Youth and Families. (2004). *Child maltreatment 2002: Reports from the states to the National Child Abuse and Neglect Data System*. Washington, DC: U.S. Government Printing Office.

Wolak, J., Mitchell, K. J., & Finkelhor, D. (2007). Unwanted and wanted exposure to online pornography in a national sample of youth Internet users. *Pediatrics, 119*, 247–257. doi:10.1542/peds.2006-1891

2

RISK FACTORS FOR
CHILD ABUSE PERPETRATION

DAVID A. WOLFE

Child abuse is an event, not a uniform disorder, and therefore it is necessary to consider multiple causes that interact unpredictably. Notwithstanding the critical role of the adult offender, child abuse is rarely caused by a single risk factor. Although risk signs and indicators are present, it is still very difficult to predict who will become abusive and who will not—child abuse may emerge in any given family if the "right" conditions exist. These causal conditions stem largely from the interaction of child, familial, and cultural influences, but it is not possible to predict with precision when they will occur (Cicchetti & Valentino, 2006).

SCOPE AND DEFINITION OF TERMS

Stress is one of those forces of nature and humankind that can convert static, stable conditions into dynamic, chaotic patterns. Physical abuse and neglect occur most often in the context of social and economic family deprivation, which can transform predisposed, high-risk parents into abusive or neglectful ones. A greater degree of stress in the social environment that the abusive parent experiences will increase the probability that violence will surface as an attempt to gain control or cope with irritating, stressful events. In the case of neglect, stress may be so severe that parents withdraw from their child-care responsibilities.

Child abuse is often enmeshed in other serious family problems, most notably parental substance abuse, financial problems, and stressful life circumstances, all of which are related to some degree to negative developmental outcomes. Given the multiple causes of abuse, social science definitions have evolved to allow greater recognition of the individual, family, and social context of maltreatment. Moreover, child abuse occurs in a relational context and may be viewed as a "relational psychopathology" resulting from a poor fit of the parent, child, and environment. Most definitions of abuse place primary importance on the relationship context in which such events occur and have their greatest psychological impact, such as developmental and psychological consequences, antecedents, and child-rearing norms.

The broader term *child maltreatment* includes physical abuse, neglect, sexual abuse, and emotional abuse. *Physical abuse* is the deliberate application of force to any part of a child's body, which results or may result in a nonaccidental injury. It may involve hitting a child a single time, or it may involve a pattern of incidents. Physical abuse also includes behavior such as shaking, choking, biting, kicking, burning, or poisoning a child, holding a child under water, or any other harmful or dangerous use of force or restraint. Child physical abuse is usually connected to physical punishment or is confused with child discipline (United Nations Secretary-General's Study on Violence Against Children, 2006). This chapter focuses on the determinants of physical abuse, although there is considerable overlap in risk factors among all forms of maltreatment. Knowledge of major risk factors for physical abuse perpetration is presented, followed by discussion of gaps and limitations. The developmental and psychological impact of abuse on the child is not within the scope of this chapter (see Chapter 4, this volume).

WHAT DO WE KNOW? KEY RISK FACTORS
FOR CHILD ABUSE PERPETRATION

The current framework is derived from a population health approach to identifying and defining key determinants of health. Theoretical and empirical findings from the literature are organized into separate sections according to five selected key determinants of health that apply to this issue (i.e., Income and Social Status, Social Support Networks, Education, Physical Environment, and Personal Adjustment and Coping Skills; see Appendix 2.1). Each determinant is discussed in terms of its composition of theoretically important variables, including some undetermined factors that merit future attention. Gender and sex differences are discussed as relevant, although such findings are often confounded with the parenting role.

A multidimensional, systems approach to understanding child abuse is built on several levels of concern and action. Thus, the current determinants of the health framework include conceptually distinct levels of individual, family, community, and cultural factors (note that some levels have been combined for brevity, and risk factors for which there are inadequate data at one or more levels are not presented; see Appendix 2.2). This approach involves consideration of critical antecedents, significant historical or developmental characteristics of the adult and child, the nature of the act, the consequences that maintain such behavior, the nature of the family or caregiving context, and the larger social system in which abuse occurs.

Income and Social Status

The first key determinant of health, income and social status, addresses child abuse risk factors stemming from the multiple influences of social deprivation, discrimination, poverty, and family and neighborhood factors.

Individual and Family Levels

Poverty and low socioeconomic status. Child maltreatment is affected by several major environmental conditions, of which low socioeconomic status (typically defined as family incomes below the poverty line, underemployment, and low education) plays a significant role. Childhood poverty is a disturbing reality for about one in six children in both the United States (U.S. Census Bureau, 2007) and Canada (Statistics Canada, 2007). Child maltreatment, especially neglect, is more common among the poor and disadvantaged. U.S. figures show that the reported incidence rate for all forms of maltreatment rises from 42/1,000 (averaged across all socioeconomic status levels) to 99/1,000 children among those from the poorest families (earning less than $15,000 per year; Sedlak & Broadhurst, 1996). This rate is 3 times greater than that of children from moderate income families ($15,000 to less than $30,000 per year), and 25 times higher compared with children in families in the highest income bracket (more than $30,000 per year). The known connection between child abuse and poverty implies that the economically based context of maltreatment—restricted child-care opportunities, crowded and unsafe housing, lack of health care, and so forth—is a powerful contributor to the high incidence rates.

Family structure. Family structure is also connected to the probability of child abuse. Children living with a single parent are at significantly greater risk of both physical abuse and neglect, most likely because of added stress, fewer resources and opportunities to share child-rearing burdens, and lower socioeconomic status than two-parent homes (Turner, Finkelhor, & Ormrod, 2007). Children living in father-only homes, in particular, are almost twice as likely to be physically abused than those living with mothers alone (Sedlak & Broadhurst, 1996). Similarly, physical abuse is more common in larger families and in stepfamilies, in which additional children in the household mean additional tasks, responsibilities, and financial demands (Turner et al., 2007).

Community Level

Neighborhood context. Child maltreatment is closely linked to structural aspects of the neighborhood and community. Variation in rates of officially reported child maltreatment was shown to relate to four determinants of community social organization: economic and family resources, residential instability, household and age structure, and geographic proximity of neighborhoods to concentrated poverty (Coulton, Crampton, Irwin, Spilsbury, & Korbin, 2007). These important dimensions of neighborhood context reflect the degree of breakdown of community social control and organization, which in turn relate to reports of child abuse. Thus, children who live in neighborhoods characterized by poverty, excessive numbers of children per adult resident, population turnover, and the concentration of single-parent families are at highest risk of maltreatment (Freisthler, Merritt, & LaScala, 2006).

Employment opportunities and loss. Similar to the link between poverty and child maltreatment, the role of unemployment and job opportunities is significant. Using unemployment rates for two different metropolitan areas, increases in the rates of physical abuse were preceded by periods of high job loss (Steinberg, Catalano, & Dooley, 1981). Male unemployment rates accounted for two thirds of the variance in total abuse and neglect rates among registered cases of maltreatment in Glasgow, Scotland (Gillham et al., 1998). These studies are correlational only and cannot explain the underlying mechanisms that account for this connection.

Societal/Cultural Level: Discrimination and Inequality

The most prominent social and cultural dimensions contributing to maltreatment stem from poverty, social isolation, and wide acceptance of corporal punishment (discussed later). These factors stem from inequality, which is arguably the major sociocultural factor contributing to maltreatment not only of children but also of many adults and members of minority groups. The extent to which a society deems any particular group as being less worthy of recognition and economic or political support represents the extent to which that group is vulnerable to violence and a host of other indignities (Chapman, Dube, & Anda, 2007).

Social Support Networks

The influence of social support networks on child abuse risk has been recognized for many years. Although these network influences are tied to income and social status, they are considered somewhat modifiable (e.g., better access to and understanding of community resources, reducing social isolation).

Individual and Family Levels

Social isolation and perceived support. Social isolation is not a singular factor but rather a set of variables linked to parents' perception of support and their informal and formal networks. Such families often lack significant social connections to others in the extended family, the neighborhood, the community, and the social agencies that are most likely to provide needed assistance (Coulton et al., 2007). Social isolation is commonly associated with other stressful living conditions, such as a lack of adequate day care, peer groups or close friends, and adequate housing. These factors play an indirect, yet significant, role in the early formation and healthy establishment of a positive versus abusive parent–child relationship. As a result, various forms of maltreatment are difficult to detect, and community agents who could promote healthy parent–child relationships are less likely to be influential.

Moves and disruptions. Families in which children are maltreated move twice as often as nonmaltreating families from similar socioeconomic backgrounds (Eckenrode, Rowe, Laird, & Braithwaite, 1995). In addition, maltreated children have less stability in terms of parental figures, which can disrupt the child's developing sense of trust and consistent supports. Disruptions in education because of frequent moves, school transfers, suspensions, and tardiness may be responsible for the academic delays noted among some abused children.

Community Level: Access to Resources

High-risk parents, especially those at risk of child abuse and woman abuse, show a marked reluctance to seek help until it is forced on them or the problem becomes major (Garbarino, 1987). The degree of accessibility to existing services may play a role in this respect. Individual and family access to public transportation, suitable forms of communication, eligibility requirements for various community services, language barriers, and other qualifying characteristics that restrict or improve access to resources have been linked indirectly to child abuse and family violence. Opportunities for disclosure of child abuse may also be hampered in the absence of access to community and school-based education and awareness.

Education

At the individual, family, and community levels, parent support is crucial. Prenatal classes, home visitation programs, and similar educational efforts to assist new parents in their new role and strengthen the parent–infant relationship serve to reduce incidents of child abuse. The importance of establishing positive early beginnings for new, inexperienced parents and their infants has received empirical support (Olds et al., 1998). Such programs aim their interventions either during pregnancy or shortly following birth, to provide new parents with basic knowledge of child care and child development. Supplemental goals may also include social support, job training, and child management and early child stimulation. However, a basic dilemma prevails: Access to education and treatment services often depends on being detected by community agents or admitting to or recognizing one's own culpability (Azar & Wolfe, 2006).

Physical Environment

The physical environment poses risk of child abuse in many ways, including homelessness, conditions in the home, and neighborhood safety.

Family Level

Homelessness. Lack of suitable shelter and a stable family environment are major issues affecting child abuse and neglect (Wekerle, MacMillan, Leung, & Jamieson, 2008). There is significantly more abuse and foster care placements among homeless children than among socioeconomically matched families with suitable shelter (McGuinness & Schneider, 2007).

Conditions in the home. Child maltreatment is associated with a lack of basic necessities that keep children safe and healthy. In a review of accidental and nonaccidental child injuries, poverty, family chaos and unpredictability, household crowding, and frequent residence changes were found to be characteristic of unintentional child injury, and risk of injury is amplified as the number of such stressors increases (Peterson & Brown, 1994). Home safety covers a wide range of important features, such as exposure to lead or other toxic substances, exposed electrical wiring, water temperature set to above 120 °F (49 °C), improper storage of medications or firearms, disrepair, and unsafe heating appliances.

Community Level: Neighborhood Structure and Safety

Neighborhood structure reflects a family's physical environment at a broader level and includes measures of instability and proximity to poverty.

Related to instability is the extent of tenure of families in the neighborhood, such as the percentage of households remaining in their current residence for less than 10 years. Neighborhood structure can also be assessed in terms of the child-care burden (the ratio of children to adults, males to females, and percentage of elderly population) and impoverishment (percentage of households that are female headed, the poverty level for the neighborhood, rate of unemployment, percentage of vacant housing units, and population loss; Korbin, Coulton, Chard, Platt-Houston, & Su, 1998). Community violence (e.g., crime, assaults, theft) and child maltreatment are mutually influential (Lynch & Cicchetti, 1998). Abused children are more likely than nonabused children to live in dangerous neighborhoods where they are exposed to further violence (Grogan-Kaylor, Ruffolo, Ortega, & Clarke, 2008).

Personal Adjustment and Coping Resources of Perpetrators

Adult offenders' personal adjustment and coping resources have received the lion's share of research on causes and risk factors relating to child abuse. This research has focused on the psychological factors that cause such behavior, as well as those that are significantly affected over the life span. Notably, child abuse seldom is caused by severe forms of adult psychopathology (Wolfe, 1999). Fewer than 10% of abusing parents have a primary psychiatric disorder that is causally linked to their abusive behavior. Nonetheless, abusive parents are likely to have a history of learning and intellectual deficits and personality disorders that impede their day-to-day abilities to cope successfully with child-related and other stressors, as described below. Also highlighted is the nascent literature that looks more specifically at characteristics of abusive fathers, as much of the past literature has been overrepresented by abusive mothers.

Individual Level

Maltreatment history. Physical and emotional abuse are significant factors in the backgrounds of children who repeat the cycle of violence, and adult offenders' experiences from their families of origin were among the first issues to stand out in early clinical studies of such individuals. Such experiences significantly increase the likelihood that an individual will become subsequently involved in coercive relationships with peers, dating partners, and their own children (Wolfe, 2006).

Stress and arousal. Child abuse researchers and practitioners have consistently described abusive parents as impulsive and exhibiting a low frustration tolerance. Negative arousal interferes with rational problem solving, such that the person's awareness of the intensity of his or her actions becomes blurred by the urgency of retaliation. This paired association between arousal and child behavior may occur gradually during everyday parent–child contact or struggles or more may occur suddenly during highly stressful, difficult encounters.

In a study by Francis and Wolfe (2008), abusive fathers reported significantly more stress directly related to parenting, with approximately 80% scoring in the elevated level on a measure assessing overall parenting-related distress. This finding indicates a poorer sense of parenting competence, role restriction, conflict with the other parent, depression, and lack of social support, compared with nonabusive fathers. Abusive fathers, similar to abusive mothers, tend to view their children more negatively, see themselves as mistreated or rejected by the child, and perceive the child as not meeting their expectations.

In addition to stress and arousal, the role of negative affect, particularly anger, has been supported in studies involving samples of abusive mothers (Mammen, Kolko, & Pilkonis, 2002). Francis and Wolfe (2008) found that abusive fathers reported higher scores than nonabusive fathers on a scale assessing outward expression of anger, which reflect the frequent aggressive expression of anger through verbal aggression or physical aggression toward other people and/or objects. More than half of the abusive fathers reported levels of the outward expression of anger that were above that of 75% of their same-sex age-related peers. Thus, the general experience of anger by abusive fathers is more likely to be associated with aggressive behavior, similar to findings with abusive mothers (Wolfe, 1999) and partner-abusing men (Norlander & Eckhardt, 2005).

Physical and psychological health. Epidemiological studies support a substantial association between child maltreatment and parental substance abuse. An interview study of 1,681 maltreating families found that almost 11% of respondents reported alcohol or drug dependence as a major family stress factor (American Association for Protecting Children, 1988). In a related study, adults with an alcohol or drug disorder were 2.7 times more likely to endorse physically abusive behaviors and 4.2 times more likely to endorse neglect behaviors toward their children (Kelleher, Chaffin, Hollenberg, & Fischer, 1994). Prospectively, parental substance abuse predicted parents' self-report of child physical abuse and neglect, controlling for several confounds including antisocial personality (Chaffin, Kelleher, & Hollenberg, 1996). Depression was a risk factor for physical abuse but not neglect, once confounds including substance abuse diagnoses were controlled. Substance abuse, overall, is significantly associated with greater recidivism, danger to the child, permanent removal of the child by courts, and noncompliance with treatment (Wekerle & Wall, 2002).

In a 17-year longitudinal study of 644 families, three factors uniquely predicted physical abuse: low maternal involvement, early separation from the mother, and perinatal problems (Brown, Cohen, Johnson, & Salzinger, 1998). Two other factors—maternal young age and maternal sociopathology—

predicted risk of physical abuse as well as risk of sexual abuse and neglect. Similarly, Bishop and Leadbeater (1999) found maternal depression, quality of social support from friends (i.e., low number of friends, contact with friends, and quality of friendship), and quality of current relationships (i.e., more negative) to be unique predictors of maltreatment status.

Mental health concerns, particularly a history of substance abuse and violent behavior, have also been identified as a risk factor in fathers' and surrogate fathers' perpetration of child abuse and neglect (Schaeffer, Alexander, Bethke, & Kretz, 2005). A history of substance abuse or dependence was identified in 85% of fathers or surrogate fathers, and approximately three quarters had a history of police involvement due to violent behavior (DeBellis et al., 2001). In contrast, mothers presented with mood and anxiety disorders, with only a third presenting with substance abuse difficulties. These researchers concluded that male caregiver mental illness as well as substance abuse was more serious and less amenable to conventional intervention than female caregiver mental illness. Substance use has also been associated with fathers' increased risk of child maltreatment as determined by their scores on the Child Abuse Potential Inventory (Ammerman, Kolko, Kirisci, Blackson, & Dawes, 1999).

In the Francis and Wolfe (2008) study, abusive fathers had less educational achievement, lower financial status, higher levels of childhood trauma, and significantly more current mental health concerns than nonabusive fathers (particularly on scales assessing depression, paranoia, and hostility), which suggests that when faced with child-related stimuli they may form quick, negative attributions and engage in behavior accordingly. They also reported a greater history of alcohol abuse, more arrests for violent offenses, and more weapon ownership, and they described themselves as more hostile and suspicious than comparison fathers.

Child-rearing style. Child maltreatment seldom involves isolated or premeditated events but rather occurs in the context of child rearing. Parents who are physically abusive tend to deliver a lot of threats or angry commands that exceed the demands of the situation when interacting with their children, rather than offer their children positive forms of guidance and praise (Azar & Wolfe, 2006). For example, studies of the everyday interactions between abusive parents and their children find that such parents express significantly less positive behavior during interactions with their children and other family members (Wolfe, 1985). Relative to other families, members of child-abusive families interact less often; when they do interact, it tends to be more negative and to involve excessive forms of verbal and physical control that exceed the demands of the situation.

Child-rearing expectations and empathy. Studies indicate that abusive parents are largely unfamiliar with their role as parents, including atypical knowledge and beliefs about normal child development and behavior (Azar,

Robinson, Hekimian, & Twentyman, 1984; Rodriguez, 2010). Deficits and distortions may play a role in parental perceptions and judgments of their child's behavior, perceptions that justify coercive or neglectful behavior. They interpret the child's behavior as being wrong and respond rapidly, without contemplating the circumstances or considering innocent explanations, which incites explosive, abusive reactions.

Unrealistic expectations and negative intent attributions can lead to greater punishment for child misbehavior and less reliance on explanation and positive teaching methods. Children are seen as deserving of harsh punishment, and its use is rationalized as a way to maintain control. Thus, maltreating parents may bring into interactions with their children a variety of negative beliefs and expectations about their children as well as about themselves as parents, leading them to misperceive or mislabel typical child behavior and respond inappropriately.

The child's role in abuse has also been carefully considered. However, with the important exception of girls being sexually abused more often than boys, no child characteristic, such as conduct problems, has been associated with the risk of maltreatment, once environmental and adult factors are controlled (U.S. Department of Health and Human Services, 2008). A child may unintentionally play a role in the continuation or escalation of abusive or neglectful relationships. For example, children with disabilities such as mental retardation or physical impairments are more likely to be abused than are their nondisabled peers (Hershkowitz & Lamb, 2007).

Abusive parents' inappropriate recognition of and responses to child needs may reflect disturbances in empathy, particularly perspective-taking and empathic concern. They lack the affective (i.e., an emotional involvement with the experience of others) as well as the cognitive component of empathy (i.e., an intellectual appreciation and recognition of the experience of others). For example, male partners who abuse their spouse and mothers who abuse their child both show lack of empathy for their victims, which interferes with their ability to recognize and meet the needs of others and leads to greater aggression (Perez-Albeniz & de Paul, 2004).

Abusive fathers indicated that they were less likely to try to consider their child's perspective and less likely to feel empathic concern for their child (Francis & Wolfe, 2008). Lower levels of perspective taking have been associated with high levels of impulsivity (Beven, O'Brien-Malone, & Hall, 2004), which serves to place the child at greater risk, particularly in the face of abusive fathers' heightened anger and general aggression. Empathy for others' emotional experience is an important component in managing any social context, including the parenting context. An appreciation of how his child may feel or view events allows the father to see the child as an individual with a unique viewpoint and feelings.

Fathers in the Francis and Wolfe (2008) study interpreted children's socioemotional signals more negatively on a measure of empathy and perceived more negative or hostile emotions on children's faces. For example, abusive fathers were more likely to label the children's facial expressions as portraying feelings of anger and disgust, which suggests they may have a hostile attribution bias and are vigilant to signs of threat. Fathers who are unable or unwilling to recognize and appreciate a child's differing viewpoint, feelings, and needs often have compromised their ability to respond to the child in a sensitive and responsive manner, and their action becomes focused on meeting their own needs rather than the needs of the child.

Although children of abusive parents may exhibit more difficult behavior as a result of dysregulation stemming from maltreatment and poor parenting, research with abusive mothers suggests that the adult's perception of the child is distorted. Studies involving only abusive mothers find that they perceive the behavior of their child (as well as other children) as more difficult and negative during behavioral/dyadic interaction tasks than independent raters (Wolfe, 1999) and overreport their child's negative behavior (Haskett, Scott, & Fann, 1995). Because abusive fathers are more likely to perceive anger and hostile intent, they may feel that they are often in the defensive position of having to manage struggles. Over time, such vigilance can lead to chronic feelings of frustration and emotion dysregulation and increase the likelihood of an aggressive or punishing response. At a minimum, the perception of anger in a child's face signals that the child is less available to meet the father's needs, which is likely to be threatening to his sense of entitlement (Scott & Crooks, 2004).

Family Level: Conflict and Violence

Family circumstances, most notably conflict and marital violence, also have a causal connection to child maltreatment. Straus and Gelles (1990) found that men who reported beating their wives were also more likely to report abusing their children (i.e., 50% of men who abused their wives three or more times in the past year also abused their children three or more times during the same period). Other studies and reviews have generally supported the estimate that in about 50% of the families in which adult partners are violent toward one another, one or both parents also have been violent toward a child at some point during the previous year (Edleson, 1999).

Domestic conflicts and violence against women most often arise during disagreements over child rearing, discipline, and each partner's responsibilities in child care (Gewirtz & Edleson, 2007). Children may be caught in the cross fire between angry adults or in some cases instigate a marital conflict by misbehaving or demanding attention. In either case, an escalating cycle of family turmoil and violence begins, whereby children's behavioral and emotional reactions to the violence create additional stress on the marital relationship, further aggravating an already volatile situation.

The physical and psychological consequences of violence, moreover, cause abused women to be less capable of responding to their children's needs, which again increases pressure on the family system (Sturge-Apple, Davies, Cicchetti, & Cummings, 2009). Tragically, not only do marital violence and family turmoil frighten and disturb children in a direct manner, but the resulting fallout from these events—ranging from changes in financial status and living quarters to loss of family unity and safety—prolongs the stress and thus the harmful impact on children's development (Margolin, 2005).

Community Level

Coordination of services. Risk of physical abuse is greater in communities that lack consistent and coordinated community efforts to assist in child maltreatment prevention and intervention. These efforts include coordinating committees to assist investigation, services, and training of personnel involved in child maltreatment. They also include public health programs that coordinate social and health-related services to families, such as home visitation by trained nursing or social work professionals (Olds et al., 1998).

Child protection. Although child protection services are available in every community, there is considerable variability in terms of their community role and effectiveness. Child welfare resources, such as the number of foster homes and specialized placement facilities, average number of cases per social worker, percentage of the total budget that is earmarked for prevention and community outreach, and similar issues, all affect rates of abuse. A second aspect of child protection involves the availability and extent of training for child welfare workers, given the critical and far-reaching role they play in each community. Finally, communities must keep track of offenders, which requires coordination at the federal and state level in addition to community efforts, because it is often discovered that they were known or suspected to have abused children in other locations prior to the current investigation. Greater exchange of relevant information between communities and agencies remains a challenge in many states and counties.

Societal/Cultural Level

Child-rearing practices. Today's parents are expected to appreciate their child's developmental strengths and limitations and to move away from total reliance on disciplinary control methods toward methods that encourage the child's emerging independence and self-control. However, hypocrisy emerges when attempting to differentiate child abuse from child discipline, because cultural norms in many countries have long accepted corporal punishment as a primary, even necessary, component of discipline. As a result, four out of five 3-year-olds in the United States are physically punished by their parents during any given year, and about one in 10 children receives discipline so severe that they are at considerable risk of physical and emotional harm (Straus & Stewart, 1999).

Whether it is acceptable to spank children has become very controversial among lay and professional audiences in more recent years (Benjet & Kazdin, 2003; Gershoff, 2002). However, there is less agreement that corporal punishment is a risk factor for child abuse, given its reliance on physical pain and its connection to emotional arousal of both parties, although its role is mostly indirect. Most parents who use physical discipline are not abusing their children in either the physical or psychological sense. However, a change in circumstances (e.g., increased stress, more difficult child behavior) can up the ante quite suddenly.

Because no universal standards exist, use of corporal punishment is often determined by local standards and parental beliefs in what defines reasonable punishment. Cultural values, historical precedent, and community standards may set the stage for one person's abuse being another person's discipline. Limited opportunities for parents to learn appropriate, noncorporal child-rearing methods and to receive necessary education and support for their role contribute to the risk of harm to children. Given increasing evidence that corporal punishment of children is harmful (Gershoff & Bitensky, 2007), a growing number of countries are choosing to abolish the practice.

Public health policies. The incidence of child maltreatment may be reduced through primary prevention efforts, which are targeted to large segments of the population regardless of any signs or symptoms of concern. Identification of the most important groups to reach is guided by epidemiological studies that point to particular characteristics indicative of subpopulations that have a problem, such as persons living in disadvantaged neighborhoods. Primary prevention is population based rather than individually based, so its successful application is reflected by reductions in the rate of the disorder in the selected population, such as a particular community or county (Wolfe, 2006).

Summary of Risk Factors

Three key elements stand out as common etiological features concerning the parent's role in child abuse and neglect: (a) the manner in which the parent interacts with the child on an everyday basis; (b) the frustration–aggression relationship that is learned by the parent in relation to child rearing, which accounts for the rapid and often uncontrollable escalation from annoyance to rage; and (c) the cognitive, social informational processes that explain the distorted beliefs and attributions underlying a parent's actions (Wolfe, 1999). Social interactional, social information processing, and arousal–aggression processes are useful in explaining the constant changes in the behavior of family members in response to events within or outside of the family unit. Child abuse can best be explained as the result of an interaction between the parent and child within a system that seldom provides alternative solutions (e.g., through exposure to appropriate parental models, education, and supports) or clear-cut restraints (e.g., maltreatment laws, sanctions, consequences). It is important to note that efforts to address the more distal events that may shape the child-rearing environment (e.g., poverty, stress) have not been successfully accomplished to date.

HOW DO WE KNOW IT? A CRITICAL ANALYSIS

The present multidimensional perspective on risk factors for child abuse perpetration is based on evidence that, much like other forms of intimate violence, such behavior is seldom due to some extremely abnormal or pathological influence. Child abuse is better described as the culmination of interrelated events both within and outside of the family rather than parental psychopathology. This argument provides the major basis for studying abusive behavior within a multilevel context of individual, family, and societal events. In addition, abusive events are often more extreme forms of everyday events and stressors that most families experience to some degree, making it difficult to pinpoint the variable or variables that lead to abuse in one family but not another.

A multidimensional perspective also involves investigation of critical antecedents, significant historical or developmental characteristics of the parent and child, the nature of the aggressive act and its impact on the child, the consequences that maintain such behavior, the nature of the family context, and the larger social system in which abuse occurs. Unfortunately, most studies of this phenomenon are incapable of examining all or most of these levels due to its complexity. Because abusive behavior is a private and illegal act that occurs at a relatively low frequency, such behavior cannot be observed and studied in its natural state. Instead, researchers study less extreme, routine interactions between parents and children that may or may not lie on the same continuum as child abuse. As measurement and analytical tools improve, however, there is an increase in studies that use multilevel modeling techniques that can better account for these interrelated processes and mechanisms (Freisthler et al., 2006).

WHERE DO WE GO FROM HERE? RECOMMENDATIONS

An important gap in child abuse research is that, with few exceptions, advances in understanding child abuse risk factors have not been translated into effective and wide-scale prevention efforts (Mikton & Butchart, 2009). Intervention and prevention should be directed toward the important issues that families face during each of the emerging developmental stages that the child and parent must endure, as opposed to attempting to repair the difficulties in the relationship later on. This approach requires a strategy that emphasizes child abuse prevention from a public health perspective, much like other circumstances that increase risk of major diseases or harm (Prinz, Sanders, Shapiro, Whitaker, & Lutzker, 2009). Such an approach reduces major challenges of current intervention and prevention programs, which are focused on identification of the most at-risk families. Public health strategies, in contrast, could redirect focus onto the identification and selection of appropriate, desirable, and attainable goals that can be addressed through community action programs, individual skills-training efforts, and similar activities (Wolfe, 1999).

Prevention of the various forms of child abuse and neglect should encourage diversity and opportunities for the development of resources and strengths among children and parents. Societal influences that play a role in child abuse and neglect, especially in circumstances in which families are exposed to major effects of poverty, health risks, and environmental conflict, require concerted efforts. The special risks and strengths of diverse cultural and ethnic groups need to be addressed, along with greater sensitivity to ethnic and cultural issues in the planning of services. A cross-cultural perspective on child abuse and neglect intervention and prevention would redirect the focus solely from individuals and families and explore societal and cultural conditions that worsen or improve these problems.

Being a victim of child abuse (as well as a child witness to woman abuse) is one of the strongest predictors of future violence in relationships. Studies of high school students reveal that exposure to violence at home is the best predictor of mental health problems (e.g., trauma-related mood and anxiety disorders), antisocial behavior, and violence in romantic relationships during adolescence (Wolfe, Scott, Wekerle, & Pittman, 2001). However, education and prevention are seldom directed at this critical connection in an effort to build positive, healthy relationships among youths, especially those at greater risk of becoming perpetrators and victims. The pathway from experiencing violence in childhood to becoming violent or abused in subsequent relationships, although significant, is by no means direct, inevitable, or irreversible. Many circumstantial events, such as the availability of a caring adult, as well as individual strengths such as an easygoing temperament and social competence, may play a role in mitigating against such outcomes.

A promising prevention direction is to introduce "healthy relationship" lessons in school, as a partnership among students, teachers, parents, and community agencies with knowledge and expertise about forms of teen dating violence and family violence (Wolfe et al., 2009). For adolescents, education must be relevant to their interests and developmental needs, actively involve their peers (not only those identified as at risk), and be introduced universally throughout elementary and secondary grades, much as health and safety lessons are introduced in many jurisdictions. Similarly, public education campaigns against child abuse and related forms of violence need to tailor awareness efforts to recognize different perspectives and needs related to demographics, such as gender, race, and social class. Communities, in particular, need to move beyond awareness and offer specific and practical strategies on what the average citizen can do about child maltreatment and domestic violence. These strategies have to be specific enough to help a friend or coworker deal with a perpetrator or victim that they know, in a manner that ensures their own safety. In addition, broader messages are needed to inform people as to what they can do for the child maltreatment issue in their own communities.

In conclusion, because child abuse is a dynamic, multicausal issue, there will never be a full understanding of its nature. Nonetheless, considerable information exists that could be very informative to education and prevention, which has not been mined. It is reasonable to conclude that prevention initiatives could focus on protective and resilient factors that promote development of strong, positive child-rearing abilities. Such resilience is accomplished by strengthening the early formation of the parent–child relationship, improving the parent's abilities to cope with stress through exposure to a mental health or social services support system, and strengthening the child's adaptive behaviors, which will contribute to his or her further emotional and psychological adjustment (Alink, Cicchetti, Kim, & Rogosch, 2009).

APPENDIX 2.1

Descriptions of the five key determinants of health used herein.

INCOME AND SOCIAL STATUS

The relative distribution of wealth, rather than the amount, is seen as a key factor that determines health status. Similarly, social status affects health by determining the degree of control people have over life circumstances and, hence, their capacity to take action. There is strong theoretical and empirical support for the significance of income and social status on rates of child maltreatment, such as the role of poverty, the neighborhood context, and the importance of social policies to thwart discrimination and inequality.

SOCIAL SUPPORT NETWORKS

Support from families, friends, and communities is important in helping people deal with difficult situations and maintaining a sense of mastery over life circumstances. The child maltreatment literature has documented the importance of such social supports in regulating the stress and isolation of families, as well as the manner in which families in need access necessary resources.

EDUCATION

Meaningful and relevant education equips people with knowledge and skills for daily living, enables them to participate in their community, and increases opportunities for employment. Community and school-based efforts make children and adults more aware of the signs and effects of maltreatment, as well as actions to take. Efforts at training, school policy, availability of prenatal and early childhood classes, and judiciary and legislative actions to deter maltreatment are described.

PHYSICAL ENVIRONMENT

Factors such as the type of housing and community safety have a major impact on health and have been implicated in rates of child maltreatment. This issue includes family- and community-level environmental factors such as homelessness, conditions in the home that impair safety and healthy development, and neighborhood structure and safety.

PERSONAL ADJUSTMENT AND COPING SKILLS

Efforts to improve one's health and personal adjustment help prevent disease and promote self-care, and effective coping skills enable people to be self-reliant, solve problems, and make choices that enhance health. Personal adjustment and coping skills fall at the level of the individual adult in the present framework, such as health problems, stress and coping resources, and psychosexual adjustment.

APPENDIX 2.2

Description of the four levels of action used herein.

INDIVIDUAL LEVEL (ADULT AND CHILD)

Abusive parents often lack the skills and resources necessary to cope effectively with child rearing and other stressful life demands, which may lead to a greater number of child behavior problems. Individual characteristics of the child (e.g., difficult behavior) also may contribute to or maintain the adult's behavior.

FAMILY LEVEL

Determinants of health at the family level include both demographic and family structure components. Childhood maltreatment often occurs in the context of multiproblem homes and neighborhoods, in which socioeconomic disadvantage, marital distress, domestic violence, and related forms of conflict or pathology have a major influence on child development. Family factors are important considerations across many of the determinants of health, such as social support networks, physical environment, and income and social status.

COMMUNITY LEVEL

Although child maltreatment is certainly not limited by the boundaries of socioeconomic status, the problem must be considered in the context of environmental stress and isolation from resources. The availability of adequate social assistance, for example, helps to combat the effects of poverty and restrictions in the child's expectable environment, such as lack of adequate day care, safety, and housing. Adults living below the poverty level, moreover, suffer greater from the effects of individual and family problems, such as substance abuse and emotional disorders. Thus, community-level variables include such issues as access to resources, employment and working conditions, educational and training opportunities, neighborhood safety, and child protection resources.

SOCIETAL/CULTURAL LEVEL

This macrolevel component to the framework involves the identification of broader social and cultural factors affecting maltreatment, such as cultural acceptance of corporal punishment, willingness to learn alternatives to corporal punishment, awareness of abuse, laws and statutes relating to children's safety and mental health, and public awareness campaigns directed at reducing the overall prevalence of child maltreatment.

REFERENCES

Alink, L. R. A., Cicchetti, D., Kim, J., & Rogosch, F. A. (2009). Mediating and moderating processes in the relation between maltreatment and psychopathology: Mother–child relationship quality and emotion regulation. *Journal of Abnormal Child Psychology, 37*, 831–843. doi:10.1007/s10802-009-9314-4

American Association for Protecting Children. (1988). *Highlights of official child neglect and abuse reporting, 1986.* Denver, CO: American Humane Association.

Ammerman, R. T., Kolko, D. J., Kirisci, L., Blackson, T. C., & Dawes, M. A. (1999). Child abuse potential in parents with histories of substance use disorder. *Child Abuse & Neglect, 23*, 1225–1238. doi:10.1016/S0145-2134(99)00089-7

Azar, S. T., Robinson, D. R., Hekimian, E., & Twentyman, C. T. (1984). Unrealistic expectations and problem-solving ability in maltreating and comparison mothers. *Journal of Consulting and Clinical Psychology, 52*, 687–691. doi:10.1037/0022-006X.52.4.687

Azar, S. T., & Wolfe, D. A. (2006). Child physical abuse and neglect. In E. J. Mash & R. A. Barkley (Eds.), *Treatment of childhood disorders* (3rd ed., pp. 595–646). New York, NY: Guilford Press.

Benjet, C., & Kazdin, A. E. (2003). Spanking children: The controversies, findings and new directions. *Clinical Psychology Review, 23*, 197–224. doi:10.1016/S0272-7358(02)00206-4

Beven, J. P., O'Brien-Malone, A., & Hall, G. (2004). Using the Interpersonal Reactivity Index to assess empathy in violent offenders. *International Journal of Forensic Psychology, 1*, 33–41.

Bishop, S. J., & Leadbeater, B. J. (1999). Maternal social support patterns and child maltreatment: Comparison of maltreating and nonmaltreating mothers. *American Journal of Orthopsychiatry, 69*, 172–181. doi:10.1037/h0080419

Brown, J., Cohen, P., Johnson, J. G., & Salzinger, S. (1998). A longitudinal analysis of risk factors for child maltreatment: Findings of a 17-year prospective study of officially recorded and self-reported child abuse and neglect. *Child Abuse & Neglect, 22*, 1065–1078. doi:10.1016/S0145-2134(98)00087-8

Chaffin, M., Kelleher, K., & Hollenberg, J. (1996). Onset of physical abuse and neglect: Psychiatric, substance abuse, and social risk factors from prospective community data. *Child Abuse & Neglect, 20*, 191–203. doi:10.1016/S0145-2134(95)00144-1

Chapman, D. P., Dube, S. R., & Anda, R. F. (2007). Adverse childhood events as risk factors for negative mental health outcomes. *Psychiatric Annals, 37*, 359–364.

Cicchetti, D., & Valentino, K. (2006). An ecological–transactional perspective on child maltreatment: Failure of the average expectable environment and its influence on child development. In D. Cicchetti & D. J. Cohen (Eds.), *Developmental psychopathology: Vol. 3. Risk, disorder, and adaptation* (2nd ed., pp. 129–201). Hoboken, NJ: Wiley.

Coulton, C. J., Crampton, D. S., Irwin, M., Spilsbury, J. C., & Korbin, J. E. (2007). How neighborhoods influence child maltreatment: A review of the literature and alternative pathways. *Child Abuse & Neglect, 31*, 1117–1142. doi:10.1016/j.chiabu.2007.03.023

De Bellis, M. D., Broussard, E. R., Herring, D. J., Wexler, S., Moritz, G., & Benitez, J. G. (2001). Psychiatric co-morbidity in caregivers and children involved in maltreatment: A pilot research study with policy implications. *Child Abuse & Neglect, 25*, 923–944. doi:10.1016/S0145-2134(01)00247-2

Eckenrode, J., Rowe, E., Laird, M., & Braithwaite, J. (1995). Mobility as a mediator of the effects of child maltreatment on academic performance. *Child Development, 66*, 1130–1142. doi:10.2307/1131803

Edleson, J. L. (1999). The overlap between child maltreatment and woman battering. *Violence Against Women, 5*, 134–154. doi:10.1177/107780129952003

Francis, K. J., & Wolfe, D. A. (2008). Cognitive and emotional differences between abusive and non-abusive fathers. *Child Abuse & Neglect, 32*, 1127–1137. doi:10.1016/j.chiabu.2008.05.007

Freisthler, B., Merritt, D. H., & LaScala, E. A. (2006). Understanding the ecology of child maltreatment: A review of the literature and directions for future research. *Child Maltreatment, 11*, 263–280. doi:10.1177/1077559506289524

Garbarino, J. (1987). Family support and the prevention of child maltreatment. In S. L. Kagan, D. R. Powell, D. Weissbourd, & E. Zigler (Eds.), *America's family support programs* (pp. 99–114). New Haven, CT: Yale University Press.

Gershoff, E. T. (2002). Corporal punishment by parents and associated child behaviors and experiences: A meta-analytic and theoretical review. *Psychological Bulletin, 128,* 539–579. doi:10.1037/0033-2909.128.4.539

Gershoff, E. T., & Bitensky, S. H. (2007). The case against corporal punishment of children: Converging evidence from social science research and international human rights law and implications for U.S. public policy. *Psychology, Public Policy, and Law, 13,* 231–272. doi:10.1037/1076-8971.13.4.231

Gewirtz, A. H., & Edleson, J. L. (2007). Young children's exposure to intimate partner violence: Towards a developmental risk and resilience framework for research and intervention. *Journal of Family Violence, 22,* 151–163. doi:10.1007/s10896-007-9065-3

Gillham, B., Tanner, G., Cheyne, B., Freeman, I., Rooney, M., & Lambie, A. (1998). Unemployment rates, single parent density, and indices of child poverty: Their relationship to different categories of child abuse and neglect. *Child Abuse & Neglect, 22,* 79–90. doi:10.1016/S0145-2134(97)00134-8

Grogan-Kaylor, A., Ruffolo, M. C., Ortega, R. M., & Clarke, J. (2008). Behaviors of youth involved in the child welfare system. *Child Abuse & Neglect, 32,* 35–49.

Haskett, M. E., Scott, S. S., & Fann, K. D. (1995). Child Abuse Potential Inventory and parenting behavior: Relationships with high-risk correlates. *Child Abuse & Neglect, 19,* 1483–1495. doi:10.1016/0145-2134(95)00107-4

Hershkowitz, I., & Lamb, M. (2007). Victimization of children with disabilities. *American Journal of Orthopsychiatry, 77,* 629–635. doi:10.1037/0002-9432.77.4.629

Kelleher, K., Chaffin, M., Hollenberg, J., & Fischer, E. (1994). Alcohol and drug disorders among physically abusive and neglectful parents in a community-based sample. *American Journal of Public Health, 84,* 1586–1590. doi:10.2105/AJPH.84.10.1586

Korbin, J. E., Coulton, C. J., Chard, S., Platt-Houston, C., & Su, M. (1998). Impoverishment and child maltreatment in African American and European American neighborhoods. *Development and Psychopathology, 10,* 215–233. doi:10.1017/S0954579498001588

Lynch, M., & Cicchetti, D. (1998). An ecological–transactional analysis of children and contexts: The longitudinal interplay among child maltreatment, community violence, and children's symptomatology. *Development and Psychopathology, 10,* 235–257. doi:10.1017/S095457949800159X

Mammen, O. K., Kolko, D. J., & Pilkonis, P. A. (2002). Negative affect and parental aggression in child physical abuse. *Child Abuse & Neglect, 26,* 407–424. doi:10.1016/S0145-2134(02)00316-2

Margolin, G. (2005). Children's exposure to violence: Exploring developmental pathways to diverse outcomes. *Journal of Interpersonal Violence, 20,* 72–81.

McGuinness, T. M., & Schneider, K. (2007). Poverty, child maltreatment, and foster care. *Journal of the American Psychiatric Nurses Association, 13,* 296–303. doi:10.1177/1078390307308421

Mikton, C., & Butchart, A. (2009). Child maltreatment prevention: A systematic review of reviews. *Bulletin of the World Health Organization, 87,* 353–361.

Norlander, B., & Eckhardt, C. (2005). Anger, hostility, and male perpetrators of intimate partner violence: A meta-analytic review. *Clinical Psychology Review, 25,* 119–152. doi:10.1016/j.cpr.2004.10.001

Olds, D., Henderson, C. R., Jr., Cole, R., Eckenrode, J., Kitzman, H., Luckey, D., . . . Powers, J. (1998). Long-term effects of nurse home visitation on children's criminal and antisocial behavior: 15-year follow-up of a randomized controlled trial. *JAMA, 280,* 1238–1244. doi:10.1001/jama.280.14.1238

Perez-Albeniz, A., & de Paul, J. (2004). Gender differences in empathy in parents at high- and low-risk of child physical abuse. *Child Abuse & Neglect, 28,* 289–300. doi:10.1016/j.chiabu.2003.11.017

Peterson, L., & Brown, D. (1994). Integrating child injury and abuse-neglect research: Common histories, etiologies, and solutions. *Psychological Bulletin, 116,* 293–315. doi:10.1037/0033-2909.116.2.293

Prinz, R. J., Sanders, M. R., Shapiro, C. J., Whitaker, D. J., & Lutzker, J. R. (2009). Population-based prevention of child maltreatment: The U.S. Triple P system population trial. *Prevention Science, 10,* 1–12. doi:10.1007/s11121-009-0123-3

Rodriguez, C. M. (2010). Personal contextual characteristics and cognitions: Predicting child abuse potential and disciplinary style. *Journal of Interpersonal Violence, 25,* 315–335. doi:10.1177/0886260509334391

Schaeffer, C. M., Alexander, P. C., Bethke, K., & Kretz, L. S. (2005). Predictors of child abuse potential among military parents: Comparing mothers and fathers. *Journal of Family Violence, 20,* 123–129. doi:10.1007/s10896-005-3175-6

Scott, K. L., & Crooks, C. (2004). Effecting change in maltreating fathers: Critical principles for intervention planning. *Clinical Psychology: Science and Practice, 11,* 95–111. doi:10.1093/clipsy/bph058

Sedlak, A. J., & Broadhurst, D. D. (1996, September). *Third national incidence study of child abuse and neglect: Final report.* Washington, DC: U.S. Department of Health and Human Services.

Statistics Canada. (2007). *Persons in low income before tax* (Cat. No. 75-202-XIE). Ottawa, Ontario, Canada: Author. Retrieved from http://www.statcan.ca/english/Pgdb/famil41a.htm

Steinberg, L. D., Catalano, R., & Dooley, D. (1981). Economic antecedents of child abuse and neglect. *Child Development, 52,* 975–985. doi:10.2307/1129102

Straus, M. A., & Gelles, R. J. (Eds.). (1990). *Physical violence in American families.* New Brunswick, NJ: Transaction Books.

Straus, M. A., & Stewart, J. H. (1999). Corporal punishment by American parents: National data on prevalence, chronicity, severity, and duration, in relation to child and family characteristics. *Clinical Child and Family Psychology Review, 2,* 55–70. doi:10.1023/A:1021891529770

Sturge-Apple, M. L., Davies, P. T., Cicchetti, D., & Cummings, E. M. (2009). The role of mothers' and fathers' adrenocortical reactivity in spillover between interparental conflict and parenting practices. *Journal of Family Psychology, 23*, 215–225. doi:10.1037/a0014198

Turner, H. A., Finkelhor, D., & Ormrod, R. (2007). Family structure variations in patterns and predictors of child victimization. *American Journal of Orthopsychiatry, 77*, 282–295. doi:10.1037/0002-9432.77.2.282

United Nations Secretary-General's Study on Violence Against Children. (2006). *World report on violence against children*. Geneva, Switzerland: United Nations. Retrieved from http://www.violencestudy.org/a553

U.S. Census Bureau. (2007). *Small area income and poverty estimates program*. Retrieved from http://www.census.gov/cgi-bin/saipe/national.cgi

U.S. Department of Health and Human Services, Administration on Children, Youth, and Families. (2008). *Child maltreatment 2006*. Washington, DC: U.S. Government Printing Office. Retrieved from http://www.acf.hhs.gov/programs/cb/pubs/cm06/index.htm

Wekerle, C., MacMillan, H. L., Leung, E., & Jamieson, E. (2008). Child maltreatment. In M. Hersen & A. M. Gross (Eds.), *Handbook of clinical psychology: Vol. 2. Children and adolescents* (pp. 856–903). Hoboken, NJ: Wiley.

Wekerle, C., & Wall, A. (2002). Introduction: The overlap between relationship violence and substance abuse. In C. Wekerle & A. Wall (Eds.), *The violence and addiction equation: Theoretical and clinical issues in substance abuse and relationship violence* (pp. 1–21). New York, NY: Brunner-Routledge.

Wolfe, D. A. (1985). Child abusive parents: An empirical review and analysis. *Psychological Bulletin, 97*, 462–482. doi:10.1037/0033-2909.97.3.462

Wolfe, D. A. (1999). *Child abuse: Implications for child development and psychopathology* (2nd ed.). Thousand Oaks, CA: Sage.

Wolfe, D. A. (2006). Preventing violence in relationships: Psychological science addressing complex social issues. *Canadian Psychology, 47*, 44–50. doi:10.1037/h0087043

Wolfe, D. A., Crooks, C. V., Jaffe, P., Chiodo, D., Hughes, R., Ellis, W., . . . Donner, A. (2009). A school-based program to prevent adolescent dating violence: A cluster randomized trial. *Archives of Pediatric and Adolescent Medicine, 163*, 692–699.

Wolfe, D. A., Scott, K., Wekerle, C., & Pittman, A. (2001). Child maltreatment: Risk of adjustment problems and dating violence in adolescence. *Journal of the American Academy of Child and Adolescent Psychiatry, 40*, 282–289. doi:10.1097/00004583-200103000-00007

3

VULNERABILITY AND PROTECTIVE FACTORS FOR CHILD ABUSE AND MALTREATMENT

ANN T. CHU, ANNARHEEN S. PINEDA, ANNE P. DePRINCE, AND JENNIFER J. FREYD

Child abuse occurs across cultures and societies, remaining a critically important public health and policy issue due to its myriad detrimental outcomes. A substantial body of research now focuses on identifying vulnerability and protective factors that moderate children's risk of abuse in the hopes of being able to understand the mechanisms underlying why and how abuse occurs and to prevent it from happening in the future. Although a comprehensive review of all possible vulnerability and protective factors of child abuse is beyond the scope of this chapter, we describe key findings from the empirical literature organized around three major sections: (a) individual (e.g., gender, gender identity/orientation, age, disability status), (b) parental and familial context (e.g., parental abuse history, parenting practices, substance abuse, co-occurring intimate partner violence [IPV], family composition), and (c) environment and social network factors (e.g., poverty, neighborhood structure, community social support, religion, cultural identity). To understand vulnerability and resilience, we draw on studies that have used diverse sampling strategies (e.g., national surveys from the general population, clinical samples, university students) and methodologies (e.g., retrospective self-report and interviews, review of medical and child welfare records, prospective study designs). Finally, we discuss future directions for, and policy implications of, this body of research.

DEFINITIONS: VULNERABILITY AND PROTECTIVE FACTORS ASSOCIATED WITH CHILDHOOD ABUSE EXPOSURE

Although researchers have identified numerous correlates of child maltreatment, many studies frame these variables as predictors of child maltreatment. However, as Stevens and Hassett (2007) pointed out, although one might understand the various factors that contribute to child abuse in identified patterns, maltreatment often occurs in multiple systems (e.g., families, neighborhoods, societies) that interact in complex and nonlinear ways that are not entirely predictable. In addition, based on findings from epidemiological studies, Finkelhor (1993) concluded that there are no identifiable factors that can absolutely protect a child from being sexually abused. We extend these ideas to propose that there are no markers—at the individual, familial, or societal level—to definitively protect a child from or predict the experience of any type of abuse or neglect. However, we can identify vulnerability factors that have been recognized to be associated with higher rates of maltreatment. For children identified to be at higher risk of child maltreatment compared with their peers, certain factors can protect them against exposure; we also include discussions of these protective factors.

Although child abuse research has advanced rapidly in recent decades to include more complex analyses and rigorous study designs, progress has at times been complicated by variations in how researchers operationalize child abuse across studies. Although researchers might uniformly agree that a 10-year-old child intentionally struck with enough force to cause broken bones has been physically abused, researchers in different countries diverge in counting spanking as physical abuse. Details within broad definitions are not always consistent. For example, the age that separates childhood abuse from adulthood abuse differs widely, with cutoffs ranging from 14 to 18 years (see Senn, Carey, & Vanable, 2008). Inclusions of specific acts of abuse also vary from study to study, with some studies including exposure, threats, and attempts and others focusing only on more severe forms of abuse. Some methodologies rely on substantiated records of abuse and/or neglect to identify abuse, whereas others rely on retrospective reporting from parents or other adult caregivers. While these methodological differences are to be expected in a relatively new area of research, arriving at more convergence will serve to improve the rigor of our scientific pursuit. Although this issue remains to be addressed by the field, for the purposes of this chapter, we include a broad range of definitions to ensure a comprehensive review of findings. Unless otherwise specified, the terms *child maltreatment* and *child abuse* refer to childhood physical, sexual, psychological, and emotional abuse; witnessing violence and neglect will be referred specifically when included in findings. We discuss studies that examine reports of childhood maltreatment, neglect, and witnessing violence that occurred before the victim's 19th birthday.

WHAT DO WE KNOW?

In this section, we review individual, parental and familial, and environmental and social network characteristics that appear to contribute to child abuse rates. A better understanding of the risk and protective factors that contribute to childhood maltreatment may guide researchers and service providers seeking to prevent future abuse.

Individual Factors

Several individual factors have emerged as potential moderators of child abuse exposure, including gender, age, and disability status. Gender appears to be a risk factor for child abuse and neglect generally. Child abuse and neglect cases reported to child protective service agencies across the nation are more likely to involve girls than boys (U.S. Department of Health and Human Services [USDHHS], 2008). However, researchers asking adult victims for retrospective reports using specific behavioral items have demonstrated striking differences in occurrence rates within abuse types and abuse characteristics by gender (e.g., Edinburgh, Saewyc, Thao, & Levitt, 2006; Goldberg & Freyd, 2006). For example, girls tend to report child sexual abuse (CSA) exposure more than boys, whether interviewed as children (as reviewed in Holmes & Slap, 1998) or in adulthood (Finkelhor, Hotaling, Lewis, & Smith, 1990; Goldberg & Freyd, 2006). A review of epidemiological studies indicates that girls are at about 2.5 to 3 times higher risk than boys of sexual abuse (Finkelhor, 1993). Researchers have also found that more adult women than adult men retrospectively reported psychological or emotional maltreatment in childhood (Goldberg & Freyd, 2006). In contrast, a review of nationally representative samples found no gender differences in relation to child physical abuse (Black, Heyman, & Slep, 2001).

The relationship between perpetrator and victim also varies based on the victim's gender. For example, adult women tended to report victimization events in childhood perpetrated by someone close, whereas adult men tended to report more childhood victimization events perpetrated by someone not close to them (Goldberg & Freyd, 2006). Perpetrators against boys were more likely to be closer in age to the victims, whereas perpetrators against girls have been reported to be older in age (Edinburgh et al., 2006). Thus, not only does gender moderate prevalence rates of broad categories of abuse, but gender effects also emerge when examining more specific relationships regarding abuse characteristics.

Findings on gender and risk are consistent with betrayal trauma theory, which highlights the gender asymmetry in abuse by close others, such as sexual abuse, and proposes that such abuse will be associated with alterations in typical information processing (DePrince & Freyd, 2002; Freyd, DePrince, & Gleaves, 2007). To the extent that girls are more likely to experience abuse by close others on whom they are dependent, they are also more likely to experience alterations in cognitive, emotional, and social information processing than their male peers. These alterations, in turn, may increase girls' risk of exposure to additional victimizations (e.g., dating, IPV) as well as negative consequences of abuse (e.g., posttraumatic stress disorder).

Researchers have argued that several alternative explanations may underlie the gender asymmetry for some forms of abuse. One is the lack of attention given to studying male sexual abuse (Romano & De Luca, 2001). Until the mid-1980s, studies specifically examining male sexual victimization rarely took place. Although researchers have increasingly started focusing on male sexual abuse since then, the study of sexually abused females continues to garner more attention than males in research studies. It is interesting that the media seem to pay particular attention to male victims relative to female victims, as is evidenced by the coverage of male victims in priest abuse compared with female victims. Furthermore, many people assume males may be more reluctant than females to disclose abuse, although the empirical support for this commonly held belief is mixed (see Tang, Freyd, & Wang, 2008). A number of factors may be involved in males' reluctance to disclose sexual abuse compared with females, including struggles with the male ethics of self-reliance, stigma of homosexuality, and less likelihood to label certain childhood sexual activities with another individual as abusive (for reviews, see Romano & De Luca, 2001; Tang et al., 2008). These factors may contribute to underestimates of male exposure and less understanding of the characteristics and outcomes associated with male sexual abuse. Alternatively, females may be socialized to perceive (and report) violations in close relationships more so than males (DePrince & Freyd, 2002). Mental health professionals also continue to be biased against the existence of male sexual abuse; thus, professionals rarely ask adult males about CSA and are reluctant to deal with child male victims (Romano & De Luca, 2001). Because systematic investigation of male sexual abuse continues to be limited, comparisons between sexually abused males and females remain difficult. Refining current methodologies will help to clarify the differences between male and female CSA prevalence rates and to effectively meet the needs of the abuse victims.

Despite girls' overrepresentation in some types of abuse and abuse contexts, males do report more frequent exposure to other forms of child abuse than females, suggesting that differences in reporting rates for high betrayal events are not due to a uniform decrease in the likelihood of males reporting.

In fact, more adult males than females reported witnessing someone being killed, committing suicide, or being severely injured as a child, in addition to being severely physical attacked in childhood (Goldberg & Freyd, 2006). Additionally, where partner and child abuse co-occur, males appear to be at elevated risk of physical abuse relative to females (Ross, 1996). Male children also reported experiencing more frequent and severe physical abuse in families with more extreme battering of the mothers, based on both child and mother reports (e.g., Jouriles & Norwood, 1995). Teasing apart these nuanced interactions between abuse and gender will not only provide more comprehensive information about the context in which abuse occurs but also help to inform more effective prevention programs.

In addition to gender, sexual identity/orientation also appears to moderate risk of child abuse. A small number of studies using community samples found that individuals identifying as lesbian, gay, or bisexual (LGB) reported higher prevalence of physical abuse by family members as well as sexual abuse by family and nonfamily members during childhood and adolescence compared with individuals identifying as heterosexual (e.g., Saewyc et al., 2006). Children and adolescents who exhibit opposite-sex–linked behaviors also reported experiencing greater child abuse and neglect (McConaghy & Silove, 1992); this may be due to the stigma associated with minority sexual orientation (Saewyc et al., 2006). Although earlier researchers had sometimes considered sexual and physical abuse to be a cause of LGB orientation, subsequent research has clearly contradicted this hypothesis. The majority of teens who identify as LGB do not report any abuse, and many teens who report sexual or physical abuse identify as heterosexual (e.g., Saewyc et al., 2006). Some studies suggest that adults identifying as bisexual appeared to be at higher risk of victimization in childhood and adolescence than gay and lesbian peers, though this finding has been inconsistent (see Saewyc et al., 2006). In the face of limited research to date, the mechanism underlying the additional risk for LGB individuals remains unclear. Some have suggested that stigma resulting from gender orientation decreases family protection and support for LGB teens (see Saewyc et al., 2006); however, many other potential links have yet to receive adequate research attention. In addition, researchers have yet to characterize the risk of child abuse faced by transgendered individuals, leaving gender identity sorely understudied in this field.

Age also moderates exposure risk. Specifically, younger children appear to be at elevated risk of some types of abuse and for severity of injuries. Nationwide data from the National Child Abuse and Neglect Data Systems (NCANDS) report that children ages 3 and younger are the most frequent victims of child fatality as a result of all types of child abuse and neglect (USDHHS, 2008). In the same nationally based data set, the overall rate of all types of child abuse and neglect was negatively correlated to the child's age.

However, these findings are based on reported cases of abuse and neglect, which may more strongly reflect trends in reporting rates than actual incidence rates.

In contrast, when examining CSA of children under the age of 18, national rates of reported CSA increase with age (Bureau of Justice Statistics, 2000). Research studies using adult retrospective reports also find similar correlations between sexual abuse rates and older age (e.g., Finkelhor, 1993; Putnam, 2003). Some researchers also suggest that age as a risk factor for CSA operates differentially for girls than for boys, with risk starting earlier and lasting longer for girls (Putnam, 2003). In the context of betrayal trauma theory, girls may be more likely to be victimized by a caregiver, whereas boys may be more likely to be victimized by a noncaregiver such as a priest, camp counselor, or coach (DePrince & Freyd, 2002; Goldberg & Freyd, 2006). Caregivers as perpetrators of female victims may have more opportunities for access to their victims, often at a younger age, than noncaregivers as perpetrators of male victims. Thus, to the extent that the relationship between perpetrator and victim may vary as a function of the victim's gender, the age of onset and duration of abuse may also differ on the basis of gender.

Children with special needs may face an elevated risk of child abuse. The NCANDS reported that among children in child protective services, those with mental or physical disabilities were 1.7 times more likely to be exposed to sexual abuse, physical abuse, or neglect than children without disabilities (USDHHS, 2008). A series of studies examining hospital files, welfare records, and school reports in both clinical and general population samples found greater rates of maltreatment among children across different types of disabilities compared with children without disabilities (for a review, see Sullivan & Knutson, 2000). Additional studies have focused on the relationship between specific disabilities and maltreatment types. For example, children with behavioral disorders have been found to be at highest risk of all types of maltreatment; neglect was the most common form of maltreatment across all types of disabilities (as reviewed in Hibbard, Desch, American Academy of Pediatrics Committee on Child Abuse and Neglect, & American Academy of Pediatrics Council on Children with Disabilities, 2007). Researchers have concluded that children with special needs are at increased risk of child abuse and neglect, although the type of maltreatment varies depending on the specific disability (Hibbard et al., 2007). Researchers also caution that thus far, available findings do not allow us to determine whether disabilities are a risk factor for or an outcome of, abuse. The developmental traumatology theory also suggests that trauma that occurs during a child's development will lead to psychopathology and impairments in cognitive and psychosocial domains (De Bellis, 2001). In turn, these conditions increase the risk of additional abuse and neglect later in life. Data from various studies provide some support for these hypotheses, such that disabilities increase risk of maltreatment at the same time that maltreatment contributes to disabilities (Hibbard et al., 2007). Teasing apart directionality may be further complicated by recurrence rates, since the NCANDS also documented that child victims with a disability were 52% more likely to experience additional victimization than child victims without a disability (USDHHS, 2008).

Studies have repeatedly shown that violence itself begets violence. Once a child is exposed to abuse, he or she is at increased risk of exposure to additional incidents. According to the NCANDS data (USDHHS, 2008), children who were victims of maltreatment were 96% more likely to experience a second substantiated event of maltreatment within 6 months than those who had not been victims previously. Additionally, studies have indicated that when a child has experienced one type of maltreatment, the likelihood of other types of maltreatment co-occurring is very high (e.g., Finkelhor, Ormrod, & Turner, 2007).

While we have so far primarily discussed gender, sexual identity/orientation, age, and disabilities as some of the documented individual characteristics that place children at elevated risk of abuse, other studies have also documented additional vulnerability factors at the individual level (e.g., temperament, perinatal risk factors). The commonality between all of these characteristics may point to important underlying vulnerabilities such as children's dependency, small size, and inability to defend themselves.

Parental and Familial Context

Rogosch and Cicchetti (2004) defined child maltreatment as parenting failures in acts of omission (i.e., neglect) or commission (i.e., abuse). Developmental traumatology theory also views child abuse and neglect as extreme forms of dysfunctional family and interpersonal functioning (De Bellis, 2001). Accordingly, numerous studies have focused on vulnerabilities in parental and familial contexts that increase risk of child maltreatment. Many researchers focus on parenting as a causal link between individual child characteristics (e.g., disabilities, young age) and maltreatment. We discuss some of the parental and familial characteristics—including abuse history, parenting practices, substance abuse, co-occurring IPV, and family composition and interaction—as contexts that place children at risk for abuse and as potential mechanisms of maltreatment.

A commonly held misconception has been that parents who were abused in childhood will necessarily continue the cycle of violence. Researchers have since documented a more complicated picture. Kaufman and Zigler's (1987) review found that only 30% ± 5% of parents with a childhood abuse history go on to abuse their children. Thus, although not all parents who have experienced maltreatment will abuse their children, childhood abuse history remains a risk factor for parental abuse of their children.

Many parental factors have been associated with increased likelihood of abuse. For example, young parental age, single parenthood, low education, low employment status, and parental psychopathology have all been found to be associated with physical abuse (as reviewed in Oliver, Kuhns, & Pomeranz, 2006). However, are there common factors underlying these relationships that drive the increased risk of physical abuse as well as additional types of maltreatment and neglect? Milner (2000) proposed a social information processing model in which negative parenting beliefs (e.g., corporal punishment) and maladaptive information processing related to child rearing (e.g., inability to integrate situational cues, unrealistic expectations with regard to child compliance) are related to risk of parental physical child abuse. A review of studies comparing mothers who are physically abusive with mothers who are not physically abusive indicated that abusive mothers were more likely to make internal and stable attributions about their children's negative behaviors and external and unstable attributions about their children's positive behaviors than nonabusive mothers (Black et al., 2001). Abusive mothers were also less likely to blame themselves for failed child–parent interactions than nonabusive mothers (Black et al., 2001). When considered within this context, the associated maternal factors listed above may exacerbate these negative parenting beliefs, attributions, or maladaptive information processing. A recent meta-analysis examining potential risk factors for child physical abuse and neglect also supports this pattern, finding a large effect size for the link between parents perceiving the child as a problem and child neglect ($r = .41$; Stith et al., 2009). Although empirical studies on the assimilation between these associated areas of research are yet to be conducted, researchers are starting to pay more attention to theories that integrate dysfunctional cognitional with additional factors (see Seng & Prinz, 2008).

Research also indicates links between parental substance abuse and child maltreatment (see Young, Boles, & Otero, 2007). An estimate by the National Committee for Prevention of Child Abuse suggests that one in 13.3 children living with a substance-abusing parent experiences severe maltreatment each year (as cited in Besinger, Garland, Litrownik, & Landsverk, 1999). Yet, what are the mechanisms that link substance use and maltreatment or neglect? Research suggests that parents of drug-exposed infants may lack the necessary skills or resources to sufficiently deal with their infants' special needs (as reviewed in Dore, Doris, & Wright, 1995). Parents with ongoing substance use may spend a significant amount of time engaging in substance-related activities (e.g., acquiring, using), which reduces the amount of available time spent on parenting, in turn increasing the likelihood of neglect or failure to protect children from maltreatment by others who have access to the child. Further, parents coping with effects of substance use may interfere with responsive parenting behaviors and increase parenting stress, again putting their children at risk of maltreatment. Future research needs to further examine these underlying mechanisms associated with substance abuse and risk of child maltreatment.

In many studies, parental stress emerges as a common—and potentially important—third variable. Stith et al.'s (2009) meta-analysis found a significant link between parents' level of stress and child neglect (effect size; $r = .38$). Under conditions of high stress, parents may be more likely to engage in rapid, automatic information processing (vs. more controlled flexible processing), which may increase the influence of basic belief structures on parenting behavior (Milner, 2000). Even beyond the main effect of stress on child abuse potential, researchers are discovering specific interactions between stress and additional life factors that contribute differentially to risk of child maltreatment. For example, the association between stress and physical child abuse potential was moderated by parents' belief in the value of corporal punishment (Milner, 2000). Specifically, among parents who strongly believed in the value of corporal punishment, level of stress was positively associated with physical child abuse potential. In contrast, level of parenting stress was not associated with physical child abuse potential among parents who reported low levels of belief in the value of corporal punishment. Looking specifically at substance abuse and parenting, Orme and Rimmer (1981) argued that outside factors, such as poverty or stress, may actually account for both substance use and the abusive behavior by caregivers. Delineating the impact of poverty and parental stress on child abuse risk is critically important to creating prevention programs. The authors argued that socioeconomic status complicates the relationship between substance abuse and child abuse because the poor and members of minority groups are overrepresented in hospital and treatment agency samples.

Family interactions and composition have also received wide attention. Findings document that partner abuse and child abuse frequently co-occur (for a review, see Herrenkohl, Sousa, Tajima, Herrenkohl, & Moylan, 2008). Although witnessing violence between parents may be considered maltreatment in and of itself (or at least potentially traumatic), literature reviews point to high co-occurrence rates (30%–60%) of documented child maltreatment and IPV (Edleson, 1999). Several factors are associated with the co-occurrence of child abuse and IPV, including lower socioeconomic status, lower parental education levels, unemployment or lower occupational status, substance use in the family, mental illness in caregivers, parenting stress, greater number of children or larger household size, and neighborhood violence (Herrenkohl et al., 2008). One hypothesized mechanism for the link between IPV and child abuse has focused on the perpetrator, if the aggression originates from the same individual. Alternatively, contextual factors, such as poverty and stress, may underlie the co-occurrence of partner and child abuse. Research has emerged to support this latter argument. For example, Margolin and Gordis (2003) found that parenting stress moderated the relationship between IPV aggression and child abuse potential such that the correlation was present in the context of high stress but not in the context of low stress. However, additional studies are needed to better understand stress as a mechanism of both IPV and maltreatment.

In related research, a large national survey of adolescents found that single-parent families reported more victimizations (from both strangers and nonstrangers) than two-parent families, even while controlling for race and socioeconomic status (Lauritsen, 2003). Various research studies as well as analyses of the NCANDS also indicate that youths living in blended households with a nonrelated parental figure are at higher risk of sexual and physical abuse as compared with youths living with two biological parents (see McRee, 2008). Additionally, Stith et al.'s (2009) meta-analysis found large effect sizes for the links between family conflict ($r = .39$) and family cohesion ($r = -.32$) to child physical abuse as well as parent–child relationship ($r = -.48$) to child neglect. These associated factors help to give a more comprehensive understanding of the type of family composition and interactions that might exert additional influence on lower microsystem (i.e., individual-based) risk factors associated with child maltreatment.

Environment and Social Network Factors

Parenting does not occur in isolation but within a wider context of community and societal relationships. Thus, a discussion of risk and protective factors associated with child abuse must necessarily include a broader ecological perspective that considers environment and social factors. We review some of the major ecological correlates (e.g., poverty, neighborhood structure, community social support, religion, cultural identity) found to contribute to higher risk of child maltreatment. We also attempt to identify areas in which more specific mechanisms might drive these broad relationships or whether the larger environmental associations influence lower level processes that together contribute to child maltreatment.

Poverty-related factors such as low income level, median residential housing/property value, unemployment, and low education have been linked to increased risk of child abuse and neglect (Coulton, Crampton, Irwin, Spilsbury, & Korbin, 2007; Ertem, Leventhal, & Dobbs, 2000). Several structural characteristics of neighborhoods that go hand-in-hand with poverty are also associated with increased child abuse risk. For example, substandard or vacant housing, overcrowding, and residential instability are also linked to child abuse risk (as reviewed in Coulton et al., 2007). Child maltreatment rates in neighborhoods also have been shown to correlate with other indicators of social distress, such as infant mortality, juvenile delinquency, violent crime, and drug trafficking (Coulton, Korbin, Su, & Chow, 1995).

Although many links between poverty-related factors and abuse have been documented, we must be cautious in interpreting these findings. First, we do not yet know the processes by which social and economic characteristics of neighborhoods relate to child maltreatment. One possibility is that geographic concentrations of social disorganization (within which child abuse is more likely to occur) result from families already possessing multiple maltreatment risk factors forced to live in poor and unstable neighborhoods (Coulton et al., 2007). Furthermore, when child protective abuse rates are used as the primary data source, it remains unclear whether more abuse actually occurs in low-income homes or whether the increased involvement of system-based representatives is more likely to result in reports of abuse in low-income families relative to more well-to-do families where abuse also occurs. For example, research studies based on community surveys find almost no differences in CSA prevalence among socioeconomic classes, but a disproportionate number of CSA cases reported to child protective services come from families with lower socioeconomic status (Finkelhor, 1993). Some researchers have suggested that professionals may feel more comfortable and confident labeling abuse among disadvantaged families, which tend to fit prevailing stereotypes about where abuse occurs (see Finkelhor, 1993). Alternatively, neighborhood chaos and social disruptions may directly influence maladaptive parenting practices, thus increasing abuse. For example, parents dealing with poverty-related stress may also be facing higher parenting stress, which leads to higher likelihood of maltreating their children (Coulton et al., 2007). Similar to the idea that within-level factors may influence each other (e.g., parental factors such as substance use and psychopathology affecting parenting practices), factors may also interact across levels (environmental context affecting parenting practices).

Neighborhood characteristics may also influence social relationships within the community, which in turn have an impact on maltreatment risk. For example, social support appears to be an important protective factor. Hunter and Kilstrom (1979) observed that parents who did not repeat child maltreatment were more likely to rely on a broad network of resources and social support, such as a positive relationship with one parent. Studies that have compared different communities based on interviews of residents, community leaders, and social service agency clients found that neighborhoods with low rates of child maltreatment reported greater social resources and community social network (as reviewed in Coulton et al., 2007). In contrast, Hashima and Amato (1994) found that the effect of poverty on punitive and unsupportive parenting behaviors was greater for parents reporting low social support.

To the extent that social support is an important protective factor, religious communities may offer parents (and children) important sources of support that protect against abuse. Religious groups also play an active and positive role in providing prevention and treatment programs for abuse victims. Parents engaging in abusive and/or neglectful behaviors tend not to be involved in community or religious activities (e.g., Polansky, Gaudin, Ammons, & Davis, 1985). However, religious beliefs can encourage and justify violent, physically abusive parenting practices (Bottoms, Nielsen, Murray, & Filipas, 2003). Thus, physical abuse may be perpetrated by adults who believe they are helping to deliver their children from sin. Taken together, religion appears to play a complex role in child abuse risk; currently, literature that identifies exact pathways in which religiosity and belief systems influence parental risk of perpetrating or rationalizing abuse remains limited.

Cultural identity also moderates abuse risk in complicated ways. Elliott and Urquiza (2006) reviewed studies examining cultural and ethnic differences in childhood maltreatment, specifically separating sexual abuse, physical abuse, and neglect. They concluded that findings across studies did not provide conclusive evidence for cultural group differences in CSA, with the exception of Asian cultures in which lower rates of CSA are reported. A similar picture emerged with physical abuse, where findings suggested various group differences, although the patterns remain inconsistent and at times contradictory. The authors attributed the inconsistency in physical abuse findings to methodological differences across studies and large within-culture and within-ethnicity variability. Although neglect was the most common form of child maltreatment according to the NCANDS (USDHHS, 2008), Elliott and Urquiza argued that the lack of studies focusing on cultural differences in neglect limits any conclusions.

Beyond pointing out cultural differences in prevalence rates, Elliott and Urquiza (2006) also reviewed cultural differences in potential mechanisms that might explain the differing child abuse rates. For example, researchers have long suggested that how one interprets differences in reports of sexual abuse by cultural groups should be informed by ethnic differences in willingness to disclose abuse as influenced by emphases on family and collectivistic beliefs, filial piety, and restraint in emotional expression. Researchers have also suggested that conservative norms in Asian cultures that frown on sexual activity act as a protective factor against CSA. Here again, reviews of studies provided no conclusive evidence regarding cultural/ethnic group differences in disclosure rates (Elliott & Urquiza, 2006). Cultural attitudes and perceptions toward sexual activities and definitions of sexual abuse remain important areas of study to further investigate cultural patterns in risk for CSA.

For physical abuse, many studies have investigated differences in parenting among caregivers of different races and ethnicities, such as differences in disciplinary strategies, expression of warmth and affection, parenting attributions, and definitions of what constitutes abuse. Differences in parenting appear to exist between cultural/ethnic groups; however, the differences also appear be influenced by a variety of factors, including acculturation levels, socioeconomic status, and neighborhood variables. Thus, any consideration of cultural identity in maltreatment, and in particular physical abuse, necessarily depends on understanding other familial, parental, and environmental factors.

Despite the inconsistency in cultural/ethnic differences in child maltreatment based on research studies, clear group differences exist in reported cases to child protective services. In 2002, African American, American Indian or Alaska Native, and multiracial children were the groups with the highest rates of maltreatment, with 19.8, 15.9, and 15.4 per 1,000 children of the same race or ethnicity, respectively (USDHHS, 2008). The next group consisted of White and Hispanic children (10.7 and 10.8 per 1,000 children of the same race or ethnicity). Asian children had the lowest victimization rate of 2.5 per 1,000 Asian children. Factors such as poverty may lead to heightened attention from state authorities and thereby disproportionately increase the number of cases reported among certain ethnic groups. Although research studies do point to variations in the child protective system's reporting of and response to reported child abuse from different cultural/ethnic backgrounds (Elliott & Urquiza, 2006), societal and familial factors (e.g., exposure to community violence, single-parent homes) continue to confound the issue. Therefore, whether ethnic differences in prevalence rates in childhood are due to actual higher incidence of abuse or reporting rates remains unclear.

HOW DO WE KNOW IT? THINKING CRITICALLY ABOUT METHODS, SAMPLES, AND ANALYSES

Throughout our review of methodological factors (e.g., samples, analyses), we offered examples that should inform interpretation of findings. Here we summarize and highlight a few central methodological issues in this literature. For example, recruitment methods have played an important role in defining what we know about vulnerability and protective factors, with pros and cons to all of the methods used. Samples recruited through child protective services give us access to reports by an outside arbiter (e.g., a caseworker) who reports on the abuse, which may help with parent and child reporting biases that may be particularly likely to lead to underreporting among some cultural groups. However, reliance on substantiated or child protective samples will likely lead us to find stronger associations between risk and poverty-related factors than in other sampling methods. Families living in poverty have more contact with system-based representatives and may, therefore, be more likely to have potentially abusive or neglectful behaviors reported to the authorities than wealthier families. Of course, many of the conditions of poverty do create terrible risks for children, such as unstable living arrangements, lack of parental education, and poor access to medical care. The interesting methodological questions become how to both understand the particular risk created by poverty and access higher socioeconomic samples outside the system where risk factors may differ.

The most common alternatives to child protective samples are parent reports or adult retrospective reports. Parent reports of abuse to researchers, including those who are mandated reporters, may increase the risk of false negatives. Adult retrospective reports of abuse may also be vulnerable to underreporting (particularly of sexual traumas by trusted others) because of high rates of false negatives (Bolen & Scannapieco, 1999). However, retrospective reports of abuse have some pronounced advantages over documented samples. Kendall-Tackett and Becker-Blease (2004) identified at least two major advantages of retrospective reports over documented samples: (a) They are less prone to missed cases and underreporting (as so few abuse cases get documented), and (b) they are more representative of most cases of abuse (in that documenting abuse requires numerous factors and has pronounced impact on the victim).

The majority of studies reviewed here involved cross-sectional, retrospective methods (i.e., the abuse already occurred). By looking primarily at samples in which abuse has already occurred, we bias our research toward identifying risk factors. Identifying risk factors is important and valuable for prevention; however, finding methods to study protective factors that kept children safe from abuse remains a challenge. To date, the majority of studies examining protective factors have focused on protective factors as part of resiliency after exposure to trauma. All too often, in studies that examine contributors to child abuse and neglect, we found that protective factors were simply the flip side of vulnerability factors identified in cross-section research. That is, if female gender is a risk factor for one type of abuse, then male gender is protective. Only a few studies identified protective factors. In these cases, traits provided buffers for parents already facing adversity and risk for engaging in abuse. For example, parental coping and social support seemed to protect against child physical abuse (see Black et al., 2001; Coulton et al., 2007). However, parental and environmental factors that may protect against CSA and neglect remain unclear. Therefore, at this time, we know little about protective factors independent of risk. Further, the cross-sectional nature of this research also means that we know little about how risk factors change over time. This is particularly important considering the tremendous cognitive, emotional, and social development that occurs in the first 18 years of life.

WHERE DO WE GO FROM HERE?

The translation of research findings into action in the form of parent education, policy changes, or prevention programs remains an important step. In this section, we present recommendations for future research and policy that may bridge some of the gaps in the current state of knowledge on and services for victims of child abuse.

Next Research Steps

Research in this field began by documenting broad group differences (e.g., gender, culture/ethnicity) and correlations (e.g., poverty, stress) associated with maltreatment rates and child maltreatment. As many researchers (e.g., Cicchetti & Lynch, 1993; Coulton et al., 2007) have suggested, we must start to use a more ecological perspective that includes all levels of analysis. These third-generation studies using more complex analyses and multiple methods will help us more fully understand the context within which child abuse happens (e.g., Banyard & Williams, 2007). Such studies may clarify nonlinear processes of risk and protective factors of child abuse, which in turn can further inform risk for further victimization and how maltreatment may unfold across the life span. Such research also has important implications for clinical practice with survivors of child maltreatment as it builds an empirical base of knowledge to identify resources for interventions that are empowering and build on survivors' strengths.

Because children change greatly during the course of development from infancy to adolescence, examining child victimization within a developmental perspective will also shed further light on changes in individual and environmental risk factors over time. According to the developmental psychopathology and developmental traumatology perspectives, researchers need to be mindful of how trauma might disrupt normal development in multiple domains of functioning as well as different physiological systems (Cicchetti & Toth, 2005; De Bellis, 2001). Characteristics that place children at risk of certain types of maltreatment may vary as a function of their developmental stage. Risk of exposure to different types of maltreatment may change as children assert greater independence from caregivers. The trauma exposure may also differentially impact various areas of functioning, depending on the timing of the developmental process. Further research is needed to minimize risk for children at all stages of development.

In addition, relatively little attention has been paid to within-group differences and even less attention paid to subpopulations (e.g., Pacific Islanders, Filipino Americans, Cuban Americans, Alaskan Natives). Studies that focus on differences between broadly defined groups ignore potentially important intragroup differences and obscure true cultural differences that affect prevalence, reporting, and experiences of child maltreatment. For example, third-generation Chinese Americans and recently immigrated Hmong refugees are both categorized as "Asian American." However, the manner in which a Hmong family perceives and addresses child maltreatment, the family's risk of engaging in child abuse, and parenting attitudes may differ widely from those of a third-generation Chinese American family (Elliott & Urquiza, 2006).

Recommendations for Policy

The studies reviewed here point to several important policy issues related to child welfare practices. For example, continued training is needed for professionals who interact with children and families across diverse settings (e.g., medical system) to recognize and assess maltreatment based on cutting-edge research on vulnerability and protective factors. Researchers such as Hibbard et al. (2007) have noted that many health workers do not receive sufficient training on the identification of risk factors, such as disabilities, for child abuse and neglect.

Because the literature on vulnerability and protective factors has been anything but static, trainings must be updated as research continues to identify vulnerability and protective factors as well as complex interactions among those factors. Training professionals to identify children who are at risk of abuse or who have been abused must, therefore, capture the complex relationship between risk factors. For example, it would be an unwelcome outcome if data on ethnicity and abuse led to focused attention on certain subgroups without considering how interactions between ethnic identity and other vulnerability/protective factors contribute to risk across and within groups. With up-to-date training, health care providers and other professionals will be in a unique position to use their knowledge to identify maltreated children as well as educate parents and families on ways to protect children. Health care professionals urgently need to learn to better use this body of research for risk assessment to prevent maltreatment from occurring, which will have to involve both policy and research agendas. For example, rigorous research methods are needed to examine whether the vulnerability and protective factors identified in documented abuse reflect actual underlying differences (e.g., between groups) versus biases in the system.

Additionally, prevention of maltreatment requires programs to systematically and comprehensively address multiple risk and protective factors, including the family and community (Herrenkohl et al., 2008). While we recommend that future research target multiple levels of influence on maltreatment, so too should policymakers address the implications of multiple system interactions. For example, mothers who are victimized by their partners may not be able to fully protect their children because leaving the abusive partner may result in loss of their economic support or increased safety risks to mothers and children. While ensuring the safety of children is paramount, policies can help to strengthen communities to support families and to reduce prevalence of child maltreatment (Coulton et al., 2007). Community social support appears to be an especially important protective factor that warrants further research to identify specific policies that can build this capacity to decrease child abuse risk.

A more collaborative team-approach response will help future data collection and provide more comprehensive responses to children who have experienced maltreatment. For example, because there is no federal mandate that information be collected on families involved in multiple systems (e.g., a family with identified child abuse that is also engaged in mandated substance treatment), the information available on how risk and protective factors interact is largely an estimate based on an interpolation of research studies. Future studies should establish accurate estimates of families who access multiple systems to more fully assess the need for services, and in turn develop appropriate capacity to respond to that need. In particular, states and communities need to fully understand the size, scope, and extent of the issue of families who are involved in systems in their jurisdictions because these factors may vary depending on geographic locations and neighborhood characteristics. Finally, we note the need for a substantial increase in federal funding for child abuse research. Freyd et al. (2005) proposed the creation of a new National Institute of Child Abuse and Neglect to help accomplish this goal. Such a bold move is justified by the economic, health, and human impact of these problems.

SUMMARY AND CONCLUSIONS

On the basis of findings from research studies and national statistics of reported child maltreatment cases, we have evidence that certain groups of children are at higher risk of maltreatment compared with their peers. These risk factors may be generally categorized as occurring at the individual, parental and familial, and environmental and societal levels. This body of research clearly illustrates that child maltreatment cannot be reduced to a single-risk model. Instead, factors across and within systems influence each other in additive and interactive ways to increase or decrease potential for child abuse and neglect. Importantly, even while we continue to gain a better understanding of the interaction between risk factors, many of the mechanisms that underlie these interactions remain poorly understood. With the important advances in the trauma field, future research studies with more nuanced research questions and sophisticated study designs and methodology will help us to address these unanswered questions. In turn, researchers and policymakers must work together to provide comprehensive and collaborative services in both the prevention and treatment of child maltreatment. To date, some prevention programs have attempted to educate parents on caretaking behaviors, attitudes, and beliefs in an effort to enhance protection against risk for abuse and neglect of their children. Researchers have also established programs to shore up social support networks within high-risk communities in efforts to prevent child abuse and neglect in those neighborhoods. However, the effectiveness of these prevention programs remains unclear. Thus, we also need to continue to monitor how to most effectively translate advances in research into prevention of abuse and neglect through policies and treatment programs.

REFERENCES

Banyard, V., & Williams, L. (2007). Women's voices on recovery: A multi-method study of the complexity of recovery from child sexual abuse. *Child Abuse & Neglect, 31*, 275–290. doi:10.1016/j.chiabu.2006.02.016

Besinger, B. A., Garland, A. F., Litrownik, A. J., & Landsverk, J. A. (1999). Caregiver substance abuse among maltreated children placed in out-of-home care. *Child Welfare Journal, 78*, 221–239.

Black, D. A., Heyman, R. E., & Slep, A. M. S. (2001). Risk factors for child physical abuse. *Aggression and Violent Behavior, 6*, 121–188. doi:10.1016/S1359-1789(00)00021-5

Bolen, R. M., & Scannapieco, M. (1999). Prevalence of child sexual abuse: A corrective meta-analysis. *Social Service Review, 73*, 281–313. doi:10.1086/514425

Bottoms, B. L., Nielsen, M., Murray, R., & Filipas, H. (2003). Religion-related child physical abuse: Characteristics and psychological outcomes. *Journal of Aggression, Maltreatment & Trauma, 8*, 87–114.

Bureau of Justice Statistics. (2000). *National crime victimization survey*. Washington, DC: U.S. Department of Justice.

Cicchetti, D., & Lynch, M. (1993). Toward an ecological/transactional model of community violence and child maltreatment: Consequences for children's development. *Psychiatry, 56*, 96–118.

Cicchetti, D., & Toth, S. L. (2005). Child maltreatment. *Annual Review of Clinical Psychology, 1*, 409–438. doi:10.1146/annurev.clinpsy.1.102803.144029

Coulton, C. J., Crampton, D. S., Irwin, M., Spilsbury, J. C., & Korbin, J. E. (2007). A review of the literature and alternative pathways. *Child Abuse & Neglect, 31*, 1117–1142. doi:10.1016/j.chiabu.2007.03.023

Coulton, C. J., Korbin, J. E., Su, M., & Chow, J. (1995). Community level factors and child maltreatment rates. *Child Development, 66*, 1262–1276. doi:10.2307/1131646

DePrince, A. P., & Freyd, J. J. (2002). The intersection of gender and betrayal trauma. In R. Kimerling, P. C. Oumette, & J. Wolfe (Eds.), *Gender and PTSD* (pp. 98–113). New York, NY: Guilford Press.

De Bellis, M. D. (2001). Developmental traumatology: The psychobiological development of maltreated children and its implications for research, treatment, and policy. *Development and Psychopathology, 13,* 539–564. doi:10.1017/S0954579401003078

Dore, M. M., Doris, J. M., & Wright, P. (1995). Identifying substance abuse in maltreating families: A child welfare challenge. *Child Abuse & Neglect, 19,* 531–543. doi:10.1016/0145-2134(95)00013-X

Edinburgh, L., Saewyc, E. M., Thao, T., & Levitt, C. (2006). Sexual exploitation of very young Hmong girls. *Journal of Adolescent Health, 39,* 111–118. doi:10.1016/j.jadohealth.2005.09.003

Edleson, J. L. (1999). Children's witnessing of adult domestic violence. *Journal of Interpersonal Violence, 14,* 839–870. doi:10.1177/088626099014008004

Elliott, K., & Urquiza, A. (2006). Ethnicity, culture, and child maltreatment. *Journal of Social Issues, 62,* 787–809. doi:10.1111/j.1540-4560.2006.00487.x

Ertem, I. O., Leventhal, J. M., & Dobbs, S. (2000). Intergenerational continuity of child physical abuse: how good is the evidence? *The Lancet, 356,* 814–819. doi:10.1016/S0140-6736(00)02656-8

Finkelhor, D. (1993). Epidemiological factors in the clinical identification of child sexual abuse. *Child Abuse & Neglect, 17,* 67–70. doi:10.1016/0145-2134(93)90009-T

Finkelhor, D., Hotaling, G., Lewis, I. A., & Smith, C. (1990). Sexual abuse in a national survey of adult men and women: Prevalence, characteristics, and risk factors. *Child Abuse & Neglect, 14,* 19–28. doi:10.1016/0145-2134(90)90077-7

Finkelhor, D., Ormrod, R. K., & Turner, H. A. (2007). Polyvictimization and trauma in a national longitudinal cohort. *Development and Psychopathology, 19,* 149–166.

Freyd, J. J., DePrince, A. P., & Gleaves, D. (2007). The state of betrayal trauma theory: Reply to McNally—conceptualizations and future directions. *Memory, 15,* 295–311. doi:10.1080/09658210701256514

Freyd, J. J., Putnam, F. W., Lyon, T. D., Becker-Blease, K. A., Cheit, R. E., Siegel, N. B., & Pezdek, K. (2005, April 22). The science of child sexual abuse. *Science, 308,* 501. doi:10.1126/science.1108066

Goldberg, L., & Freyd, J. J. (2006). Self-reports of potentially traumatic experiences in an adult community sample: Gender differences and test-retest stabilities of the items in a Brief Betrayal-Trauma Survey. *Journal of Trauma & Dissociation, 7*(3), 39–63. doi:10.1300/J229v07n03_04

Hashima, P. Y., & Amato, P. R. (1994). Poverty, social support, and parental behavior. *Child Development, 65,* 394–403. doi:10.2307/1131391

Herrenkohl, T. I., Sousa, C., Tajima, E. A., Herrenkohl, R. C., & Moylan, C. A. (2008). Intersection of child abuse and children's exposure to domestic violence. *Trauma, Violence & Abuse, 9,* 84–99. doi:10.1177/1524838008314797

Hibbard, R. A., Desch, L. W., American Academy of Pediatrics Committee on Child Abuse and Neglect, & American Academy of Pediatrics Council on Children With Disabilities. (2007). Maltreatment of children with disabilities. *Pediatrics, 119,* 1018–1025. doi:10.1542/peds.2007-0565

Holmes, W. C., & Slap, G. B. (1998). Sexual abuse of boys: Definition, prevalence, correlates, sequelae, and management. *JAMA, 280,* 1855–1862. doi:10.1001/jama.280.21.1855

Hunter, R. S., & Kilstrom, N. (1979). Breaking the cycle in abusive families. *The American Journal of Psychiatry, 136,* 1320–1322.

Jouriles, E. N., & Norwood, W. D. (1995). Physical aggression toward boys and girls in families characterized by the battering of women. *Journal of Family Psychology, 9,* 69–78. doi:10.1037/0893-3200.9.1.69

Kaufman, J., & Zigler, E. (1987). Do abused children become abusive parents? *American Journal of Orthopsychiatry, 57,* 186–192.

Kendall-Tackett, K., & Becker-Blease, K. A. (2004). The importance of retrospective findings in child maltreatment research. *Child Abuse & Neglect, 28,* 723–727. doi:10.1016/j.chiabu.2004.02.002

Lauritsen, J. L. (2003). *How families and communities influence youth victimization.* Washington, DC: U.S. Department of Justice, Office of Justice Programs, Office of Juvenile Justice and Delinquency Prevention.

Margolin, G., & Gordis, E. B. (2003). Co-occurrence between marital aggression and parents' child abuse potential: The impact of cumulative stress. *Violence and Victims, 18,* 243–258. doi:10.1891/vivi.2003.18.3.243

McConaghy, N., & Silove, D. (1992). Do sex-linked behaviors in children influence relationships with their parents? *Archives of Sexual Behavior, 21,* 469–479. doi:10.1007/BF01542271

McRee, N. (2008). Child abuse in blended households: Reports from runaway and homeless youth. *Child Abuse & Neglect, 32,* 449–453.

Milner, J. S. (2000). Social information processing and child physical abuse: Theory and research. In D. J. Hansen (Ed.), *Nebraska Symposium on Motivation: Vol. 46. Motivation and child maltreatment* (pp. 39–84). Lincoln, NE: University of Nebraska Press.

Oliver, W. J., Kuhns, L. R., & Pomeranz, E. S. (2006). Family structure and child abuse. *Clinical Pediatrics, 45,* 111–118. doi:10.1177/000992280604500201

Orme, T. C., & Rimmer, J. (1981). Alcoholism and child abuse: A review. *Journal of Studies on Alcohol, 42,* 273–287.

Polansky, N. A., Gaudin, J. M., Ammons, P. W., & Davis, K. B. (1985). The psychological ecology of the neglectful mother. *Child Abuse & Neglect, 9,* 265–275. doi:10.1016/0145-2134(85)90019-5

Putnam, F. W. (2003). Ten-year research update review: Child sexual abuse. *Journal of the American Academy of Child and Adolescent Psychiatry, 42,* 269–278. doi:10.1097/00004583-200303000-00006

Rogosch, F. A., & Cicchetti, D. (2004). Child maltreatment and emergent personality organization: Perspectives from the five-factor model. *Journal of Abnormal Child Psychology, 32,* 123–145. doi:10.1023/B:JACP.0000019766.47625.40

Romano, E., & De Luca, R. V. (2001). Male sexual abuse: A review of effects, abuse characteristics, and links with later psychological functioning. *Aggression and Violent Behavior, 6,* 55–78. doi:10.1016/S1359-1789(99)00011-7

Ross, S. M. (1996). Risk of physical abuse to children of spouse abusing parents. *Child Abuse & Neglect, 20,* 589–598. doi:10.1016/0145-2134(96)00046-4

Saewyc, E. M., Skay, C. L., Pettingell, S. L., Reis, E. A., Bearinger, L., Resnick, M., . . . Combs, L. (2006). Hazards of stigma: The sexual and physical abuse of gay, lesbian, and bisexual adolescents in the United States and Canada. *Child Welfare, 85,* 195–213.

Seng, A. C., & Prinz, R. J. (2008). Parents who abuse: What are they thinking? *Clinical Child and Family Psychology Review, 11,* 163–175. doi:10.1007/s10567-008-0035-y

Senn, T. E., Carey, M. P., & Vanable, P. A. (2008). Childhood and adolescent sexual abuse and subsequent sexual risk behavior: Evidence from controlled studies, methodological critique, and suggestions for research. *Clinical Psychology Review, 28,* 711–735. doi:10.1016/j.cpr.2007.10.002

Stevens, I., & Hassett, P. (2007). Applying complexity theory to risk in child protection practice. *Childhood, 14,* 128–144. doi:10.1177/0907568207072535

Stith, S. M., Liu, T., Davies, C., Boykin, E. L., Alder, M. C., Harris, J. M., . . . Dees, J. E. M. E. G. (2009). Risk factors in child maltreatment: A meta-analytic review of the literature. *Aggression and Violent Behavior, 14,* 13–29. doi:10.1016/j.avb.2006.03.006

Sullivan, P. M., & Knutson, J. F. (2000). Maltreatment and disabilities: A population-based epidemiological study. *Child Abuse & Neglect, 24,* 1257–1273. doi:10.1016/S0145-2134(00)00190-3

Tang, S. S., Freyd, J. J., & Wang, M. (2008). What do we know about gender in the disclosure of child sexual abuse? *Journal of Psychological Trauma, 6*(4), 1–26. doi:10.1080/19322880802096442

U.S. Department of Health and Human Services. (2008). *Child maltreatment 2006: Reports from the states to the National Child Abuse and Neglect Data System.* Washington, DC: US Government Printing Office.

Young, N. K., Boles, S. M., & Otero, C. (2007). Parental substance use disorders and child maltreatment: Overlap, gaps, and opportunities. *Child Maltreatment, 12,* 137–149. doi:10.1177/1077559507300322

4

PSYCHOLOGICAL, HEALTH, BEHAVIORAL, AND ECONOMIC IMPACT OF CHILD MALTREATMENT

ERNESTINE C. BRIGGS, RICHARD THOMPSON,
SARAH OSTROWSKI, AND RUBY LEKWAUWA

For the nearly 3 million children in the United States at risk of child abuse and neglect each year (U.S. Department of Health and Human Services [USDHHS], 2010), the consequences are extraordinarily complex. Some youths will exhibit considerable psychological, behavioral, or physical problems, whereas others will emerge relatively unscathed. These outcomes are further complicated by the economic costs of abuse, neglect, and other adversities. This chapter examines myriad psychological, behavioral, health, and economic consequences associated with child abuse and neglect. To fully understand these outcomes associated with child abuse and neglect, it is imperative that we also explore the variations in definition and assessment, the larger context in which they occur, and alternative explanations for the links that we have identified.

DEFINITION AND ASSESSMENT OF CHILD ABUSE AND NEGLECT

A major barrier to the assessment, treatment, and prevention of child abuse and neglect or child maltreatment is the lack of clear definitions. Definitions and classifications of *child maltreatment* vary across time, cultures, and professional disciplines (Cicchetti & Manly, 2001). However, over the past few years advances have been made concerning maltreatment definitions, theories, and research designs. Generally speaking, maltreatment includes acts of omission or commission by a parent or caretaker that results in death, serious physical or emotional harm, sexual abuse, or exploitation. Further, different types of maltreatment have been found to have differential effects on an array of child outcomes. Rates of comorbidity among subtypes of maltreatment have also been found to range from 46% to 90% (Higgins & McCabe, 2000). Consequently, researchers have begun to examine different types of maltreatment separately in addition to examining the chronicity, severity, and frequency of the event. Knowledge of the type of maltreatment can increase understanding of the nature and extent of the maltreatment. In turn, this can help with the selection of the type of resources needed to prevent, investigate, and decrease the negative consequences of maltreatment (English, 2003).

To date, *child sexual abuse* (CSA) has received the most research attention despite being the least prevalent (approximately 8.8%) and the most under-reported form of abuse (Finkelhor & Jones, 2006). Sexual abuse can include a range of behaviors from fondling, genital exposure, intimate kissing, and forced masturbation to oral, penile, or digital penetration of the mouth, vagina, or anus. Child prostitution, pornography, and "ritual" abuse also fit under the rubric of sexual abuse. Research based on data from the National Child Abuse and Neglect Data System (NCANDS) suggests that children are most vulnerable to CSA between the ages of 8 and 12 years (USDHHS, 2008). Moreover, there were minimal differences in rates of reported CSA across cultures, with the exception of Asian countries, in which lower levels of CSA were found for Asians than other minorities (Chen, Dunne, & Wang, 2003).

Child physical abuse is frequently defined as when a parent or caregiver beats, shakes, scalds, bites, or otherwise inflicts injury on a child. Research on child physical abuse has typically focused on child-rearing and discipline techniques. Although corporal punishment is accepted by some, many classify any injury beyond immediate redness as abuse (Dubowitz & Bennett, 2007). Prevalence rates of child physical abuse range from 8% to 16% (USDHHS, 2010) and differ on the basis of race and ethnicity. Higher rates of child physical abuse have been found for African Americans and Asian Americans compared with non-Latino Whites, Latinos, and, mixed-race children (USDHHS, 2005, 2010).

Child neglect is generally classified by an omission of care, such as health care, supervision, education, and meeting the child's emotional and physical needs. Child neglect is often associated with a constellation of environmental and individual caregiver factors, such as poverty, residential instability, relatively young caregiver age, single parenthood, chaotic family functioning, domestic violence, low parental warmth, caregiver's history of abuse, caregiver depression, caregiver substance abuse, and lack of parenting and problem-solving skills. Some consider neglect to be a precursor to other types of maltreatment. Although conceptual and operational definitions of neglect have been the source of much discussion and debate (Dubowitz et al., 2005), it is by far the most prevalent form of child maltreatment. According to the NCANDS data (USDHHS, 2005, 2010), neglect accounts for approximately 49.9% of all child maltreatment reports, and this rate ranges by ethnicity from 48% to 71%, with African Americans disproportionately represented in these figures.

Emotional abuse, also known as *verbal abuse* and *psychological maltreatment*, includes a range of acts by parents or caretakers such as using extreme forms of punishment (e.g., confinement in a closet), threatening or terrorizing a child, and belittling a child. Emotional abuse is difficult to define and, therefore, to diagnose reliably; as a result, there is considerable variation between different states in their rates of evaluation and reporting of emotional abuse. Researchers tend to agree that the rates generally reported for emotional abuse (approximately 7.3%; USDHHS, 2010) underestimate the true scope of the problem.

Of course, there is by no means a consensus as to what is meant by the term *child abuse and neglect* (or, for that matter, the broader term *maltreatment*). Importantly, the literature reviewed here is informed by several different perspectives on what constitutes maltreatment. In particular, the definition of neglect is very difficult and still controversial. Does it refer to a specific set of parental behaviors or omissions or to a broader failure to meet children's needs (Dubowitz et al., 2005)? There is no obvious answer to this question, and lumping neglect with maltreatment or abuse does not help to clarify, given that neglect may not always covary with abuse. Moreover, emotional abuse and neglect are very difficult to define and, thus, to assess.

There are, however, a variety of ways of understanding maltreatment. An initial, and fundamental, question is whether to treat maltreatment as a dichotomy (did maltreatment occur, yes or no?). As suggested earlier, one can examine the different types of maltreatment separately, or at least treat them as separate dimensions. However, there are more sophisticated approaches than a typological one. One can further examine the impact of the severity of maltreatment generally or of each form of maltreatment separately. A related approach is to focus on maltreatment that has been officially recognized as such by child protective services, whether as a proxy for severity or because of particular practical or theoretical concerns. However, substantiation is a complex and multidetermined process; in addition to the severity or certainty of the alleged maltreatment, substantiation is also influenced by administrative factors and by demographics (King, Trocme, & Thatte, 2003).

The temporal pattern of maltreatment may be another important dimension to consider when defining child maltreatment. Some researchers have simply examined whether maltreatment occurred more than once and used this to define chronicity. Others have examined the age of the child at the first instance of maltreatment as an important predictor of child outcomes. Moreover, few studies to date have examined whether the risks, antecedents, and consequences associated with maltreatment are the same across various developmental periods (e.g., early childhood, adolescence). A more complex understanding of the temporal pattern of maltreatment would take into account the relation of experience of children's maltreatment to their developmental stages, as well as examine the timing and extent of maltreatment across different developmental periods (English, 2003).

WHAT DO WE KNOW? CONSEQUENCES OF CHILD ABUSE AND NEGLECT

The sequelae associated with child abuse and neglect have been well documented in the literature. Adverse consequences for children's development have been identified in multiple domains, including psychological, cognitive, social, behavioral, and physical. For many children, these effects extend far beyond childhood into adolescence and may persist into adulthood. It should be noted, however, that the nature and severity of symptoms vary from child to child such that some will be asymptomatic whereas others will be on the other end of the continuum, demonstrating severe distress that meets diagnostic criteria for a mental health disorder. Moreover, several studies have concluded that children's level of functioning declines as the number and frequency of stressors increase. Differing outcomes in abused children may be due to abuse-related characteristics. For instance, psychological impairment is likely to occur if the abuse takes place over a long period of time, if the perpetrator has a close affective relationship with the child, if coercion and force are used, and if the abuse involved penetration (Black, Dubowitz, & Harrington, 1994). In this section, we describe some of the more common psychological, behavioral, and health outcomes associated with child abuse and neglect.

Psychological Outcomes

Substantial evidence documents the deleterious impact of child maltreatment and other victimization experiences on psychological or emotional functioning. Indeed, child abuse and neglect have been associated with myriad adverse outcomes, including higher rates of depression, suicidal thoughts and attempts, lowered self-esteem, substance use, anxiety, separation anxiety, and posttraumatic stress disorder (PTSD; Wang & Holton, 2007). There is increasing evidence that different types of maltreatment are associated with differential sequelae; however, few studies have examined the long-term outcomes of various types of child abuse in a single population.

Many studies examining child abuse have focused primarily on anxiety-related symptoms (development of fears and worries). Children who were abused by a close adult relative tend to exhibit more anxiety, depression, somatic complaints, and withdrawal symptoms compared with children assaulted by a more distant perpetrator (Black et al., 1994). Variables such as parental reaction following the disclosure might explain these behavioral disturbances. For example, Chaffin, Wherry, and Dykman (1997) found an association between perceived social support from parents, externalizing behaviors, and global self-worth, suggesting that children may experience fewer behavioral difficulties and higher feelings of self-worth when they feel supported by their parents.

Numerous empirical studies have also examined the association between child maltreatment and PTSD. PTSD includes an array of arousal, avoidance, and reexperiencing symptoms and has been linked with maltreatment, exposure to violence, and other victimization experiences. In addition to the psychosocial consequences of maltreatment, children with chronic PTSD appear to have a number of biological abnormalities, including altered levels of catecholamines and cortisol that may also have an impact on a child's developing brain and leave her or him vulnerable to other maladaptive responses (Watts-English, Fortson, Gibler, Hooper, & De Bellis, 2006).

In addition to the psychological outcomes noted earlier, youths may experience an array of social difficulties, including insecure attachments with caregivers, which may lead to difficulties in developing trusting relationships with peers and adults later in life. These difficulties may stem from a decreased ability to regulate emotions or attention. Additionally, youths may experience difficulties with cognitive and academic functioning, including deficits in attention, abstract reasoning, language development, and problem-solving skills (Sroufe, Egeland, Carlson, & Collins, 2005).

Behavioral Outcomes

Research on the effects of child maltreatment suggests a number of potential short- and long-term consequences. In addition to disruptions in normative developmental tasks, abused and neglected youths may exhibit numerous externalizing behavioral problems that fit into the general categories of aggressive acting out and self-destructive behavior (Cooley-Quille, Boyd, Frantz, & Walsh, 2001). Specifically, these behavioral outcomes include aggressive and violent behaviors, conduct disorders, delinquent behaviors, and school-related behavioral problems. Moreover, an overwhelming proportion of abused children are diagnosed with comorbid disorders (e.g., PTSD, depression, conduct disorders). Many youths are also likely to engage in high-risk behaviors, such as alcohol and substance use, early initiation of cigarette use, multiple sexual partners, and other risky and reckless behaviors. Child abuse victims report significantly more antisocial behavior, regardless of which type of abuse was reported, higher levels of suicidal ideation, and greater numbers of suicide attempts (Silverman, Reinherz, Giaconia, 1996; Yates, Carlson, & Egeland, 2008). The life-threatening consequences of child maltreatment underscore the pressing need for timely prevention and intervention strategies.

Physical Health Outcomes

For some children who have experienced abuse, the most acute and direct physical health consequences may be readily apparent; for others, the effects of abuse and neglect persist well into adulthood (Springer, Sheridan, Kuo, & Carnes, 2007). The type of health-related consequence varies by the type of abuse, ranging from bruises, burns, contusions, and fractures in the case of physical abuse to sexually transmitted infections, tears, and pregnancy in the case of sexual abuse. Other health consequences documented in the literature include delayed physical growth, neurological damage, chronic fatigue, altered immune function, hypertension, obesity, and in extreme cases death (Wang & Holton, 2007). Some of these conditions are amenable to curative treatments, whereas others are not. In addition, maltreated children tend to have longer hospital stays, worse medical outcomes, and higher hospital charges than other children admitted to the hospital. Although many health consequences of child abuse are readily seen in pediatric clinics, research suggests that child abuse leaves its mark on physical health outcomes long after the inciting trauma.

It is clear that adult men and women with a history of any form of child abuse have poorer overall physical health as assessed by health-care utilization rates, self-report, and chart reviews. While men and women with a history of childhood abuse are likely to have decreased general health (i.e., decreased daily function due to illness, increased lifetime surgeries, more days spent in bed, more dysfunction due to pain), they are also more likely to exhibit specific conditions than their counterparts without a trauma history. Indeed, several studies have documented an increased rate of a range of health problems, including fibromyalgia, chronic pelvic pain, and irritable bowel syndrome (Wang & Holton, 2007). Moreover, more recent studies have documented the association between adverse childhood experiences, such as maltreatment, and premature death (Brown et al., 2009).

Many studies have shown a clear relation between childhood abuse and health outcomes in adult settings, but it must be mentioned that this does not occur in a vacuum. Rather, abuse occurs in the larger context of familial and social structures. Factors such as parental divorce, early parental loss, parental psychopathology, parental education, and exposure to community/domestic violence are each known to be associated with poor health outcomes in children and adolescents. These psychosocial and contextual factors notwithstanding, Springer et al. (2007) concluded that even after controlling for age, sex, family background, and childhood adversity, childhood abuse was associated with poor physical health over time.

Given the association between childhood abuse and poor health outcomes later in life, understanding the pathways through which this association occurs is important. There have been several theories posited as to why the relation between childhood abuse and health consequences exists and the mechanisms and pathways that further explain this relation. Several emotional, behavioral, social/interpersonal, cognitive, and biological pathways have been identified (Kendall-Tackett, 2002). Children and adults who have been abused are at increased risk of developing psychiatric disorders, including major depression (Springer et al., 2007), which can affect sleep quality and cardiovascular health, among other things. Moreover, children who have experienced childhood abuse are more likely to engage in behaviors associated with poor health outcomes, namely, problematic substance use and risky sexual behaviors (Felitti et al., 2001). Socially, children with a history of abuse are more likely to experience difficulties in interpersonal relationships and report lower levels of social support, which in turn has been linked to an increase risk of mortality and poor health outcomes (Smith & Christakis, 2008). Similarly, a history of abuse can also affect biological functioning, including marked dysregulation of the hypothalamic–pituitary–adrenal axis and sympathetic nervous system that can persist long after the initial abuse. Disruptions in these neurohormonal systems have been demonstrated to have an impact on the immune system (Haddad, 2008), thus increasing the risks for conditions associated with chronic inflammation and/or infectious diseases. Due to the complex ways in which violence affects the individual, family, and community, it is likely that multiple pathways account for the negative health outcomes seen in those who have a history of maltreatment and other traumatic events.

Economic Costs of Child Maltreatment

Although the personal costs of child abuse and neglect for children and their families are quite significant, the indirect and direct costs to society at large are staggering. As noted earlier, child abuse and neglect are associated with an array of devastating psychological, behavioral, and physical health consequences. Moreover, maltreatment has a similar adverse effect on societal health and functioning (Hagele, 2005). Most notable are the plethora of social and public health problems associated with maltreatment, including community and domestic violence, delinquency, mental health disorders, alcohol and illicit substance use, obesity, suicide, and teen pregnancy. These outcomes, in turn, are associated with increased utilization of public and private resources (Hagele, 2005; Wang & Holton, 2007).

A cost analysis of child maltreatment conducted by Prevent Child Abuse America in 2007 suggests that the estimated annual costs of child maltreatment in the United States exceed $103.8 billion (Wang & Holton, 2007). This relatively conservative estimate includes projected expenditures for mental health services, hospitalizations secondary to serious physical injury, child welfare services, law enforcement, special education, juvenile delinquency, criminal justice, health care, and lost productivity. Although this figure is quite sizable, it does not include the numerous costs that are incalculable across these service systems related to both the family and society, as well as the intangible costs of pain, suffering, and diminished quality of life associated with maltreatment and other traumatic events. At a time of growing economic concern, it is expected that maltreatment rates will increase as limited resources shrink further. Therefore, it is critical to consider both the estimated expenditures and the intangible costs when allocating finite resources to prevent and respond to maltreatment (Wang & Holton, 2007).

It is important not simply to list what is known about the impact of child abuse and neglect but also to critically examine the strength of the evidence for what is known, and to point to areas in which more knowledge is needed. To that end, we briefly examine the larger context in which maltreatment occurs and alternative explanations for the links that we have discussed. We also examine the role of race and ethnicity as well as identify some potential next steps.

Larger Context of Abuse and Neglect

One of the most robust obstacles to understanding the impact of child abuse and neglect involves the need to disentangle its effects from those of its larger context. Child abuse and neglect tend not to occur in isolation. Rather, there are family, community, and societal correlates of child maltreatment, such that maltreatment is usually not the only negative experience that children have. Thus, deciding the degree to which a particular negative outcome results from maltreatment rather than other forms of interpersonal or community violence, family dysfunction, chronic adversity, or poverty remains difficult. Some statistical approaches have been attempted, but to truly disentangle this phenomenon is more complicated than it seems. A full review of the contextual factors that are associated with both maltreatment and child outcomes is beyond the scope of this chapter. Nevertheless, we offer an overview of some of the contextual factors that must be considered.

At the family level, family dysfunction is intimately entangled with child maltreatment. Other forms of family violence, such as intimate partner violence, are also at elevated risk of occurring in the homes of maltreated children (Knickerbocker, Heyman, Slep, Jouriles, & McDonald, 2007) and predispose them to a host of negative outcomes. Indeed, roughly half of families with official reports of maltreatment have at least some indication of intimate partner violence (English, Edleson, & Herrick, 2005). Research also suggests that parents who maltreat their children tend to have lower levels of social support, have less contact with their families of origin, receive less help from their families, and feel lonely and isolated. Moreover, parental mental health issues, such as depression and PTSD, are likely to be present in many maltreating families and may lead to an increased risk of potentially negative outcomes (Famularo, Fenton, Kinscherff, Ayoub, & Barnum, 1994). Additional contributing risk factors for child abuse include a child with a disability, child genetic predisposition and temperament, quality of the family and extended social support networks, and degree of family and social tolerance of specific levels and types of family violence (Famularo et al., 1994). All of these variables may interact in complex ways, resulting in varying levels of risk.

Both family income and family structure (e.g., density, single-parent household, extended networks) have also been linked to poor child outcomes and maltreatment. More recent research suggests that family economic hardship, rather than family income per se, is what is especially salient for child outcomes (Gershoff, Aber, Raver, & Lennon, 2007). Economic conditions and other community-level factors can also co-occur with maltreatment and negative child outcomes. Indeed, poverty at the community level, not just the family level, also predicts child maltreatment and a host of negative child outcomes (Coulton, Crampton, Irwin, Spilsbury, & Korbin, 2007).

Several other community-level risk factors are also important to consider when examining the relation between maltreatment and outcomes, such as neighborhood safety and cohesion. In particular, maltreated children are more likely than other children to be exposed to dangerous neighborhoods and community violence, which in turn is linked to negative child outcomes. A host of other facets of community life are entwined with maltreatment risk; indeed, community factors as arcane as the number of alcohol outlets (i.e., liquor stores) in an area are predictive of child maltreatment rates (Freisthler, Gruenewald, Remer, Lery, & Needell, 2007). Similarly, isolation from more formal systems of social support, such as social groups, community organizations, and other community resources, has also been linked to maltreatment and an array of unfavorable outcomes. In sum, maltreatment is often one of several social risks faced by children, which tend to co-occur and result in negative outcomes (Larson, Russ, Crall, & Halfon, 2008).

Alternative Explanations: Mediators and Moderators

To further complicate our understanding of the impact of maltreatment, it is likely to have both proximal and distal outcomes associated with it. In many cases, the effect on the distal outcomes is explained by (or mediated through) the effect on more proximal outcomes. One potential mediator is the way that maltreated children represent the world, themselves, and others. Global views of the world as unsafe, others as untrustworthy, and themselves as worthless can have profound implications for many areas of development and may explain some of the outcomes associated with child maltreatment. Testing the mediation effects of schema is somewhat difficult, however, particularly when using retrospective data. A more distal mediator that is potentially important is revictimization. Adults who have a history of child abuse (especially, but not solely, sexual abuse) are also at risk of further violence victimization as adults, usually through intimate partner violence. In turn, recent violence victimization can have a great impact on many indicators of mental health; thus, revictimization may explain some of the long-term effects of maltreatment. Finally, another potential mediator may be emotional distress; maltreatment may lead to generalized emotional distress, which in turn predicts more specific negative psychosocial outcomes (Whiffen & MacIntosh, 2005).

A related question is one of moderation. Why do some abused or neglected children have a host of negative outcomes, whereas others have none? At the heart of this question is the issue of resilience, that is, thriving in the face of adversity (McGloin & Widom, 2001; Sroufe et al., 2005). There are many factors that apparently help to reduce the negative impact of child maltreatment. At the community level, neighborhood cohesion and social support of families may help to protect children from the worst of the effects (Saluja, Kotch, & Lee, 2003). Conversely, the level of criminal activity in the community appears to moderate the link between maltreatment and criminal or violent behavior; the link between maltreatment and delinquent behavior is especially strong when children remain in crime-ridden neighborhoods (Schuck & Widom, 2005). Other factors that operate at the family or individual level (family stability, parental warmth, child cognitive strength, and positive relationships with nonrelated adults) all appear to be protective (Haskett, Nears, Sabourin Ward, & McPherson, 2006). Finally, it is important to note that interventions can be seen as moderators, if they are effective. There is some limited evidence that appropriate treatment can improve child outcomes, but more research is needed to understand how these work.

HOW DO WE KNOW IT?

Aside from the issue of how maltreatment is defined, as discussed at the beginning of this chapter, is the issue of how it is to be assessed, and when. Traditionally, researchers have often relied on official reports of maltreatment from child protective services. However, this approach has important limitations; many cases of child maltreatment go unreported to the authorities. Indeed, even fatalities from child abuse are likely to be underreported (Herman-Giddens et al., 1999), and there are likely to be biases at different levels of the reporting process (Fluke, Yuan, Hedderson, & Curtis, 2003).

If official reports are the traditional way of assessing maltreatment, the most common are retrospective reports, usually by adults (Paz, Jones, & Byrne, 2005). In most research, adults are asked about their experiences of being maltreated as children, and particular outcomes of interest are assessed contemporaneously. Then, the relation between these reports of maltreatment and of outcomes is examined. There are several problems with this approach. Recollections can change over time and can be influenced by current mood and social context (Paz et al., 2005). In particular, there is evidence that someone who has reported a history of child abuse at one point may not report that same history later on, and vice versa (Aalsma, Zimet, Fortenberry, Blythe, & Orr, 2002).

Because of the limitations of such retrospective reports, more recent research has focused on assessing children with a history of maltreatment prospectively (e.g., Runyan, Hunter, et al., 1998). This approach avoids some of the problems mentioned earlier but does not completely mitigate them (Kendall-Tackett & Becker-Blease, 2004). First, there is the problem of identifying children who have been maltreated, as noted previously: Should the children be identified using child protective services records or through self-reports or parent reports from high-risk or general population samples? Regardless of which approach is used, more severe forms of maltreatment are more likely to be detected, either through self-report or administrative report (Kendall-Tackett & Becker-Blease, 2004). Additionally, self-report, whether retrospectively or close to the time that maltreatment has occurred, is not a panacea. Several pitfalls associated with self-reports of maltreatment must be considered and avoided if possible, or at least mitigated; there are also biases attendant in self-reports of maltreatment (Hanson et al., 2003). Labeling a given set of experiences as maltreatment involves attributions, and many youths often do not describe actual instances of physical or sexual abuse as being abuse (Gibb, Alloy, & Abramson, 2003). In general, it is important to ask behaviorally specific questions about children's experiences, which can help in minimizing some of these biases (DiLillo et al., 2006). More recent research, including the Minnesota Longitudinal Study (Sroufe et al., 2005) and the Longitudinal Studies of Child Abuse and Neglect (LONGSCAN; Runyan, Curtis, et al., 1998), have been increasingly likely to use such behaviorally specific questions in eliciting self-reports on maltreatment experience from children.

There has been considerable debate regarding the overrepresentation of racial and ethnic minorities among children victimized by child abuse and neglect. What the extant research shows, however, is a more complicated picture encompassing both over- and underrepresentation depending on the racial/ethnic group, the location of study, the level of aggregation (county, state, or nation), the type of maltreatment, and the stage in the child welfare processing sequence (i.e., report, investigation, substantiation, service determination; Carter, 2003). Causal debates notwithstanding, the numbers indicate that the victimization rate is highest for African Americans, Native Americans/Alaskans, and children of multiple races. European Americans and Latinos have moderate rates of victimization, whereas Asian Americans have relatively low victimization rates (USDHHS, 2010).

Implicit in the discussion thus far has been the issue of race and child maltreatment. Because race influences maltreatment and its effects, it can influence the results found, depending on the racial/ethnic makeup of the sample used. First, as noted earlier, there are some biases in the process by which children are reported as maltreated. Some of these biases are racial; African American children are disproportionately more likely to be reported to child protective services (Fluke et al., 2003). Because of this apparent bias, there appears to be a lower threshold for reporting African American children to child protective services; thus, African American children reported as maltreated are less likely than other reported children to have experienced severe forms of maltreatment (Lau et al., 2003). An examination of the effects of race on judgments of parenting behavior found some evidence of widespread racial bias in such judgments (Berger, McDaniel, & Paxson, 2005). Specifically, when observing similar parental behavior engaged in by both African American and White parents, observers tended to rate the parental behavior of African American parents as more aggressive.

Race also appears to influence how children fare once they are reported as maltreated. For example, African American children are more likely than other children in child protective services to be removed from the home and less likely to be reunited with their families. Similarly, African American children in child welfare are less likely to receive mental health services than other children, further complicating our understanding of the impact of these services (Garland et al., 2005). It is interesting that this pattern of negative consequences associated with maltreatment tends to persist for children of color (for a review, see Cohen, Deblinger, Mannarino, & deArellano, 2001). Indeed, the biases in reporting to child protective services, along with the disparities in treatment of children who are in the system, have led some to argue that the biases attendant in child welfare are a civil rights issue (Roberts, 2003). This issue is not uniquely an American one; similar arguments have been made regarding ethnic minority populations in other countries. In sum, ethnicity and race are extremely complex variables that encompass social roles, norms, mores, and policies that may moderate the definitions and consequences of child abuse and neglect (Ferrari, 2002). Consequently, it is crucial to consider cultural factors in the assessment and intervention of child abuse and neglect.

WHERE DO WE GO FROM HERE?

As we have discussed in the preceding sections, there is much more still to be learned about the effects of child maltreatment on children. In particular, complications in the definition and assessment of maltreatment make results from different studies difficult to integrate. Further, the mechanisms by which maltreatment influences child outcomes remain poorly understood, as do the factors that promote resilience. Finally, biases at different points in the process of child maltreatment reporting and responding further complicate efforts at understanding. Future research must begin with a multidimensional understanding of maltreatment that takes into account severity, typology, and timing.

Margolin (2005) issued a call for a more sophisticated understanding of children's exposure to violence. A similar need is evident with regard to child maltreatment. Specifically, there is a need to move beyond documenting the bivariate effects and to carefully study the mechanisms that explain or disrupt these links. Margolin proposed three perspectives that may explain the influence of exposure to violence, and there are likely to be parallels with regard to child maltreatment: (a) developmental psychopathology, with an emphasis on how maltreatment interacts with children's developmental capacities; (b) trauma theory, which posits maltreatment as a trauma and many of the negative outcomes as symptoms of posttraumatic stress; and (c) family systems theory, which focuses on the family context, noting that maltreatment marks broad family dysfunctionality. Going forward, the most fruitful approach is likely to be an integration of these perspectives.

Few studies to date have been large prospective longitudinal studies aimed at examining the multiple factors that address both the etiology and consequences of maltreatment and other potentially traumatic events. Future research efforts will benefit from the collaborative nature of studies such as LONGSCAN that allow for examination of multiple ecological and contextual factors that may influence critical developmental capacities and extend our understanding of concomitant traumatic and stressful events while providing insight to family functioning and other contextual factors.

As referenced earlier, LONGSCAN (Runyan, Curtis, et al., 1998) is a consortium of research studies operating under common by-laws and procedures. It was initiated in 1990 with grants from the National Center on Child Abuse and Neglect through a coordinating center at the University of North Carolina and five satellite sites. Although each project can stand alone on its own merits, through the use of common assessment measures, similar data collection methods and schedules, and pooled analyses, LONGSCAN is a collaborative effort that is truly greater than the sum of its parts. The coordinated LONGSCAN design permits a comprehensive exploration of many critical issues in child abuse and neglect on a combined sample of sufficient size for unprecedented statistical power and flexibility ($N = 1,354$). Built into the design is also the ability to replicate and extend findings across a variety of ethnic, social, and economic subgroups.

The goal of LONGSCAN is to follow the children and their families until the children themselves become young adults. Comprehensive assessments of children, their parents, and their teachers are scheduled to occur at child ages 4, 6, 8, 12, 14, 16, 18, and 20 years (see Figure 4.1). All data are collected from multiple sources, including parents, teachers, children/adolescents, and record reviews at least every 2 years. Yearly telephone interviews allow the sites to track families and assess yearly service utilization and other important life events. Much of the data collected through LONGSCAN are publicly available through the National Data Archive on Child Abuse and Neglect; currently all data through age 12 are publicly available, and eventually all of the data will be available for public use and secondary data analyses. Researchers interested in utilizing the data for secondary data analyses are encouraged to access additional information from http://www.iprc.unc.edu/longscan/.

Another innovative collaborative endeavor that has significant potential for influencing the fields of family violence and traumatic stress is the National Child Traumatic Stress Network (NCTSN). Established by Congress in 2000, the NCTSN is supported through funding from the Donald J. Cohen National Child Traumatic Stress Initiative, administered by the USDHHS, Center for Mental Health Services, Substance Abuse and Mental Health Services Administration. The mission of the NCTSN is to raise the standard of care and improve access to services for traumatized children, their families, and communities throughout the United States. The NCTSN comprises more than 85 academic and community-based service centers across the United States, including the University of California, Los Angeles–Duke University National Center for Child Traumatic Stress (the colocated coordinating center). Merging expertise and knowledge in the areas of child development, traumatic stress, clinical interventions, and cultural and family perspectives, the NCTSN serves as a national resource for developing and disseminating evidence-based interventions, trauma-informed services, and professional and public education.

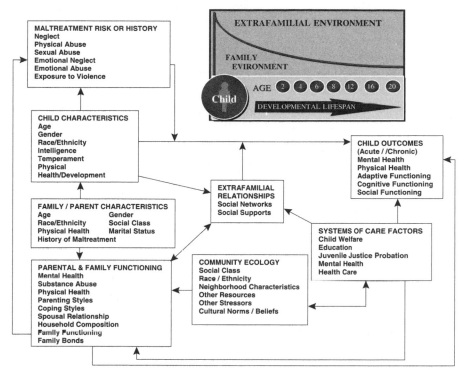

LONGSCAN'S Ecological – Developmental Conceptual Model

Figure 4.1. An overview of the Longitudinal Studies of Child Abuse and Neglect (LONGSCAN) ecological–developmental conceptual model. From "LONGSCAN— A Consortium for Longitudinal Studies of Maltreatment and the Life Course of Children," by D. K. Runyan, P. A. Curtis, W. M. Hunter, M. M. Black, J. B. Kotch, S. Bangdiwala, H. Dubowitz, D. English, M. D. Everson, and J. Landsverk, 1998, *Aggression and Violent Behavior, 3,* p. 281. Copyright 1998 Elsevier. Reprinted with permission.

The NCTSN has a number of resources and products developed by experts in the field to assist with (a) disseminating, implementing, and adopting evidence-based and promising practices; (b) enhancing access to and quality of clinical services; and (c) standardizing assessment and treatment monitoring protocols via a unique quality improvement data initiative with more than 10,000 cases. The NCTSN is a unique resource that will not only assist with bridging the gap between science and practice for communities and families most in need but also create a unique data source to explore some of the aforementioned complex relationships among maltreatment, trauma, and a host of psychological, behavioral, and physical outcomes.

Another important goal for future research will be to further investigate the effectiveness of intervention approaches that have been developed for the prevention, early intervention, and treatment of child abuse and neglect. Given the profound costs to children, families, and society, it is imperative that we begin to use evidence-based interventions and other promising practices to minimize the effects on psychosocial functioning. To this end, several researchers have begun to evaluate the results of several evidence-based interventions aimed at decreasing the impact of child maltreatment. One such example that summarizes promising practices and evidence-based interventions is titled *Closing the Quality Chasm in Child Abuse Treatment: Identifying and Disseminating Best Practices* (Chadwick Center, 2004). Another similar resource, titled *Child Physical and Sexual Abuse: Guidelines for Treatment*, was developed by Saunders, Berliner, and Hanson (2004) with support from the Office for Victims of Crime. This document delineates the clinical and research basis for available interventions used to address child maltreatment and other forms of violence. A similar resource that summarizes interventions in general and culturally adapted interventions, in particular, is available from the NCTSN website (http://www.nctsn.org). Additional resources that will advance our understanding of effective interventions are critical to reducing the impact of maltreatment.

Fortunately, solutions do indeed exist that either minimize the impact or in some cases prevent child maltreatment and other forms of violence. Although some of these solutions have been noted earlier, there is no single algorithm or solution that will fully address such a complex problem as maltreatment. Rather, a multilevel strategy is needed that consists of a combination of approaches, including the following: (a) examination of data collected as part of longitudinal, prospective research; (b) development of effective prevention initiatives, interventions, and services; (c) culturally competent practices; (d) training and dissemination efforts; (e) collaborative and strategic partnerships that span across services systems; and (f) public policies to support funding for additional child maltreatment and traumatic stress research, intervention, training, and collaboration.

In conclusion, we have learned a tremendous amount about child maltreatment and its effects on children and families, yet there is much more to be done. Approaches that capitalize on collaboration and use integrated, ecologically based, prospective longitudinal approaches will be most informative as researchers continue to unravel the complex relations that besiege child maltreatment and its related effects. Similarly, policies and funding to support these efforts will lessen the price we will all have to pay as a result of child abuse and other forms of violence.

REFERENCES

Aalsma, M. C., Zimet, G. D., Fortenberry, J. D., Blythe, M., & Orr, D. P. (2002). Reports of childhood sexual abuse by adolescents and young adults: Stability over time. *Journal of Sex Research, 39,* 259–263. doi:10.1080/00224490209552149

Berger, L. M., McDaniel, M., & Paxson, C. (2005). Assessing parenting behaviors across racial groups: Implications for the child welfare system. *Social Service Review*, *79*, 653–688.

Black, M., Dubowitz, H., & Harrington, D. (1994). Sexual abuse: Developmental differences in children's behavior and self-perception. *Child Abuse & Neglect*, *18*, 85–95.

Brown, D. W., Anda, R. F., Tiemeier, H., Felitti, V. J., Edwards, V. J., Croft, J. B., & Giles, W. H. (2009). Adverse childhood experiences and the risk of premature mortality. *American Journal of Preventive Medicine*, *37*, 389–396. doi:10.1016/ j.amepre.2009.06.021

Carter, J. (2003, June). *Celebrating foster care: Back to the foundations*. Paper presented at the annual conference of the Foster Care Association of Victoria, Melbourne, Victoria, Australia.

Chadwick Center. (2004). *Closing the quality chasm in child abuse treatment: Identifying and disseminating best practices*. Retrieved from http://www.chadwickcenter.org/ Documents/Kaufman%20Report/ChildHosp-NCTAbrochure.pdf

Chaffin, M., Wherry, J., & Dykman, R. (1997). School age children's coping with sexual abuse: Abuse stresses and symptoms associated with four coping strategies. *Child Abuse & Neglect*, *21*, 227–240. doi:10.1016/S0145-2134(96)00148-2

Chen, J., Dunne, M. P., & Wang, X. W. (2003). Childhood sexual abuse: An investigation among 239 male high school students. *Chinese Mental Health Journal*, *17*, 345–347.

Cicchetti, D., & Manly, J. (2001). Editorial: Operationalizing child maltreatment: Developmental processes and outcomes. *Development and Psychopathology*, *13*, 755–757.

Cohen, J. A., Deblinger, E., Mannarino, A., & deArellano, M. (2001). The importance of culture in treating abused and neglected children: An empirical review. *Child Maltreatment*, *6*, 148–157. doi:10.1177/1077559501006002007

Cooley-Quille, M., Boyd, R. C., Frantz, E., & Walsh, J. (2001). Emotional and behavioral impact of exposure to community violence in inner-city adolescents. *Journal of Clinical Child Psychology*, *30*, 199–206. doi:10.1207/S15374424JCCP3002_7

Coulton, C. J., Crampton, D. S., Irwin, M., Spilsbury, J. C., & Korbin, J. E. (2007). How neighborhoods influence child maltreatment: A review of the literature and alternative pathways. *Child Abuse & Neglect*, *31*, 1117–1142. doi:10.1016/ j.chiabu.2007.03.023

DiLillo, D., Fortier, M. A., Hayes, S. A., Trask, E., Perry, A. R., Messman-Moore, T., . . . Nash, C. (2006). Retrospective assessment of childhood sexual and physical abuse: A comparison of scaled and behaviorally specific approaches. *Assessment*, *13*, 297–312. doi:10.1177/1073191106288391

Dubowitz, H., & Bennett, S. (2007). Physical abuse and neglect of children. *The Lancet*, *369*, 1891–1899. doi:10.1016/S0140-6736(07)60856-3

Dubowitz, H., Newton, R. R., Litrownik, A. J., Lewis, T., Briggs, E. C., Thompson, R., . . . Feerick, M. M. (2005). Examination of a conceptual model of child neglect. *Child Maltreatment, 10,* 173–189.

English, D. J. (2003). The importance of understanding a child's maltreatment experience cross-sectionally and longitudinally. *Child Abuse & Neglect, 27,* 877–882. doi:10.1016/S0145-2134(03)00145-5

English, D. J., Edleson, J. L., & Herrick, M. E. (2005). Domestic violence in one state's child protective caseload: A study of differential case dispositions and outcomes. *Children and Youth Services Review, 27,* 1183–1201. doi:10.1016/j.childyouth.2005.04.004

Famularo, R., Fenton, T., Kinscherff, R., Ayoub, C., & Barnum, R. (1994). Maternal and child post traumatic stress disorder in cases of child maltreatment. *Child Abuse & Neglect, 18,* 27–36. doi:10.1016/0145-2134(94)90093-0

Felitti, V. J., Anda, R. F., Nordenberg, D., Williamson, D. F., Spitz, A. M., Edwards, V., . . . Marks, J. S. (2001). Relationship of childhood abuse and household dysfunction to many of the leading causes of death in adults. In K. Franey, R. Geffner, & R. Falconer (Eds.), *The cost of child maltreatment: Who pays? We all do* (pp. 53–69). San Diego, CA: Family Violence and Sexual Assault Institute.

Ferrari, A. M. (2002). The impact of culture upon child rearing practices and definitions of maltreatment. *Child Abuse & Neglect, 26,* 793–813. doi:10.1016/S0145-2134(02)00345-9

Finkelhor, D., & Jones, L. (2006). Why have child maltreatment and child victimization declined? *Journal of Social Issues, 62,* 685–716. doi:10.1111/j.1540-4560.2006.00483.x

Fluke, J. D., Yuan, Y.-Y. T., Hedderson, J., & Curtis, P. A. (2003). Disproportionate representation of race and ethnicity in child maltreatment: Investigation and victimization. *Children and Youth Services Review, 25,* 359–373. doi:10.1016/S0190-7409(03)00026-4

Freisthler, B., Gruenewald, P. J., Remer, L. G., Lery, B., & Needell, B. (2007). Exploring the spatial dynamics of alcohol outlets and child protective services referrals, substantiations, and foster care entries. *Child Maltreatment, 12,* 114–124. doi:10.1177/1077559507300107

Garland, A. F., Lau, A. S., Yeh, M., McCabe, K. M., Hough, R. L., & Landsverk, J. A. (2005). Racial and ethnic differences in utilization of mental health services among high-risk youths. *American Journal of Psychiatry, 162,* 1336–1343. doi:10.1176/appi.ajp.162.7.1336

Gershoff, E. T., Aber, J. L., Raver, C. C., & Lennon, M. C. (2007). Income is not enough: Incorporating material hardship into models of income associations with parenting and child development. *Child Development, 78,* 70–95. doi:10.1111/j.1467-8624.2007.00986.x

Gibb, B. E., Alloy, L. B., & Abramson, L. Y. (2003). Global reports of childhood maltreatment versus recall of specific maltreatment experiences: Relationships with dysfunctional attitudes and depressive symptoms. *Cognition and Emotion*, *17*, 903–915.

Haddad, J. J. (2008). On the mechanisms and putative pathways involving neuro-immune interactions. *Biochemical and Biophysical Research Communications, 370*, 531–535. doi:10.1016/j.bbrc.2008.04.012

Hagele, D. M. (2005). The impact of maltreatment on the developing child. *North Carolina Medical Journal, 66*, 356–359. Retrieved from http://www.ncmedical journal.com/sept-oct-05/Hagele.pdf

Hanson, R. F., Kievit, L. W., Saunders, B. E., Smith, D. W., Kilpatrick, D. G., Resnick, H. S., & Ruggiero, K. J. (2003). Correlates of adolescent reports of sexual assault: Findings from the National Survey of Adolescents. *Child Maltreatment, 8*, 261–272. doi:10.1177/1077559503257087

Haskett, M. E., Nears, K., Sabourin Ward, C., & McPherson, A. V. (2006). Diversity in adjustment of maltreated children: Factors associated with resilient functioning. *Clinical Psychology Review, 26*, 796–812. doi:10.1016/j.cpr.2006.03.005

Herman-Giddens, M. E., Brown, G., Verbiest, S., Carlson, P. J., Hooten, E. G., Howell, E., & Butts, J. D. (1999). Underascertainment of child abuse mortality in the United States. *JAMA, 282*, 463–467. doi:10.1001/jama.282.5.463

Higgins, D. J., & McCabe, M. P. (2000). Relationships between different types of maltreatment during childhood and adjustment in adulthood. *Child Maltreatment, 5*, 261–272. doi:10.1177/1077559500005003006

Kendall-Tackett, K. (2002). The health effects of childhood abuse: Four pathways by which abuse can influence health. *Child Abuse & Neglect, 26*, 715–729. doi:10.1016/S0145-2134(02)00343-5

Kendall-Tackett, K., & Becker-Blease, K. (2004). The importance of retrospective findings in child maltreatment research. *Child Abuse & Neglect, 28*, 723–727. doi:10.1016/j.chiabu.2004.02.002

King, G., Trocme, N., & Thatte, N. (2003). Substantiation as a multitier process: The results of a NIS-3 analysis. *Child Maltreatment, 8*, 173–182. doi:10.1177/1077559503254143

Knickerbocker, L., Heyman, R. E., Slep, A. M. S., Jouriles, E. N., & McDonald, R. (2007). Co-occurrence of child and partner maltreatment: Definitions, prevalence, theory, and implications for assessment. *European Psychologist, 12*, 36–44. doi:10.1027/1016-9040.12.1.36

Larson, K., Russ, S. A., Crall, J. J., & Halfon, N. (2008). Influence of multiple social risks on children's health. *Pediatrics, 121*, 337–344. doi:10.1542/peds.2007-0447

Lau, A. S., McCabe, K. M., Yeh, M., Garland, A. F., Hough, R. L., & Landsverk, J. (2003). Race/ethnicity and rates of self-reported maltreatment among high-risk youth in public sectors of care. *Child Maltreatment, 8*, 183–194. doi:10.1177/1077559503254141

Margolin, G. (2005). Children's exposure to violence: Exploring developmental pathways to diverse outcomes. *Journal of Interpersonal Violence, 20*, 72–81. doi:10.1177/0886260504268371

McGloin, J. M., & Widom, C. S. (2001). Resilience among abused and neglected children grown up. *Development and Psychopathology, 13*, 1021–1038. doi:10.1017/S095457940100414X

Paz, I., Jones, D., & Byrne, G. (2005). Child maltreatment, child protection and mental health. *Current Opinion in Psychiatry, 18*, 411–421. doi:10.1097/01.yco.0000172061.93896.26

Roberts, D. E. (2003). Child welfare and civil rights. *University of Illinois Law Review, 2003*, 171–182.

Runyan, D. K., Curtis, P. A., Hunter, W. M., Black, M. M., Kotch, J. B., Bangdiwala, S., ... Landsverk, J. (1998). LONGSCAN— A consortium for longitudinal studies of maltreatment and the life course of children. *Aggression and Violent Behavior, 3*, 275–285.

Runyan, D. K., Hunter, W. M., Socolar, R. R. S., Amaya-Jackson, L., English, D., Landsverk, J., ... Matthew, R. M. (1998). Children who prosper in unfavorable environments: The relationship to social capital. *Pediatrics, 101*, 12–18. doi:10.1542/peds.101.1.12

Saluja, G., Kotch, J., & Lee, L.-C. (2003). Effects of child abuse and neglect: Does social capital really matter? *Archives of Pediatrics & Adolescent Medicine, 157*, 681–686. doi:10.1001/archpedi.157.7.681

Saunders, B. E., Berliner, L., & Hanson, R. F. (2004). *Child physical and sexual abuse: Guidelines for treatment* (Revised Report). Charleston, SC: National Crime Victims Research and Treatment Center. Retrieved from http://www.musc.edu/ncvc

Schuck, A. M., & Widom, C. S. (2005). Understanding the role of neighborhood context in the long-term criminal consequences of child maltreatment. *American Journal of Community Psychology, 36*, 207–222. doi:10.1007/s10464-005-8615-1

Silverman, A. B., Reinherz, H. Z., & Giaconia, R. M. (1996). The long term sequelae of child and adolescent abuse. *Child Abuse & Neglect, 20*, 709–723. doi:10.1016/0145-2134(96)00059-2

Smith, K. P., & Christakis, N. A. (2008). Social networks and health. *Annual Review of Sociology, 34*, 405–429. doi:10.1146/annurev.soc.34.040507.134601

Springer, K. W., Sheridan, J., Kuo, D., & Carnes, M. (2007). Long-term physical and mental health consequences of childhood physical abuse: Results from a large population-based sample of men. *Child Abuse & Neglect, 31*, 517–530. doi:10.1016/j.chiabu.2007.01.003

Sroufe, L. A., Egeland, B., Carlson, E. A., & Collins, W. A. (2005). *The development of the person: The Minnesota study of risk and adaptation from birth to adulthood.* New York, NY: Guilford Press.

U.S. Department of Health and Human Services, Children's Bureau, Administration on Children, Youth, and Families. (2005). *National Child Abuse and Neglect Data System (NCANDS)*. Washington, DC: U.S. Government Printing Office.

U.S. Department of Health and Human Services, Children's Bureau, Administration on Children, Youth, and Families. (2008). *Child maltreatment 2006*. Washington, DC: U.S. Government Printing Office.

U.S. Department of Health and Human Services, Children's Bureau, Administration on Children, Youth, and Families. (2010). *Child maltreatment 2008*. Washington, DC: U.S. Government Printing Office.

Wang, C.-T., & Holton, J. (2007). *Total estimated cost of child abuse and neglect in the United States: Economic impact study*. Chicago, IL: Prevent Child Abuse America. Retrieved from http://member.preventchildabuse.org/site/DocServer/cost_analysis.pdf?docID=144

Watts-English, T., Fortson, B. L., Gibler, N., Hooper, S. R., & De Bellis, M. D. (2006). The psychobiology of maltreatment in childhood. *Journal of Social Issues, 62*, 717–736. doi:10.1111/j.1540-4560.2006.00484.x

Whiffen, V. E., & MacIntosh, H. B. (2005). Mediators of the link between childhood sexual abuse and emotional distress: A critical review. *Trauma, Violence & Abuse, 6*, 24–39. doi:10.1177/1524838004272543

Yates, T. M., Carlson, E. A., & Egeland, B. (2008). A prospective study of child maltreatment and self injurious behavior in a community sample. *Development and Psychopathology, 20*, 651–671. doi:10.1017/S0954579408000321

II

SEXUAL VIOLENCE

5

PREVALENCE OF SEXUAL VIOLENCE

LORI ANN POST, BRIAN J. BIROSCAK, AND GIA BARBOZA

Social problems have been characterized as consisting of social situations involving a substantial number of persons and constituting a threat to social well-being, as defined by the mores of the group, and which must be dealt with in an organized and concerted way (Bossard, 1934). Such a definition suggests that *pervasiveness* is a primary determinant of whether a phenomenon is considered a social problem. Whereas the pervasiveness of violence against women factored into the passage of the Violence Against Women Act of 1994 and its subsequent reauthorization (U.S. Department of Justice, Office on Violence Against Women, n.d.), the pervasiveness of a problem among the populace also factors into the setting of research agendas (e.g., the Centers for Disease Control and Prevention's Injury Research Agenda; National Center for Injury Prevention and Control, 2002) and the development of prevention priorities (e.g., Healthy People 2010; Centers for Disease Control and Prevention, 2001a). This chapter examines the current state of knowledge regarding the pervasiveness of sexual violence against women and children.

SCOPE OF CHAPTER: KEY TERMS

There are myriad possible questions to address in a chapter on the pervasiveness of sexual violence, ranging from the seemingly basic—for example, "What is violence?"—to more nuanced details—for example, "Is there a meaningful difference between violence and aggression?" Unfortunately, there is not enough space here to cover all of the topics of interest. As a result, only major issues of definition and measurement are addressed. We argue that to address a social problem, one must have data of acceptable quality to assist with planning and evaluating prevention efforts. This process begins with defining the concept at hand, determining how to operationalize that definition, and finally, identifying valid and reliable measures of those concepts.

Sexual Violence: Definitions

The World Health Organization (2002) has defined *sexual violence* as including

> any sexual act, attempt to obtain a sexual act, unwanted sexual comments or advances, or acts to traffic, or otherwise directed, against a person's sexuality using coercion, by any person regardless of their relationship to the victim, in any setting, including but not limited to home and work. (p. 149)

Coercion encompasses a broad spectrum of actions ranging from physical and psychological intimidation to nonconsensual sexual contact that occurs as a result of voluntary or involuntary intoxication (World Health Organization, 2002). The Centers for Disease Control and Prevention, on the other hand, has defined sexual violence as including

> nonconsensual completed or attempted penetration of the vagina or anus, nonconsensual completed or attempted oral sex, nonconsensual intentional touching of a sexual nature, or nonconsensual non-contact acts of a sexual nature such as voyeurism and verbal or behavioral sexual harassments. (Basile, Hertz, & Back, 2007, p. 8)

These definitions suggest a number of activities that qualify as sexual violence, including rape (completed or attempted), sex trafficking, unwanted touching, sexual harassment, threats, intimidation, peeping, and taking nude photos without consent. Global studies on sexual violence often include traditional harmful practices such as female genital cutting, obligatory inspections for virginity, and forced marriage.

Definitions of sexual violence suggest that sexual coercion exists along a continuum ranging from forcible rape to verbal pressure to engage in sexual acts against one's will. But traditional conceptualizations of sexual violence tend to be restricted to culturally disvalued types of sexual coerciveness. Therefore, despite the fact that these definitions seem transparent, the operational criterion used in practice for measuring the occurrence of sexual violence is, in reality, a social construct with public policy implications. Although socially unacceptable forms of coercion (e.g., rape) are criminalized, more acceptable forms of coercion are not only culturally tolerated but also sometimes condoned.

Sexual Violence: Prevalence Versus Incidence

In the course of measuring the pervasiveness of sexual violence, researchers must make a number of decisions, including but not limited to determining whether they should measure incidence and/or prevalence, and in the case of the latter, deciding whether to measure period or lifetime prevalence (or both). *Incidence*, in its simplest form, refers to the number of instances of illness commencing, or injuries (or sexual violence episodes) occurring during a given period in a specified population, and is typically reported as the number of cases per 1,000 or 100,000 (Last, 1995). Unlike incidence measures, which focus on the number of events, prevalence measures focus on the status of persons with respect to disease, injury, disability, or some other attribute (including sexual violence victimization) and are reported as a percentage of cases in a sample or population.[1] There are a number of prevalence subtypes, but the two most commonly used measures are *lifetime prevalence*—defined as the total number of persons known to have had the attribute or experience at some point in their lives—and *period prevalence*—defined as the number of persons known to have had the attribute at any time during a specified period (usually the previous year; Last, 1995).

Inclusion/Exclusion Criteria

We restricted our review to studies that measured the frequency of sexual violence against female adolescents and adults. Where possible, we only present data on sexual violence against persons age 12 years and older, using data collected within the United States. Data also must have been collected either via census or according to a national probability sample. In the case of sampling, priority was given to authors who provided measures of precision (e.g., confidence intervals). To provide readers with a contemporary review

---

[1]For a more detailed treatment of incidence and prevalence measures, see Rothman and Greenland's (1998) chapter on measures of disease frequency.

of sexual violence, data must have been collected within the past decade (see Table 5.1).[2]

WHAT WE KNOW

This section presents contemporary findings regarding the occurrence of sexual violence against women and children in the United States. Findings are presented in the following order: general population data for adult females, criminal justice system data, health care system data, college studies data, and adolescent studies data. In the subsequent section (How We Know It), we delve into the intricacies of each data source.

Adult Female Population Data

We identified only two published sources of general population data collected within the past decade that measured the prevalence of sexual violence among women living in the United States: the Second Injury Control and Risk Survey (ICARIS-2; Basile, Chen, Black, & Saltzman, 2007) and the Drug-Facilitated, Incapacitated, and Forcible Rape National Study (DAFR/IR; Kilpatrick, Resnick, Ruggiero, Conoscenti, & McCauley, 2007).

Conducted from July 2001 to February 2003, the ICARIS-2 collected data on experiences of U.S. residents 18 years and older and descriptive information about the relationship of the parties and age at first reported victimization. In the sexual violence module of the ICARIS-2, respondents were asked the following regarding unwanted sexual activity: "During the past 12 months, have you experienced any sexual activity when you did not want to, including touch that made you uncomfortable?" The estimated past-year prevalence of unwanted sexual activity was 2.5%. This corresponds to a nationwide estimate of 2,736,065 adult females. (No estimate of precision was provided.) In response to the question, "Have you ever been forced to have sex?" 10.6% of women, or an estimated 11,711,718 adult females, reported experiencing forced sex in their lifetime.

The DAFR/IR collected data in a national telephone household sample of 3,001 women on both lifetime and past-year prevalence of rape, forcible rape, drug-facilitated rape, and intoxicated rape (Kilpatrick et al., 2007). *Forcible rape* was defined as any unwanted sexual act involving oral, anal, or

---

[2]We exclude four of the most frequently cited sources of data—the National Women's Study (National Victim Center, 1992), the National Violence Against Women Survey (Tjaden & Thoennes, 2000), the Sexual Experiences Survey (Koss, Gidycz, & Wisniewski, 1987), and the National College Women's Sexual Victimization Study (Fisher, Cullen, & Turner, 2000)—because they do not meet our time period requirements.

TABLE 5.1
Studies Measuring Sexual Violence

Study	Unit of analysis	Target population	Type of sexual violence covered	Best account for	Incidence or prevalence
		General population surveys			
ICARIS-2	Individuals (females)	All females in the United States age 18 years and older	Forcible sex; unwanted sexual activity	Females in the United States	2.5% annual; 10.6% lifetime
DAFR/IR	Individuals (females)	All females in the United States age 18 years and older	Forcible rape; drug- and alcohol-facilitated rape	Females in the United States	18% lifetime
		Criminal justice			
UCR	Aggregate; reporting agency	All law enforcement agencies; 98% reporting	Limited number reported and recorded crimes	Commercial and business victims	92,455 past year or 60/100,000
NCVS	Victimization, individuals and households	Individuals in households	Household and personal crimes	Household and personal crimes not reported to police	176,450 past year or 1.4/1,000
		College studies			
ACHA-NCHA	Students in classrooms	All students attending college or university	Crimes on college campuses	Female college students at participating colleges	1,153,680 lifetime or 11.5%; 501,600 past year, 5%
DAFR/IR	College students	U.S. college students	Crimes on college campuses	Female college students in U.S. colleges	20,200,000 lifetime, 16%; 1,100,000, 0.6% past year

(continues)

TABLE 5.1
Studies Measuring Sexual Violence   (Continued)

Study	Unit of analysis	Target population	Type of sexual violence covered	Best account for	Incidence or prevalence
			Health studies		
NHAMCS	Medical record	Visits to emergency rooms in noninstitutional, short-stay hospitals (excluding federal, military, and Veterans Affairs hospitals)	Rape and sexual assault based on International Classification of Diseases codes	Individuals who visit emergency departments (or individuals without insurance/ low income)	158,504 emergency departments visits; 4.2% of all emergency departments visits
NEISS-AIP	Medical record	Injuries treated in hospital emergency departments	Completed or attempted rape, completed or attempted sodomy, any other completed or attempted assault of a sexual nature with physical force and abusive sexual contact derived from hospital records	Individuals who visit emergency departments (or individuals without insurance/ low income)	93,381 visits over 2 years
			Adolescent studies		
YRBSS	Adolescents	Adolescents in Grades 9–12 in school	Household and personal crimes	High school students in the United States	11.3% lifetime

Note. ICARIS-2 = Second Injury Control and Risk Survey; DAFR/IR = Drug-Facilitated, Incapacitated, and Forcible Rape National Study; UCR = Uniform Crime Reporting; NCVS = National Crime Victimization Survey; ACHA-NCHA = American College Health Association–National College Health Assessment; NHAMCS = National Hospital Ambulatory Medical Care Survey; NEISS-AIP = National Electronic Injury Surveillance System–All Injury Program; YRBSS = Youth Risk Behavior Surveillance System.

vaginal penetration involving force, threat of force, or injury. *Incapacitated rape* was similarly defined except that the sexual act in question took place after the victim's voluntary consumption of drugs and/or alcohol. *Drug- and alcohol-facilitated rape*, on the other hand, was defined as committing an unwanted sexual act against the victim after intentionally providing her with drugs and/or alcohol. Kilpatrick et al. (2007) found 18% of women reported any lifetime experience of rape, which included forcible sexual penetration (16.1%) as well as penetrations involving drugs, alcohol, or other incapacities (5%). Using the 2005 census data, the authors estimated that 20.2 million (18%) women had experienced forced sex in their lifetime, 18 million (16.1%) women had a history of forcible rape, 2.6 million (2.3%) women had a history of drug-facilitated rape, 3.1 million (2.8%) women had a history of incapacitated rape, and 1.1 million (0.6%) had experienced rape in the year prior.

Criminal Justice Studies

Although not all forms of sexual violence rise to the level of being considered criminal (at least not in all jurisdictions), the U.S. criminal justice system has a long history of measuring the nature and extent of sexual violence. In contrast to general population survey data not specifically devoted to crime and victimization, there are two ongoing, nationwide criminal justice data collection efforts that measure sexual violence: the Uniform Crime Reporting (UCR) Program and the National Crime Victimization Survey (NCVS).

UCR data are based on annual law enforcement submissions that are compiled into data sets for use in administration, operation, and management. Nearly 17,000 law enforcement agencies submit data to the Federal Bureau of Investigation according to procedures spelled out in a detailed handbook (U.S. Department of Justice, Federal Bureau of Investigation, 2004). The UCR Program defines forcible rape conceptually as the carnal knowledge of a female forcibly and against her will. According to the UCR Handbook: "There is carnal knowledge if there is the slightest penetration of the sexual organ of the female (vagina) by the sexual organ of the male (penis)" (U.S. Department of Justice, Federal Bureau of Investigation, 2004, p. 149). Completed assaults as well as attempts to rape by force or threat of force are included; however, statutory rape (without force) and other sex offenses are excluded from this measure. The UCR Program counts one offense for each female victim of a rape, attempted rape, or assault with intent to rape, regardless of the victim's age.[3] In 2006, an estimated 92,455 forcible rapes were reported to law enforcement, which corresponds to a nationwide rate of 60.9 offenses per 100,000 female inhabitants (U.S. Department of Justice, Federal Bureau of Investigation, 2007).

---

[3]We were not able to restrict our review of sexual violence to persons age 12 years or older for this measure.

The NCVS, formerly called the National Crime Survey, was implemented nationwide in 1973 (National Archive of Criminal Justice Data, n.d.). The NCVS is an annual survey of a nationally representative sample of approximately 49,000 households (about 100,000 persons). Developed after the UCR Program to capture offenses not reported to police, the NCVS was designed to achieve four objectives: (a) to provide information about the victims and consequences of crime, (b) to estimate crimes not reported to the police, (c) to provide uniform measures of selected types of crimes, and (d) to permit assessments of trend and comparisons by area (National Archive of Criminal Justice Data, n.d.). It defines rape/sexual assault conceptually as forced sexual intercourse, including both psychological coercion and physical force (Catalano, 2006). Household respondents are asked whether anyone has attacked or threatened them in the 6-month period preceding the 1st day of the month of the interview and includes the response option: "Any rape, attempted rape or other type of sexual attack" (U.S. Department of Commerce, 2004). Respondents are also asked the following question: "Have you been forced or coerced to engage in unwanted sexual activity by (a) Someone you didn't know before, (b) A casual acquaintance, or (c) Someone you know well?" For the year 2005, an estimated 176,540 rapes/sexual assaults were committed in the United States, which corresponds to an incidence rate of 1.4 rapes/sexual assaults per 1,000 females age 12 and older (U.S. Department of Justice, Office of Justice Programs, 2006). The breakdown for 2005 was 66,670 rapes (0.5 per 1,000), 48,340 attempted rapes (0.4 per 1,000), and 61,530 assaults (0.5 per 1,000).

Health Care Studies

Two ongoing, nationwide data collection efforts include measurements of sexual violence treated within the health care system: the National Hospital Ambulatory Medical Care Survey (NHAMCS) and the National Electronic Injury Surveillance System–All Injury Program (NEISS-AIP). The NHAMCS is an annual survey based on a nationwide sample of visits made to emergency departments (EDs) and outpatient clinics in the United States. Data are collected on the patient record form (National Center for Health Statistics, 2007). Sexual assault is determined according to NHAMCS codes for rape and sexual abuse, International Classification of Diseases codes for rape and sexual assault, and a verbatim text field related to the reason for the ED visit. In 2003, sexual assault and rape of females age 12 years and older accounted for an estimated 158,504 ED visits (Straight & Heaton, 2007).

The NEISS-AIP is a surveillance system operated by the U.S. Consumer Product Safety Commission that collects data from medical records for ED visits for nonfatal injuries treated in a nationally representative subsample of

66 NEISS hospitals. Data coders classify nonfatal injuries as sexual assault according to a broad definition: some indication in the record of a probable or possible assault of a sexual nature, including completed or attempted rape, completed or attempted sodomy, and any other completed or attempted assault of a sexual nature with physical force and abusive sexual contact (U.S. Consumer Product Safety Commission, 2000). During the 2-year period 2001–2002, sexual assault and rape of females age 10 years and older accounted for an estimated 93,381 ED visits. This figure represents 4.2% of all assault visits to EDs (Saltzman et al., 2007).

College Studies

Female college students represent one of the most extensively studied populations with respect to sexual violence. The past decade saw two nationwide surveys of college campuses intending to measure sexual violence victimization: the American College Health Association–National College Health Assessment (ACHA-NCHA) and the DAFR/IR.

The ACHA-NCHA is a survey instrument designed to collect information on a broad range of students' health behaviors, indicators, and perceptions (American College Health Association, 2005). Although North American postsecondary institutions self-selected to participate, the ACHA-NCHA spring 2006 reference group reported here includes data from only those institutions that used random sampling techniques, which yielded a final data set consisting of 94,806 students on 117 campuses. The researchers had gender data for 91,379 students, 63.4% ($n = 57,903$) of whom were female. ACHA-NCHA obtained data from females on four forms of sexual violence within the past school year: verbal threats for sex against their will ($n = 2,246$; 3.9%); sexual touching against their will ($n = 6,179$; 10.7%); attempted sexual penetration against their will ($n = 2,081$; 3.6%); and sexual penetration against their will ($n = 1,028$; 1.8%).

The DAFR/IR study, introduced earlier, represents the first comprehensive study of both the lifetime and past-year prevalence of rape among a national sample of 2,000 female students selected from a representative national list of women attending 4-year colleges and universities (Kilpatrick et al., 2007). The study represents the first and most comprehensive national data on the prevalence, characteristics, and impact of drug- and alcohol-facilitated rape and incapacitated rape among U.S. college women. Results show that approximately 1,153,680, or 11.5%, of undergraduate women enrolled in the study had been raped during their lifetime. The 11.5% prevalence estimate included forcible sexual penetration (8.7%) as well as penetrations involving drugs, alcohol, or other incapacities (6.4%). Using the 2005 census data, the authors estimated that approximately 501,600 (5%) of college women had experienced a rape in the year prior to the survey. The DAFR/IR study further found that 6.4% of female college students, or an estimated 375,000 college women, have been victims of drug- and alcohol-facilitated rape/incapacitated rape at some time during their lifetime. By including drug- and alcohol-facilitated rape/incapacitated rape in rape prevalence estimates, Kilpatrick and colleagues (2007) identified an additional 164,000 rapes.

Adolescent Studies

In many cases, the college years are not the first time that a young woman has been sexually victimized. Although the adult Behavioral Risk Factor Surveillance System does not currently generate nationwide estimates for sexual violence, its youth counterpart, the Youth Risk Behavior Surveillance System (YRBSS), asks questions about sexual violence of all high school respondents. The YRBSS, conducted biennially since 1991, monitors priority health risk behaviors via national, state, and local school-based surveys of students in Grades 9 through 12 (Centers for Disease Control and Prevention, 2008). The YRBSS asks one question related to sexual violence: "Have you ever been physically forced to have sexual intercourse when you did not want to?" For 2007, the estimated percentages of females' affirmative responses to the question by Grades 9 to 12 were 9.2% (confidence interval [CI] = 7.3%–11.5%), 13.1% (CI = 10.6%–16.0%), 12.0% (CI = 9.8%–14.5%), and 10.9% (CI = 9.2%–12.8%), respectively.

For the sake of completeness, we note here that the National Survey of Adolescents (NSA), originally carried out in 1995 (Kilpatrick et al., 2000), was replicated in 2005 (Danielson et al., 2010). Just like the original, the NSA replication study was a national household probability sample and an oversample of urban-dwelling adolescents ages 12 to 17 years. Complete parent and adolescent telephone interviews were obtained from 3,614 cases. However, weighted prevalence estimates of adolescent female sexual abuse were not provided. In all, 269 adolescents (males and females) reported having experienced at least one incident of sexual abuse, defined as

> (a) episodes that involved forced vaginal or anal penetration by an object, finger, or penis; (b) episodes of forced oral sex; (c) episodes in which another person touched the adolescent's genitalia against their will; or (d) episodes in which the adolescent was forced to touch another's genitalia. (Danielson et al., 2010, p. 102)

In a separate publication based on NSA replication study data, sexual assault in the context of adolescent dating violence was 0.9% (Wolitzky-Taylor et al., 2008).

HOW WE KNOW IT

Before proceeding with a critical analysis of the above-mentioned data, we would like to emphasize that it is not our intent to minimize or invalidate the experiences of sexual violence victims. Rather, it is our intent to help advance knowledge regarding the pervasiveness of sexual violence in the United States by examining current data that are used for setting policy, planning prevention initiatives, and evaluating the sum of our efforts. The critical evaluation of researchers' methods, samples, analyses, and so on leads to recommendations for improvement. It is beyond the scope of this chapter to critique in full all the sources we reviewed. Thus, selected examples that highlight the major issues are given.[4]

Adult Female Population Data

The ICARIS-2 (Basile, Chen, et al., 2007) provides national survey estimates of the prevalence of unwanted sexual activity and forced sex among adults in the United States. The past-year prevalence of unwanted sexual activity was estimated using the following measure: "During the past 12 months, have you experienced any sexual activity when you did not want to, including touch that made you uncomfortable?" Basile, Chen, et al. (2007) did not define sexual activity in their publication, and it is not clear whether respondents interpreted the term identically. Furthermore, might some participants have responded affirmatively if they had consensual sex with their partner in the past year when they really did not feel like having sex? It is unclear what these issues mean in terms of the measurement validity of sexual violence data reported from ICARIS-2, as the authors' publication does not mention whether validity was evaluated. Lastly, although the past-year prevalence estimate of 2.5% is based on data from a probability-based national survey, the authors did not provide confidence intervals for this estimate to indicate the range within which the true value likely falls. This could be problematic, especially considering that the resultant estimate of 2.7 million women experiencing unwanted sexual activity in the past 12 months is based on only 136 affirmative responses.

The lifetime prevalence of forced sex was estimated based on responses to the question, "Have you ever been forced to have sex?" defined as

> any type of vaginal, oral, or anal penetration or intercourse in situations
> against your will. It also includes situations where you were unable to
> give consent for any reason, such as age, drugs, alcohol, sleep or mental

---

[4]For more information on research issues involving sensitive topics, such as sexual violence, see Rosenbaum and Langhinrichsen-Rohling (2006); for information on the limits of random-digit dialing methods, see Simon, Mercy, and Barker (2006).

disability. These incidents may have involved anyone known or unknown to you. (Basile, Chen, et al., 2007, p. 440)

Respondents answering in the affirmative would include women reporting past incidents of child sexual abuse. In fact, an estimated 20.6% to 30.5% of women were younger than 12 years old at the time of first forced sex. This question is so broad in scope that it is of questionable utility. Similar to the other sexual violence question, the authors' estimate of 11.7 million victims is based on only 577 women's responses, and no confidence interval is provided.

Criminal Justice Studies

The UCR and NCVS are the two prominent data sources used to study sexual violence. A number of authors have critically analyzed sexual violence data arising from the UCR Program and the NCVS. Both data sets differ in terms of the population sampled and the definition of sexual assault used (Ruback & Menard, 2001). Differences in sampled populations result from the UCR's reliance on citizens reporting the crime to the police. There is widespread discrepancy, however, between the reporting of crime and its occurrence. For example, less than 40% of rape and attempted rape victims are believed to report the crime to the police (Rand & Catalano, 2007).

Part I crimes, including forcible rape, are counted in the UCR only if these crimes are both reported and recorded by police. Substantial undercounting in the UCR results from state law variations regarding the components of sexual assault and victimization. Some forms of sexual violence, for example, those classified as Part II crimes, are included in the UCR only after an arrest has been made. Finally, under the hierarchy rule, if multiple crimes are committed in a single incident, only the most serious is counted (Maxfield & Babbie, 2007). For example, if a woman is raped and then murdered, only the most serious crime—murder—is recorded in the UCR.

The NCVS relies on victim surveys, which are based on self-report and offer at least three clear advantages over data collected from the UCR. First, victim surveys allow researchers to obtain information on crimes that were not reported to the police. Second, they make it possible to measure incidents that police may not have recorded as crimes. Finally, they provide data on victims, offenders, and the incident itself (Maxfield & Babbie, 2007). The limitations associated with the NCVS are those commonly found in surveys based on self-report. Inaccurate recall, telescoping, serial victimization, and underestimating incidents in which the victim and offender know each other are common sources of bias associated with information of a sensitive nature, including estimates of sexual violence provided by the NCVS.

In addition to comparing estimates derived from each source (e.g., Catalano, 2006), previous reviewers have compared data from the NCVS with those from other commonly used surveys such as the National Violence Against Women Survey, or NVAWS (e.g., Kelley, 2002). Generally speaking, it is not possible to directly compare estimates across different surveys given methodological differences. However, if differences in sampling methods are properly accounted for, such comparisons may indeed be possible. According to Bachman (2000), for example, "general magnitude estimates of physical assault against women across surveys converge when the definitions of victim (e.g., female 18 years of age or older) and offender (e.g., lone male offender) are controlled" (p. 7). Nevertheless, estimates for rape from the NVAWS remain significantly higher than those reported by the NCVS. Moreover, compared with the NCVS, the NVAWS results in a larger proportion of intimate-perpetrated rapes and physical assaults, a finding attributed to the "more graphic behavioral-specific screening questions used by the NVAWS to uncover these victimizations" (Bachman, 2000, p. 7).

Health Care Studies

NHAMCS and NEISS-AIP sexual violence data are both obtained via chart review methods (Saltzman et al., 2007). Because of this similarity, it might seem reasonable to assume that NEISS-AIP and NHAMCS national estimates afford comparative information about medically treated episodes of sexual violence. Indeed, the NHAMCS and the NEISS-AIP use similar definitions of what constitutes injury. The estimates of sexual violence provided by these two data sources, however, are very different. For example, in two separate studies reviewed for this chapter, one study provided an ED estimate based on 1 year of NHAMCS data that were 1.7 times larger than a different study that used 2 years of NEISS-AIP data. The most likely source of divergence in these two surveys is attributable to differences in sample design and survey instrumentation and procedures. For example, the NHAMCS samples visits to 500 hospital outpatient and EDs, whereas the NEISS-AIP survey samples 500,000 medical records from 66 hospital EDs. Moreover, the NHAMCS estimate includes both initial ED visits and revisits for the same injury, whereas the NEISS-AIP estimate includes only initial ED visits (Centers for Disease Control and Prevention, 2001b).

The NHAMCS data use external cause of injury "e-codes" derived from information in the medical record to identify intent or manner of injury (accident, self-inflicted, or intentional assault) and mechanism (e.g., firearm, cutting, unarmed brawl) in injury cases (Saltzman et al., 2007). Despite the fact that the coding follows well-defined protocols, the decision regarding injury classification is highly subjective, possibly resulting in low intercoder agreement. According to Cohen and Lynch (2007),

> if the hospital staffs who abstract the data do not distinguish between thwarted offenders and victims among patients, or between intended and unintended injuries, the NHAMCS data will overstate visits due to assault victimizations. On the other hand, if the staff uses a more stringent definition of assault, then this might understate these events. (p. 194)

They further stated that "coding practices of the NHAMCS suggest a reluctance to inappropriately designate an injury as intentional when there is inadequate information in the record" (Cohen & Lynch, 2007, p. 194).

Both the NEISS-AIP and NHAMCS are limited by the quality of the original hospital records. The medical record typically contains only the information necessary for proper medical diagnosis and treatment. Given that the circumstances surrounding sexual violence perpetration might not always be necessary features of medical intervention, they are not likely to be recorded in the medical record (Cohen & Lynch, 2007). Part of the problem, therefore, with relying on medical records is that there will be large amounts of missing data for some variables. The small annual numbers compound the missing data problem further and make statistical analyses difficult. In this situation, the most reliable estimates are derived by combining data across years to provide more stable estimates (Lohr, 1999).

College Studies

Psychometric analyses of the ACHA-NCHA have been described by the American College Health Association (2004, 2005). The series of comparisons and statistical analyses relied heavily on information from various independent sources to achieve the goal of demonstrating the reliability and validity of the ACHA-NCHA. These analyses have included comparing relevant percentages, performing reliability checks, and conducting validity analyses that compare the results of the ACHA-NCHA with a nationally representative database. Despite the sophisticated method of triangulation used to establish validity and reliability, the results of the ACHA-NCHA are not generalizable to all college and/or university students in the United States.

According to the American College Health Association (2007), there are at least four reasons for the lack of external validity. First, although the students themselves were randomly selected, data were collected at self-selected institutions rather than from a random sample of schools. Second, because nonmember institutions were charged a fee to participate, association members were probably overrepresented in the study. Third, institutions that participated might have been inclined to view health-related behaviors as being more or less salient than institutions that chose not to participate. Finally, the method and manner of data collection varied significantly across institutions, with some choosing to administer web-based as opposed to paper surveys or to collect data from a random sample of students as opposed to students in randomly selected classrooms. Thus, ACHA-NCHA data are primarily useful for making comparisons across schools that are represented in the study. Consequently, the data are best suited to identify populations at high risk for sexual violence on campus, to develop and evaluate programs that address the problem of sexual assault on campus, and to allocate resources dedicated to end crimes of a sexual nature on college campuses.

Adolescent Studies

Despite the fact that the YRBSS asks students about dating violence in the context of other health risk behaviors, including smoking, sexual behavior, dietary habits, alcohol and drug use, accidental injuries, and physical fights with peers, research has suggested that it is both reliable and valid (Brener, Collins, Kann, Warren, & Williams, 1995). Several studies address the interrelationship between the YRBSS data, and each study provides evidence of the measures' reliability. For example, results from studies based on YRBSS data that explored characteristics associated with gender and age and differences between in-school youths and dropouts were consistent with other research. Generally speaking, in comparison studies of school-based surveys and other methodologies, researchers have found that student reporting of health risk behaviors is associated with greater privacy/anonymity and more objective and reliable measures.

Nevertheless, the victimization estimates provided by the YRBSS differ significantly from other data sources. Some obvious differences are that most surveys include broader age ranges and definitions of sexual violence. The YRBSS taps violence of a physical nature only. Inconsistencies across surveys are likely also due to sampling frames and the manner in which the surveys are conducted. The YRBSS, for example, exclusively represents American high school students who complete an anonymous paper-and-pencil instrument in relative privacy within a classroom environment. Furthermore, the forced sexual intercourse measure used in the YRBSS is asking about lifetime prevalence. Therefore, this includes childhood as well as adolescent sexual abuse.

KNOWLEDGE GAPS

One theme that emerges from our critical analysis of contemporary sexual violence data is whether multiple, behaviorally specific questions versus global questions of sexual violence provide more accurate measures in terms of validity and reliability. One widely acknowledged finding common to the measurement literature is that reliability assessments depend on question wording. The relative benefits that specific versus global questions have on survey responses have not been addressed in the sexual violence literature (Hodgson & Kelley, 2002). In general, specific questions, such as those with a defined time frame, have been shown to produce more accurate assessments than global questions, for example, queries about "usual" or "typical" behavior (Belson, 1981), whereas global questions are considered more reliable.[5] Specific questions offer the advantage of providing diagnostic feedback about the most effective policies that can be implemented in order to change behaviors associated with, and to reduce the occurrence of, sexual violence (Conway & Cassidy, 2001).

On the one hand, there is a clear need to obtain the most accurate data possible; on the other hand, the scope of measurement must be able to identify a wide range of behaviors and be useful to myriad stakeholders, including victims, advocates, researchers, and policymakers. Although understanding the appropriate scope of measurement deserves emphasis, it is important to acknowledge that there is a clear tradeoff associated with the form of the question being asked and the nature of the elicited response. For example, survey questions commonly ask about sexual violence victimization that has taken place during the "previous 6 months" or "within the past year" irrespective of whether the behavior fits the legal definition of *criminal*. Asking questions in this way keeps resulting prevalence estimates relevant, current, and useful for public policy problem solving and implementation. This approach is also useful for circumventing problems associated with the social construction of crime and underreporting due to culturally biased interpretations of what constitutes criminal behavior. Nevertheless, responses to these types of questions encompass both behaviors that would be reported to the police and behaviors that would not. By counting events that would not be considered crimes, the effort to be more inclusive overestimates the prevalence of sexual violence from a legal standpoint and hence might not be useful to criminal justice authorities (but would be useful to advocates of sexual violence prevention).

Research cannot be divorced from the social context in which it is conducted. Similarly, existing attitudes, norms, and stereotypes cannot be divorced from one's ability to quantify sexual violence as a social problem. Some forms of sexual violence victimization are culturally defined and exist in a context of more subtle forms of cultural and gendered aggression that are

---

[5]An example of a global question is the following, taken from the NCVS: "Other than any incidents already mentioned, has anyone attacked or threatened you in any of these ways . . ." An example of a specific question taken from the NVAWS is as follows: "Has a man or boy ever made you have sex by using force or threatening to harm you or someone close to you? Just so there is no mistake, by sex we mean putting a penis in your vagina?"

more or less severe. Two examples are legal or cultural definitions of sexual assault and coercion or the role of female choice as a motivating factor for rape. For this reason, we know little about how the prevalence of rape and other forms of sexual violence compare among different racial and ethnic groups or even between males and females. At this time, estimates of sexual violence based on race and/or ethnicity vary widely and are inconclusive, and studies based on adolescents do not cover a broad enough range of coercive behaviors (e.g., YRBSS).

Knowledge regarding the value of lifetime prevalence figures is also lacking. Given what is known about the extent of childhood sexual abuse, many researchers believe that the appropriate measure of sexual violence should be *adult* lifetime prevalence. Moracco, Runyan, Bowling, and Earp (2007), for example, argued that to accurately reflect the chronic nature of sexual violence, point estimates should be supplemented with adult lifetime estimates of victimization. Because lifetime prevalence is, by definition, more inclusive than past-year prevalence, they may be more valid. Keeping measurement methods consistent and relevant, while challenging, is necessary to avoid inconsistencies in reporting the occurrence of sex-based crimes.

Finally, an unresolved question pertains to the role of communication and how changes in technology—for example, abandoning landline telephones in favor of mobile phones or spending more time on the Internet—will affect efforts to measure sexual violence against women. Telephone surveys are under-inclusive because they do not reach people who do not have landlines, such as women who are homeless, women in jails and prisons, women in drug treatment facilities, and women in the military. Excluding individuals in these environments assumes particular salience given that they may be at higher risk of sexual assault.

WHERE DO WE GO FROM HERE? RECOMMENDATIONS

Our recommendations fall under two categories: those pertaining to (a) current data and data collection systems and (b) future data collection efforts.

Current Data

The existing lack of agreement about the cultural and legal definitions of sexual violence results in prevalence estimates that are misunderstood, misapplied, and misinformed. Legal and cultural definitions based on multiple indicators must be standardized. Discussions of rape as a social problem will be facilitated when researchers, policymakers, and criminal justice authorities have all defined the problem similarly, based on informed definitions of what constitutes sexual violence. However, until the gaps in our knowledge can be debated, definitions refined, and improved measures implemented, there will be a need to make sound use of existing data and surveillance systems. At present, no one data source measures the full magnitude of violence against women. Our discussion about the limitations of current measures suggests several reasons for this. First, there is clearly a lack of consensus about the definition of violence against women. Sexual assault incorporates a broader range of sexual abuse and levels of severity, but definitions between studies vary, making comparisons and prevalence estimates difficult. Other features of the research design that will result in different estimates include how the question is framed as well as the manner and method in which the data are collected. In sum, our critical analysis of existing data reveals the multiple ways in which the sampling frames, which can limit the external validity or generalizability of findings, reliance on self-report data, the time order (e.g., cross-sectional or longitudinal), and the decision to limit measures to more or less specific items, are all factors that explain differing rates of sexual victimization across studies and affect our ability to accurately gauge the incidence and prevalence of sexual victimization.

Thus, given current data limitations, the magnitude of sexual violence against women is best estimated by the use of triangulation across multiple data sets. For example, as Table 5.1 shows, significant underreporting occurs by focusing on one subpopulation to the exclusion of another. Crime victimization surveys that best account for household and personal crimes not reported to the police supplement crime statistics generated by law enforcement agencies. In addition, sexual violence publications often contain statements like, "the lifetime prevalence of rape is 15% among women and 2% among men." Such figures are typically derived from singular surveys—for example, the National Violence Against Women Survey conducted about 15 years ago (Tjaden & Thoennes, 2000)—and include no indications of the precision of the estimate. An improvement would be to report estimates derived via systematic review studies (meta-analysis) or life table methods. Clearly, no single current data source will suffice to provide a comprehensive understanding of the nature of sexual violence. Rather, multiple independent sources of data are needed to explore the issue of sexual violence and to aid in the credibility and dependability of estimates of its occurrence.

Future Data

Improved data collection systems will support policymakers, researchers, public health practitioners, advocates, service providers, and media professionals by providing more timely and accurate estimates of the incidence and prevalence of sexual violence against women and children (Washington State Department of Health, 2008). The Centers for Disease Control and Prevention's Injury Research Agenda (National Center for Injury Prevention and Control, 2002) calls for institutionalized surveillance of sexual violence, in addition to other forms of violence against women and children. To measure the scope of violence against women, data collection efforts must be amended to include women of a variety of different backgrounds and socioeconomic statuses. For example, much of the current knowledge regarding sexual violence comes from studies involving college-age students. Moreover, the sampling frames tend to include college women who are currently enrolled in school. Therefore, women who are not enrolled in school, and who may be the most vulnerable to sexual violence perpetration, are not included in the analysis. In addition, most current investigations are limited to women who speak English, and therefore individuals whose primary language is not English tend to be underrepresented.

Current data collection efforts—for example, random-digit dialing surveys—are often insensitive to the needs of victims and/or are not culturally appropriate. Collecting data in this manner underestimates the occurrence of sexual violence because people may often be reluctant to report their victimization experience(s) to researchers, especially over the phone. Again, this will require broadening current definitions of rape to include socially acceptable forms of rape. Future studies should use alternative communication technologies that have been shown to be effective in eliciting accurate responses to sensitive questions. In addition, sophisticated statistical methodologies, such as capture–recapture, may prove useful for estimating the prevalence of sexual violence among these "hidden" populations (Boyle, Kirkbride, & Jones, 2005; Gondolf, Chang, & Laporte, 1999).

Victimization surveys best supplement crime reports; however, a significant number of states do not collect information on domestic and sexual violence offenses. To remedy this, first, future studies should standardize definitions across states in the types of victims included in reporting requirements to facilitate making comparisons or aggregating data at a national level. Second, future studies should link law enforcement data with other relevant sources such as from health care providers, employers, colleges, and emergency departments to paint a more detailed portrait of sexual violence.

Finally, current data sets make it difficult to monitor changes in the incidence and prevalence of violence against women over time. Most estimates of sexual violence are derived from retrospective, cross-sectional studies. Therefore, we know very little about the occurrence of sexual victimization over time. Nor do we have information on revictimization. To adequately address these questions, future data collection efforts should be directed toward collecting prospective, longitudinal data.

Rape and all forms of sexual violence remain vastly underreported and undercounted in the United States. In this chapter, we devoted considerable effort to establishing that no one data source currently provides estimates of the magnitude of sexual violence against women that are likely to meet the needs of all users. Therefore, organized and comprehensive changes to the manner in which sexual violence against women is measured must be forthcoming. At the very least, this will require universal agreement about the definition of violence against women, the restructuring of cultural norms and new social constructions regarding appropriate sexual behaviors, more sophisticated methods of data collection, and survey measurements that provide valid and reliable indicators of the prevalence and incidence of sexual violence.

REFERENCES

American College Health Association. (2004). *National college health assessment: Reliability and validity analyses 2000*. Baltimore, MD: Author.

American College Health Association. (2005). The American College Health Association National College Health Assessment (ACHA-NCHA), spring 2003 reference group report. *Journal of American College Health, 53*, 199–210.

American College Health Association. (2007). American College Health Association National College Health Assessment spring 2006 reference group data report (abridged). *Journal of American College Health, 55*, 195–206. doi:10.3200/JACH.55.4.195-206

Bachman, R. (2000). *Violence against women: Synthesis of research for criminal justice policymakers*. Washington, DC: U.S. Department of Justice, National Institute of Justice.

Basile, K. C., Chen, J., Black, M. C., & Saltzman, L. E. (2007). Prevalence and characteristics of sexual violence victimization among U.S. adults, 2001–2003. *Violence and Victims, 22*, 437–448. doi:10.1891/088667007781553955

Basile, K. C., Hertz, M. F., & Back, S. E. (2007). *Intimate partner violence and sexual violence victimization assessment instruments for use in healthcare settings: Version 1* (Vol. 1). Atlanta, GA: Centers for Disease Control and Prevention, National Center for Injury Prevention and Control.

Belson, W. A. (1981). *The design and understanding of survey questions*. Aldershot, England: Gower.

Bossard, J. H. S. (1934). *Social change and social problems*. New York, NY: Harper & Brothers.

Boyle, A., Kirkbride, J., & Jones, P. (2005). Record linkages of domestic assault victims between an emergency department and the police. *Journal of Epidemiology and Community Health, 59*, 909–910. doi:10.1136/jech.2004.028597

Brener, N. D., Collins, J. L., Kann, L., Warren, C. W., & Williams, B. I. (1995). Reliability of the Youth Risk Behavior Survey Questionnaire. *American Journal of Epidemiology, 141,* 575–580.

Catalano, S. M. (2006). *The measurement of crime: Victim reporting and police recording.* New York, NY: LFB Scholarly.

Centers for Disease Control and Prevention. (2001a). *Healthy People 2010: Focus area 15—Injury and violence prevention.* Retrieved from http://www.healthypeople. gov/Document/HTML/Volume2/15Injury.htm

Centers for Disease Control and Prevention. (2001b). National estimates of nonfatal injuries treated in hospital emergency departments—United States, 2000. *Morbidity and Mortality Weekly Report, 50,* 340–346.

Centers for Disease Control and Prevention. (2008). Youth Risk Behavior Surveillance—United States, 2007. *Morbidity and Mortality Weekly Report, 57*(No. SS-4), 1–131.

Cohen, J., & Lynch, J. P. (2007). Exploring differences in estimates of visits to emergency rooms for injuries from assaults using the NCVS and NHAMCS. In J. P. Lynch & L. A. Addington (Eds.), *Crime statistics: Revisiting the divergence of the NCVS and UCR* (pp. 183–222). Cambridge, England: Cambridge University Press.

Conway, M., & Cassidy, M. F. (2001). *Evaluating trainer effectiveness: Tips, tools and intelligence for trainers.* Alexandria, VA: American Society for Training & Development.

Danielson, C. K., Macdonald, A., Amstadter, A. B., Hanson, R., de Arellano, M. A., Saunders, B. E., & Kilpatrick, D. G. (2010). Risky behaviors and depression in conjunction with or in the absence of lifetime history of PTSD among sexually abused adolescents. *Child Maltreatment, 15,* 101–107. doi:10.1177/ 1077559509350075

Fisher, B. S., Cullen, F. T., & Turner, M. G. (2000). *The sexual victimization of college women.* Washington, DC: U.S. Department of Justice, Office of Justice Programs, National Institute of Justice.

Gondolf, E. W., Chang, Y. F., & Laporte, R. (1999). Capture-recapture analysis of batterer reassaults: An epidemiological innovation for batterer program evaluation. *Violence and Victims, 14,* 191–202.

Hodgson, J. F., & Kelley, D. S. (Eds.). (2002). *Sexual violence: Policies, practices, and challenges in the United States and Canada.* Westport, CT: Praeger.

Kelley, D. S. (2002). The measurement of rape. In J. F. Hodgson & D. S. Kelley (Eds.), *Sexual violence: Policies, practices, and challenges in the United States and Canada* (pp. 15–34). Westport, CT: Praeger.

Kilpatrick, D. G., Acierno, R., Saunders, B., Resnick, H. S., Best, C. L., & Schnurr, P. P. (2000). Risk factors for adolescent substance abuse and dependence: Data from a national sample. *Journal of Consulting and Clinical Psychology, 68,* 19–30. doi:10.1037/0022-006X.68.1.19

Kilpatrick, D. G., Resnick, H., Ruggiero, K., Conoscenti, L., & McCauley, J. (2007). *Drug facilitated, incapacitated, and forcible rape: A national study*. Washington, DC: U.S. Department of Justice.

Koss, M. P., Gidycz, C. A., & Wisniewski, N. (1987). The scope of rape: Incidence and prevalence of sexual aggression and victimization in a national sample of higher education students. *Journal of Consulting and Clinical Psychology, 55*, 162–170. doi:10.1037/0022-006X.55.2.162

Last, J. M. (Ed.). (1995). *A dictionary of epidemiology* (3rd ed.). New York, NY: Oxford University Press.

Lohr, S. L. (1999). *Sampling: Design and analysis*. Pacific Grove, CA: Brooks/Cole.

Maxfield, M., & Babbie, E. (2007). *Research methods for criminal justice and criminology*. Belmont, CA: Wadsworth.

Moracco, K. E., Runyan, C. W., Bowling, J. M., & Earp, J. A. L. (2007). Women's experiences with violence: A national study. *Women's Health Issues, 17*, 3–12. doi:10.1016/j.whi.2006.03.007

National Archive of Criminal Justice Data. (n.d.). *National Crime Victimization Survey resource guide*. Retrieved from http://www.icpsr.umich.edu/NACJD/NCVS/

National Center for Health Statistics. (2007). *NHAMCS description*. Retrieved from http://www.cdc.gov/nchs/about/major/ahcd/nhamcsds.htm

National Center for Injury Prevention and Control. (2002). *CDC injury research agenda*. Atlanta, GA: Centers for Disease Control and Prevention.

National Victim Center. (1992). *Rape in America: A report to the nation*. Charleston, SC: Author.

Rand, M., & Catalano, S. M. (2007). *Criminal victimization, 2006*. Washington, DC: Bureau of Justice Statistics.

Rosenbaum, A., & Langhinrichsen-Rohling, J. (Eds.). (2006). Meta-research on violence and victims: The impact of data collection methods on findings and participants [Special issue]. *Violence and Victims, 21*(4).

Rothman, K. J., & Greenland, S. (1998). Measures of disease frequency. In K. J. Rothman & S. Greenland (Eds.), *Modern epidemiology* (2nd ed., pp. 29–46). Philadelphia, PA: Lippincott Williams & Wilkins.

Ruback, B. R., & Menard, K. S. (2001). Rural-urban differences in sexual victimization and reporting: Analyses using UCR and crisis center data. *Criminal Justice and Behavior, 28*, 131–155. doi:10.1177/0093854801028002001

Saltzman, L. E., Basile, K. C., Mahendra, R. R., Steenkamp, M., Ingram, E., & Ikeda, R. (2007). National estimates of sexual violence treated in emergency departments. *Annals of Emergency Medicine, 49*, 210–217. doi:10.1016/j.annemergmed.2006.10.015

Simon, T. R., Mercy, J. A., & Barker, L. (Eds.). (2006). Can we talk? Importance of random-digit-dial surveys for injury prevention research [Theme issue]. *American Journal of Preventive Medicine, 3*(5).

Straight, J. D., & Heaton, P. C. (2007). Emergency department care for victims of sexual offense. *American Journal of Health-System Pharmacists, 64*, 1845–1850. doi:10.2146/ajhp060346

Tjaden, P., & Thoennes, N. (2000). *Full report of the prevalence, incidence, and consequences of violence against women: Findings from the National Violence Against Women Survey*. Washington, DC: U.S. Department of Justice, Office of Justice Programs.

U.S. Consumer Product Safety Commission. (2000). *NEISS coding manual 2000*. Washington, DC: Author.

U.S. Department of Commerce, Economics and Statistics Administration. (2004). *National Crime Victimization Survey: NCVS-1 basic screen questionnaire*. Retrieved from http://www.ojp.usdoj.gov/bjs/pub/pdf/ncvs104.pdf

U.S. Department of Justice, Federal Bureau of Investigation. (2004). *Uniform crime reporting handbook*. Clarksburg, WV: Uniform Crime Reporting Program. Retrieved from http://www.fbi.gov/ucr/handbook/ucrhandbook04.pdf

U.S. Department of Justice, Federal Bureau of Investigation, Criminal Justice Information Services Division. (2007). *Forcible rape: Crime in the United States 2006*. Retrieved from http://www.fbi.gov/ucr/cius2006/offenses/violent_crime/forcible_rape.html

U.S. Department of Justice, Office of Justice Programs, Bureau of Justice Statistics. (2006). *Criminal victimization in the United States: Statistical tables*. Retrieved from http://www.ojp.usdoj.gov/bjs/abstract/cvusst.htm

U.S. Department of Justice, Office on Violence Against Women. (n.d.). *Federal laws and legislation*. Retrieved from http://www.ovw.usdoj.gov/regulations.htm

Washington State Department of Health. (2008). *Washington State injury and violence prevention guide*. Olympia, WA: Author.

Wolitzky-Taylor, K. B., Ruggiero, K. J., Danielson, C. K., Resnick, H. S., Hanson, R. F., Smith, D. W., & Kilpatrick, D. G. (2008). Prevalence and correlates of dating violence in a national sample of adolescents. *Journal of the American Academy of Child and Adolescent Psychiatry, 47*, 755–762. doi:10.1097/CHI.0b013e318172ef5f

World Health Organization. (2002). Sexual violence. In E. G. Krug, L. L. Dahlberg, J. A. Mercy, A. B. Zwi, & R. Lozano (Eds.), *World report on violence and health* (pp. 147–182). Geneva, Switzerland: Author.

6

RISK FACTORS FOR
SEXUAL VIOLENCE

RAYMOND A. KNIGHT AND JUDITH SIMS-KNIGHT

The aim of this chapter is to identify and briefly discuss those situational, dispositional, and life course variables that increase the probability of sexually coercive behavior. We focus on male perpetrators, who commit the great majority of acts of sexual violence. We do not include the literature on predicting the risk of recidivism of offenders who have been adjudicated for sexual crimes or any discussion of modern evolutionary explanations of ultimate causation. Finally, because those who target children as sexual victims differ substantially in etiology, disposition, risk factors, and life course from those who sexually coerce peers and women (e.g., Bard et al., 1987; Knight & Thornton, 2007), we focus only on the risk factors for the latter.

The intention of the chapter is practical. The strategy of trying to reduce sexually aggressive behavior only by treating and managing offenders is costly to survivors and to society and has yielded at best modest efficacy (e.g., Hanson et al., 2002). Consequently, society must pursue the more promising approaches to reducing sexually coercive behavior that lie in prevention and early intervention. Such strategies require well-founded models of etiology and developmental course to guide the fashioning of interventions and policies.

It is our intent in this chapter (a) to review the factors that are correlated with increasing the risk that a male will become sexually aggressive (i.e., what we know), (b) to identify the methodological problems in the extant research and the gaps in our knowledge that must be addressed (i.e., how we know it and what we need to know), and (c) to speculate about the general parameters of interventions that are likely to be more successful in decreasing the probability that sexually coercive behavior will develop (i.e., where we go from here).

WHAT DO WE KNOW?

In this chapter, we define *risk factors* broadly as any variables for which there is consistent evidence that men who score high on these factors are more likely to exhibit sexually coercive behavior. The methodology of most current research (cross-sectional, correlative) does not permit claims about which risk factors cause men to rape or to become persistent rapists and which are simply correlative. Consequently, for this chapter, we divide the factors into three descriptive clusters: (a) situational variables that immediately precede the assault and are correlated with the probability that rape will occur (e.g., alcohol use, distorted perceptions), (b) attributes and dispositional characteristics of the perpetrator that constitute cross-temporally stable traits that hypothetically influence the probability of sexually coercive behavior (e.g., hypersexuality), and (c) developmental and biological antecedents that are the likely etiological factors that contribute to the formation of the traits. Because of page limitations and our focus on individual etiology, we forgo consideration of rape-supportive social contexts (White, 2009).

Concurrent Risk Factors for Rape

Substantial research has been devoted to the concurrent correlates of rape. These studies have frequently used academic samples of convenience rather than criminal samples, and until recently most have predominantly focused on samples in the United States (Hines, 2007). Several reviews of these studies exist (e.g., Malamuth, 2003; Murnen, Wright, & Kaluzny, 2002). We summarize the most consistent factors that have emerged from these studies and might be considered concurrent risk factors. They can be divided into four categories: rape-supportive attitudes, cognitive–perceptual proclivities that distort communication in relationships, the effects of alcohol, and perpetrator use of pornography.

Rape-Supportive Attitudes

A number of scales that assess a variety of masculine ideological beliefs hypothesized to support sexually coercive behavior have been studied. These were generated from feminist sociocultural models of rape, and their early success in accounting for "rape proclivity" (Pollard, 1994), their clear relevance to intervention, and the ease with which they could be administered to academic samples contributed to their popularity. These tap a variety of beliefs focusing on the adversarial nature of men's relationships with women, on stereotypical ideas about sex roles, on negative notions about masculinity, and on rape myths that support coercion.

In a meta-analysis examining 11 different measures of masculine ideology across 39 studies, Murnen et al. (2002) found that although all but one measure of masculine ideology were significantly associated with sexual aggression, the strongest support emerged for Malamuth, Sockloskie, Koss, and Tanaka's (1991) hostile masculinity and Mosher and Sirkin's (1984) hypermasculinity scales, both of which assess hostile beliefs about women, the desire to be in control, and an acceptance of violence against women. Measures of simple gender adherence, which did not include the hostility and acceptance of aggression components, were not, however, strong predictors of sexually coercive behavior. In a cross-cultural, 38-site study, Hines (2007) examined the roles of adversarial sexual beliefs, the status of women in society, and prior sexual victimization as risk factors for sexually coercive behavior against both women and men. No support was found for the feminist theory that lower status of women in society covaried with sexual violence against women, but only one operationalization of the status of women was tested. In contrast, Hines found support that both adversarial attitudes about relationships and having been the victim of sexual abuse were related to sexual aggression in both genders, across cultures, and across samples.

These rape-supportive attitudes have fared less well in discriminating sex offenders in criminal samples, in which rapists have not been found to differ from controls in their endorsement of these beliefs (e.g., Drieschner & Lange, 1999). Recent studies using the Multidimensional Inventory of Development, Sex, and Aggression (MIDSA, 2008), however, have suggested that the failure to find rape-supportive attitudes in incarcerated rapists might be due to their defensive suppression of such nonsocially desirable attitudes in assessment situations. In the MIDSA studies a computerized inventory was administered to a variety of samples with substantial assurances of confidentiality to reduce response defensiveness. Consistent with the results from noncriminal samples, rapists were found to score significantly higher than community controls on both the MIDSA Hostility Toward Women and Negative Masculinity scales (MIDSA, 2008).

Distorted Perceptions

In acquaintance rape, sexually coercive behavior occurs within a social context that requires the active selection and processing of information. Several studies have suggested that males likely to rape may have perceptual biases that lead to specific misperceptions of women's communications. Drieschner and Lange (1999) grouped these into three hypothetical classes of perception: (a) the tendency to overperceive friendly behavior as seductive and assertive behavior as hostile; (b) a positivity bias that in ambiguous situations transforms negative, dismissive communications into encouragement; and (c) a general set to mistrust women's communications and perceive them as hostile. Support has continued to accrue for these hypotheses, especially the overperception of sexual intent in women's behavior, which is particularly prevalent in sexually coercive men and men who endorse sex role stereotypes (Farris, Treat, Viken, & McFall, 2008). Moreover, the processes that may be problematic in misperceptions have been further specified. First, Farris, Viken, Treat, and McFall (2006) demonstrated that men who believed that rape was justifiable and who blamed women for victimization had more difficulty distinguishing between sexual interest and other affect categories, particularly when women were dressed provocatively. Second, Yoon and Knight (2008) found that self-reported sexually coercive males had more difficulty disattending from sexual stimuli to complete a cognitive task than noncoercive males. Their difficulty disattending from sexual stimuli was correlated with scales measuring impulsivity and emotional dysregulation rather than scales assessing callous manipulativeness and hypersexuality, suggesting that such perceptual deficiencies may be related to emotional dysregulation problems. More recent data in our laboratory also suggest the covariation of disattention difficulties with high sexual compulsivity.

Alcohol Use

Whether its role is facilitative or causative, whether it serves as an excuse, a precipitant, or a manipulative device, there is no doubt that alcohol use and abuse play a significant, multifaceted role in sexually coercive behavior in both college and criminal samples (e.g., Abbey, Zawacki, Buck, Clinton, & McAuslan, 2004; Prentky & Knight, 1991). In almost 50% of sexual assaults the perpetrator has been found to have imbibed alcohol, and at the time of a sexual assault approximately one half of victims have been found to be using alcohol (Abbey et al., 2004). As one might predict, there is a high correlation between perpetrator and victim drinking (Ullman, Karabatsos, & Koss, 1999). Alcohol's impairment of inhibitory controls, its exacerbation of communication misinterpretations, its disruption of higher order cognitive processing (e.g., decision-making abilities), and its interaction with existing personality characteristics (e.g., trait aggression) have all been invoked as reasons for alcohol's relation to sexually aggressive behavior (Abbey et al., 2004). In addition, in a prospective study, Abbey and McAuslan (2004) found that males who reported consuming larger quantities of alcohol when dating and prior to having consensual sex manifested greater persistence in their sexually coercive behavior.

Alcohol abuse not only correlates with increased frequency of sexual coercion but also affects the outcome of the assault. Perpetrator alcohol use has been found to increase violence for both rapists and child molesters (Hamdi & Knight, 2010). Abbey, Clinton-Sherrod, McAuslan, Zawacki, and Buck (2003) found that the amount of alcohol consumed during an assault correlated both with perpetrator aggressiveness and with the severity of the outcome (i.e., whether coitus was achieved). Higher perpetrator alcohol consumption was positively related to higher violence, but the relation to severity was curvilinear—increasing at lower levels of alcohol consumption, reaching a plateau at moderate levels, and decreasing at high levels. Abbey et al. also found a positive correlation between the amount of alcohol consumed by the victim and outcome severity, suggesting that more intoxicated victims faced a greater risk of completed rape. Alcohol use may inhibit the victim's ability to detect sexually aggressive signals and to respond in an effective fashion.

Pornography Use

In a meta-analysis of 46 studies, Oddone-Paolucci, Genius, and Violato (2000) determined that exposure to explicit sexual materials (pornography) was correlated with moderate effect sizes with a variety of negative outcomes, including increased sexual perpetration and endorsement of rape myths. Reviews of the literature (e.g., Malamuth, Addison, & Koss, 2000) confirm the consistency of the correlation between pornography use and sexually coercive behavior.

Work by Malamuth (see Malamuth & Huppin, 2005) has attempted to integrate field correlative research and laboratory experimental strategies and to provide a model of the likely effects of pornography on sexually aggressive attitudes and behavior. Field studies have suggested that males who are high on particular risk factors, such as a high frequency of sexual and hostile fantasies, a high attraction to impersonal sex, and aggressive/dominance motivation, are significantly more likely to acknowledge both greater exposure to and preference for various kinds of pornography. Consistent with these results, research on the MIDSA (2008) across three independent samples (juvenile sex offenders, adult sex offenders, and community nonoffenders) has found that scores on scales that measure both conventional heterosexual and violent pornography use were consistently related to scales assessing hypersexuality and sexual preoccupation and to paraphilic behavior and fantasies. In addition, across the three samples, high scores on these pornography scales consistently correlated with facets of psychopathy and with higher anger and aggression.

Experimental studies have suggested that not only are males with a higher proclivity to sexually coercive behavior more likely to be drawn to excessive pornography use, but they are also more likely to be influenced by their exposure to such materials (e.g., Malamuth et al., 2000). After viewing a rape portrayal in which a woman showed signs of sexual arousal, males with a high self-reported proclivity to sexual aggression against women were more likely to rate women as deriving pleasure from such assaults. In contrast, males low in the likelihood of raping showed no such effect. This putative effect of pornography on sexual coercion has been supported by field studies that have found that pornography predicts sexually coercive behavior, even after critical risk factors have been partialed out. Among males who reported high hostility toward women and were attracted to impersonal sex, which are both risk factors for sexually coercive behavior, those who used pornography frequently were more likely to have engaged in sexual aggression than those high on these risk factors who did not use pornography (Vega & Malamuth, 2007). Thus, it appears that males high on factors that would put them at high risk to be sexually coercive are more drawn to pornography than males without such characteristics, and these high-risk males might have their sexually coercive proclivities disinhibited by their exposure to and use of such materials.

Attributes and Dispositional Characteristics of the Perpetrator

In contrast with the concurrent characteristics, attributes and dispositional characteristics represent more enduring, cross-temporally stable, core traits that contribute to sexually aggressive behavior.

Historical Perspective

Early studies attempting to identify the correlates of sexually coercive behavior against women among college students initially examined the contributions of various components of psychopathy and antisocial behavior. Scales that assess antisocial tendencies and psychopathy were found to correlate with sexually coercive behavior in college students (e.g., Koss & Dinero, 1988). Such scales, however, did not contribute independently to the discrimination of sexually coercive college males beyond the contribution of more highly correlating scales (e.g., sexual conservatism, rape myths). The slightly higher predictive potency and apparently greater explanatory potential of these alternative attitude scales led subsequent researchers studying noncriminal samples to focus their predictive models on these more sexual-aggression congruent attitudes and behaviors (Malamuth, 2003) and to speculate that different models might be appropriate for criminal and noncriminal populations.

Working predominantly with college samples, Malamuth and colleagues (for a review, see Malamuth, 2003) proposed and tested a two-path confluence model. They posited that sexual aggression against women resulted from the interaction of two paths: hostile masculinity, which as we noted earlier constitutes a cluster of negative attitudes about relationships and women, and impersonal sexuality, which is measured by the age of first intercourse experience and the number of sexual partners since age 14. We initially replicated Malamuth's two-path model with sex offenders but found that it accounted for only a small portion of the variance of sexually coercive behavior (Knight & Sims-Knight, 2003, 2004). We were able to explain more variance by adding a third path, behavioral impulsivity, which included alcohol use, and by broadening the hostile masculinity attitudes to the latent disposition with which it correlated, callousness–unemotionality (CU), a more general personality characteristic that forms the first factor of the Psychopathy Checklist—Revised (PCL-R; Hare, 2003). We also measured the impersonal sexuality path with a latent trait identified by sexual preoccupation, sexual compulsivity, and hypersexuality. A schematic version of our three-path model is presented in Figure 6.1. We validated our model on committed sex offenders, generic criminals, juveniles who sexually offend (JSOs), college students, and

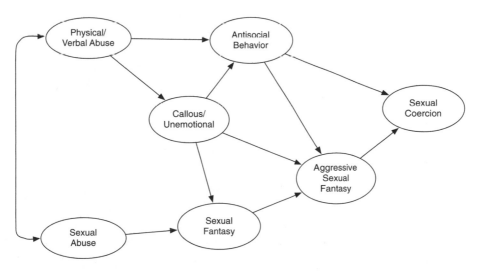

Figure 6.1. Path model of the antecedents of sexual coercion found in sexual offenders and community males.

noncriminal community controls and showed that the revised model yielded better fit statistics than Malamuth's model (Knight & Sims-Knight, 2003, 2004). The consistent predictive potency of this model across criminal and community samples supports the hypothesis that a unified theory of sexual coercion can be generated. Malamuth (2003) subsequently introduced dominance–narcissism, which would also map onto the CU latent trait, as an important predictor and has acknowledged a stronger role for impulsivity/antisocial behavior.

Although future research will undoubtedly require revisions in both the observed measures and the model itself, the general parameters of the three antecedent latent traits can be described. As depicted in Figure 6.1, these three traits include hypersexuality/impersonal sex (Sexual Fantasy in Figure 6.1), the arrogant–deceitful CU characteristics of psychopathy, and antisocial behavioral tendencies. The latter two traits provide a rich theoretical link to a vast research literature on the genetic, cognitive, affective, and personality correlates of psychopathy (e.g., Knight & Guay, 2006) that can only be referred to in this chapter.

Hypersexuality/Sociosexuality

The notion that some aspect of sexual drive or sexual appetitive behavior is a critical component of sexual aggression (e.g., Malamuth 2003) and may be an underlying component of other volitional impairments of sexual behavior (Kafka & Hennen, 2003) has found considerable empirical support. A number of investigations have found that sexually coercive males have consensual sex at an earlier age and have more consensual sex partners than do noncoercive males (e.g., Koss & Dinero, 1988). Knight, Ronis, Prentky, and Kafka (2009) found that sexual drive and preoccupation discriminated sexually coercive males from noncoercive males in both community and general criminal samples. Regardless of criminal status or age (juvenile or adult), sexually coercive males reported higher levels of sexual drive, frequency of sexual behavior, and sexual deviance on the MIDSA (2008) than noncoercive males. Hypersexuality covaries with a number of negative attributes, including components of negative affect like mood and anxiety disorders and increased substance abuse and impulse-related problems (e.g., Långström & Hanson, 2006).

There is, however, considerable debate about what the core construct underlying this dimension is. For example, Malamuth (2003) postulated that the proclivity to engage in promiscuous/impersonal sex is the critical construct. He described the dimension of impersonal sex as similar to the concept of *sociosexuality*, a hypothetical dimension of willingness to engage in sexual activity in the relative absence of attachment or emotional ties. In contrast, Knight and Cerce (1999) found that a different aspect of sexuality—sexual drive, preoccupation, and compulsivity—was important in sexual coercion and also covaried with pornography use, expressive aggression toward women, sadism, pervasive anger, and offense planning for both adult and juvenile sex offenders. This drive and fantasy aspect of sexuality appears to be equally important in both juvenile and adult samples (MIDSA, 2008).

Antisocial and Impulsivity Tendencies

Antisocial behavior in its manifold guises has consistently been shown to be a covariate of sexually coercive behavior, especially against women (Knight & Guay, 2006; Prentky & Knight, 1991). Both juveniles and adults who sexually coerce have been characterized as high in impulsivity and antisocial behavior (MIDSA, 2008). The importance of antisocial behavior and impulsivity in predicting sexual aggression in noncriminal samples has been supported in a number of other studies (e.g., Calhoun, Bernat, Clum, & Frame, 1997). Persistently sexually coercive males among college students have also been distinguished by their adolescent delinquency (Abbey & McAuslan, 2004). It is not surprising that our adding of this path to Malamuth's two-path model increased substantially the percentage of coercive sexual behavior accounted for (Knight & Sims-Knight, 2003, 2004). The link of this component to alcohol abuse (e.g., Krueger, Markon, Patrick, Benning, & Kramer, 2007) ties it directly to the concurrent risks described previously, and its congruence with an externalizing syndrome and emotional lability (e.g., Krueger, 2006) and its strong link to genetic etiology (Waldman & Rhee, 2006) enhance its potential as a primary prevention target.

Callousness–Unemotionality

Studies examining the differentiating characteristics of both juvenile and adult sex offenders have found that rapists have higher scores on scales measuring the CU component of psychopathy. Caputo, Frick, and Brodsky (1999) compared a group of JSOs with a group of violent juvenile non-sex offenders and a group of juvenile offenders with only "noncontact" property and drug offenses on the Psychopathy Screening Device, a youth version of the PCL-R. Compared with the non-sex offenders, the juvenile sex offenders had higher scores on the factor that corresponded to the PCL-R CU factor, reflecting less guilt and empathy and greater emotional restriction. Kim, Guay, and Knight (2007) found that rapists scored higher than child molesters on the overall CU factor of the PCL-R and on both the interpersonal and affective facets it comprises. Both juvenile and adult sex offenders also scored significantly higher than noncriminal community males on scales measuring the CU factor (MIDSA, 2008). Because in our operationalization of Malamuth's model, we (Knight & Sims-Knight, 2003, 2004) found that scales measuring negative masculinity and hostility toward women covaried with the scales developed to index the PCL-R interpersonal facet (MIDSA, 2008), we incorporated these two scales into the broader construct of the CU path of our structural equation model (SEM) of etiology (for a summary, see Knight & Guay, 2006). Evidence that this component is consistent over time, even in juveniles (Lynam, Caspi, Moffitt, Loeber, & Stouthamer-Loeber, 2007), and that it shows some evidence of genetic transmission (see Genetic Antecedents section) supports its potential as a target for primary prevention interventions.

Developmental and Biological Antecedents

As one moves from narrower, concurrent risk factors to broader hypothetical traits and finally to the purported earliest developmental and biological antecedents, the amount of supportive research diminishes. Within the domain of the risk factors that are most distal, research on early abuse antecedents is far more prevalent than research on biological risk factors. Indeed, we provide supportive studies with sex offenders to bolster the former, but we have to access research with other populations to support speculations about the latter.

It has long been established that the backgrounds of sex offenders are characterized by disrupted family relationships, violence, and neglect (Bard et al., 1987). Lisak and Roth (1990) found that such problematic family backgrounds were not limited to offenders. Unincarcerated, self-identified sexually coercive males disclosed more negative relationships with both parents, but particularly fathers, than did nonsexually aggressive men. Abusive experiences play an important role in the SEMs of etiology applied to both criminal and community samples (Knight & Sims-Knight, 2003, 2004). The negative developmental antecedents that have received the most empirical support are sexual abuse and physical abuse/antipathy. We discuss each in turn.

Sexual Abuse

Generic sex offenders appear to have been sexually victimized in childhood more often than the general population or other types of offenders (Jespersen, Lalumière, & Seto, 2009), and such abuse has been found to covary with the characteristics of their future perpetration, such that youths who have been abused repeat sexually aggressive behaviors that were used by their own victimizers (Burton, 2003). Histories of sexual abuse have been found to be more prevalent among JSOs than other delinquent groups (e.g., Zakireh, Ronis, & Knight, 2008). Moreover, the experience of being sexually abused has been found to predict both revictimization (Hines, 2007) and perpetration (Hines, 2007; White & Smith, 2004), even among noncriminal samples.

Isolating the specific effects of sexual abuse from other pathogenic properties of family environment, such as physical abuse, neglect, and general family disruption, has been difficult because different types of abuse tend to covary (e.g., Knight & Sims-Knight, 2003, 2004). In addition, many studies have not used optimal control groups, and outcome measures have been neither standardized nor normed. Finally, sexual abuse is a complex phenomenon, fraught with multiple definitional and assessment problems. Consequently, the immediate and long-term covariates of childhood sexual abuse that have been identified must be interpreted cautiously.

Physical and Verbal Abuse

In the literature on adult sex offenders, a high incidence of childhood physical abuse has been reported among both rapists and child molesters (Bard et al., 1987). In a study of the relation of early maltreatment to offense characteristics, physical abuse was found to covary with the frequency and level of nonsexual unsocialized aggression among sex offenders (Prentky et al., 1989). In our SEM model (Knight & Sims-Knight, 2003, 2004), physical/verbal abuse was found to be a significant antecedent of the CU path in multiple samples that vary in age, criminality, and sex offender status.

Being physically abused or observing family violence has also been hypothesized to contribute to the development of sexual violence in adolescence. Consistent with these speculations, JSOs have been found to have experienced more abuse than other delinquent groups. For example, Lewis, Shanok, and Pincus (1981) found that whereas 75% of their violent JSOs had been physically abused, only 29% of other delinquents had experienced such abuse. Physical abuse was not, however, unique to JSOs. In this same study, an equal percentage of violent non-sex offenders had also been physically abused. Similarly, observing domestic violence appears to be associated with violence in general and not specifically with sexual violence (Spaccarelli, Bowden, Coatsworth, & Kim, 1997). Thus, it seems clear that children who experience physical abuse are likely to exhibit higher-than-average aggression in adolescence and adulthood, but this aggression is not necessarily sexual.

Although noncriminal samples have been less frequently studied, physical abuse has been implicated in their sexually coercive behavior (White & Smith, 2004). It has been found to cause children to detach emotionally and is correlated with dissociation and with personality disorders (e.g., Goldman, D'Angelo, DeMaso, & Mezzacappa, 1992). In Malamuth's (1998) theoretical model of sexual coercion, harsh early environments, which include physical abuse, play a prominent antecedent role in sexually coercive behavior, both potentially locking a person into short-term mating strategies and increasing the probability of a hostile masculinity associative network and aggressive and antisocial behavior. Malamuth cited literature supporting both hypotheses.

Genetic Antecedents

Genetic influences on sexual aggression have not been studied directly. Nonetheless, genetic antecedents of many of the risk factors for sexual aggression (antisocial behaviors, psychopathy, criminality/delinquency, aggressive behaviors, alcohol use and misuse) have been studied, and thus genetic factors can at least indirectly be implicated in sexual aggression. In addition, studies of aggression and sexual aggression often have common environmental correlates (e.g., physical abuse as a developmental factor), suggesting shared genetic influences.

Traditionally, genetic influences have been studied in humans by the use of twin and adoption studies. Substantial heredity estimates have been found for antisocial personality, conduct disorder, and aggressive behavior, although methodological weaknesses may have inflated the results (see Pérusse & Gendreau, 2005). In addition, attention-deficit/hyperactivity disorder (ADHD), which is a correlate of the antisocial path described earlier and a frequent trait in JSOs (for a review, see MIDSA, 2008), has been shown to have a genetic contribution (e.g., McLoughlin, Ronald, Kuntsi, Asherson, & Plomin, 2007).

The nature of genetic influences has been clarified by research that uses the newly developed techniques for identifying polymorphisms in individual genes. This research has found that genes interact with the environment, so that only individuals who possess the deleterious gene allele and suffer abusive early environments develop the negative traits. Although the technique has not yet been applied to sexual aggression, interactions have been found and replicated with ADHD, conduct disorder, antisocial disorder, and alcohol dependency, all of which are risk factors for sexual aggression. The genes that have been studied all play a role in monoamine neurotransmitters.

The first convincing study (Caspi et al., 2002) was a prospective study of the interaction between harmful early environment and the MAOA gene in boys (it is an X-linked trait) who were 26 years of age at the time of the outcome. They found a significant interaction indicating that the boys who had the low-activity MAOA allele and were severely maltreated were more aggressive than either the low-activity MAOA boys who were not maltreated or the high-activity MAOA boys whether they were maltreated or not. Although not all attempts to replicate this study have been successful, a meta-analysis by Kim-Cohen et al. (2006) suggests that the relationship is real. Furthermore, comparable findings have emerged from studies of the serotonin transporter gene (5HHTLPR) in rhesus monkeys (for a review, see Suomi, 2005). The primate research is important for two reasons. First, it confirms experimentally the interaction found in human nonexperimental studies. Second, it suggests characteristics of the outcome variables that provide intriguing hypotheses to be tested in humans. Young monkeys with low levels of *5-HIAA* metabolite in their spinal fluid tended to exhibit inappropriate aggressive and social behaviors from an early age. These males were typically driven out of their natal troop prior to 3 years of age, long before puberty when male macaques usually leave their natal troop. Such monkeys lacked the social skills to join another troop, and most failed to survive to adulthood. This pattern of findings is suggestive of the highly impulsive, aggressive characteristics of antisocial personality.

It should be noted that the same interaction between *5HTTLPR* and childhood adversity has been found in humans with other outcome measures. The most evidence has accrued with depression (for a review, see Caspi & Moffitt, 2006), but it has also been found with behavioral inhibition at 8 years of age (Fox et al., 2005).

Most studies in this area use omnibus measures of child adversity, but Beaver (2008) explored the interaction with a single type of abuse of particular importance in sexual aggression: child sexual abuse. Using a summary index of three dopaminergic genes (*DAT*, *DRD2*, and *DRD4*) and violent adolescent delinquency as the outcome, Beaver found the predicted interaction between child sexual abuse and genetic liability; that is, children who were at genetic risk and suffered childhood sexual abuse were significantly more likely to become violent delinquents.

In addition to research exploring an interaction between genetic polymorphisms and environmental adversity, correlations between gene polymorphisms and other traits have been found. For example, the *5HHTLPR* gene is related to anxiety-related behavioral traits and amygdala responses (Hariri et al., 2002). Alcohol consumption in early adulthood has been found to be related to *MAOA*, *5HTTLPR*, *DAT1*, *DRD4*, and *DRD2* (Guo, Wilhelmsen, & Hamilton, 2007). Caspi et al. (2008) found in three distinct samples that the *COMT* dopaminergic gene polymorphism differentiated between ADHD boys who did and did not exhibit antisocial behaviors. Although none of these studies assessed sexual aggression, research has found that a low level of serotonin activity is related to enhanced sexual behavior as well as impulsivity and behavioral lability (Spoont, 1992), and monoamines have been implicated in sexual appetitive disorders (Kafka, 2003a).

All of the above-described human genetic research is correlational. Its causal validity is, however, boosted by animal studies, such as the experimental manipulation of the environment in the rhesus monkey studies described earlier and experimental manipulation of genes in knockout gene studies, which we have not discussed. Although these research strategies are not possible with humans, evidence of the gene effects can be inferred indirectly from experimental studies of the effectiveness of medications. Medications such as antidepressants presumably counteract the effects of the deleterious monoamine gene alleles. In a meta-analysis of experimental and repeated measures studies, such drugs have been found to reduce aggressiveness (Connor, Boone, Steingard, Lopez, & Melloni, 2003), and evidence supports their efficacy in treating disinhibited sexual motivation or sexual appetitive behavior disorders (e.g., Kafka, 2003a). Comparable strategies could be used in gene–environment studies. Of course, genetic polymorphisms cannot be experimentally manipulated in humans, but some alternative interpretations (gene–environment correlations) can be tested.

HOW DO WE KNOW IT, AND WHAT DO WE NEED TO KNOW?

The vast majority of the research we reviewed examining the risk factors for sexually coercive behavior has been cross-sectional, has often used samples of convenience and self-report measures, and when assessing early stressors and developmental events, has relied on retrospective rather than prospective strategies. Consequently, these studies are vulnerable to myriad methodological criticisms that have been leveled at multiple levels at such research. Especially vigorous have been the debates about the use of self-report to assess issues related to psychopathy and sexuality (e.g., Lilienfeld & Fowler, 2006) and the distortions inherent in retrospective data (e.g., Widom, Raphael, & DuMont, 2004). More recent data have, however, come to the defense of self-report in these domains (MIDSA, 2008; Walters, 2006), and retrospective report, which may be more accurate than some critics have proposed (Hardt & Rutter, 2004), has been defended as contributing an important piece to the developmental picture (Kendall-Tackett & Becker-Blease, 2004).

Although the research reviewed has identified some of the risk variables that might be critical in an eventual causative model of sexual coercion, the current data support only their correlative and not their causative status. Future research must focus on the critical specifications of both causality and the underlying mechanisms responsible for coercive behavior. Toward that end, it is essential that a number of issues be addressed (e.g., Moffitt, 2005). Most crucial are the direction of causality and potential common causes. The current research in this area is almost always cross-sectional and retrospective. Establishing the temporal antecedence of variables (e.g., by longitudinal studies) can disentangle the direction of causality (does A cause B or does B cause A?). In correlational designs, common causes, that is, variables that may be the true cause of both risk factor and outcome, always lurk as possibilities. A combination of designs—experiments with animals, laboratory analog studies with humans, intervention research, and causal-analytic techniques of correlational research such as SEM—all can help to determine whether risk factors are truly causative. To use these designs effectively, researchers must ferret out the operative characteristics of risk factors and, more important, the core mechanisms involved and how they affect sexual coercion. Moderating variables must be identified. Moreover, it is important to explore and uncover the etiology of causal risk factors themselves, so that proposed models extend to the earliest dispositional and developmental roots. Finally, risk factors are likely to have multiple effects, and it is likely that more than one path is responsible for an outcome (i.e., equifinality). A comprehensive causal model requires the identification of all the effects of a risk factor and all of the causal paths that can lead to a sexually coercive outcome. The models that are generated and tested will have to be sufficiently complex to reflect the complicated developmental processes we are studying.

The example of the hypothesized causative role of hypersexuality illustrates these methodological conundrums. We have suggested that it is a critical causative trait in sexual coercion, but we have yet to establish convincingly its temporal priority relative to other factors in the proposed causative models (e.g., is it the result of or a contributor to sexual abuse or to an emotionally detached adaptation?). Its interaction with other domains must be specified (e.g., is an interaction with psychopathy necessary for hypersexuality to lead to coercion? How does it interface with pornography use and abuse?). The operative components of this risk factor that lead to coercion remain speculative (e.g., arousal, impersonality of the sexual drive, distortion of attitudes or perceptions). Its etiology and underlying processes remain largely unexplored (e.g., Bailey, Kirk, Zhu, Dunne, & Martin, 2000; Kafka, 2003b). Its relation to other outcomes is just beginning to be examined (Kafka & Hennen, 2003). It is clear that the research on the etiology of sexual coercion needs to be supplemented with the arsenal of etiologic strategies and longitudinal designs that have been applied in other domains of deviant behavior (e.g., Moffitt, 2005). It is only through the convergence of multiple research perspectives that the most efficacious models will emerge.

WHERE DO WE GO FROM HERE?

Future developments require advances in both basic research and improved, effective prevention. The latter depends on advances in the former.

Basic Research on Developmental Antecedents

Despite the obvious gaps in our knowledge about the etiology and course of sexually aggressive behavior against women, definite consistencies have emerged in the risk factors data reviewed. Figure 6.2 presents a speculative

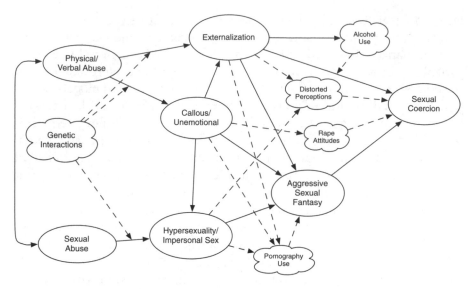

Figure 6.2. Hypothetical integration of the concurrent risk factors and the genetic determinants into the path model of the antecedents of sexual coercion. Ovals represent the latent traits and developmental antecedents that have been tested in extant structural equation models (SEMs). Clouds represent hypothetical constructs, either concurrent correlates of rape or speculative genetic antecedents, that have not been directly tested in SEMs.

model of all the factors discussed in this chapter. It builds on the SEM of Figure 6.1 (ovals), introducing more likely underlying traits (i.e., externalizing for antisocial behavior) and incorporating the current covariates and genetic interactions (clouds) we have reviewed. As can be seen in the figure, alcohol abuse is related to the externalization path, which involves impulsivity and emotional lability. Distorted perceptions are hypothesized to mediate between both externalization and hypersexuality and sexual coercion. Negative masculinity and adversarial relationship attitudes have been found to covary with components of the CU path and are hypothesized to mediate between CU and sexual coercion. Pornography use correlates with the hypersexuality, CU, and externalization paths and is hypothesized to disinhibit aggressive sexual fantasies. The distal abuse experiences are hypothesized to interact with genetic dispositions. Thus, the concurrent covariates of rape proclivity map onto cross-temporally stable traits. All of these dispositional trait paths are intertwined with developmental antecedents and interacting genetic influences whose Gordian knots must be unraveled if maximally efficacious preventative interventions are going to be created. The empirical investigation of the basic processes underlying sexually aggressive behavior and the mapping of their developmental trajectories are essential.

Rape Prevention

The majority of the rape prevention programs that target males have been aimed at acquaintance rape and have applied a skills-based approached aimed at improving sexual relationship knowledge and dating behavior and countering rape-supportive attitudes (see Gidycz, Orchowski, & Edwards, 2011, in *Violence Against Women and Children, Volume 2: Navigating Solutions*). Although some evidence indicates that such programs have a small but positive effect on changing problematic rape attitudes, little or no evidence has emerged that they reduce sexually coercive behavior. Indeed, the attitudes changed in male-oriented programs often subsequently rebound to the level that the males had prior to the intervention, and the positive effects of interventions appear to diminish as the length of the follow-up increases (Anderson & Whiston, 2005).

Although better success might follow from a concerted effort to develop longer, more comprehensive, multilevel prevention strategies that include peer, community, and societal levels, it could also be argued that such programs have yielded suboptimal results because they target correlates rather than causes. We must continue to attempt to work to change society's attitudes about the legitimacy of violence as a solution to problems, and we must continue to attack rape-supportive attitudes about male–female relationships, but the data reviewed here suggest that our preventative efforts will open new horizons.

Essential to any truly primary prevention intervention is a well-established, empirically based model of etiology and course that discriminates causal factors from risk factors. Just as efforts to prevent antisocial activity in general have been curtailed by the limits of our understanding of its causes (Moffitt, 2005), likewise any endeavors to prevent sexual aggression will be limited by our ignorance of its etiology and course. The history of attempts to prevent antisocial behavior is littered with failed programs (e.g., peer-group interventions, the DARE [Drug Abuse Resistance Education] program) that have targeted risk factors that were correlative but not causative. Only studies that attempt to disentangle genetic and environmental influences or studies that are able to manipulate environmental impacts will allow us to develop more effective prevention programs. The full panoply of behavior–genetic research methods (e.g., Moffitt, 2005) and prospective studies that incorporate genetic analyses must be directed at this problem. The creation of effective sexual aggression primary prevention programs that efficiently target the most vulnerable at the critical developmental stages rests on the foundation of such knowledge. Although we cannot alter the genetic makeup of vulnerable individuals, the single-gene research suggests that we can prevent the negative expression of aberrant genes by eliminating or reducing the stressful and punishing environments that trigger them.

The two prime candidates for prevention of the development of traits that lead to rape are physical abuse and sexual abuse. If subsequent research indicates that they are truly causal factors, and if interventions can be developed that at least reduce the incidence of such abuse, then the potential would exist to lessen the deleterious effects of harmful genes, thereby preventing the development of traits that lead to rape. Promising programs such as the Chicago Child–Parent Centers program that provide child and family support for disadvantaged families have demonstrated the long-term educational, criminal justice, and economic benefits of early-childhood intervention programs (Reynolds & Temple, 2006). Parent management training programs have had some success at reducing problematic aggressive child behavior, but more research is needed (Duncan & Magnuson, 2006). No early intervention programs have specifically targeted or measured sexually coercive behavior. Although such primary prevention programs have the greatest potential to reduce the incidence of rape, effecting widespread reduction in child abuse unfortunately may require interventions that extend beyond programs that target changes in the family (for a discussion, see Hay & Jones, 1994).

If we cannot effect a truly primary prevention that averts the onset of negative, maladaptive characteristics, we can and must focus our attention on secondary prevention, in which we identify problems at the earliest ages possible and intervene to prevent these children from becoming offenders. Impulsivity and antisocial tendencies and CU characteristics are measurable behavioral dispositions in childhood (Lynam et al., 2007; Moffitt, 2005). Interventions into sexual proclivities should also begin early. McClintock and Herdt (1996) demonstrated that in both males and females, both homosexual and heterosexual, sexual attraction begins around 10 years of age. They posited that this sexual attraction is caused by the rise in sex hormones between the ages of 6 and 11 years as a result of the maturation of the adrenal glands. Thus, prevention programs directed at hypersexuality, as well as those for CU traits, impulsivity, and antisocial behavior, should not wait until the individuals are of college age but should attack these traits when they are truly in their formative stages.

Research must be directed at the identification of early risk factors associated with subsequent sexual aggression and clarify their causative role. For practical implementation, reliable and valid measures of these factors must be generated so that vulnerable children can be identified, possibly in the context of efficient mental health checkups, so that effective interventions can be initiated and studied. In addition to responding to obviously vulnerable children whose manifest behavior indicates the presence of risk factors or whose reported abuse history is known, we should also implement additional assessment strategies. Sequential assessments, such as computerized self-report screening questionnaires followed by more thorough evaluations for potential high-risk youths, should be developed and evaluated using the strategies suggested for other problematic domains (Fox, Halpern, & Forsyth, 2008). Age-appropriate interventions that target the most likely causative risks must be fashioned and tested (see Durlak, Fuhrman, & Lampman's 1991 meta-analysis in which they found cognitive behavioral therapy more effective for adolescents than for younger children). Some intervention research targeting aggression in teenagers indicates the potential effectiveness of such strategies (e.g., Lochman, Powell, Whidby, & Fitzgerald, 2006).

Finally, we have argued that programs that focus on college students may be suboptimal both because they are too late and because they focus on correlated but not causative factors. The data reviewed suggest that such programs may be improved if two things were done. First, discriminating measures of proximal and trait correlates of sexually aggressive behavior need to be developed. Second, males with high trait vulnerability should be triaged into programs that specifically address their problematic proclivities (e.g., impulsivity, hypersexuality, emotional dysregulation), and the males with low trait but high attitudinal risk could be streamed into traditional programs. The latter group is more likely to have acquired their negative attitudes from a problematic male culture. Hypothetically, programs specifically targeting core causative problems should be more effective.

REFERENCES

Abbey, A., Clinton-Sherrod, A. M., McAuslan, P., Zawacki, T., & Buck, P. O. (2003). The relationship between the quantity of alcohol consumed and the severity of sexual assaults committed by college men. *Journal of Interpersonal Violence, 18,* 813–833. doi:10.1177/0886260503253301

Abbey, A., & McAuslan, P. (2004). A longitudinal examination of male college students' perpetration of sexual assault. *Journal of Consulting and Clinical Psychology, 72,* 747–756. doi:10.1037/0022-006X.72.5.747

Abbey, A., Zawacki, T., Buck, P. O., Clinton, A. M., & McAuslan, P. (2004). Sexual assault and alcohol consumption: What do we know about their relationship and what types of research are still needed? *Aggression and Violent Behavior, 9,* 271–303. doi:10.1016/S1359-1789(03)00011-9

Anderson, L. A., & Whiston, S. C. (2005). Sexual assault education programs: A meta-analytic examination of their effectiveness. *Psychology of Women Quarterly, 29,* 374–388. doi:10.1111/j.1471-6402.2005.00237.x

Bailey, J. M., Kirk, K. M., Zhu, G., Dunne, M. P., & Martin, N. G. (2000). Do individual differences in sociosexuality represent genetic or environmentally contingent strategies? Evidence from the Australian twin registry. *Journal of Personality and Social Psychology, 78,* 537–545. doi:10.1037/0022-3514.78.3.537

Bard, L. A., Carter, D. L., Cerce, D. D., Knight, R. A., Rosenberg, R., & Schneider, B. (1987). A descriptive study of rapists and child molesters: Developmental, clinical, and criminal characteristics. *Behavioral Sciences & the Law, 5,* 203–220. doi:10.1002/bsl.2370050211

Beaver, K. M. (2008). The interaction between genetic risk and childhood sexual abuse in the prediction of adolescent violent behavior. *Sexual Abuse, 20,* 426–443. doi:10.1177/1079063208325204

Burton, D. (2003). Male adolescents: Sexual victimization and subsequent sexual abuse. *Child & Adolescent Social Work Journal, 20,* 277–296. doi:10.1023/A:1024556909087

Calhoun, K. S., Bernat, J. A., Clum, G. A., & Frame, C. L. (1997). Sexual coercion and attraction to sexual aggression in a community sample of young men. *Journal of Interpersonal Violence, 12,* 392–406. doi:10.1177/088626097012003005

Caputo, A. A., Frick, P. J., & Brodsky, S. L. (1999). Family violence and juvenile sex offending: The potential mediating role of psychopathic traits and negative attitudes toward women. *Criminal Justice and Behavior, 26,* 338–356. doi:10.1177/0093854899026003004

Caspi, A., Langley, K., Milne, B., Moffitt, T. E., O'Donovan, M., Owen, M. J., . . . Thapar, A. (2008). A replicated molecular genetic basis for subtyping antisocial behavior in children with attention deficit/hyperactivity disorder. *Archives of General Psychiatry, 65,* 203–210. doi:10.1001/archgenpsychiatry.2007.24

Caspi, A., McClay, J., Moffitt, T. E., Mill, J., Martin, J., Craig, I. W., . . . Poulton, R. (2002, August 2). Role of genotype in the cycle of violence in maltreated children. *Science, 297,* 851–854. doi:10.1126/science.1072290

Caspi, A., & Moffitt, T. E. (2006). Gene–environment interactions in psychiatry: Joining forces with neuroscience. *Nature Reviews Neuroscience, 7,* 583–590. doi:10.1038/nrn1925

Connor, D. F., Boone, R. T., Steingard, R. J., Lopez, I. D., & Melloni, R. H., Jr. (2003). Psychopharmacology and aggression: II. A meta-analysis of nonstimulant medication effects on overt aggression-related behaviors in youth with SED (serious emotional and behavioral disorders). *Journal of Emotional and Behavioral Disorders, 11,* 157–168. doi:10.1177/10634266030110030301

Drieschner, K., & Lange, A. (1999). A review of the cognitive factors in the etiology of rape: Theories, empirical studies and implications. *Clinical Psychology Review, 19,* 57–77. doi:10.1016/S0272-7358(98)00016-6

Duncan, G. J., & Magnuson, K. (2006). Costs and benefits from early investments to promote human capital and positive behavior. In N. E. Watt, C. Ayoub, R. H. Bradley, J. E. Puma, & W. A. LeBoeuf (Eds.), *The crisis in youth mental health: Vol. 4. Critical issues and effective programs* (pp. 27–51). Westport, CT: Praeger.

Durlak, J. A., Fuhrman, T., & Lampman, C. (1991). Effectiveness of cognitive–behavior therapy for maladapting children: A meta-analysis. *Psychological Bulletin, 110,* 204–214. doi:10.1037/0033-2909.110.2.204

Farris, C., Treat, T. A., Viken, R. J., & McFall, R. M. (2008). Sexual coercion and the misperception of sexual intent. *Clinical Psychology Review, 28*, 48–66. doi:10.1016/j.cpr.2007.03.002

Farris, C., Viken, R. J., Treat, T. A., & McFall, R. M. (2006). Heterosocial perceptual organization: Application of the choice model of sexual coercion. *Psychological Science, 17*, 869–875. doi:10.1111/j.1467-9280.2006.01796.x

Fox, J. K., Halpern, L. F., & Forsyth, J. P. (2008). Mental health checkups for children and adolescents: A means to identify, prevent, and minimize suffering associated with anxiety and mood disorders. *Clinical Psychology: Science and Practice, 15*, 182–211. doi:10.1111/j.1468-2850.2008.00129.x

Fox, N. A., Nichols, K. E., Henderson, H. A., Rubin, K., Schmidt, L., Hamer, D., . . . Pine, D. S. (2005). Evidence for a gene–environment interaction in predicting behavioral inhibition in middle childhood. *Psychological Science, 16*, 921–926. doi:10.1111/j.1467-9280.2005.01637.x

Gidycz, C. A., Orchowski, L. M., & Edwards, K. M. (2011). Primary prevention for sexual violence. In M. P. Koss, J. W. White, & A. E. Kazdin (Eds.), *Violence against women and children, Vol. 2: Navigating solutions* (pp. 159–180). Washington, DC: American Psychological Association.

Goldman, S. J., D'Angelo, E. J., DeMaso, D. R., & Mezzacappa, E. (1992). Physical and sexual abuse histories among children with borderline personality disorder. *American Journal of Psychiatry, 149*, 1723–1726.

Guo, G., Wilhelmsen, K., & Hamilton, N. (2007). Gene–lifecourse interaction for alcohol consumption in adolescence and young adulthood: Five monoamine genes. *American Journal of Medical Genetics, 144B*, 417–423. doi:10.1002/ajmg.b.30340

Hamdi, N., & Knight, R. A. (2010). *The effects of intoxication on the sexual violence of rapists and child molesters.* Manuscript submitted for publication.

Hanson, R. K., Gordon, A., Harris, A. J. R., Marques, J. K., Murphy, W., Quinsey, V. L., & Seto, M. C. (2002). First report of the collaborative outcome data project on the effectiveness of psychological treatment for sex offenders. *Sexual Abuse, 14*, 169–194. doi:10.1177/107906320201400207

Hardt, J., & Rutter, M. (2004). Validity of adult retrospective reports of adverse childhood experiences: Review of the evidence. *Journal of Child Psychology and Psychiatry, and Allied Disciplines, 45*, 260–273. doi:10.1111/j.1469-7610.2004.00218.x

Hare, R. D. (2003). *The Psychopathy Checklist—Revised technical manual* (2nd ed.). Toronto, Ontario, Canada: Multi-Health Systems.

Hariri, A. R., Mattay, V. S., Tessitore, A., Kolachana, B., Fera, F., Goldman, D., . . . Weinberger, D. R. (2002, July 19). Serotonin transporter genetic variation and the response of the human amygdala. *Science, 297*, 400–403. doi:10.1126/science.1071829

Hay, T., & Jones, L. (1994). Societal interventions to prevent child abuse and neglect. *Child Welfare, 73*, 379–403.

Hines, D. A. (2007). Predictors of sexual coercion against women and men: A multi-level, multinational study of university students. *Archives of Sexual Behavior, 36,* 403–422. doi:10.1007/s10508-006-9141-4

Jespersen, A. F., Lalumière, M. L., & Seto, M. C. (2009). Sexual abuse history among adult sex offenders and non-sex offenders: A meta-analysis. *Child Abuse & Neglect, 33,* 179–192. doi:10.1016/j.chiabu.2008.07.004

Kafka, M. P. (2003a). The monoamine hypothesis for the pathophysiology of paraphilic disorders: An update. In R. A. Prentky, E. Janus, & M. Seto (Eds.), *Sexual coercion: Understanding and management* (pp. 86–94). New York, NY: New York Academy of Sciences.

Kafka, M. P. (2003b). Sex offending and sexual appetite: The clinical and theoretical relevance of hypersexual desire. *International Journal of Offender Therapy and Comparative Criminology, 47,* 439–451. doi:10.1177/0306624X03253845

Kafka, M. P., & Hennen, J. (2003). Hypersexual desire in males: Are males with paraphilias different from males with paraphilia-related disorders? *Sexual Abuse, 15,* 307–321. doi:10.1177/107906320301500407

Kendall-Tackett, K. A., & Becker-Blease, K. (2004). The importance of retrospective findings in child maltreatment research. *Child Abuse & Neglect, 28,* 723–727. doi:10.1016/j.chiabu.2004.02.002

Kim, J., Guay, J. P., & Knight, R. A. (2007, April). *The efficacy of the factors of psychopathy for predicting recidivism in sexual offender.* Poster presented at the 2nd Biannual Meeting of the Society for the Scientific Study of Psychopathy, St. Petersburg, FL.

Kim-Cohen, J., Caspi, A., Taylor, A., Williams, B., Newcombe, R., Craig, I. W., & Moffitt, T. E. (2006). MAOA, maltreatment, and gene–environment interaction predicting children's mental health: New evidence and a meta-analysis. *Molecular Psychiatry, 11,* 903–913. doi:10.1038/sj.mp.4001851

Knight, R. A., & Cerce, D. D. (1999). Validation and revision of the Multidimensional Assessment of Sex and Aggression. *Psychologica Belgica, 39,* 187–213.

Knight, R. A., & Guay, J. P. (2006). The role of psychopathy in sexual offenders against women. In C. J. Patrick (Ed.), *Handbook of psychopathy* (pp. 512–532). New York, NY: Wiley.

Knight, R. A., Ronis, S. T., Prentky, R. A., & Kafka, M. (2009). *The role of sexual motivation in sexually coercive behavior.* Manuscript submitted for publication.

Knight, R. A., & Sims-Knight, J. E. (2003). Developmental antecedents of sexual coercion against women: Testing of alternative hypotheses with structural equation modeling. In R. A. Prentky, E. Janus, & M. Seto (Eds.), *Sexual coercion: Understanding and management* (pp. 72–85). New York, NY: New York Academy of Sciences.

Knight, R. A., & Sims-Knight, J. E. (2004). Testing an etiological model for male juvenile sexual offending against females. *Journal of Child Sexual Abuse, 13,* 33–55. doi:10.1300/J070v13n03_03

Knight, R. A., & Thornton, D. (2007). *Evaluating and improving risk assessment schemes for sexual recidivism: A long-term follow-up of convicted sexual offenders* (Final Report NCJ 217618). Retrieved from http://nij.ncjrs.gov/publications

Koss, M. P., & Dinero, T. E. (1988). Predictors of sexual aggression among a national sample of male college students. In R. A. Prentky & V. L. Quinsey (Eds.), *Human sexual aggression: Current perspectives* (pp. 133–147). New York, NY: New York Academy of Sciences.

Krueger, R. F. (2006). Perspectives on the conceptualization of psychopathy: Toward an integration. In C. J. Patrick (Ed.), *Handbook of psychopathy* (pp. 193–202). New York, NY: Wiley.

Krueger, R. F., Markon, K. E., Patrick, C. J., Benning, S. D., & Kramer, M. D. (2007). Linking antisocial behavior, substance use, and personality: An integrative quantitative model of the adult externalizing spectrum. *Journal of Abnormal Psychology, 116,* 645–666. doi:10.1037/0021-843X.116.4.645

Långström, N., & Hanson, R. K. (2006). High rates of sexual behavior in the general population: Correlates and predictors. *Archives of Sexual Behavior, 35,* 37–52. doi:10.1007/s10508-006-8993-y

Lewis, D. O., Shanok, S. S., & Pincus, J. H. (1981). Juvenile male sexual assaulters: Psychiatric, neurological, psychoeducational, and abuse factors. In D. O. Lewis (Ed.), *Vulnerabilities to delinquency* (pp. 89–105). New York, NY: SP Medical & Scientific Books.

Lilienfeld, S. O., & Fowler, K. A. (2006). The self-report assessment of psychopathy: Problems, pitfalls, and promises. In C. Patrick (Ed.), *Handbook of psychopathy* (pp. 107–132). New York, NY: Guilford Press.

Lisak, D., & Roth, S. (1990). Motives and psychodynamics of self-reported, unincarcerated rapists. *American Journal of Orthopsychiatry, 60,* 268–280. doi:10.1037/h0079178

Lochman, J. E., Powell, N. R., Whidby, J. M., & Fitzgerald, D. P. (2006). Aggressive children: Cognitive–behavioral assessment and treatment. In P. C. Kendall (Ed.), *Child and adolescent therapy: Cognitive–behavioral procedures* (pp. 33–81). New York, NY: Guilford Press.

Lynam, D. R., Caspi, A., Moffitt, T. E., Loeber, R., & Stouthamer-Loeber, M. (2007). Longitudinal evidence that psychopathy scores in early adolescence predict adult psychopathy. *Journal of Abnormal Psychology, 116,* 155–165. doi:10.1037/0021-843X.116.1.155

Malamuth, N. M. (1998). An evolutionary-based model integrating research on the characteristics of sexually coercive men. In J. Adair, K. Dion, & D. Belanger (Eds.), *Advances in psychological science: Vol. 1. Social, personal, and developmental aspects* (pp. 151–184). Hove, England: Psychology Press/Erlbaum.

Malamuth, N. M. (2003). Criminal and noncriminal sexual aggressors: Integrating psychopathy in a hierarchical-mediational confluence model. In R. A. Prentky, E. S. Janus, & M. C. Seto (Eds.), *Sexually coercive behavior: Understanding and management* (Vol. 989, pp. 33–58). New York, NY: Annals of the New York Academy of Sciences.

Malamuth, N. M., Addison, T., & Koss, M. (2000). Pornography and sexual aggression: Are there reliable effects and can we understand them? *Annual Review of Sex Research, 11,* 26–91.

Malamuth, N. M., & Huppin, M. (2005). Pornography and teenagers: The importance of individual differences. *Adolescent Medicine Clinics, 16,* 315–326. doi:10.1016/j.admecli.2005.02.004

Malamuth, N. M., Sockloskie, R. J., Koss, M. P., & Tanaka, J. S. (1991). Characteristics of aggressors against women: Testing a model using a national sample of college students. *Journal of Consulting and Clinical Psychology, 59,* 670–681.

McClintock, M. K., & Herdt, G. (1996). Rethinking puberty: The development of sexual attraction. *Current Directions in Psychological Science, 5,* 178–183. doi:10.1111/1467-8721.ep11512422

McLoughlin, G., Ronald, A., Kuntsi, J., Asherson, P., & Plomin, R. (2007). Genetic support for the dual nature of attention deficit hyperactivity disorder: Substantial genetic overlap between the inattentive and hyperactive-impulsive components. *Journal of Abnormal Child Psychology, 35,* 999–1008. doi:10.1007/s10802-007-9149-9

Moffitt, T. E. (2005). The new look of behavioral genetics in developmental psychopathology: Gene–environment interplay in antisocial behaviors. *Psychological Bulletin, 131,* 533–554. doi:10.1037/0033-2909.131.4.533

Mosher, D. L., & Sirkin, M. (1984). Measuring a macho personality constellation. *Journal of Research in Personality, 18,* 150–163.

Multidimensional Inventory of Development, Sex, and Aggression (MIDSA). (2008). *MIDSA clinical manual.* Bend, OR: Augur Enterprises. Retrieved from http://www.midsa.us

Murnen, S. K., Wright, C., & Kaluzny, G. (2002). If "boys will be boys," then girls will be victims? A meta-analytic review of the research that relates masculine ideology to sexual aggression. *Sex Roles, 46,* 359–375. doi:10.1023/A:1020488928736

Oddone-Paolucci, E., Genius, M., & Violato, C. (2000). A meta-analysis of published research on the effects of pornography. In C. Violato, E. Oddone-Paolucci, & M. Genius (Eds.), *The changing family and child development* (pp. 48–59). Aldershot, England: Ashgate.

Pérusse, D., & Gendreau, P. L. (2005). Genetics and the development of aggression. In R. E. Tremblay, W. W. Hartup, & J. Archer (Eds.), *Developmental origins of aggression* (pp. 223–241). New York, NY: Guilford Press.

Pollard, P. (1994). Sexual violence against women: Characteristics of typical perpetrators. In J. Archer (Ed.), *Male violence* (pp. 170–194). London, England: Routledge.

Prentky, R. A., & Knight, R. A. (1991). Identifying critical dimensions for discriminating among rapists. *Journal of Consulting and Clinical Psychology, 59,* 643–661. doi:10.1037/0022-006X.59.5.643

Prentky, R. A., Knight, R. A., Sims-Knight, J. E., Straus, H., Rokous, F., & Cerce, D. (1989). Developmental antecedents of sexual aggression. *Development and Psychopathology, 1,* 153–169. doi:10.1017/S0954579400000328

Reynolds, A. J., & Temple, J. A. (2006). Impacts of the Chicago Child–Parent Centers on child and family development. In N. E. Watt, C. Ayoub, R. H. Bradley, J. E. Puma, & W. A. LeBoeuf (Eds.), *The crisis in youth mental health: Vol. 4. Critical issues and effective programs* (pp. 229–249). Westport, CT: Praeger.

Spaccarelli, S., Bowden, B., Coatsworth, J. D., & Kim, S. (1997). Psychosocial correlates of male sexual aggression in a chronic delinquent sample. *Criminal Justice and Behavior, 24,* 71–95. doi:10.1177/0093854897024001005

Spoont, M. R. (1992). Modulatory role of serotonin in neural information processing: Implications for human psychopathology. *Psychological Bulletin, 112,* 330–350. doi:10.1037/0033-2909.112.2.330

Suomi, S. J. (2005). Genetic and environmental factors influencing the expression of impulsive aggression and serotonergic functioning in Rhesus monkeys. In R. E. Tremblay, W. W. Hartup, & J. Archer (Eds.), *Developmental origins of aggression* (pp. 63–82). New York, NY: Guilford Press.

Ullman, S. E., Karabatsos, G., & Koss, M. P. (1999). Alcohol and sexual aggression in a national sample of college men. *Psychology of Women Quarterly, 23,* 673–689. doi:10.1111/j.1471-6402.1999.tb00391.x

Vega, V., & Malamuth, N. M. (2007). Predicting sexual aggression: The role of pornography in the context of general and specific risk factors. *Aggressive Behavior, 33,* 104–117. doi:10.1002/ab.20172

Waldman, I. D., & Rhee, S. H. (2006). Genetic and environmental influences on psychopathy and antisocial behavior. In C. Patrick (Ed.), *Handbook of psychopathy* (pp. 205–228). New York, NY: Wiley.

Walters, G. D. (2006). Risk-appraisal versus self-report in the prediction of criminal justice outcomes: A meta-analysis. *Criminal Justice and Behavior, 33,* 279–304. doi:10.1177/0093854805284409

White, J. W. (2009). A gendered approach to adolescent dating violence: Conceptual and methodological issues. *Psychology of Women Quarterly, 33,* 1–15. doi:10.1111/j.1471-6402.2008.01467.x

White, J. W., & Smith, P. H. (2004). Sexual assault perpetration and reperpetration: From adolescence to young adulthood. *Criminal Justice and Behavior, 31,* 182–202. doi:10.1177/0093854803261342

Widom, C. S., Raphael, K. G., & DuMont, K. A. (2004). The case for prospective longitudinal studies in child maltreatment research: Commentary on Dube,

Williamson, Thompson, Felitti, and Anda (2004). *Child Abuse & Neglect, 28,* 715–722. doi:10.1016/j.chiabu.2004.03.009

Yoon, J., & Knight, R. A. (2008, August). *Processing bias for sexual material in sexually aggressive males: Disattending from sexual material and covariates of these deficits.* Poster presented at the 116th Annual Convention of the American Psychological Association, Boston, MA.

Zakireh, B., Ronis, S. T., & Knight, R. A. (2008). Individual beliefs, attitudes, and victimization histories of male juvenile sexual offenders. *Sexual Abuse: Journal of Research and Treatment, 20,* 323–351. doi:10.1177/1079063208322424

7

VULNERABILITY AND PROTECTIVE FACTORS FOR SEXUAL ASSAULT

SARAH E. ULLMAN AND CYNTHIA J. NAJDOWSKI

Approximately one in five women are victims of sexual assault during their adult lives (for a review, see Chapter 5, this volume), including unwanted sexual contact, sexual coercion, attempted rape, and completed rape resulting from threat, force, or incapacitation from alcohol or drugs (either willingly or unwillingly consumed). We use the term *sexual assault* because the studies reviewed here focus on this specific form of sexual violence against women. In this chapter, we examine vulnerability factors that increase women's risk of being a victim of sexual assault as well as protective factors that reduce the risk of being assaulted. We also discuss how these factors affect the likelihood that women who have experienced sexual assault will be revictimized. In cross-sectional research, it can be difficult to distinguish factors that increase the likelihood of experiencing an assault from consequences of such experiences. Thus, although we review some cross-sectional studies (some of which are on college students), we focus on recent longitudinal studies that have prospectively examined vulnerability and protective factors for sexual assault in representative samples of women.

WHAT DO WE KNOW?

This review of vulnerability and protective factors is organized using a social ecological model, which includes societal factors at the macro level; situational factors at the mesolevel; and individual, relationship, and family factors at the micro level.

Vulnerability Factors

Vulnerability factors are those that increase women's risk of experiencing sexual assault. By identifying relevant vulnerability factors, we gain important insight into why some women face a greater risk of experiencing sexual assault due to societal, situational, and individual variables. Understanding and targeting these factors is necessary to reduce women's risk of sexual assault and to develop appropriate prevention and intervention programs.

Macro Level: Societal Factors

Although existing studies examining macrolevel vulnerability factors are limited because of use of cross-sectional designs, they suggest that certain structural factors increase risk of sexual assault. For example, the alienating conditions of urban life may contribute to higher rates of sexual assault rates in urban compared with rural areas (Baron & Straus, 1989). Sexual assault perpetrators are more likely to be known by their victims in rural areas, whereas perpetrators are more likely to be strangers in urban areas, and assaults perpetrated by strangers are more likely to be reported to authorities (Menard, 2005). Thus, the excess and distinctive risk of sexual assault in urban areas, although real, may be partially accounted for by a greater rate of stranger-perpetrated assaults.

On a broader scale, correlational analyses have found that sexual assault is more frequent in states in which there is more social disorganization (hence fewer social constraints against assault), unemployment, and economic inequality (Baron & Straus, 1989). Relations between geographical location and sexual assault prevalence may be explained in part by regional differences in cultural attitudes and practices. For example, cultural support for violence is an important factor that influences sexual assault prevalence across states (Baron & Straus, 1989), and cultural spillover theory maintains that norms that favor violence for socially legitimate purposes (e.g., capital punishment) tend to be generalized to other social contexts and increase the likelihood of sexual assault (Baron & Straus, 1989). Research also suggests that greater consumption of pornography in the population relates to greater sexual assault prevalence (Baron & Straus, 1989). Other cultural factors associated with sexual assault risk include acceptance of rape myths and traditional beliefs about sex roles (e.g., men should pay for dates), which may engender women's passivity with men in sexual situations and men's willingness and likelihood of being sexually aggressive with women (Muehlenhard, 1988).

General attitudes toward women also appear to be important in predicting sexual assault (e.g., Hines, 2007). Indeed, research suggests that gender inequality is a significant factor that contributes to sexual assault. For example, sexual assault is most prevalent in cities and states in which gender inequality is greatest in terms of the proportion of men to women in the population as well as in economic, educational, political, and legal institutions (Baron & Straus, 1989). Feminist theory argues that the unequal social status of women relative to men may be a root cause of sexual assault. According to social disorganization theory, gender inequality in society may lead to more sexual assault because women's issues receive less attention and support. Evidence regarding these hypotheses is mixed, however, with some studies actually showing positive relations between gender equality and higher sexual assault rates (e.g., Austin & Kim, 2000), supporting a "backlash" hypothesis. That is, women may be more likely to experience sexual assault as they gain greater equality, perhaps because they are exposed to more risky situations and potential perpetrators by virtue of their greater participation in society, or because men are threatened by women and commit sexual assault to maintain inequality (e.g., male dominance). Contradictory findings regarding the relations between gender inequality and sexual assault prevalence may result from differences in level of analysis (macro level vs. individual level; Martin, Vieraitis, & Britto, 2006), type of assault (e.g., acquaintance perpetrated vs. stranger perpetrated; Pazzani, 2007), or simply how gender inequality has been operationalized in studies (e.g., women's actual status vs. their status relative to men; Martin et al., 2006). For instance, Martin et al. (2006) found that higher absolute achievements in economic, educational, employment, and occupational domains were associated with less sexual assault among women, but as women's achievements in these domains approached men's (i.e., relative status, gender equality), sexual assault rates increased.

Meso Level: Situational Factors

Although broader societal factors have a significant impact on women's vulnerability to experiencing sexual assault, it is also important to consider more proximal situational factors that affect sexual assault risk. Being on a date, attending a party, or going to a bar increases women's vulnerability to experiencing sexual assault, particularly by acquaintances and strangers or men whom women do not know well. This may be because alcohol is more common in these situations, as are men's misperceptions of women's sexual interest (for a review, see Abbey, Ross, McDuffie, & McAuslan, 1996).

Isolated or private locations are also riskier contexts for sexual assault as opposed to public places, where informal social control (e.g., other people, passing cars) may reduce risk (Ullman, 2007). Spontaneous social situations may also be riskier than those that are planned, as well as dates in which men take greater control, women are more passive, and more drinking is involved (Ullman, 2007). Further research is needed, however, to understand exactly how these risky situations contribute to women's greater risk of experiencing sexual assault.

Micro Level: Individual Factors

Much more research has examined microlevel factors pertaining to individual women's vulnerability to sexual assault. Having a history of victimization may set the stage for increasing a woman's risk of experiencing further sexual assault, so researchers are studying why this link exists. Previous research has also found links between victimization and trauma history, family dynamics, sexual attitudes and behavior, risk perception, mental health, and alcohol and drug use/abuse. Each of these factors is a potential mediator of the effect of prior victimization on future risk of sexual assault, but each also relates to vulnerability to experiencing sexual assault in women with no history of abuse or sexual assault. Next, we review the research discussing the relations between each factor and risk of either a first incident or repeated experience of sexual assaults.

Prior victimization history. The single greatest factor that increases women's vulnerability for experiencing sexual assault is having previously experienced abuse or assault. Sexual, physical, or emotional abuse in either childhood or adolescence predicts greater risk of sexual assault in women, especially if there is a history of early or severe abuse or multiple abuse types (Acierno, Resnick, Kilpatrick, Saunders, & Best, 1999; Jankowski, Leitenberg, Henning, & Coffey, 2002; Messman-Moore & Brown, 2004; Smith, White, & Holland, 2003). Further, research suggests that child sexual abuse victims who are revictimized as adolescents are more likely than others to experience additional revictimization as adults (Himelein, 1995; Smith et al., 2003). Experiencing an assault during adulthood also increases the likelihood of future victimization (e.g., Livingston, Testa, & VanZile-Tamsen, 2007). For example, having a history of relationship conflict, including interpersonal violence and emotional abuse in dating relationships, is associated with women's risk of sexual assault (e.g., Messman-Moore, Coates, Gaffey, & Johnson, 2008; Testa, VanZile-Tamsen, & Livingston, 2007). Thus, both distal and proximal victimization experiences are important factors to consider for understanding women's vulnerability to adult sexual assault.

Trauma history. A history of other stressors or traumas (e.g., crime victimization) may also create vulnerability to sexual assault, possibly through their effects on problem drinking (Ullman & Najdowski, 2009) or mental health sequelae (Hedtke et al., 2008). Bursik and Grasmick (1993) suggested that social disorganization theory explains this link because socially disorganized communities typically have higher crime rates, and women may experience sexual assault in the context of other crimes. Although research has not consistently supported social disorganization theory as an explanation for sexual assault (Pazzani, 2007), it may be more applicable to assaults perpetrated by strangers, which are likely to be similar to other crimes that occur in disadvantaged communities. Less research has examined how other traumatic experiences such as combat, disaster exposure, or community violence contribute to sexual assault risk, yet some work has illustrated such connections (e.g., Miller, 2008).

Family dynamics. Family factors also affect women's vulnerability to experiencing sexual assault. Among child sexual abuse victims, Siegel and Williams (2001) found that girls who ran away from home and whose family backgrounds included having a mother who had been arrested were at significantly increased risk of adolescent victimization compared with other girls. Similarly, unmarried adult victims of child sexual abuse who reported having mothers who were unavailable because of emotional problems, medical illnesses, or alcohol/drug use problems were at higher risk of retraumatization, including sexual assault, compared with other women (Banyard, Williams, & Siegel, 2003). Women's perceptions of their childhood family environments also influence sexual assault risk. For example, sexual assault appears to be more common among women who report lower levels of paternal care/warmth (Jankowski et al., 2002), concern and support between family members, and family expressiveness (Messman-Moore & Brown, 2004).

Attitudes: Gender, sex, and rape myths. Attitudes have long been thought to relate to sexual victimization risk, although research has not determined that this is actually the case. Some studies have shown that attitudes toward sexuality are related to women's risk of assault (e.g., Himelein, 1995; Koss & Dinero, 1989). For example, Himelein (1995) found that having more liberal sexual attitudes prospectively predicted sexual assault in college women. Less sexually conservative women in Himelein's study also tended to report more consensual sexual experiences, however, which also increase risk for sexual assault, as discussed later. Conclusions regarding relations between attitudes and sexual assault risk are also precluded because prevention programs designed to change attitudes about rape myths and toward women generally have a limited impact on sexual assault risk as revealed by the few studies that have examined their effects (for review, see Staggs & Schewe, 2011, in *Violence Against*

Women and Children, Volume 2: Navigating Solutions). Existing research might have failed to find consistent and convincing relations between attitudes and sexual assault risk because such effects have not yet been delineated to a specific enough degree. For instance, Kalof (2000) found that over a 2-year period, different types of rape-supportive attitudes had unique effects on vulnerability to specific forms of sexual victimization among college women. Overall, discrepancies in the research support Koss and Dinero's (1989) argument that attitudes and behaviors do not render women "uniquely vulnerable to victimization" (p. 249), although more fine-grained analyses may be required to fully understand how attitudes influence sexual assault risk.

Risk-taking behaviors. Although Siegel and Williams (2001) found that sexually precocious behaviors did not predict increased risk of victimization during adolescence, numerous longitudinal studies using both college and community samples have revealed that the tendency to engage in risky or impulsive sexual behaviors, including having many prior sexual partners, poses a risk of experiencing sexual assault for adult women (e.g., Combs-Lane & Smith, 2002; Siegel & Williams, 2001; Testa et al., 2007). Even intentions to engage in risk-taking behaviors (e.g., accepting a ride from a stranger) strongly predict prospective risk of sexual victimization (Combs-Lane & Smith, 2002). Risk-taking behaviors may also mediate the effect of past abuse on risk for future victimization. For example, compared with nonabused women, women who had experienced child sexual abuse, especially severe abuse, had relationships with more partners who were sexually risky and aggressive (Testa, VanZile-Tamsen, & Livingston, 2005). To the extent that exposure to more and riskier partners increases women's risk of prospective sexual assault, these results suggest one pathway by which prior victimization may lead to future sexual assault.

Risk perception. In addition to actually engaging in risky behaviors, failures to perceive risk in a situation or detect danger cues are associated with increased vulnerability for experiencing sexual assault (see Gidycz, McNamara, & Edwards, 2006). Research suggests that it is not only risk perception that matters, however, but also the ability and willingness to act when a threat is recognized, which can be affected by women's thoughts and emotions at the time of an attack (Gidycz, Rich, Orchowski, King, & Miller, 2006). Longitudinal studies have revealed that both lower levels of risk recognition and delayed responses to risk in hypothetical situations predict both an initial experience of sexual assault and revictimization in college women (Messman-Moore & Brown, 2006).

Mental health. Women with intellectual disabilities are more likely to be victims of sexual assault than are women who are not intellectually disabled (Petersilia, 2001). Schizophrenia, depression, and dissociation are also associated with increased risk of sexual assault (e.g., Banyard et al., 2003). In addition to chronic mental health conditions, psychological distress experienced as a consequence of abuse or assault (e.g., posttraumatic stress disorder, low self-esteem, guilt, self-blame) may confer risk of sexual assault (e.g., Livingston et al., 2007). Greater risk among women experiencing these conditions might result from an increased likelihood of being targeted by perpetrators who view them as vulnerable. Alternatively, or perhaps in addition, such women may be less likely or able to detect risk and resist assault (e.g., Acierno et al., 1999). Research suggests that women's attempts to cope with symptoms (i.e., "self-medicate") by using sex, alcohol, or drugs mediate the effect of psychological distress on subsequent sexual assault risk (Messman-Moore, Ward, & Brown, 2009). Treating psychological symptoms, including those resulting from prior victimization, may help women to avoid risk of future assault, particularly by reducing risky behaviors and alcohol/drug use that lead perpetrators to target them.

Alcohol and drug use/abuse. Several cross-sectional and longitudinal studies using both community and college samples have shown that alcohol use, particularly heavy use, is a robust risk factor for the sexual assault of women (e.g., Gidycz et al., 2007; Messman-Moore et al., 2009; Parks, Hsieh, Bradizza, & Romosz, 2008; Siegel & Williams, 2001; Testa et al., 2007). For example, Parks et al. (2008) collected daily diary data from college women for 8 weeks using interactive voice response technology. Women were more likely to be targets of sexual aggression on heavy drinking days compared with nondrinking days, although sexual aggression was not associated with severity of psychological symptoms, number of sexual partners, or prior victimization. Gidycz et al. (2007), in contrast, found that college women's risk of experiencing further sexual assault over several months increased as a function of both level of drinking and history and severity of prior sexual victimization. Nonvictimized women were not likely to be assaulted during the study regardless of alcohol use, but compared with nonvictimized nondrinkers, heavy-drinking women who were victims of severe assault were 10 times more likely to experience further sexual assault. Thus, drinking may confer immediate risk for sexual assault, whereas factors such as psychological symptoms, number of partners, and prior victimization may only show effects over longer time periods.

Fewer studies have examined the role of drug use in women's experiences of sexual assault, but those that have suggest that it increases women's risk for assault. In fact, one study found that drug use (specifically marijuana use), but not alcohol use, predicted sexual victimization in a large sample of young women and men (Martino, Collins, & Ellickson, 2004). In contrast, a prospective study of a representative sample of women showed that neither alcohol nor drug use predicted subsequent assault (Acierno et al., 1999), although the study did not assess sexual assault perpetrated against women who were given alcohol/drugs or who were too intoxicated to resist attack. Research should take both alcohol and drug use into consideration to better understand their unique effects on sexual assault risk.

Alcohol and drug use may reduce women's intentions and abilities to resist unwanted sexual advances (see, e.g., Testa, VanZile-Tamsen, Livingston, & Buddie, 2006). It is also dangerous for women because of the possibility of being assaulted while incapacitated by alcohol or drugs. Kaysen, Neighbors, Martell, Fossos, and Larimer (2006) studied the incidence of incapacitated rape, or rape due to a woman being incapacitated by alcohol, among college women and men over the course of 3 years. Incapacitated rape was prospectively predicted by heavier alcohol consumption and more negative alcohol-related consequences. Further, alcohol use increased following victimization, suggesting a dangerous cycle of relations between alcohol use and sexual victimization. This is consistent with Najdowski and Ullman's (2009) research showing that (a) problem drinking is greater among sexually victimized women who also have a history of child sexual abuse, (b) problem drinking increases the likelihood of being revictimized over 1 year, and (c) revictimization in turn exacerbates problem drinking. Problem drinking and alcohol dependence among victims of sexual assault may be predicted by beliefs that drinking will relieve tension and help them to cope with distress (Ullman, Filipas, Townsend, & Starzynski, 2005; Ullman & Najdowski, 2009; for a review of victims' motives for using alcohol and/or drugs, see Chapter 8, this volume). Unfortunately, these beliefs may inadvertently put victimized women at even greater risk of experiencing future incapacitated rape.

Demographics. Just being a woman is a vulnerability factor for experiencing sexual assault—85% of victims of sexual assault are women (Bureau of Justice Statistics, 1984)—but many other demographic variables are also associated with increased risk of sexual assault. Research has shown that younger, ethnic minority (specifically, African American or Native American), unmarried, or separated women are more likely to be sexually victimized than other women, according to National Crime Victimization Survey (NCVS) data (Rennison, 2002). However, other analyses of older NCVS data showed that low-income, older, White suburban women were at greater risk of experiencing sexual assault compared with other women (Avakame, 1999), whereas divorce related to less assault perpetrated by acquaintances but not strangers in the National Violence Against Women Survey (Pazzani, 2007). Lesbian and bisexual women appear to be at similar or slightly higher risk of sexual assault compared with heterosexual women (Balsam, Rothblum, & Beauchaine, 2005). Among college women, membership in a sorority is also a factor that increases risk of sexual assault (Mohler-Kuo, Dowdall, Koss, & Wechsler, 2004), presumably because sorority members are more likely to attend parties, which increases their risk. Compared with other women, women with lower incomes are more vulnerable to being assaulted, as are women in shelters or homeless women (Acierno et al., 1999; Banyard et al., 2003). Women with lower education and unemployment are at greater risk of experiencing sexual assault, according to both national and international victimization surveys (Avakame, 1999). Finally, women who live away from home are more likely to experience sexual assault compared with women who live with their parents (Buddie & Testa, 2005). This is true even after controlling for other risk factors (e.g., number of sexual partners) that might be increased due to the absence of parental monitoring for women who live away from home compared with women who live with their parents.

Summary of Vulnerability Factors

In summary, a number of vulnerability factors relate to women's risk of experiencing sexual assault, with most research focusing on predictors at the individual level. Still, little research exists to explain why various demographic characteristics relate to assault risk. Such characteristics are most likely proxies for other behaviors and lifestyle circumstances that increase women's risk of being victimized, and more research is needed to identify potential mediators of these relations. Ecological and contextual factors that may also contribute to risk of sexual assault in women also warrant further study. Research is needed on risk factors for different subgroups of women in different contexts so we can better understand how individual factors (e.g., women's characteristics and histories of experiencing sexual assaults) and behaviors (e.g., alcohol or drug use, sexual behavior) translate into risk for sexual assault in different situational and structural contexts. In addition, existing research highlights the need to directly examine the effects of contextual factors and consequences associated with early victimization (i.e., in childhood and adolescence) that in turn increase women's risk of revictimization as adults. Multilevel studies of risk factors using nested designs that incorporate macrolevel structures, mesolevel situations, and microlevel individual factors are needed as existing studies have examined only one level of analysis at a time.

Protective Factors

Although in general much less research has focused on protective factors, researchers have identified several variables that reduce women's risk of experiencing sexual assault, particularly in the presence of risk. These are reviewed in the following sections with macrolevel factors reviewed first, followed by mesolevel and microlevel factors.

Macro Level: Societal Factors

Little empirical research has documented macrolevel protective factors, but results of international surveys show that Western industrialized regions like the United States and Europe have lower rates of violence against women compared with developing regions like Africa and Latin America (del Frate, 2007). Such macrolevel differences may be due to greater economic and educational opportunities (known to relate to less risk of sexual assault) and greater control over fertility for women in developed countries. Sanday's (1981) comparison of societies that were rape-prone versus rape-free provides some anthropological evidence about how macrolevel factors affect sexual assault rates. Societies that value women and feminine qualities of caring, nurturing, and valuing of nature also socialize men to respect women, and these qualities are associated with lower rates of violence against women (Sanday, 1981). Research is needed to better understand how macrolevel factors may reduce sexual assault and how meso- and microlevel factors operate within different social structural locations and societies.

Meso Level: Situational Factors

A promising approach to prevention is focusing on men and women as bystanders to change social norms in a rape-supportive peer culture. This involves teaching how to intervene to deter sexual assault from being committed, to stop peers from expressing prorape attitudes, and to support someone who discloses experiences of sexual assault. Also, research has examined social support following assault as a factor protecting against psychological sequelae, but it appears that social support may prevent women from even being victimized.

Bystander intervention. Research suggests that the presence of bystanders reduces the likelihood that an attack on a woman will result in completed rape (Ullman, 2007) and may even reduce women's risk of being attacked in the first place. Banyard, Moynihan, and Plante (2007) evaluated a sexual assault prevention program that taught college women and men how to intervene safely and effectively in cases of sexual assault by, for example, interrupting situations that could lead to assault before it happens or during an incident. Compared with a control group, program participants were less accepting of rape myths and more willing or likely to engage in bystander behaviors, felt more confident about being an active bystander, and were more likely to have actually engaged in bystander behaviors, with most effects persisting for a year. Although this research suggests that prevention programs focusing on bystander intervention are promising, more work is needed to determine if bystanders reduce sexual assault in the community as well as on college campuses over the long term. Such interventions imply the need for and may in fact facilitate changes in social norms that support sexual assault, which can then reinforce efforts to make assault prevention a collective community responsibility, not simply the responsibility of individual women to avoid on their own.

Social support and social integration. There is some indication that social support is related to lower risk of sexual victimization and revictimization in victims of intimate partner violence and sexual assault. For example, Banyard et al. (2003) found that victims of child sexual abuse who reported greater satisfaction with their relationships with friends or spouses were less likely to experience additional traumas, including sexual assault. Also, some research shows that involvement in religions characterized by high religious integration and regulation relates to lower sexual assault rates (Stack & Kanavy, 1983). Among women who have already experienced sexual assault, those who receive more positive reactions from social support network members to whom they disclose are at lower risk of experiencing further victimization over the course of 1 year (Ullman & Najdowski, in press). Thus, social support appears to reduce risk for first as well as subsequent experiences of sexual assault.

Micro Level Factors

Avoiding high-risk behaviors may be an important strategy for women to reduce their personal risk of sexual assault. Although perpetrators are always responsible for assault, it is still important to consider how women's behaviors may protect them from high-risk situations and contexts in which sexual assault is more likely. In addition, being able to detect and respond to risk appropriately can significantly improve women's chances to avoid assault. We consider these factors as well as the potential role of coping strategies in protecting women from sexual assault.

Avoiding risk behaviors. Clear evidence suggests that self-protection is important for reducing sexual assault risk (Ullman, 2007). Women who restrict their participation in risky activities, do not engage in sexual activity, and abstain from drinking may have lower risk of experiencing sexual assault, at least by acquaintances and strangers, although data are needed to demonstrate that such behaviors in fact reduce women's victimization risk. Sexual assault that occurs within dating and romantic relationships may not be altered by such behavioral restrictions, however. Thus, although the media and police often advocate behavioral restriction, it cannot eliminate women's risk of being assaulted. Further, it is problematic to recommend that women restrict their full participation in social life and society to avoid assault. Despite this, engaging in fewer risky behaviors does reduce women's risk of some forms of sexual assault (e.g., alcohol related, stranger perpetrated) to at least some extent.

Risk perception. It has been argued that perceiving risk accurately is protective against sexual assault, although it is not clear that improving risk recognition alone will reduce sexual assault incidence (Gidycz, McNamara, & Edwards, 2006). To illustrate, Gidycz et al. (2007) found that despite being more likely to recognize their increased risk of future assault, heavy drinkers were more likely to experience sexual assault compared with non-drinkers. Brown, Messman-Moore, Miller, and Stasser (2005) suggested that "heightened risk perception may be an accurate assessment of risk that actually precedes victimization experience" (p. 963). Thus, effective programs are needed to teach women how to use the ability to recognize risk to protect themselves from being sexually assaulted. Existing research suggests that these programs do not yet exist. For example, despite feeling more likely to recognize unwanted sexual behaviors and increasing protective behaviors, college women who completed a prevention program were no less likely to be assaulted than women in a control group (Gidycz, Rich, et al., 2006).

Sexual assertiveness. Sexual assertiveness may protect women from experiencing sexual assault. In support, Livingston et al. (2007) found that sexual assertiveness reduced risk of sexual assault in their large community sample of women. Of importance for understanding revictimization, sexual assault decreased sexual refusal assertiveness over time. Relatedly, sexual refusal self-efficacy, self-competence, and perceived control each may play roles in reducing risk for sexual assault in women (Gidycz, Van Wynsberghe, & Edwards, 2008; Testa et al., 2007). Research also shows that the ability to communicate about and avoid misperceptions regarding one's sexual intent reduces women's risk of sexual assault (Abbey et al., 1996; Testa, Livingston, Vanzile-Tamsen, & Frone, 2003). Thus, future research should examine ways to instill sexual assertiveness and skills for communicating about sex in women to reduce sexual assault incidence, particularly among women who have already been victimized.

Resistance and self-defense. A significant body of research shows that actively resisting (e.g., using forceful verbal and physical resistance strategies) sexual assault attempts reduces the likelihood of their success (for a review, see Ullman, 2007). For example, screaming, fighting, and fleeing all appear to enhance sexual assault avoidance without increasing physical injury risk to women (Ullman, 2007). Conversely, not resisting or engaging in nonforceful verbal resistance (e.g., pleading, begging, reasoning) is an ineffective strategy for preventing sexual assault (Ullman, 2007). Studies examining the efficacy of risk reduction programs emphasizing resistance and/or self-defense training to reduce the likelihood of sexual assault have yielded mixed findings, however. For example, Turchik, Probst, Chau, Nigoff, and Gidycz (2007) and Gidycz et al. (2008) examined college women's intentions to use different resistance tactics when attacked and their actual utilization of strategies in assault incidents reported several weeks later. Gidycz et al. reported that women's intentions to utilize assertive resistance strategies (e.g., physically fight) predicted their actual use, but Turchik et al. did not observe this effect. Future studies using consistent operationalizations of resistance tactics are needed to disentangle relations between women's intentions for resistance and strategies actually implemented so that prevention programs can target and encourage the use of strategies that are most effective in protecting women from being sexually assaulted.

Coping strategies. A great deal of research has examined coping in the aftermath of sexual assault, but few studies have examined relations between women's coping strategies and future sexual assault risk. Ullman and Najdowski (in press) found no link between sexual assault victims' coping strategies and further revictimization over 1 year, but more research is needed, particularly to test whether the strategies nonvictimized women use to cope with other stressors influence their risk of sexual assault. Attempts to reduce women's reliance on coping by engaging in sexual behavior or using drugs or alcohol to reduce distress or self-medicate may be helpful, because both of these forms of coping increase sexual assault and revictimization risk (e.g., Messman-Moore et al., 2008). Research should examine whether adaptive coping strategies (e.g., help seeking) protect women from being victimized. Such coping strategies may reduce sexual assault risk, for example, by strengthening women's links to social support networks or reducing women's alcohol or drug use or contact with risky sexual partners.

Summary of Protective Factors

Although less research has been conducted on protective factors that reduce women's risk of experiencing sexual assault than on risk factors, currently it appears that the presence of bystanders willing to intervene to stop an attack, perceiving one's risk of assault, avoiding risky behaviors (e.g., heavy drinking), having greater sexual refusal assertiveness or self-efficacy, engaging in resistance if threatened or attacked, and, possibly, having social support and coping strategies can reduce women's risk of sexual assault. Research on protective factors is in its infancy, however, and little prospective research exists on what helps protect women from sexual assault. Although societal factors like development status of nations and higher valuation and status of women may be macrolevel protective factors, such evidence is descriptive and correlational in nature and requires more rigorous research to understand fully.

HOW DO WE KNOW IT? A CRITICAL ANALYSIS
OF THE RESEARCH

Research has examined risk and protective factors for sexual assault, but it is important to understand the challenges researchers face when studying this personal issue and limitations of research methods (e.g., study design, sampling strategies) to evaluate the significance of individual study findings. For example, a key limitation is that much of what we know is based on cross-sectional studies and nonrepresentative samples, precluding us from drawing inferences and generalizing findings to women in the general population. Despite such limitations, is there agreement among researchers in the field? What findings are still up for debate?

Challenges in Studying Correlates of Sexual Assault

The topic of sexual assault is difficult to study for several reasons. First, studies rely on victims reporting or acknowledging sexual assault experiences, which they do not always do. Reporting is especially low for nonstereotypic assaults (Menard, 2005). A further challenge involves the need to understand vulnerability and protective factors for sexual assault in context. This need is highlighted by research demonstrating that risk factors differ as a function of who the perpetrator is (i.e., stranger, acquaintance, intimate partner), type of sexual assault, the level of force involved, whether drug or alcohol use is involved, and even across subgroups of ethnic groups (e.g., Kalof, 2000; Messman-Moore et al., 2008; Pazzani, 2007; Testa et al., 2003; Testa et al., 2007). For example, Testa et al. (2007) found that sexual assault perpetrated by an intimate partner was predicted by drug use but not heavy drinking, whereas sexual assault perpetrated by a nonintimate perpetrator was predicted by heavy drinking but not drug use. Thus, unique risk factors emerged as a function of perpetrator identity. Currently, we know more about vulnerability factors than protective factors, but research demonstrates the importance of taking context into account to gain a more complete understanding of how effects may vary.

Gaps and Weaknesses in Existing Knowledge

Existing studies have a number of limitations related to methodology, samples, and analyses. One problem with existing research related to sexual assault risk is that most studies are not longitudinal. Cross-sectional research precludes the ability to determine whether variables are predictors or consequences of sexual assault. Of those studies that are longitudinal, many use homogeneous samples, composed predominantly of White college students.

Although most research has focused on college women and risk of acquaintance rape, an important high-risk group, sexual assault is also prevalent in the community, and we know less about behavioral and situational risk factors for assault in community-residing women. In particular, more knowledge is needed about factors that increase or reduce risk of sexual assault perpetrated by known offenders for women in the community. Most research has not distinguished between different kinds of perpetrators, but we cannot assume that risk and protective factors are the same for all perpetrator types. Thus, studies using large, representative, and diverse samples of women in terms of age, race, and socioeconomic status, which also take characteristics of victimization experiences into consideration, are needed to better understand vulnerability and protective factors for sexual assault among women in the broader community.

Given that college women are younger, more privileged, and typically higher functioning compared with other women, it is likely that the contexts and factors related to their assaults differ from those of older, less privileged, and psychologically distressed women in society. Given the clear association between women's lower status and increased sexual assault risk, it is important that attention also focus on vulnerable socioeconomic groups. Longitudinal studies should also concentrate on subgroups of women who are at high risk for sexual assault, such as those with mental health problems or physical disabilities, who may be unable to avoid risk factors for sexual assault. And although most research on sexual assault is focused on women in college or in the community, research on women in high-risk contexts in which sexual assault is common, such as prison or the military, is also important.

Better measures of relevant risk factors as well as theoretically driven research are needed to understand how vulnerability and protective factors play a role in risk of assault. Especially lacking is research on protective factors, although some studies suggest that they exist and that integrating such factors in prevention efforts may reduce sexual assault. The field has yet to develop integrated theoretical models to test multiple levels of vulnerability and protective factors that relate to sexual assault. As yet, there is not enough research integrating such factors ranging from the ecological to the individual level, nor is there adequate work on how individual-level factors affect sexual assault risk in different situational contexts and social structures. This should be an important focus of future research, as we already know that risk of different types of assault by different perpetrators also varies according to women's contexts and age (i.e., college vs. community samples). Finally, although more is known about characteristics of sexually aggressive men (see Chapter 6, this volume) than about factors related to women's risk of sexual victimization, it is important to keep in mind that without data on perpetrators, attempts to identify risk and protective factors in women may fall short, at least in identifying root causes that help in developing primary prevention. Such research is critically important for secondary prevention and treatment, however, as it can help us to determine who is at risk, in what circumstances, and why, so interventions target appropriate factors and address women who face the greatest risk of sexual assault. Thus, longitudinal studies are needed of large representative samples of women from the community to better understand the role of individual, contextual, and ecological risk and protective factors for sexual assault, including data on perpetrators.

Consensus and Conflicting Positions

There is consistency across several studies showing that women's lower absolute status (e.g., greater poverty, low education, unemployment) is a risk factor for sexual assault, using both macrolevel state and microlevel individual data. These results support feminist theory suggesting that women's lower status in society is related to higher sexual assault rates, whereas social disorganization theory has had less support, particular with regard to known offenders (Pazzani, 2007). There is also little disagreement regarding behavioral risk factors for sexual assault, although some have suggested that personality factors, attitudes, and beliefs are important, whereas others have argued they are not significant risk factors. It is likely that personality differences between women who have been sexually assaulted and those who have not are actually effects of being assaulted (McMullin, Wirth, & White, 2007), but this is difficult to know without longitudinal research examining personality factors and victimization over time, which is currently lacking.

WHERE DO WE GO FROM HERE? RECOMMENDATIONS FOR FUNDING PRIORITIES AND POLICY CHANGE

Although further exploration of factors contributing to and reducing the incidence of sexual assault is required, there is a great deal of research already available on which funding priorities and policies can be based in efforts to reduce sexual assault among women. Beginning at the macro level, women's status (e.g., education, employment) within and between societies has been found to be inversely related to sexual assault rates. Research on this issue is cross-sectional and limits conclusions that can be drawn, but improving women's position in society should lead to lower assault rates, although some increase in assault may occur while the relative status of men and women is shifting due to men's backlash against women's status gains.

Research also suggests that prior victimization plays a significant role in women's risk of adult sexual assault. Thus, prevention of abuse and assault, especially during childhood and adolescence, is particularly important for reducing assault risk. Sexual assault prevalence rates obtained in community samples have not declined or changed over the past 20 years (see Chapter 5, this volume), suggesting that prevention efforts have not addressed underlying factors adequately to reduce sexual assault in women. Although research is still needed to understand why risk of sexual assault is higher for women abused in childhood and adolescence, the existence of this link clearly implies that child abuse prevention should be linked to sexual assault prevention and that research must take a life-span perspective to understand how early experiences increase risk of later revictimization. This is important given the young age at which most women experience sexual assault. Longitudinal research on risk of revictimization may in fact help to identify risk and protective factors that also apply to women's risk for first experiences of sexual assault.

Currently much less funded is research examining risk and protective factors as compared with treatment and prevention of sexual assault. Such research is expensive and time-consuming, yet identifying risk and protective factors from such studies should consequently help to inform better treatment and prevention strategies for sexual assault. More research on women from the community is needed to better understand factors related to their risk of sexual assault. We know that women differentially situated in the social structure (e.g., those having lower socioeconomic status and living in poorer neighborhoods) face different risks of violence in general, and research is needed to determine whether this is also true of sexual assault. This work must be focused on understanding which women face risk of what types of assault in which specific contexts.

Finally, public policies are needed to address women's underreporting of sexual assault, provide a more supportive response to victims, and create services in places women feel comfortable going to for assistance in the community. Often women delay reporting their sexual assault experiences and/or seeking help, especially when they know the offender. As a consequence, our knowledge about sexual assault risk and protective factors is probably biased toward assaults perpetrated by strangers and men less well known to women, except for research on date and acquaintance rape in college women. Thus, policies ensuring that women have services and assistance available to them, while providing obvious benefits to victims of sexual assault, may also increase reporting of atypical rapes as well as our knowledge of factors related to them. A new generation of research on risk and protective factors for different types of sexual assault in different subgroups of women in the population is needed to provide a better empirical basis for effective prevention and treatment initiatives.

REFERENCES

Abbey, A., Ross, L. T., McDuffie, D., & McAuslan, P. (1996). Alcohol, misperception, and sexual assault: How and why are they linked? In D. M. Buss & N. M. Malamuth (Eds.), *Sex, power, conflict: Evolutionary and feminist perspectives* (pp. 138–161). New York, NY: Oxford University Press.

Acierno, R., Resnick, H., Kilpatrick, D. G., Saunders, B., & Best, C. L. (1999). Risk factors for rape, physical assault, and posttraumatic stress disorder in women: Examination of differential multivariate relationships. *Journal of Anxiety Disorders, 13*, 541–563. doi:10.1016/S0887-6185(99)00030-4

Austin, R. L., & Kim, Y. S. (2000). A cross-national examination of the relationship between gender equality and official rape rates. *International Journal of Offender Therapy and Comparative Criminology, 44*, 204–221. doi:10.1177/0306624X00442006

Avakame, E. (1999). Females' labor force participation and rape: An empirical test of the backlash hypothesis. *Violence Against Women, 5*, 926–949. doi:10.1177/10778019922181554

Balsam, K. F., Rothblum, E., & Beauchaine, T. P. (2005). Victimization over the life span: Comparison of lesbian, gay, bisexual, and heterosexual siblings. *Journal of Consulting and Clinical Psychology, 73*, 477–487. doi:10.1037/0022-006X.73.3.477

Banyard, V. L., Moynihan, M. M., & Plante, E. G. (2007). Sexual violence prevention through bystander education: An experimental evaluation. *Journal of Community Psychology, 35*, 463–481. doi:10.1002/jcop.20159

Banyard, V. L., Williams, L. M., & Siegel, J. A. (2003). Retraumatization among adult women sexually abused in childhood: Exploratory analyses in a prospective study. *Journal of Child Sexual Abuse, 11*, 19–48. doi:10.1300/J070v11n03_02

Baron, L., & Straus, M. A. (1989). *Four theories of rape in American society: A state-level analysis*. New Haven, CT: Yale University Press.

Brown, A. L., Messman-Moore, T. L., Miller, A. G., & Stasser, G. (2005). Sexual victimization in relation to perceptions of risk: Mediation, generalization, and temporal stability. *Personality and Social Psychology Bulletin, 31*, 963–976. doi:10.1177/0146167204274101

Buddie, A. M., & Testa, M. (2005). Rates and predictors of sexual aggression among students and nonstudents. *Journal of Interpersonal Violence, 20*, 713–724. doi:10.1177/0886260505276073

Bureau of Justice Statistics. (1984). *The National Crime Survey: Methodological studies*. Washington, DC: U.S. Department of Justice.

Bursik, R., & Grasmick, H. (1993). *Neighborhoods and crime: The dimensions of effective community control*. New York, NY: Maxwell Macmillan.

Combs-Lane, A. M., & Smith, D. W. (2002). Risk of sexual victimization in college women: The role of behavioral intentions and risk-taking behaviors. *Journal of Interpersonal Violence, 17*, 165–183. doi:10.1177/0886260502017002004

del Frate, A. (2007). Victimization: An international perspective. In R. C. Davis, A. Lurigio, & S. Herman (Eds.), *Victims of crime* (3rd ed., pp. 233–252). Thousand Oaks, CA: Sage.

Gidycz, C. A., Loh, C., Lobo, T., Rich, C., Lynn, S. J., & Pashdag, J. (2007). Reciprocal relationships among alcohol use, risk perception, and sexual victimization: A prospective analysis. *Journal of American College Health, 56*, 5–14. doi:10.3200/JACH.56.1.5-14

Gidycz, C. A., McNamara, J. R., & Edwards, K. M. (2006). Women's risk perception and sexual victimization: A review of the literature. *Aggression and Violent Behavior, 11*, 441–456. doi:10.1016/j.avb.2006.01.004

Gidycz, C. A., Rich, C. L., Orchowski, L., King, C., & Miller, A. K. (2006). The evaluation of a sexual assault self-defense and risk-reduction program for college women: A prospective study. *Psychology of Women Quarterly, 30*, 173–186. doi:10.1111/j.1471-6402.2006.00280.x

Gidycz, C. A., Van Wynsberghe, A., & Edwards, K. M. (2008). Prediction of women's utilization of resistance strategies in a sexual assault situation: A prospective study. *Journal of Interpersonal Violence, 23*, 571–588. doi:10.1177/0886260507313531

Hedtke, K. A., Ruggiero, K. J., Fitzgerald, M. M., Zinzow, H. M., Saunders, B. E., Resnick, H. S., & Kilpatrick, D. G. (2008). A longitudinal investigation of interpersonal violence in relation to mental health and substance use. *Journal of Consulting and Clinical Psychology, 76*, 633–647. doi:10.1037/0022-006X.76.4.633

Himelein, M. J. (1995). Risk factors for sexual victimization in dating. *Psychology of Women Quarterly, 19*, 31–48. doi:10.1111/j.1471-6402.1995.tb00277.x

Hines, D. A. (2007). Predictors of sexual coercion against women and men: A multilevel, multinational study of university students. *Archives of Sexual Behavior, 36*, 403–422. doi:10.1007/s10508-006-9141-4

Jankowski, M. K., Leitenberg, H., Henning, K., & Coffey, P. (2002). Parental caring as a possible buffer against sexual revictimization in young adult survivors of child sexual abuse. *Journal of Traumatic Stress, 15*, 235–244. doi:10.1023/A:1015259412746

Kalof, L. (2000). Vulnerability to sexual coercion among college women: A longitudinal study. *Gender Issues, 18*, 47–58. doi:10.1007/s12147-001-0023-8

Kaysen, D., Neighbors, C., Martell, J., Fossos, N., & Larimer, M. E. (2006). Incapacitated rape and alcohol use: A prospective analysis. *Addictive Behaviors, 31*, 1820–1832. doi:10.1016/j.addbeh.2005.12.025

Koss, M. P., & Dinero, T. E. (1989). Discriminant analysis of risk factors for sexual victimization among a national sample of college women. *Journal of Consulting and Clinical Psychology, 57*, 242–250. doi:10.1037/0022-006X.57.2.242

Livingston, J. A., Testa, M., & VanZile-Tamsen, C. (2007). The reciprocal relationship between sexual victimization and sexual assertiveness. *Violence Against Women, 13,* 298–313. doi:10.1177/1077801206297339

Martin, K., Vieraitis, L., & Britto, S. (2006). Gender equality and women's absolute status: A test of the feminist models of rape. *Violence Against Women, 12,* 321–339. doi:10.1177/1077801206286311

Martino, S. C., Collins, R. L., & Ellickson, P. L. (2004). Substance use and vulnerability to sexual and physical aggression: A longitudinal study of young adults. *Violence and Victims, 19,* 521–540. doi:10.1891/vivi.19.5.521.63684

McMullin, D., Wirth, R., & White, J. (2007). The impact of sexual victimization on personality: A longitudinal study of gendered attributes. *Sex Roles, 56,* 403–414. doi:10.1007/s11199-006-9179-8

Menard, K. S. (2005). *Reporting sexual assault: A social ecology perspective.* New York, NY: LFB Scholarly Publishing.

Messman-Moore, T. L., & Brown, A. L. (2004). Child maltreatment and perceived family environment as risk factors for adult rape: Is child sexual abuse the most salient experience? *Child Abuse & Neglect, 28,* 1019–1034. doi:10.1016/j.chiabu.2004.05.003

Messman-Moore, T. L., & Brown, A. L. (2006). Risk perception, rape, and sexual revictimization: A prospective study of college women. *Psychology of Women Quarterly, 30,* 159–172. doi:10.1111/j.1471-6402.2006.00279.x

Messman-Moore, T. L., Coates, A. A., Gaffey, K. J., & Johnson, C. F. (2008). Sexuality, substance use, and susceptibility to victimization: Risk for rape and sexual coercion in a prospective study of college women. *Journal of Interpersonal Violence, 23,* 1730–1746. doi:10.1177/0886260508314336

Messman-Moore, T. L., Ward, R. M., & Brown, A. L. (2009). Substance use and PTSD symptoms impact the likelihood of rape and revictimization in college women. *Journal of Interpersonal Violence, 24,* 499–521. doi:10.1177/0886260508317199

Miller, J. (2008). Respect yourself, protect yourself: Sexual coercion and violence. In J. Miller (Ed.), *Getting played: African American girls, urban inequality, and gendered violence* (pp. 114–150). New York, NY: New York University Press.

Mohler-Kuo, M., Dowdall, G. W., Koss, M. P., & Wechsler, H. (2004). Correlates of rape while intoxicated in a national sample of college women. *Journal of Studies on Alcohol, 65,* 37–45.

Muehlenhard, C. M. (1988). Misinterpreted dating behaviors and the risk of date rape. *Journal of Social and Clinical Psychology, 6,* 20–37.

Najdowski, C. J., & Ullman, S. E. (2009). Prospective effects of sexual victimization on PTSD and problem drinking. *Addictive Behaviors, 34,* 965–968. doi:10.1016/j.addbeh.2009.05.004

Parks, K. A., Hsieh, Y.-P., Bradizza, C. M., & Romosz, A. M. (2008). Factors influencing the temporal relationship between alcohol consumption and experiences with aggression among college women. *Psychology of Addictive Behaviors, 22*, 210–218. doi:10.1037/0893-164X.22.2.210

Pazzani, L. M. (2007). The factors affecting sexual assaults committed by strangers and acquaintances. *Violence Against Women, 13*, 717–749. doi:10.1177/1077801207 302699

Petersilia, J. R. (2001). Crime victims with developmental disabilities: A review essay. *Criminal Justice and Behavior, 28*, 655–694. doi:10.1177/009385480102 800601

Rennison, C. M. (2002). *Rape and sexual assault: Reporting to police and medical attention, 1992–2000* (No. NCJ 194530). Washington, DC: U.S. Department of Justice.

Sanday, P. R. (1981). The sociocultural context of rape: A cross-cultural study. *Journal of Social Issues, 37*, 5–27. doi:10.1111/j.1540-4560.1981.tb01068.x

Siegel, J. A., & Williams, L. M. (2001). *Risk factors for violent victimization of women: A prospective study*. Washington, DC: U.S. Department of Justice.

Smith, P. H., White, J. W., & Holland, L. J. (2003). A longitudinal perspective on dating violence among adolescent and college-age women. *American Journal of Public Health, 93*, 1104–1109. doi:10.2105/AJPH.93.7.1104

Staggs, S. L., & Schewe, P. A. (2011). Primary prevention of domestic violence. In M. P. Koss, J. W. White, & A. E. Kazdin (Eds.), *Violence against women and children, Vol. 2: Navigating solutions* (pp. 237–258). Washington, DC: American Psychological Association.

Stack, S., & Kanavy, M. J. (1983). The effect of religion on forcible rape: A structural analysis. *Journal for the Scientific Study of Religion, 22*, 67–74. doi:10. 2307/1385592

Testa, M., Livingston, J. A., Vanzile-Tamsen, C., & Frone, M. R. (2003). The role of women's substance use in vulnerability to forcible and incapacitated rape. *Journal of Studies on Alcohol, 64*, 756–764.

Testa, M., VanZile-Tamsen, C., & Livingston, J. A. (2005). Childhood sexual abuse, relationship satisfaction, and sexual risk taking in a community sample of women. *Journal of Consulting and Clinical Psychology, 73*, 1116–1124. doi:10.1037/0022-006X.73.6.1116

Testa, M., VanZile-Tamsen, C., & Livingston, J. A. (2007). Prospective prediction of women's sexual victimization by intimate and nonintimate male perpetrators. *Journal of Consulting and Clinical Psychology, 75*, 52–60. doi:10.1037/0022-006X.75.1.52

Testa, M., VanZile-Tamsen, C., Livingston, J. A., & Buddie, A. M. (2006). The role of women's alcohol consumption in managing sexual intimacy and sexual safety motives. *Journal of Studies on Alcohol, 67*, 665–674.

Turchik, J. A., Probst, D. R., Chau, M., Nigoff, A., & Gidycz, C. A. (2007). Factors predicting the type of tactics used to resist sexual assault: A prospective study of college women. *Journal of Consulting and Clinical Psychology, 75*, 605–614. doi:10.1037/0022-006X.75.4.605

Ullman, S. E. (2007). A 10-year update on "Review and critique of empirical studies of rape avoidance." *Criminal Justice and Behavior, 34,* 411–429. doi:10.1177/0093 854806297117

Ullman, S. E., Filipas, H. H., Townsend, S. M., & Starzynski, L. L. (2005). Trauma exposure, posttraumatic stress disorder and problem drinking in sexual assault survivors. *Journal of Studies on Alcohol, 66,* 610–619.

Ullman, S. E., & Najdowski, C. J. (2009). Revictimization as a moderator of psychosocial risk factors for problem drinking in female sexual assault survivors. *Journal of Studies on Alcohol and Drugs, 70,* 41–49.

Ullman, S. E., & Najdowski, C. J. (in press). Prospective changes in attributions of self-blame and social reactions to women's disclosures of adult sexual assault. *Journal of Interpersonal Violence.*

8

HEALTH AND ECONOMIC CONSEQUENCES OF SEXUAL VIOLENCE

SANDRA L. MARTIN, REBECCA J. MACY, AND SIOBHAN K. YOUNG

This chapter presents research concerning the effects of sexual violence on women's psychological health, physical health, and behavioral health, as well as research on the economic consequences of this violence. Although sexual violence may be defined in many ways, most studies described here focus on sexual assault or rape. Moreover, the studies allow examination of the impact of sexual violence separate from other types of violence. This chapter focuses on violence during adulthood; however, because most sexual violence research on adults also includes adolescents, some of the reviewed studies include adults and teens.

This is not a comprehensive literature review but rather an overview, illustrated with selected research findings. We examine the methods commonly used in these studies and note the gaps in our knowledge. We conclude with recommendations regarding emerging research priorities and methods that may be useful for future studies.

WHAT DO WE KNOW?

Sexual violence against women often results in multiple health problems in the areas of psychological health, physical health, and behavioral health, resulting in enormous financial costs for both the sexual violence survivors and society.

Psychological Health

Women who experience sexual violence during adulthood are more likely than nonvictimized women to evidence many types of psychological problems, including posttraumatic stress disorder (PTSD), anxiety, depression, and suicide ideation and attempts. For example, research with a random sample of 2,876 insured women (ages 18–64 years) found that intimate partner sexual violence survivors were twice as likely as the other women to have high levels of depressive symptoms (Bonomi, Anderson, Rivara, & Thompson, 2007). A survey of 1,152 women (ages 18–65) from family practice clinics found that intimate partner sexual violence survivors were twice as likely to report symptoms of PTSD, anxiety, and depression; moreover, they were four times more likely to have attempted suicide (Coker et al., 2002). A national sample of 3,632 female military veterans found that those sexually assaulted in the military were more likely to evidence depression (Hankin et al., 1999; Skinner et al., 2000), and a study of Gulf War veterans (including 336 women) found that women with PTSD were more likely to have been sexually assaulted during deployment (Kang, Dalager, Mahan, & Ishii, 2005). A study of battered women in shelters found that those who had experienced intimate partner rape were more likely to have symptoms of depression, PTSD, and suicidal ideation (Weaver et al., 2007). Many other studies also have found elevated psychological symptoms among sexual violence survivors (Breitenbecher, 2006; Ullman, Filipas, Townsend, & Starzynski, 2006).

Variation in Psychological Outcomes

Most female sexual violence survivors experience negative psychological sequelae immediately after the event, with many, but not all, significantly recovering within a year (Dancu, Riggs, Hearst-Ikeda, Shoyer, & Foa, 1996; Kimerling & Calhoun, 1994; Rothbaum, Foa, Riggs, Murdock, & Walsh, 1992). In light of this variation, research has examined variables that may moderate or mediate links between sexual violence and the severity and duration of psychological sequelae. Some such variables include women's histories of violence (revictimization); violence severity; the social relationship of the perpetrator and survivor; women's coping strategies, self-blame, and cognitive processing concerning the event; the social reactions that women receive from others when they disclose information concerning their victimization experiences; and women's demographic characteristics.

Violence History/Revictimization

Women who have previously experienced violence often evidence poorer psychological health outcomes in response to a new sexual violence incident. For example, a survey of 1,300 adult women in Washington state found that those who had experienced multiple sexual assaults had higher levels of depression and PTSD symptoms than did women who had experienced one or no sexual assaults (Casey & Nurius, 2005). A study of 117 recent rape victims recruited through police, hospital, and victim services found that those who were sexually abused as children were more likely to also have been previously physically and sexually victimized as adults, which in turn was associated with greater PTSD severity 1 month after the current rape (Nishith, Mechanic, & Resick, 2000). A survey of 600 adult female sexual assault survivors found that those with a prior trauma history reported more PTSD symptoms (Ullman, Filipas, Townsend, & Starzynski, 2007). It is not clear why chronic victimization influences psychological responses to a new traumatic incident; however, continuous victimization may affect women's physiological stress reactions (e.g., cortisol responses), which in turn may affect women's psychological responses to trauma (Resnick, Yehuda, & Acierno, 1997; Resnick, Yehuda, Pitman, & Foy, 1995).

Sexual Violence Severity

Women who experience more severe sexual violence often have more severe psychological symptoms and are slower to recover from the trauma (Rothbaum et al., 1992). For example, a survey of a media-recruited sample of 323 adult women who were sexually assaulted at age 14 or older found that those who believed that their life was in danger during the assault were more likely to evidence high levels of PTSD symptoms (Ullman & Filipas, 2001). Similar results have been found with other samples (Ullman et al., 2006).

Social Relationship of the Perpetrator and Survivor

Findings are equivocal as to whether women with closer social ties to the perpetrator (e.g., married) experience more negative psychological sequelae in response to sexual violence, with research often finding associations for one type of psychological problem but not for others. For instance, a study of 96 female undergraduates who were sexually assaulted at age 12 or older found that after controlling for violence severity, there were greater levels of PTSD-related hyperarousal and intrusion symptoms among those assaulted by marital partners, followed by acquaintances, sexual intimates, and dating partners; however, this effect was not seen for PTSD-related avoidance symptoms (Culbertson & Dehle, 2001). A survey of 700 women who were sexually assaulted at age 14 or older found that those assaulted by relatives reported the highest level of PTSD symptoms, followed by those assaulted by strangers, partners/husbands, and lastly acquaintances; however, no differences were found between the groups in terms of depression symptoms (Ullman et al., 2006). These PTSD findings may be at least partially explained by the fact that assaults by strangers were more severe in nature compared with assaults by other persons.

Coping Strategies, Self-Blame, and Cognitive Processing

Considerable research has examined whether women's coping strategies relate to their psychological health following sexual violence. For example, a study of 17- to 65-year-old women, including 103 recent rape victims and 112 recent victims of nonsexual assault, found that those who used positive distancing as a coping strategy (assessed by items such as "accepted the next best thing to what you wanted") had lower PTSD levels 3 months postassault than women who used wishful thinking (assessed by items such as "wished you could change the way you felt"; Valentiner, Foa, Riggs, & Gershuny, 1996). Other research has found elevated PTSD symptoms among sexual assault survivors who used avoidance coping strategies, such as behavioral disengagement, denial, and self-distraction (Ullman, 1996; Ullman et al., 2007).

There is growing evidence that female survivors who blame themselves for the sexual violence often experience poorer psychological health. For instance, a longitudinal study of 171 female sexual assault survivors (age 16 and older) at a hospital emergency room found that behavioral self-blame for the assault (assessed via survey items such as "I used poor judgment") was positively correlated with psychological distress up to 1 year postassault (Frazier, 2003). Similarly, a survey of 224 female college students who experienced sexual violence found that women had more symptoms of psychological distress if they endorsed characterological self-blame for the assault, as assessed via survey items such as "I am stupid" (Breitenbecher, 2006).

Other research has examined how women's conceptualization or understanding of the event may mediate psychological responses to sexual violence. For example, a cross-sectional study of 253 female sexual assault survivors found that cognitive-affective processing mediated the women's psychological responses to the violence (Koss, Figueredo, & Prince, 2002).

Social Reactions

Much research has found that women who experience negative social reactions from others when they disclose sexual violence victimization have poor psychological outcomes; however, fewer studies have found links between positive social reactions in response to such disclosure and women's psychological health (Ullman & Filipas, 2001; Ullman et al., 2007). One study that found effects of both negative and positive social reactions was a survey of a convenience sample of 155 adult rape survivors that found an association between negative social reactions and elevated psychological symptoms, and an association between positive social reactions (feeling listened to and believed) and better psychological health (Ullman, 1996).

A few studies consider potential positive psychological outcomes, such as women's psychological growth, in response to surviving such trauma. For example, a survey of 55 female college sexual assault survivors found that those who received negative support postassault were more likely to have PTSD symptoms, whereas those who received positive support were more likely to score high on the Perceived Benefits Scale, an assessment measuring subjective positive life changes (e.g., increased self-efficacy, caring) after trauma (Borja, Callahan, & Long, 2006).

Demographics

Some research has examined women's demographic characteristics related to their psychological responses to sexual violence. This research shows that women who were sexually assaulted at younger ages are more likely to evidence suicide ideation (Ullman & Brecklin, 2002) and PTSD symptoms (M. W. Miller & Resnick, 2007; Ullman et al., 2007). Findings are equivocal as to whether psychological responses to sexual violence vary by race or ethnicity (McFarlane, Malecha, Gist, et al., 2005; M. W. Miller & Resnick, 2007; Ullman & Brecklin, 2002; Ullman et al., 2007) or education levels (M. W. Miller & Resnick, 2007; Ullman & Filipas, 2001; Ullman et al., 2007). Several studies have not found women's income, employment, or marital/relationship status to be related to the psychological outcomes of adult female sexual assault survivors (M. W. Miller & Resnick, 2007; Ullman & Brecklin, 2002; Ullman et al., 2007).

Physical Health

Sexual violence may result in myriad physical health problems, including injuries, gynecologic and reproductive health problems, headaches, gastrointestinal problems, sleep disturbances, functional limitations/disabilities, and even death.

Sexual Assault–Related Death

In 2005, 3.7% of all female homicide victims within the 16 U.S. states in the National Violent Death Reporting System experienced rape/sexual assault at the time of death (S. Smith, personal communication, September 5, 2008). Although sexual assault survivors are more likely than others to have suicidal thoughts and attempts, we could not locate empirical information concerning the prevalence of completed suicides in response to sexual violence.

Injury

Many women survivors of sexual violence experience injuries. For instance, the National Violence Against Women Survey (a national sample of 8,000 women) found that a third of those raped since age 18 were injured, with the most common injuries being scratches/bruises/welts, broken bones/dislocated joints, and head/spinal cord injuries (Tjaden & Thoennes, 2000). The National Women's Study (a longitudinal study of more than 4,000 U.S. women) had similar results, finding that 24% of 714 rape survivors sustained minor injuries and that 4% sustained major injuries (Kilpatrick, Edmunds, & Seymour, 1992). Clinic-based investigations of sexual assault often find a higher prevalence of injuries, perhaps because many less injured survivors do not seek health care after the violence (Tjaden & Thoennes, 2000). For example, a study of 819 female sexual assault survivors (age 15 and older) seen at a hospital found that 52% had general body injuries (bruises, abrasions, fractures, and intracranial trauma injuries) and 20% had genital-anal trauma (Sugar, Fine, & Eckert, 2004).

Gynecologic and Reproductive Health

Not only are female sexual violence survivors affected by injuries, including genital injuries, but they also may evidence many types of gynecologic symptoms. A study of three randomly selected samples of more than 4,000 U.S. women found positive associations between sexual assault and dysmenorrhea, menorrhagia, and sexual dysfunction (Golding, Wilsnack, & Learman, 1998). Comparable findings have been noted in other samples (Campbell, Lichty, Sturza, & Raja, 2006; Frayne et al., 1999).

Positive associations have been found between sexual violence against women and sexually transmitted infections (STIs), including gonorrhea, chlamydia, syphilis, herpes simplex virus, human papillomavirus, and human immunodeficiency virus (Kalichman, Sikkema, DiFonzo, Luke, & Austin, 2002; McFarlane, Malecha, Watson, et al., 2005; Reynolds, Peipert, & Collins, 2000; Zierler, Witbeck, & Mayer, 1996). Such infections may lead to other serious problems, including pelvic inflammatory disease, chronic pelvic pain, infertility, cervical cancer, and AIDS.

Although it is clear that high percentages of sexual assault survivors have STIs, it is difficult to estimate the rate of sexual assault–induced STIs

(Reynolds et al., 2000). Such estimation is complicated because women's risk of infection varies by their susceptibility, the type of sexual assault, and the organisms being transmitted. Moreover, women do not always seek health care immediately following the assault to allow for timely STI screening, nor do they always attend follow-up visits to allow for the detection of new STIs. One clinic-based study found that 43% of 204 female rape survivors seen within 72 hr of the incident had an STI acquired prior to the rape; approximately 20% of the women who were STI-negative at the initial exam had developed a rape-induced STI by the 2-week follow-up (Jenny et al., 1990).

Sexual violence may result in pregnancy. The National Women's Study estimated a national rape-related pregnancy rate of 5% per rape among females ages 12 to 45, with almost half of the pregnancy-related rapes perpetrated by the survivors' husbands or boyfriends (Holmes, Resnick, Kilpatrick, & Best, 1996). Rape-induced pregnancy may be prevalent among women frequently who were sexually assaulted by intimate partners, with one study finding that 20% of 100 intimate partner sexual assault survivors reported such pregnancies (McFarlane, Malecha, Watson, et al., 2005).

Although it is clear that pregnant women may experience sexual violence, little research has focused on how this violence affects gestation and pregnancy outcomes. One study that did examine this found that 2% of 5,734 sexual assault survivors seen at a hospital were pregnant during the violence; no spontaneous abortions or deliveries occurred during the 4 weeks post-assault, but many women delivered low birth weight infants (24%) and preterm infants (16%; Satin, Hemsell, Stone, Theriot, & Wendel, 1991). Another study of a convenience sample of 118 women pregnant during the past year found that 60% of the 30 who miscarried experienced intimate partner sexual violence during the past year, compared with 27% of the 88 who delivered infants (Morland, Leskin, Block, Campbell, & Friedman, 2008).

Sexual violence may affect women's sexuality and their desire for children. A national sample of 3,632 female veterans found that those sexually assaulted while in the military were less likely to be satisfied with their sex life and were less likely to desire children (Skinner et al., 2000). Similar results have been found in other research (Wingood & DiClemente, 1998).

Headaches

Headaches are common among female sexual violence survivors, in part due to the head injuries that often occur during assaults (Tjaden & Thoennes, 2000). A study of 167 treatment-seeking adult rape survivors found headaches to be the most common physical symptom, affecting 86% of women (Clum, Nishith, & Resick, 2001). Data from 5,284 women in the Epidemiologic Catchment Area study found that sexual assault survivors, especially young women and those assaulted during childhood, commonly reported headaches (Golding, 1999).

Gastrointestinal Problems

Studies from many settings have found associations between women's sexual violence experiences and gastrointestinal problems. A survey of 3,543 female outpatients of Veterans Administration health care centers showed that those sexually assaulted while in the military were more likely to have gastrointestinal problems (Frayne et al., 1999). A study of 239 adult female gastroenterology patients found that 41% had been raped, with 61% first raped at age 14 or older (Leserman et al., 1996). Many types of gastrointestinal symptoms (e.g., nausea, indigestion) also have been noted among rape survivors (Clum et al., 2001).

Sleep

Adult female sexual assault survivors often experience insomnia and nightmares (Clum et al., 2001; Frayne et al., 1999). They also may frequently have sleep-disordered breathing and sleep-related movement disorder symptoms (Krakow et al., 2000).

Functional Limitations and Disabilities

Sexual violence may so negatively affect women's health that it impairs their ability to conduct routine daily activities. A survey of a representative sample of 9,830 North Carolina women found that those who experienced sexual violence during adulthood were more likely to report functional impairment in the past month due to a physical or mental health problem (Martin et al., 2008). Similar findings have emanated from clinic-based studies, with one investigation of 237 adult female patients showing higher levels of disability in multiple functional areas (e.g., mobility, body care) among rape victims (Leserman et al., 1996). Vision and hearing problems have also been found to be elevated in sexual assault survivors (Frayne et al., 1999).

Variation in Physical Health Outcomes

Women often vary in terms of their physical health responses to sexual violence. Although many sexual assault survivors show significant improvement in physical health within a year (Kimerling & Calhoun, 1994), some women continue to experience poor physical health years after the event. Many of the same factors that have been related to women's psychological responses to sexual violence have been related to women's physical responses to sexual violence, including violence severity, the relationship of the perpetrator to the survivor, and social reactions from others (Campbell et al., 2006; Jones, Rossman, Wynn, Dunnuck, & Schwartz, 2003; Kimerling & Calhoun, 1994; Sugar et al., 2004).

Some research has examined how women's cognitive processing of violent events may mediate their physical health responses to sexual violence. For example, research with a media-recruited sample of 18- to 45-year-old women (40 who acknowledged being raped, 29 who did not acknowledge being raped even though they reported violent experiences that met the legal definition of rape, and 20 nonviolated women) found that both groups of rape survivors had more physical health complaints, with the greatest number among those who acknowledged the rape (Conoscenti & McNally, 2006). Other research also has found some support that cognitive processing may mediate physical responses to violence (Koss et al., 2002).

Research also has linked women's psychological responses to sexual violence with their physical responses to this violence. For instance, a study of 76 adult treatment-seeking female sexual assault survivors with chronic PTSD found that those with the most severe PTSD symptoms reported the most physical health symptoms (Zoellner, Goodwin, & Foa, 2000). Other variables that have been found to mediate associations between sexual victimization during adulthood and physical health include current levels of stress and experiential avoidance (being unwilling to experience negative emotions, thoughts, and memories, as well as engaging in behaviors that temporarily reduce these negative feelings; Palm & Follette, 2008).

Finally, some research has examined potential relations between women's demographic characteristics and their physical health following sexual assault. Patterns of sexual assault injuries (Jones et al., 2003; Sugar et al. 2004), rape-related pregnancy rates (Holmes et al., 1996), and headaches (Golding, 1999) have been found to differ by women's ages at the time of sexual violence. Other research has shown that sexual violence adversely affects many aspects of women's physical health, regardless of race/ethnicity, education, income, or marital/relationship status (Campbell et al., 2006; Frayne et al., 1999; Golding, 1999; Irwin et al., 1995; Leserman et al., 1996; Martin et al., 2008; Zoellner et al., 2000).

Behavioral Health

Many studies have found links between adult women's experiences of sexual violence and their engagement in high-risk health behaviors, all of which threaten women's health and some of which increase women's likelihood of revictimization. Although several types of high-risk behaviors have been studied in relation to sexual violence, this discussion examines the most commonly studied behaviors: alcohol and drug use, tobacco use, and unsafe sex behaviors.

Alcohol and Drugs

Many studies have found links between trauma and substance use and abuse (Stewart, 1996), including studies of women's experiences of sexual violence during adulthood. For instance, the National Violence Against Women Survey found prescription drug use elevated among women sexually assaulted during adulthood (Kaukinen & DeMaris, 2005). A mailed survey of a national sample of 3,632 women veterans found that those sexually assaulted while in the military were twice as likely to screen positive for alcohol abuse and to report that substance use interfered with readjustment to civilian life (Hankin et al., 1999; Skinner et al., 2000). A study of 540 undergraduate women found that marijuana use was more common among those sexually assaulted at age 14 or older (Gidycz, Orchowski, King, & Rich, 2008). In addition, study of a convenience sample of 1,104 women recruited from the streets and other public areas found that crack cocaine use was more common among those raped in the past year (Irwin et al., 1995).

Some studies have used a retrospective recall approach to examine whether women's substance use or abuse began before or after their experiences of sexual violence. One such study asked 100 intimate partner sexual assault survivors whether they increased substance use after the most recent assault; results showed that women repeatedly assaulted increased alcohol use but not drug use (McFarlane, Malecha, Gist, et al., 2005). Another recall study found that 28 traumatized crash survivors reported decreases in alcohol use after the event, whereas 29 traumatized sexual assault survivors reported increases in alcohol use after the event (Deliramich & Gray, 2008). A recall study of 75 female bodybuilders (10 raped at age 14 or older) found that 34% of nonvictims and 70% of rape victims used anabolic steroids, with the rape survivors reporting that they started steroid use postrape to enhance their defensive ability (Gruber & Pope, 1999).

Few prospective longitudinal investigations have examined the timing of women's sexual assault experiences during adulthood relative to their use of substances. The Welfare, Children, and Families project studied 2,402 low-income women over a 2-year period and found that sexual coercion experiences at the first assessment predicted increases in the women's frequency of intoxication at the follow-up assessment (Hill, Schroeder, Bradley, Kaplan, & Angel, 2009). In another longitudinal study (Testa & Livingston, 2000) of a media-recruited sample of 93 single women ages 20 to 35 years who were high risk (heavy drinkers who had more than one male sex partner in the past year), greater alcohol use at the initial assessment was predictive of sexual aggression at follow-up; however, sexual aggression at the initial assessment was not linked to alcohol use at follow-up. The National Women's Study analyzed the timing of substance use (including alcohol and drugs) and violent assault (including rape and/or physical violence) among 3,006 women (Kilpatrick, Acierno, Resnick, Saunders, & Best, 1997). This analysis is different from the others reported in this chapter in that it did not separately examine the impact of sexual violence disentangled from physical violence; however, it is included because there are few methodologically rigorous studies of the timing of violence and substance use among women. This study found that violent assault led to women's increased use of both alcohol and drugs. Drug use, but not alcohol use, increased women's probability of violent assault. Thus, violence enhanced alcohol and drug use among women, but only among drug users did this turn into a cycle in which more drug use led to more violence, which in turn led to more drug use.

Tobacco Use

Tobacco use has been found to be elevated among female sexual violence survivors. A survey of 281 women randomly selected from North Carolina registered voters found a positive correlation between frequency of forced sex by male partners in the past year and women's levels of cigarette use (Smith, Thornton, DeVellis, Earp, & Coker, 2002). Similar findings have been noted in other samples (Gidycz et al., 2008; McFarlane, Malecha, Gist, et al., 2005).

Unsafe Sex Behaviors

Growing research documents positive associations between women's experiences of sexual violence and their engagement in unsafe sex practices, including having multiple sex partners, not negotiating condom use with sex partners, having sex with men not using condoms, trading sex for money/drugs, and having sex with an HIV-infected partner. For example, a study of 540 undergraduate women found that those sexually assaulted at age 14 or older were more likely to have multiple sex partners (Gidycz et al., 2008). Research with a convenience sample of 165 African American women recruited from a low-income neighborhood found that those raped after age 15 were less likely to negotiate condom use with sex partners and were more likely to frequently engage in sex with men not using condoms (Wingood & DiClemente, 1998). A study of 1,104 women recruited from the streets and public areas found that those raped in the past year were more likely to have traded sex for money/drugs and to have had sex with HIV-infected men during the past year (Irwin et al., 1995).

Some research has investigated the timing of women's experiences of sexual violence and their risky sex behaviors. A cross-sectional investigation of a media-recruited convenience sample of 102 female rape survivors (assaulted at age 18 or older) asked women how their sexual behaviors had changed after the rape and found that 48% became less risky, 18% became somewhat more risky, and 34% became much more risky (Campbell, Sefl, & Ahrens, 2004).

Variation in Behavioral Health Outcomes

Some research has examined variables potentially related to women's behavioral responses to sexual violence. These studies have found the highest levels of risky behaviors among survivors with repeated victimizations, who blame themselves for the violence and who experienced negative social reactions from others when they disclosed information about the assault (Ullman, Filipas, Townsend & Starzynski, 2005). In addition, researchers have posited that the psychological trauma of sexual violence, often assessed by PTSD symptoms, contributes to women's increased engagement in risky health behaviors. Although there has been little study of whether women's behavioral responses to sexual violence vary by their demographic characteristics, one study found that females who were assaulted at younger ages were more likely to exhibit riskier sex behaviors (Campbell et al., 2004), and another study found that minority women were more likely than Caucasian women to use substances after being sexually assaulted (Kaukinen, & DeMaris, 2005).

Economic Cost

Each of the few investigations of the financial costs of sexual violence takes into account tangible costs (e.g., medical care). For instance, a study using the National Violence Against Women Survey, the Medical Expenditure Panel Survey, and other sources estimated that each of the 322,230 intimate partner rapes of U.S. females in 1995 cost $992, including costs of medical/mental health care, ambulance, and lost productivity (Max, Rice, Finkelstein, Bardwell, & Leadbetter, 2004). This translates to a total annual cost of $319.7 million.

Some studies have estimated the cost of sexual violence taking into consideration both tangible and intangible costs (e.g., survivors' quality of life). For example, using data from the National Women's Health Study, the National Crime Victimization Survey, and other sources, one study estimated that each of the 1,467,000 rapes/sexual assaults of men and women in 1993 costs $87,000, with approximately $5,000 being due to tangible costs and approximately $82,000 being due to intangible costs (T. R. Miller, Cohen, &

Wiersema, 1996). This translates to a total U.S. cost of $127 billion for the rape/sexual assault of adult women and men, the highest annual victim cost of all the crimes studied. Unlike the other studies in this chapter, this study grouped together male and female survivors for their analysis. However, only 17% of the survivors were male; thus, most of this cost was associated with the sexual assault of women.

A Michigan investigation estimated both tangible and intangible costs of two types of sexual offenses against adult women: rape/sexual assault and sexual offense homicide (Post, Mezey, Maxwell, & Wibert, 2002). Using data from the 1996 Violence Against Michigan Women Survey, the U.S. Census Bureau, the Federal Bureau of Investigation Supplementary Homicide Files, and estimates of costs from study by T. R. Miller et al. (1996), this study estimated the 1996 cost of each of the 61,581 incidents of Michigan women's rape/sexual assault to be $108,447 (a cost higher than T. R. Miller et al.'s estimate due to adjustments for the study year and the higher costs in Michigan). They estimated the cost of each of the 5 incidents of women's sex-offense homicide to be $3,664,750. This translates to an annual cost of $6.6 billion for sexual violence against women in Michigan ($6,678,275,000 for rape/sexual assault and $18,324,000 for sexual offense homicide).

HOW DO WE KNOW IT?

As can be seen from these highlighted studies, many methods have been used to examine the health and economic consequences of sexual violence against women. We now describe some of the more commonly used methods, noting both their strengths and limitations.

Definition and Assessment of Sexual Violence and Health

Although there are many forms of sexual violence, most research examines sexual assault and rape. Thus, little is known about how other forms of sexual violence affect women's health.

A few studies in this area assess sexual violence using data from multiple sources (e.g., survivor reports plus forensic exams); however, most studies assess sexual violence based solely on survivors' self-reported data. Although self-reports often provide the best information researchers can gather concerning these offenses, exclusive reliance on self-reports may result in underdetection of sexual violence because some women will not disclose such information because of embarrassment, shame, or concern about what will happen to themselves or their families.

Although some studies use a single question to ask about sexual violence, most studies use psychometrically sound, standardized instruments comprising multiple questions. Moreover, most assessments do not use emotionally loaded terms such as *rape* that may be defined very differently by different people but instead ask about specific types of behaviors. Some assessments ask women to recall violence experiences throughout their lifetimes. Given that recall is imperfect, it may bias the study findings. Moreover, scoring procedures used by retrospective recall instruments vary, with different age cut-points used to classify sexual violence during "childhood" versus "adulthood," making comparisons across studies difficult.

Finally, not all studies gather information on contextual factors of the violence, such as violence severity, social relationship of the survivor and perpetrator, location at which the incident occurred, and so on. Ignoring these potentially important aspects of sexual violence misses a window of opportunity in which we could learn more about these acts, information that could be helpful to those who develop violence prevention and intervention strategies.

Many of the concerns regarding instruments used to assess sexual violence also pertain to instruments used to assess psychological, physical, and behavioral health. There is great reliance on women's self-reports to assess their health status, although some investigations do incorporate clinical assessments. Some studies use one question to ask about health, but many use psychometrically sound, multiple-item health assessments. Some assessments ask women to recall both their previous and current health status, thus placing the studies at risk of recall bias.

Study Designs

Although all the studies discussed here are interested in the question of how women's experiences of sexual violence affect their health, the vast majority of studies are cross-sectional in nature rather than prospective longitudinal investigations that can truly determine the timing of sexual violence in relation to health outcomes. Some cross-sectional studies have gathered information on the timing of violence and health by asking women to recall when the violence first occurred and when the health symptoms first occurred. Such retrospective approaches supply important information; however, reliance on memories limits these investigations. Even when prospective longitudinal study designs are used, they are often of a short duration (several months or a year), leaving one unsure of how sexual violence affects women's health throughout their lifetimes. Moreover, longitudinal studies often suffer from loss to follow-up. Because those lost often have poorer outcomes, ignoring such information will lead to biased estimates of the true extent of women's health problems associated with sexual violence.

Samples

A few investigations of sexual violence and women's health have studied nationally representative samples of women, but more often research has studied convenience samples recruited through health clinics, sexual violence services, or the media. Such recruitment methods limit the generalizability of the research findings. Another generalizability concern is that many studies have a relatively low response rate. Thus, we are unsure as to whether study participants are representative of all women.

Some studies include comparison groups of women who have not experienced sexual violence; however, many studies focus exclusively on violence survivors. With no comparison group, we are often unsure whether the health outcomes are truly attributable to sexual violence.

Finally, many investigations have fairly small sample sizes, limiting their statistical power to detect true effects. Even when studies involve large samples, the statistical power can be low if there are few participants in the categories of interest (sexual violence survivors).

Methods Used in Studies of the Economic Cost of Violence

All of the economic investigations reviewed here documented some tangible costs of sexual violence (e.g., health care costs) but did not consider other tangible costs (e.g., judicial system costs). Thus, these studies underestimate the true tangible costs of sexual violence. It is extremely difficult (if not impossible) to put a financial price tag on women's suffering. However, failure to include such intangible costs, as in one of the investigations reviewed here (Max et al., 2004), results in an underestimate of the true cost of such violence.

None of the economic studies included violence-related costs that unfold over time. Although many survivors show substantial recovery within a year's time, health difficulties may resurface years later if women's memories of violence are triggered by new experiences.

WHERE ARE THE GAPS AND WEAKNESSES IN EXISTING KNOWLEDGE?

Research has greatly enhanced our understanding of the health and economic consequences of sexual violence against women. Yet, many questions remain unanswered. There is a dearth of information concerning the prevalence of violent death among sexually assaulted women, including homicide and suicide. This information is important to inform the development of violence prevention and intervention programs and policies.

Although it is known that many female adult sexual violence survivors experience psychological, physical, and/or behavioral health problems, how these problems co-occur is less clear. For example, is a subset of survivors afflicted with multiple problems?

We have limited understanding of how chronic violence victimization affects women's physiological responses to a new incident of sexual violence, information that might help to explain why women's histories of violence are statistically associated with differential psychological, physical, and behavioral health outcomes in response to new violence incidents. Moreover, there is no information on the potential role played by gene–environment interactions, even though one study suggests that such interactions may underlie some of the differential psychological outcomes seen among adults who were severely abused as children (Binder et al., 2008).

Little is known about how cognitive processes mediate women's psychological, physical, and behavioral responses to sexual violence. Learning more about this could help inform development of interventions to mitigate the negative health consequences of such violence. Although there is a wealth of research demonstrating positive associations between women's experiences of sexual violence and their psychological, physical, and behavioral health, few studies clearly document the timing of sexual violence in relation to health outcomes.

There has been relatively little study of women's demographic characteristics (e.g., race/ethnicity, age) and other characteristics (e.g., sexual orientation, disability status) related to health outcomes of sexual violence. Although most studies describe their samples using demographic data, these data are less frequently included in statistical analyses to determine whether they are related to women's responses to sexual violence.

Research has examined the impact of physical violence during pregnancy on women's health and birth outcomes (these studies are not reviewed here because they focused on physical rather than sexual violence). However, information is scant regarding how sexual violence during pregnancy may impact women's health and pregnancy outcomes.

We do not have a precise estimate of the true financial cost of sexual violence against women. The little research that has been done in this area is compelling. However, the studies have been somewhat restricted, not considering some of the many costs related to violence.

WHAT ARE THE NEXT STEPS?

Given the gaps in our knowledge, further study is encouraged in several areas. Research is needed to enhance our understanding of the following: sexual assault–related homicides and suicides of women; physiological and cognitive factors related to women's psychological, physical, and behavioral responses to sexual violence; the timing of women's sexual violence experiences in relation to their psychological, physical, and behavioral health; how women's demographic and other characteristics are related to their health and behavioral responses to sexual violence; the impact of sexual violence during pregnancy; and the economic costs of sexual violence.

To address these knowledge gaps, we encourage national health surveillance systems to include (or refine) their documentation of sexual violence victimization so as to allow examination of the impact of sexual violence on women's health. For example, sexual violence information could be better integrated into the Violent Death Reporting System, the Behavioral Risk Factor Surveillance System, and the Pregnancy Risk Assessment and Monitoring System.

Because we have learned much from nationally representative surveys of violence against women, we encourage funders to invest in new investigations of similar scope (e.g., the National Intimate Partner and Sexual Violence Survey currently under way). Moreover, oversampling high-risk groups and groups about whom we know little (e.g., women with disabilities) would be helpful, as would be incorporating a longitudinal component.

We encourage researchers to carefully consider how they define and assess sexual violence. Ideally, studies should gather information concerning a wide range of different types of this violence from multiple sources of information using standardized, psychometrically sound, multiple-question assessments that capture information on the context of the violence. To clearly document the timing of women's sexual violence experiences in relation to their health outcomes, researchers are urged to use prospective, longitudinal investigations rather than relying on cross-sectional approaches with retrospective recall.

Researchers are encouraged to use rigorous scientific methods to select and recruit large, representative study samples. The use of sampling techniques, coupled with effective strategies to enhance response rates, would greatly improve the generalizability of study findings. Large samples would allow researchers to use sophisticated statistical analyses to assess a variety of potentially confounding, modifying, and mediating factors. Moreover, researchers are urged to include a nonviolated comparison group in their studies to allow determination of whether the observed effects can truly be attributed to sexual violence victimization. Finally, because financial resources are required to conduct groundbreaking research on sexual violence against women, we encourage the agencies that fund such work to consider making the investigation of sexual violence against women a top priority.

In closing, we wish to emphasize that the recent growth in understanding of the health and economic consequences of sexual violence against women is impressive, and we thank the many researchers in this field for their diligence and devotion to this important work.

REFERENCES

Binder, E. B., Bradley, R. G., Liu, W., Epstein, M. P., Deveau, T. C., Mercer, K. B., . . . Ressler, K. J. (2008). Association of FKBP5 polymorphisms and childhood abuse with risk of posttraumatic stress disorder symptoms in adults. *JAMA, 299,* 1291–1305. doi:10.1001/jama.299.11.1291

Bonomi, A. E., Anderson, M. L., Rivara, F. P., & Thompson, R. S. (2007). Health outcomes in women with physical and sexual intimate partner violence exposure. *Journal of Women's Health, 16,* 987–997. doi:10.1089/jwh.2006.0239

Borja, S. E., Callahan, J. L., & Long, P. J. (2006). Positive and negative adjustment and social support of sexual assault survivors. *Journal of Traumatic Stress, 19,* 905–914. doi:10.1002/jts.20169

Breitenbecher, K. H. (2006). The relationships among self-blame, psychological distress, and sexual victimization. *Journal of Interpersonal Violence, 21,* 597–611. doi:10.1177/0886260506286842

Campbell, R., Lichty, L. F., Sturza, M., & Raja, S. (2006). Gynecological health impact of sexual assault. *Research in Nursing & Health, 29,* 399–413. doi:10.1002/nur.20155

Campbell, R., Sefl, T., & Ahrens, C. E. (2004). The impact of rape on women's sexual health risk behaviors. *Health Psychology, 23,* 67–74. doi:10.1037/0278-6133.23.1.67

Casey, E. A., & Nurius, P. S. (2005). Trauma exposure and sexual revictimization risk: Comparisons across single, multiple incident, and multiple perpetrator victimizations. *Violence Against Women, 11,* 505–530. doi:10.1177/1077801204274339

Clum, G. A., Nishith, P., & Resick, P. A. (2001). Trauma-related sleep disturbance and self-reported physical health symptoms in treatment-seeking female rape victims. *Journal of Nervous and Mental Disease, 189,* 618–622. doi:10.1097/00005053-200109000-00008

Coker, A. L., Smith, P. H., Thompson, M. P., McKeown, R. E., Bethea, L., & Davis, K. E. (2002). Social support protects against negative effects of partner violence on mental health. *Journal of Women's Health & Gender-Based Medicine, 11,* 465–476. doi:10.1089/15246090260137644

Conoscenti, L. M., & McNally, R. J. (2006). Health complaints in acknowledged and unacknowledged rape victims. *Journal of Anxiety Disorders, 20,* 372–379. doi:10.1016/j.janxdis.2005.03.001

Culbertson, K. A., & Dehle, C. D. (2001). Impact of sexual assault as a function of perpetrator type. *Journal of Interpersonal Violence, 16,* 992–1007. doi:10.1177/088626001016010002

Dancu, C. V., Riggs, D. S., Hearst-Ikeda, D., Shoyer, B. G., & Foa, E. B. (1996). Dissociative experiences and posttraumatic stress disorder among female victims of criminal assault and rape. *Journal of Traumatic Stress, 9*, 253–267. doi:10.1002/jts.2490090208

Deliramich, A. N., & Gray, M. J. (2008). Changes in women's sexual behavior following sexual assault. *Behavior Modification, 32*, 611–621. doi:10.1177/0145445508314642

Frayne, S. M., Skinner, K. M., Sullivan, L. M., Tripp, T. J., Hankin, C. S., Kressin, N. R., & Miller, D. R. (1999). Medical profile of women Veterans Administration outpatients who report a history of sexual assault occurring while in the military. *Journal of Women's Health & Gender-Based Medicine, 8*, 835–845. doi:10.1089/152460999319156

Frazier, P. A. (2003). Perceived control and distress following sexual assault: A longitudinal test of a new model. *Journal of Personality and Social Psychology, 84*, 1257–1269. doi:10.1037/0022-3514.84.6.1257

Gidycz, C. A., Orchowski, L. M., King, C. R., & Rich, C. L. (2008). Sexual victimization and health-risk behaviors. *Journal of Interpersonal Violence, 23*, 744–763. doi:10.1177/0886260507313944

Golding, J. M. (1999). Sexual assault history and headache: Five general population studies. *Journal of Nervous and Mental Disease, 187*, 624–629. doi:10.1097/00005053-199910000-00006

Golding, J. M., Wilsnack, S. C., & Learman, L. A. (1998). Prevalence of sexual assault history among women with common gynecologic symptoms. *American Journal of Obstetrics and Gynecology, 179*, 1013–1019. doi:10.1016/S0002-9378(98)70208-X

Gruber, A. J., & Pope, H. G., Jr. (1999). Compulsive weight lifting and anabolic drug abuse among women rape victims. *Comprehensive Psychiatry, 40*, 273–277. doi:10.1016/S0010-440X(99)90127-X

Hankin, C. S., Skinner, K. M., Sullivan, L. M., Miller, D. R., Frayne, S., & Tripp, T. J. (1999). Prevalence of depressive and alcohol abuse symptoms among women VA outpatients who report experiencing sexual assault while in the military. *Journal of Traumatic Stress, 12*, 601–612. doi:10.1023/A:1024760900213

Hill, T. D., Schroeder, R. D., Bradley, C., Kaplan, L. M., & Angel, R. J. (2009). The long-term health consequences of relationship violence in adulthood: An examination of low-income women from Boston, Chicago, and San Antonio. *American Journal of Public Health, 99*, 1645–1650. doi:10.2105/AJPH.2008.151498

Holmes, M. M., Resnick, H. S., Kilpatrick, D. G., & Best, C. L. (1996). Rape-related pregnancy: Estimates and descriptive characteristics from a national sample of women. *American Journal of Obstetrics and Gynecology, 175*, 320–325. doi:10.1016/S0002-9378(96)70141-2

Irwin, K. L., Edlin, B. R., Wong, L., Faruque, S., McCoy, H. V., Word, C., . . . Holmberg, S. D. (1995). Urban rape survivors: Characteristics and prevalence of human immunodeficiency virus and other sexually transmitted infections. *Obstetrics and Gynecology, 85*, 330–336. doi:10.1016/0029-7844(94)00425-D

Jenny, C., Hooton, T. M., Bowers, A., Copass, M. K., Krieger, J. N., Hillier, S. L., . . . Holmes, K. K. (1990). Sexually transmitted diseases in victims of rape. *New England Journal of Medicine, 322,* 713–716.

Jones, J. S., Rossman, L., Wynn, B. N., Dunnuck, C., & Schwartz, N. (2003). Comparative analysis of adult versus adolescent sexual assault: Epidemiology and patterns of anogenital injury. *Academic Emergency Medicine, 10,* 872–877. doi:10.1111/j.1553-2712.2003.tb00631.x

Kalichman, S. C., Sikkema, K. J., DiFonzo, K., Luke, W., & Austin, J. (2002). Emotional adjustment in survivors of sexual assault living with HIV-AIDS. *Journal of Traumatic Stress, 15,* 289–296. doi:10.1023/A:1016247727498

Kang, H., Dalager, N., Mahan, C., & Ishii, E. (2005). The role of sexual assault on the risk of PTSD among Gulf War veterans. *Annals of Epidemiology, 15,* 191–195. doi:10.1016/j.annepidem.2004.05.009

Kaukinen, C., & DeMaris, A. (2005). Age at first sexual assault and current substance use and depression. *Journal of Interpersonal Violence, 20,* 1244–1270. doi:10.1177/0886260505277732

Kilpatrick, D. G., Acierno, R., Resnick, H. S., Saunders, B. E., & Best, C. L. (1997). A 2-year longitudinal analysis of the relationship between violent assault and substance use in women. *Journal of Consulting and Clinical Psychology, 65,* 834–847. doi:10.1037/0022-006X.65.5.834

Kilpatrick, D. G., Edmunds, C. N., & Seymour, A. K. (1992). *Rape in America: A report to the nation.* Arlington, VA: National Victim Center & Medical University of South Carolina.

Kimerling, R., & Calhoun, K. S. (1994). Somatic symptoms, social support, and treatment seeking among sexual assault victims. *Journal of Consulting and Clinical Psychology, 62,* 333–340. doi:10.1037/0022-006X.62.2.333

Koss, M. P., Figueredo, A. J., & Prince, R. J. (2002). Cognitive mediation of rape's mental, physical and social health impact: Tests of four models in cross-sectional data. *Journal of Consulting and Clinical Psychology, 70,* 926–941. doi:10.1037/0022-006X.70.4.926

Krakow, B., Germain, A., Tandberg, D., Koss, M., Schrader, R., Hollifield, M., . . . Edmond, T. (2000). Sleep breathing and sleep movement disorders masquerading as insomnia in sexual-assault survivors. *Comprehensive Psychiatry, 41,* 49–56. doi:10.1016/S0010-440X(00)90131-7

Leserman, J., Drossman, D. A., Li, Z., Toomey, T. C., Nachman, G., & Glogau, L. (1996). Sexual and physical abuse history in gastroenterology practice: How types of abuse impact health status. *Psychosomatic Medicine, 58,* 4–15.

Martin, S. L., Rentz, E. D., Chan, R. L., Givens, J., Sanford, C. P., Kupper, L. L., . . . Macy, R. J. (2008). Physical and sexual violence among North Carolina women: Associations with physical health, mental health, and functional impairment. *Women's Health Issues, 18,* 130–140. doi:10.1016/j.whi.2007.12.008

Max, W., Rice, D. P., Finkelstein, E., Bardwell, R. A., & Leadbetter, M. S. (2004). The economic toll of intimate partner violence against women in the United States. *Violence and Victims, 19*, 259–272. doi:10.1891/vivi.19.3.259.65767

McFarlane, J., Malecha, A., Gist, J., Watson, K., Batten, E., Hall, I., & Smith, S. (2005). Intimate partner assault against women and associated victim substance use, suicidality and risk factors for femicide. *Issues in Mental Health Nursing, 26*, 953–967. doi:10.1080/01612840500248262

McFarlane, J., Malecha, A., Watson, K., Gist, J., Batten, E., Hall, I., & Smith, S. (2005). Intimate partner sexual assault against women: Frequency, health consequences, and treatment outcomes. *Obstetrics and Gynecology, 105*, 99–108.

Miller, M. W., & Resnick, P. A. (2007). Internalizing and externalizing subtypes in female sexual assault survivors: Implications for the understanding of complex PTSD. *Behavior Therapy, 38*, 58–71. doi:10.1016/j.beth.2006.04.003

Miller, T. R., Cohen, M. A., & Wiersema, B. (1996). *Victim costs and consequences: A new look*. Washington, DC: U.S. Department of Justice, National Institute of Justice.

Morland, L. A., Leskin, G. A., Block, C. R., Campbell, J. C., & Friedman, M. J. (2008). Intimate partner violence and miscarriage: Examination of the role of physical and psychological abuse and posttraumatic stress disorder. *Journal of Interpersonal Violence, 23*, 652–669. doi:10.1177/0886260507313533

Nishith, P., Mechanic, M. B., & Resick, P. A. (2000). Prior interpersonal trauma: The contribution to current PTSD symptoms in female rape victims. *Journal of Abnormal Psychology, 109*, 20–25. doi:10.1037/0021-843X.109.1.20

Palm, K. M., & Follette, V. M. (2008). Sexual victimization and physical health: An examination of explanatory mechanisms. *Journal of Child Sexual Abuse, 17*, 117–132. doi:10.1080/10538710801916309

Post, L. A., Mezey, N. J., Maxwell, C., & Wibert, W. N. (2002). The rape tax: Tangible and intangible costs of sexual violence. *Journal of Interpersonal Violence, 17*, 773–782. doi:10.1177/0886260502017007005

Resnick, H. S., Yehuda, R., & Acierno, R. (1997). Acute post-rape plasma cortisol, alcohol use, and PTSD symptom profile among recent rape victims. *Annals of the New York Academy of Sciences, 821*, 433–436. doi:10.1111/j.1749-6632.1997.tb48298.x

Resnick, H. S., Yehuda, R., Pitman, R. K., & Foy, D. W. (1995). Effect of previous trauma on acute plasma cortisol level following rape. *American Journal of Psychiatry, 152*, 1675–1677.

Reynolds, M. W., Peipert, J. F., & Collins, B. (2000). Epidemiologic issues of sexually transmitted diseases in sexual assault victims. *Obstetrical & Gynecological Survey, 55*, 51–57. doi:10.1097/00006254-200001000-00023

Rothbaum, B. O., Foa, E. B., Riggs, D., Murdock, T., & Walsh, W. (1992). A prospective examination of post-traumatic stress disorder in rape victims. *Journal of Traumatic Stress, 5*, 455–475. doi:10.1002/jts.2490050309

Satin, A. J., Hemsell, D. L., Stone, I. C., Jr., Theriot, S., & Wendel, G. D., Jr. (1991). Sexual assault in pregnancy. *Obstetrics and Gynecology, 77,* 710–714.

Skinner, K. M., Kressin, N., Frayne, S., Tripp, T. J., Hankin, C. S., Miller, D. R., & Sullivan, L. M. (2000). The prevalence of military sexual assault among female veterans' administration outpatients. *Journal of Interpersonal Violence, 15,* 291–310. doi:10.1177/088626000015003005

Smith, P. H., Thornton, G. E., DeVellis, R., Earp, J., & Coker, A. L. (2002). A population-based study of the prevalence and distinctiveness of battering, physical assault, and sexual assault in intimate relationships. *Violence Against Women, 8,* 1208–1232. doi:10.1177/107780102320562691

Stewart, S. H. (1996). Alcohol abuse in individuals exposed to trauma: A critical review. *Psychological Bulletin, 120,* 83–112. doi:10.1037/0033-2909.120.1.83

Sugar, N. F., Fine, D. N., & Eckert, L. O. (2004). Physical injury after sexual assault: Findings of a large case series. *American Journal of Obstetrics and Gynecology, 190,* 71–76. doi:10.1016/S0002-9378(03)00912-8

Testa, M., & Livingston, J. A. (2000). Alcohol and sexual aggression: Reciprocal relationships over time in a sample of high-risk women. *Journal of Interpersonal Violence, 15,* 413–427. doi:10.1177/088626000015004005

Tjaden, P. G., & Thoennes, N. (2000). *Extent, nature, and consequences of intimate partner violence: Findings from the National Violence Against Women Survey* (Publication NCJ 181867). Washington, DC: U.S. Department of Justice, Office of Justice Programs.

Ullman, S. E. (1996). Social reactions, coping strategies, and self-blame attributions in adjustment to sexual assault. *Psychology of Women Quarterly, 20,* 505–526. doi:10.1111/j.1471-6402.1996.tb00319.x

Ullman, S. E., & Brecklin, L. R. (2002). Sexual assault history and suicidal behavior in a national sample of women. *Suicide & Life-Threatening Behavior, 32,* 117–130. doi:10.1521/suli.32.2.117.24398

Ullman, S. E., & Filipas, H. H. (2001). Predictors of PTSD symptom severity and social reactions in sexual assault victims. *Journal of Traumatic Stress, 14,* 369–389. doi:10.1023/A:1011125220522

Ullman, S. E., Filipas, H. H., Townsend, S. M., & Starzynski, L. L. (2005). Trauma exposure, posttraumatic stress disorder and problem drinking in sexual assault survivors. *Journal of Studies on Alcohol, 66,* 610–619.

Ullman, S. E., Filipas, H. H., Townsend, S. M., & Starzynski, L. L. (2006). The role of victim–offender relationship in women's sexual assault experiences. *Journal of Interpersonal Violence, 21,* 798–819. doi:10.1177/0886260506288590

Ullman, S. E., Filipas, H. H., Townsend, S. M., & Starzynski, L. L. (2007). Psychosocial correlates of PTSD symptom severity in sexual assault survivors. *Journal of Traumatic Stress, 20,* 821–831. doi:10.1002/jts.20290

Valentiner, D. P., Foa, E. B., Riggs, D. S., & Gershuny, B. S. (1996). Coping strategies and posttraumatic stress disorder in female victims of sexual and nonsexual assault. *Journal of Abnormal Psychology, 105,* 455–458. doi:10.1037/0021-843X.105.3.455

Weaver, T. L., Allen, J. A., Hopper, E., Maglione, M. L., McLaughlin, D., McCullough, M. A., . . . Brewer, T. (2007). Mediators of suicidal ideation within a sheltered sample of raped and battered women. *Health Care for Women International, 28,* 478–489. doi:10.1080/07399330701226453

Wingood, G. M., & DiClemente, R. J. (1998). Rape among African American women: Sexual, psychological and social correlates predisposing survivors to risk of STD/HIV. *Journal of Women's Health, 7,* 77–84. doi:10.1089/jwh.1998.7.77

Zierler, S., Witbeck, B., & Mayer, K. (1996). Sexual violence against women living with or at risk for HIV infection. *American Journal of Preventive Medicine, 12,* 304–310.

Zoellner, L. A., Goodwin, M. L., & Foa, E. B. (2000). PTSD severity and health perceptions in female victims of sexual assault. *Journal of Traumatic Stress, 13,* 635–649. doi:10.1023/A:1007810200460

III

DOMESTIC VIOLENCE

9

PREVALENCE OF DOMESTIC VIOLENCE

JULIA L. PERILLA, CAROLINE LIPPY, ALVINA ROSALES,
AND JOSEPHINE V. SERRATA

The World Health Organization (WHO; 2002) referred to violence as a "universal scourge that tears at the fabric of communities" (p. 1). Violence against women by intimate partners—often called *domestic violence* (DV), *intimate partner violence*, or *wife battering*—accounts for a major portion of the violence that occurs worldwide. The definition of DV itself has been the focus of debate and scholarship. The American Psychological Association (1996) defines *domestic violence* as the range of physical, sexual, and emotional maltreatment by one family member against another. The Centers for Disease Control and Prevention (CDC) uses the term *intimate partner violence* to refer to physical, sexual, or psychological harm by a current or former partner or spouse and includes both heterosexual and same-sex couples, whether or not they engage in sexual intimacy, and defines *battering* as repeated abuse (Saltzman, Fanslow, McMahon, & Shelley, 1999).

In this chapter, we use the term *domestic violence* to refer to the violence (physical, verbal, sexual, or stalking) that women—in relationship with a man or a woman—experience from their intimate partners.[1] We begin with

---

[1]Despite its high prevalence, teen dating violence is not addressed in this chapter. This issue warrants a separate discussion because it differs in many important ways from the DV featured in adult relationships.

an overview of what is known about DV both worldwide and in the United States and how available statistics were obtained. We briefly discuss current controversies about prevalence rates, including how the theoretical approach of researchers affects the research process and outcome, as well as the limited information available about violence in marginalized communities. We also provide a critical analysis of methods, samples, and limitations of the literature we cite, and we end the chapter with a discussion of gaps in current literature and recommendations for future directions in the field.

WHAT WE KNOW

The World Report on Violence and Health (WHO, 2002) indicates that DV happens in all countries, cultures, and social classes. However, women in relationship with men who have low levels of education and low income, and who engaged in aggressive or delinquent behavior as adolescents, are at greater risk of experiencing DV at some point in their lives. Based on 48 large surveys from around the world, the WHO (2002) reported that 10% to 69% of women indicated that they had been physically assaulted by their partners at some point in their lives. Other researchers report findings from 50 studies throughout the world in which 10% to 52% of women reported physical violence and 10% to 30% reported sexual violence from their intimate partner during their lives (Heise & García-Moreno, 2002). The WHO (2005) Multi-Country Study on Women's Health and Domestic Violence Against Women, which used standardized population-based surveys with 24,097 women ages 15 to 49 years in 15 sites in 10 countries, found prevalence rates of physical or sexual violence or both of 15% to 71% lifetime and 4% to 54% in the previous year (García-Moreno, Jansen, Ellsberg, Heise & Watts, 2006). Clearly, DV affects women throughout the world. As we discuss in the following subsection, the United States is no exception.

United States

Table 9.1 provides findings from major national surveys on DV conducted in the United States. As can be seen, rates of DV vary mostly among studies that use different questions, samples, and definitions of DV. We address these critical methodological issues in the "How Do We Know It?" section of this chapter.

Physical Violence

National surveys on DV prevalence have focused almost exclusively on physical violence. Using the Conflict Tactics Scale (CTS; Straus, 1979), three

Survey name, year	Author(s) (date)	Type of abuse	Instrument method	Sample	Findings
National Family Violence Survey, 1975	Straus (1979)	PhV VrA	CTS in person	2,143 households; 1,071 women	Prior year PhV: 12.1%
National Family Violence Survey, 1985	Straus and Gelles (1990)	PhV VrA	CTS via telephone	3,520 households; 1,909 women Oversampled African Americans and Latinos	Prior year PhV: 11.3% VrA: 75%
National Alcohol and Family Violence Survey, 1992	Kaufman Kantor, Jasinski, and Aldarondo (1994); Aldarondo, Kaufman Kantor, and Jasinski (2002)	PhV VrA	CTS in person	1,192 households; 653 women Oversampled Latinos	Prior year PhV: 13.2% VrA: Not reported
National Crime Victimization Survey, 1992–1993	Bachman and Saltzman (1995)	PhV SxA	Domestic violence questions in survey in person	Approx. 100,000 women	Prior year PhV: 29% SxA: 26%
National Violence Against Women Survey, 1995–1996	Tjaden and Thoennes (2000)	PhV SxA Stkg	CTS via telephone	8,000 women	Lifetime PhV: 20.4% SxA: 4.5% Stkg: 4.1%

(continues)

TABLE 9.1
Major Population-Based Surveys in the United States on Domestic Violence Against Women *(Continued)*

Survey name, year	Author(s) (date)	Type of abuse	Instrument method	Sample	Findings
Women's Experience With Violence national study, 1997	Moracco, Runyan, Bowling, and Earp (2007)	PhV SxA Stkg	Questions about 6 types of violence via telephone	1,800 women	Lifetime PhV: 23.4% SxA: 14.3 StkgF: 42.7% StkgC: 25.3%
Commonwealth Fund Survey of Women's Health, 1998	Plichta and Falik (2001)	PhV SxA	CTS via telephone	2,850 women Oversampled African Americans, Asians, Latinas	Lifetime PhV: 31% SxA: Not reported
Centers for Disease Control and Prevention's Behavioral Risk Factor Surveillance System, 2006	Green, Tsai, and Floyd (2008)	PhV SxA	8 questions in survey via telephone	7,432 women	Lifetime PhV: 28.5% SxA: Not reported

Note. PhV = physical violence; VrA = verbal abuse; CTS = Conflict Tactics Scale; SxA = sexual abuse; Stkg = stalking; StkgF = followed; Stkg C = repeatedly contacted.

national studies at the University of New Hampshire (UNH) National Research Laboratory found the lowest rates of physical violence against women by their male partners during the previous year: the 1975 National Family Violence Survey (Straus, Gelles, & Steinmetz, 1980), the 1985 National Family Violence Survey (Straus & Gelles, 1986), and the 1992 National Alcohol and Family Violence Survey (Kaufman Kantor, Jasinski, & Aldarondo, 1994; see Table 9.1). Completion rates for each of these surveys (in chronological order) were 65%, 84%, and 75.4%. As shown in Table 9.1, all three found remarkably similar rates of DV against women (11.3%–13.2%).[2]

Verbal Abuse

As mentioned previously, early national surveys focused their exploration of DV on physical violence, although Straus and his colleagues (Kaufman Kantor et al., 1994; Straus & Gelles, 1986) collected verbal abuse data with the original version of the CTS. However, a review of the literature provides little information on the prevalence of verbal abuse. In one of the few articles available, using data from the 1985 National Family Violence Survey, Straus and Sweet (1992) reported a high (74%) incidence rate of male-to-female verbal abuse. The dearth of scientific literature on the topic is surprising, given the connection that is known to exist between verbal abuse and physical violence (Stets, 1990).

Sexual Abuse

Prior to the National Crime Victimization Survey (NCVS) in 1996, questions about sexual abuse by an intimate partner were not included in national surveys. It is not clear if this omission reflected the then prevailing idea that a husband had the right to have sex with his wife at will or a lack of awareness by researchers about this type of violence against women by their partner. By the mid-1980s, there was increasing concern about the difficulty of estimating rates of sexual assault against women in intimate relationships given the reluctance of survivors to report this type of victimization to police and interviewers. Scientists and researchers from the Bureau of Justice Statistics (BJS) and the CDC collaborated in a 10-year project to redesign the NCVS instrument. The revision enhanced the accuracy of capturing rape and sexual assault incidents by intimate partners, obtaining substantially more incidents of all categories of violence, including sexual abuse (Bachman & Saltzman, 1995). The NCVS found the highest (26%) lifetime prevalence rate for sexual abuse by an intimate; other studies produced rates of 4.5% and 14.3% (see Table 9.1).

---

[2]It is important to note that one cannot compare findings from the national surveys that collected only previous-year data with those of lifetime prevalence studies.

Stalking

We found only two national studies that included questions about stalking, despite the frequency with which survivors of DV report this type of abuse. The two studies used very different questions and criteria to determine stalking and, not surprisingly, obtained significantly different rates. The Women's Experience With Violence national study (Moracco, Runyan, Bowling, & Earp, 2007) asked two questions about stalking behaviors and reported individual rates for each question. One question asked if the participant had ever been followed by a man (prevalence rate: 42.7%). The other asked whether someone had contacted the participant repeatedly (prevalence rate: 25.3%). In contrast, the National Violence Against Women (NVAW) survey (Tjaden & Thoennes, 2000) asked participants if they had ever experienced any of eight stalking behaviors (e.g., followed or spied on, unsolicited phone calls). Respondents who answered yes to any question were asked if they had this experience on more than one occasion and if they had felt frightened or in danger as a result of the behavior. Respondents who were victimized more than once and who were very frightened or feared bodily harm were counted as stalking victims. This survey found a 4.1% lifetime prevalence rate for stalking.

As we discuss later, national surveys provide only a broad-brush picture of DV prevalence in the United States. To enhance our understanding and produce knowledge that is accurate and relevant to specific groups in the United States' very heterogeneous society, we must focus on specific groups and communities, which often are underrepresented in research, practice, and policy. Next, we present a sampling of what is known about DV against women in specific communities, highlighting differences and similarities that have been found.

Specific Communities

In this section, we provide brief synopses of current knowledge about DV in cultural groups, within-group comparisons, immigrants and refugees, and sexual minorities. Obviously, these short descriptions offer only a cursory overview of each community, and interested readers are urged to use the cited literature as a starting point for more in-depth information about the occurrence of DV in each of these communities.

Cultural Groups

Extant literature on DV has underrepresented ethnic minority groups. The earliest DV surveys limited their sample representation to Caucasian participants and people of color (including African American, Asian, and Hispanics), making no distinction among people in the latter group (Brice-Baker,

1994). African American, Latinos/Hispanics, Asian/Pacific Islanders, and American Indian/Alaska Natives have been included as distinct groups in more recent national surveys (e.g., Tjaden & Thoennes, 2000).

DV prevalence studies report a wide range of findings for minority groups. Lifetime prevalence rates for Asian/Pacific Islander women range from 12.8% to 61% (Tjaden & Thoennes, 2000; Yoshihama, 1999); for Hispanic/Latinas, the range is 13.4% to 25.7% (Kaufman et al., 1994); for African Americans, 17.4% to 26.3% (Tjaden & Thoennes, 2000); and for American Indians/Native Alaskans, 30.7% to 91% (Oetzel & Duran, 2004). Results from the NVAW survey (1995–1996) revealed that Asian/Pacific Islander women reported the lowest lifetime prevalence rates (12.8%), whereas American Indian/Alaska Native women were found to have the highest (30.7%) prevalence rates of all ethnic/racial groups studied. Lifetime prevalence rates for Latina/Hispanic (21.3%), African American (26.3%), and Caucasian (22.1%) women were not significantly different from one another (Tjaden & Thoennes, 2000).

McFarlane, Groff, Watson, and Watson (2005) oversampled Hispanic and African American women in a study that included 7,443 women ages 18 to 44 years. Women were recruited from community clinics in southern Texas; 25% of women were African American and 67% were Hispanic. Researchers found that 5.3% of Hispanic women and 6.0% of African American women had experienced DV in the previous year. Another study with 1,577 Asian individuals, 55.0% of whom were women, found that 15.3% of the women had experienced intimate partner violence in the previous year (Leung & Cheung, 2008). Although of interest to communities regarding local prevalence rates, prior-year rates of DV cannot be compared with lifetime prevalence rates found by the national surveys.

In agreement with Aldarondo and Castro-Fernandez (2008), moreover, Tjaden and Thoennes (2000) suggested that it is inappropriate to draw categorical conclusions about rates of DV among diverse cultural groups from data obtained in national surveys. It appears that DV has both universal and culture-specific elements that may play important roles in its antecedents, dynamics, and effects (Perilla, 1999). The Asian/Pacific Islander group, for example, includes remarkably diverse subpopulations that have very distinct ethnic, religious, historical, philosophical, and social values that may have important roles in the dynamics of DV. These cultural distinctions are often glossed over or completely ignored in the construction of pan-ethnic categories. For the most part, national surveys have not obtained data with this level of nuance; gathering these data could enhance our contextual understanding of DV among people who are not part of the majority group.

Researchers have also determined the importance of considering social and economic factors (e.g., poverty, high levels of conflict, excessive alcohol use, childhood exposure to violence) in DV prevalence studies and how they interact with cultural factors (e.g., Aldarondo & Castro-Fernandez, 2008; Yick & Oomen-Early, 2008). Aldarondo and Castro-Fernandez (2008) found that socioeconomic factors such as poverty and alcohol abuse predicted DV; a higher preponderance of these factors have been identified in certain minority groups in the United States, including African Americans, Latinos, and Native Americans (Malley-Morrison & Hines, 2004).

Within-Group Comparisons

In efforts to elucidate potential differences within pan-ethnic groups, researchers have recently begun to examine within-group differences by collecting specific demographic and socioeconomic data. Leung and Cheung (2008) examined various national subgroups within the broad and commonly labeled "Asian" group. They found that among 1,577 Asian (Chinese, Taiwanese, Vietnamese, Indian, Korean, Filipino, and Japanese) respondents residing in the greater Houston area, 15.3% of women reported experiencing DV in the previous year. However, further analyses by ethnicity revealed substantially different rates for subgroups: 22.4% for Vietnamese, 21.8% for Filipinos, 19.5% for Indians, 19.5% for Koreans, 9.7 % for Japanese, and 9.7% for Chinese. It is clear the aggregate data of large populations encompassing such diverse subgroups do not provide the level of detail necessary to obtain a clear understanding of within-group DV prevalence rates.

The group designated as "African American" or "Black" also contains immense internal diversity, including people whose ancestors were brought to the United States centuries ago as well as more recent immigrants from Africa and the Caribbean, with clearly distinct historical, cultural, and social experiences (Malley-Morrison & Hines, 2004). Thus, the dynamics of DV and the implications for addressing this problem in each population may require different strategies. Unfortunately, African Americans are underrepresented in the literature, and published prevalence data examining within-group ethnic differences are largely unavailable. Given the high prevalence rates among African Americans, researchers have investigated risk factors associated with DV. West (2002) suggested that the demographic profile of women most frequently abused is African American, young, divorced or separated, impoverished, and residing in urban areas. However, Benson, Wooldredge, Thistlethwaite, and Fox (2004) found that controlling for income and neighborhood characteristics reduced differences in DV across race. Of serious concern is the disproportionate representation of African Americans in domestic homicide rates. Between 1976 and 1999, African Americans represented 43% of all domestic homicide victims, yet they only represented 12% of the population (Williams, Oliver, & Pope, 2008). Although current literature does not provide a clear picture of African American within-group differences, it is clear that DV has had a serious impact on the entire community and that those who are impoverished are especially affected.

The American Indian/Native Alaskan group may also have significant within-group variation in prevalence rates given the ethnic, historical, and social differences among the tribes and nations; unfortunately, there is little research on specific groups. As mentioned earlier, national prevalence rates for American Indians/Alaska Natives is 30.7% (higher than any other ethnic group; Tjaden & Thoennes, 2000). One of the few DV studies with a specific American Indian group (Navajos) found 52.0% lifetime and 16.4% previous-year prevalence among 341 women participants (Fairchild, Fairchild, & Stoner, 1998). This study suggests that for American Indian/Alaskan Native people, studies with pan-ethnic groups do not produce accurate and useful information to address DV in their specific communities.

Like other pan-ethnic groupings, Latinos/Hispanics are very heterogeneous. Tracing their origins to countries throughout Latin America, Spain, and Portugal, Latinos/Hispanics also vary among themselves considerably depending on their length of residence in the United States. Three national DV surveys have oversampled Latinos/Hispanics to obtain prevalence rates for non-Caucasian groups: the 1985 National Family Violence Survey, the National Alcohol and Family Violence Survey (NAFVS), and the Commonwealth Fund Survey of Women's Health. However, only the NAFVS explored within-group differences in the Latino/Hispanic population. Using the NAFVS data, Aldarondo, Kaufman Kantor, and Jasinski (2002) found significant differences among Puerto Rican (20.4%), Mexican American (17.9%), Mexican (10.5%), and Cuban American (2.5%) couples' reports of male-to-female DV. These data provide clear evidence of the importance of exploring within-group differences to gain a more nuanced understanding of how groups differ in their rates of DV.

Immigrants and Refugees

Like many women in the United States, immigrant and refugee women are at high risk of experiencing DV. Of special relevance to this chapter, many immigrant and refugee women do not participate in national surveys for numerous reasons, including language barriers, cultural beliefs about talking to strangers about private issues, and the classifications used in the studies. For example, immigrants and refugees from Eastern Europe, Africa, and the Middle East either are not included in national samples or are often misclassified as "White" despite the remarkable differences in their history, ethnicity, religious background, immigration status, and other key variables. Finally, immigrants and refugees often experience unique forms of DV that are not captured by existing DV scales. Specifically, immigration status is a common and powerful control mechanism used against immigrant women to force them to stay in the relationship (Dutton, Orloff, & Hass, 2000).

Sexual Minorities

DV among sexual minorities is an area of research that has only gained attention in recent decades. Many obstacles have prevented greater inclusion of this population within the DV movement. Even same-sex partners themselves can endorse stereotypes assuming the egalitarian nature of same-sex relationships, making even some sexual minorities reluctant to include themselves within DV efforts (Elliott, 1996). Additionally, the DV movement itself was reluctant to incorporate sexual minorities because of their potential threat to many gender-based feminist views of DV. Domestic violence among partners of the same gender challenges theories that explain DV as the sole result of patriarchy and inequality between men and women. The need to incorporate sexual minorities in our efforts is demonstrated by studies showing that DV in sexual minority relationships occurs at approximately the same rate as in heterosexual relationships (Elliott, 1996; Turell, 2000). However, much like the national and intranational statistics for heterosexuals, the range of violence found by specific studies in this community varies widely.

HOW DO WE KNOW IT?

As seen in the previous section, DV prevalence rates reported in the literature differ considerably due to the methods used. In turn, the theoretical and philosophical stance of a researcher greatly influences methodological choices. We begin this section with a short discussion of how theoretical and philosophical positions affect current knowledge about DV prevalence and then examine some methodological issues that exercise the greatest effects on prevalence rates. These include issues with definition, instruments, sampling, and method of data collection. Significant debate exists in the field about each issue, and where researchers settle on each debate greatly affects the approach they use and ultimately the rates of DV they find.

Theoretical/Philosophical Stances

Two primary positions have been used by researchers exploring the prevalence of DV: feminism and family systems theory. At the beginning of the DV movement, an unambiguous message regarding the urgency of addressing DV as a gender-based phenomenon was essential. Women were seen as victims, men as perpetrators. Most studies using this perspective were conducted with small samples, mainly in shelters and community organizations. Participants seldom, if ever, were asked about their own use of violence against their partners. Although some academic researchers used this theoretical stance for their studies of DV, most proponents of the feminist perspective were practitioners for whom the high prevalence rates that were found matched the realities of their everyday work with survivors.

At the same time, family systems researchers who subscribed to the idea of dynamic and reciprocal family violence began conducting large-scale national surveys that used the CTS, which asked questions about experience and perpetration of specific behaviors with intimate partners. Proponents of this stance were academic researchers who focused on theory and methods rather than on applied work. The consistent gender symmetry of their findings supported their theoretical beliefs about violence in families—that women were just as violent as men.

It is not surprising that these differing viewpoints and findings spark deep and at times highly acerbic arguments that hold academic, political, practical, and policy implications. The reluctance of some feminist proponents to explore the use of violence by women in their intimate relationships was often the result of a disinclination to step back from a gender analysis that had served the movement well. This stance signaled to some an unwillingness to bring the entirety of survivors' experience to light, and it was used by family systems proponents to advance their own position. Family systems proponents have produced an impressive number of studies (both large national surveys and smaller studies) that find gender symmetry and are currently being used to challenge laws, policies, scholarship, and services targeting only women.

Definitions

Despite the attempt by the CDC and other federal institutions to standardize the terms used to study DV, there still is enormous variation in how researchers conceptualize and explore this topic. As mentioned earlier, both the American Psychological Association (1996) and the CDC (Saltzman et al., 1999) have included physical, sexual, and psychological/emotional maltreatment or harm by an intimate partner in their definition of DV. However, most national studies fall short of gathering data on this broad range of behaviors, focusing exclusively on physical and, more recently, sexual violence in intimate relationships.

The seriousness of verbal abuse has been well documented. It is known to co-occur with and be a marker for increased physical violence and has been found to have significant deleterious effects (Stets, 1990). Despite the fact that verbal abuse has been captured by the CTS since the first version in the 1970s, a search for literature regarding verbal abuse produces a remarkably low number of scientific articles. This reflects the lack of dialogue in the field about this important aspect of DV. Data about verbal abuse were not collected by the NVAW survey, nor are they collected by the annual NCVS conducted by the BJS. To our knowledge, data will not be collected by the more recent Behavioral Risk Factor Surveillance System. This is a serious oversight; excluding verbal abuse from the definition of DV will affect prevalence rates and obscure our understanding of DV by ignoring a serious aspect of this phenomenon.

In addition, to date, only two national surveys have included stalking as one of the behaviors that define DV. As described previously, the NVAW survey (Tjaden & Thoennes, 2000) found a 4.1% prevalence rate for stalking, whereas the Women's Experience With Violence national study produced very high prevalence rates for each of the two questions asked (42.7% and 25.3% lifetime; 5.9% and 5.5% prior year). This is a good example of how significantly different rates between two studies may be an artifact of the broad versus narrow definition of stalking used in each one, which still leaves us with no clear understanding of the frequency with which women are stalked by their intimate partner.

Instrument Issues

Straus and his colleagues at the University of New Hampshire (UNH) were the first to conduct DV prevalence studies with national representative samples. The CTS (Straus, 1979) was originally developed for this purpose and became the most widely used DV research instrument worldwide. After strong critiques from the field about the inability of the CTS to capture a more accurate picture of DV, the instrument was modified as the Revised Conflict Tactics Scales (CTS2; Straus, Hamby, Boney-McCoy, & Sugarman, 1996).

The pivotal role of instruments in determining DV prevalence is well illustrated by the differing rates of violence produced in the UNH studies and the BJS study. The different instrument used in each study resulted in drastically different rates of violence. The UNH studies used the first version of the CTS, which only included items on physical and verbal violence (Desai & Saltzman, 2001). In contrast, the BJS redesigned the NCVS (Bachman & Saltzman, 1995) in 1992 to include items on women's experience of rape and sexual assault.

Although the CTS2 includes seven questions regarding sexual abuse, many researchers and practitioners still raise concerns about the validity of the data produced by the CTS2, especially its inability to capture the surrounding context of the violence it taps. The scale asks about the frequency with which respondents experience and/or perpetrate specific violent acts with their partner during an argument or a conflict. Thus, the CTS2 can quantify acts of violence but can do little to contextualize them. Although the scale includes questions on the resulting injury of the violence, many researchers point out how more information is needed to understand the meaning and motive of the violence perpetrated (e.g., Dasgupta, 2002; DeKeseredy & Schwartz, 2001). None of these changes have been considered in the gender symmetry debate.

Additionally, many researchers raise the issue of reporting bias in the completion of the CTS, with men exhibiting a tendency to underreport their perpetration of DV (DeKeseredy, Saunders, Schwartz, & Alvi, 1997; Kimmel, 2002). The fact that the CTS is a retrospective scale potentially exacerbates this trend. Asking participants to reflect back on their experience and use of violence over the course of the year may further decrease the accuracy of the reports. As Kimmel (2002) described, "retrospection may not be completely reliable because memory often serves our current interests but is unlikely to provide an accurate rendition of what actually happened" (p. 1343).

With so many limitations of the CTS, the most widely used DV instrument, it is clear that the field needs to broaden its tools. Researchers are increasingly describing the need to investigate DV using a mixed-method approach that utilizes qualitative methodologies as well as quantitative ones (DeKeseredy & Schwartz, 2001). Incorporating more opportunities for participants to describe their experience of violence in their own words would address several limitations of the quantitative studies that currently dominate the field. Using qualitative methods can help contextualize the violence reported by participants, illuminating critical pieces of information, including the motive, meaning, and impact of the violent act. This would help to understand the nature of the violence and even whether the act should be deemed an act of DV in the first place (Smith, Tessaro, & Earp, 1995).

Another significant advantage of adding qualitative components is that this allows research to tap more comprehensively into the experiences of the real experts in the field. No one can describe the experiences of participants better than they can; providing participants the opportunity to describe their experiences in their own voice expands the potential for researchers and practitioners to learn from the men and women we study. Qualitative methods allow participants to describe their experiences of violence, which raises a central issue in this type of work: determining who has the right to decide what should be considered DV. Quantitative measures with closed questions permit researchers to define the acts that make up DV, and these definitions may not accurately represent participants' experiences (Gondolf & Beeman, 2003). Qualitative methods can create more equilibrium in the power differential between researcher and participant by not imposing an a priori definition of DV.

A danger in using strictly quantitative instruments is that it increases the risk of creating theories that make sense from an academic perspective but that have not been validated by the men and women with whom we conduct our research. An example of this is the DV typologies created by Johnson (2006) that are used, in part, to explain the discrepant prevalence rates found between studies. Johnson, synthesizing extensive quantitative data, uses his typologies to show that the field may be tapping different types of DV with the different methodologies used. Although many laud Johnson's theory and have tested it using more quantitative studies (Graham-Kevan, 2007), no study to date appears to have validated the typologies using qualitative methods. This means, in essence, that researchers have not openly asked participants if they agree with the typologies or if the typologies map onto their experiences of violence.

Sampling, Data Collection, and Dissemination Issues

The differing rates of DV across communities underscore the importance for researchers to consider what groups are being sampled to create knowledge about DV. The literature contains many problematic sampling issues, including what groups are over- and undersampled, the interaction of data collection methods with sampling strategies, and the treatment of identity by different sampling methods. Exploration of the issues helps to explain previously identified rates of DV and can also provide a road map for future directions for the field.

One of the most cited sampling issues is also the most obvious: who gets included or excluded in studies on DV. This issue is fundamental to the external validity of the research conducted. The use of college samples in the study of DV is a significant limitation to our understanding of this social problem (Kimmel, 2002), especially because the great majority of studies that use the CTS have been conducted with these populations. For example, Archer's (2002) well-known meta-analysis of sex differences in aggression between heterosexual partners includes 76 articles that use the CTS. Of these, 71.1% were conducted with college (45) and high school (nine) samples, something of extreme concern when attempting to determine an issue as controversial as gender symmetry in DV. There is substantial evidence that the expression of violence in relationships changes over the course of the life span, and violence in relationships in early adulthood seems in particular to differ from violence in later relationships (O'Leary et al., 1989). The use of teen and college-age populations in studies on the prevalence of DV threatens the external validity of the findings not only because developmental factors in college and high school samples may act as confounders but also because students do not represent the population as a whole.

Another critique raised about sampling in DV research involves the representation of minorities. Especially for the large-scale, national studies, appropriate representation of minority communities has remained largely elusive, in part due to sampling and reporting procedures. Several of the national studies dichotomize their sample into White/non-White (e.g., Straus & Gelles, 1990; Straus & Kaufman Kantor, 1994; Straus & Sweet, 1992); some even forgo discussion of demographics in publications in which race is not the central topic (e.g., Straus & Gelles, 1990; Straus & Sweet, 1992). This is true even when the study oversampled minority groups. By overlooking or downplaying the effects of demographic differences within their sample, researchers of some of the large national studies diminish the generalizability of their findings, and they often do not cite this as a limitation of their studies (e.g., Straus & Kaufman Kantor, 1994). In contrast, many of the authors cited in the "Specific Communities" section recognize the importance of within-group differences, being careful not to crudely homogenize identities (e.g., speaking broadly about Latinos, Asians, women, etc.; Aldarondo & Castro-Fernandez, 2008; Kaufman Kantor et al., 1994; McFarlane et al., 2005; Oetzel & Duran, 2004; Tjaden & Thoennes, 2000). Given the increasing diversity in the U.S. population, the exclusion of samples that reflect the heterogeneity of our society is problematic because of its potential impact on applied work and policymaking.

Some of the more common data collection methodologies exacerbate this dilemma. Telephone surveys, for example, immediately exclude participation from individuals who may not have phones because of limited financial resources, unstable housing arrangements, or exclusive use of cell phones (Blumberg & Luke, 2007). Many researchers criticize this methodology for being biased even within populations who own landline telephones. Analyses reveal lower response rates to telephone surveys from racial/ethnic minorities and people with lower levels of education (Link & Kresnow, 2006). These demographic characteristics also largely correspond to individuals at greater risk of experiencing DV (Malley-Morrison & Hines, 2004), which makes the decreased presence of these groups in prevalence studies all the more problematic.

Cultural concerns regarding face-to-face interview methods also exist. In many communities, discussions with strangers about private issues such as DV are not considered culturally appropriate (Malley-Morrison & Hines, 2004), which strains the external validity of research studies that use this method. For example, the completion rate in the 1975 National Family Violence Survey was 65% (Straus & Gelles, 1990) and 75.4% for the 1992 NAFVS (Kaufman Kantor et al., 1994). Both studies used in-person interviewing. Participation or completion rates in other national studies were not readily available, so it is difficult to make comparisons across studies. Nevertheless, attrition rates in national "representative" samples could create a bias that should, at the very least, be mentioned and discussed in dissemination efforts. Using data collection methods that exclude or at least significantly reduce the participation of entire communities means creating knowledge about DV that only pertains to certain groups. This has serious implications for the validity of the rates of violence found in studies and affects the cultural appropriateness of services and policies created on the basis of this knowledge.

The issues of sampling techniques and data collection methods point to an overarching limitation in the research on DV prevalence: its oversimplification of identity. Many of the more common sampling and data collection methods construct identities in overly simplified ways. By sampling for and identifying participants on the basis of their racial/ethnic identity using broad categories like White, Black, Asian, and Latino, the opportunity for a more nuanced understanding of the interaction between race/ethnicity and DV becomes exceedingly difficult. Many researchers describe the importance of seeing individuals as embedded within intersecting hierarchies determined on the basis of their age, race/ethnicity, sexual orientation, class, immigration status, and so on (Crenshaw, 2005). How all of these identities interact to situate an individual within society influences an individual's experience and reporting of DV; however, to begin to examine the intersectionality of identity will require an alteration of the methodologies used by researchers in the field.

As this section points out, many of the "facts" of the previous section must be significantly qualified to address the limitations of the methods used by researchers. Consistent with research across all disciplines, study findings within this area reflect the methodological decisions of the researcher, which are often informed by his or her own theoretical or philosophical stance. Decisions regarding instruments and the sampling technique greatly affect the prevalence rates of DV that researchers find. In addition to the qualifications of the "things we know" based on the limitations outlined previously, the next section provides further qualifications in its description of the numerous gaps in our current knowledge of DV.

WHERE DO WE GO FROM HERE?

An in-depth review of this literature was a difficult task. As we discussed in this chapter, current knowledge about DV against women is often contradictory, difficult to understand, and clearly insufficient to address in a more informed and in-depth manner the plight of the women affected by this social problem. Despite these serious flaws, these data are being used as a solid scientific basis for interventions, policy, and funding. Our review of extant literature on prevalence rates uncovered gaps in several key areas of interest to researchers, advocates, and policymakers. These gaps include definitions of DV, theoretical/philosophical stances, sampling procedures, instrumentation, interpretation and dissemination of findings, and the role that diversity plays in the occurrence and effects of DV in the U.S. population.

We are not yet at a place where prevalence data alone can provide a full picture of the insidiousness of DV in U.S. society. For one thing, despite the presence of clear definitions that could be used to standardize our research, applied, and policy efforts, large national surveys and smaller community-based studies do not use common definitions, resulting in data that are confusing, difficult to interpret, and incomplete. Future studies that purport to advance our knowledge and increase the relevance of our findings must include the many forms of DV. Research will need to become much more nuanced and comprehensive to capture the complexity of DV and help us draw blueprints for its elimination. Specifically, our field must advance beyond national surveys that produce impressive but often contradictory numbers about physical violence. We must take into consideration and explore the rates and the connections between physical violence and verbal abuse, and their joint association with sexual abuse and stalking. In other words, until we begin to see DV in a comprehensive manner that includes all forms of violence against women within a relationship, we will continue to analyze, research, and address only pieces of women's reality.

In terms of sampling, our review of current literature provided clear evidence about the need for the field to advance beyond what has been considered representative samples of the U.S. population. As stated earlier, most national studies have not been inclusive enough to provide the degree of accuracy we need to determine how specific groups (beyond the currently used pan-ethnic categories) are affected and—most important—how DV needs to be addressed in these diverse settings. Rather than additional large surveys that generally tap White populations and perhaps oversample pan-ethnic groupings, smaller focused studies that explore within-group differences may be much more relevant and important to our work. This purposeful and careful sampling must also include ethnic and sexual minority groups that have not previously been included. In addition, research on dating violence conducted with high school or college populations is a valid and interesting field of its own and should continue to be studied. However, its inclusion in meta-analytic studies regarding DV not only will prevent the advancement of knowledge we need to eradicate this social issue but also creates confounding information that does disservice to the field. In addition, DV researchers need to engage in dialogue about current sampling strategies, discussing the need for transparency regarding participation rates in randomly selected samples and the limitations of such samples.

Undoubtedly, the CTS has helped advance the field of DV by serving as a tool that allows researchers to collect and compare data across studies from throughout the world. This has in turn produced an astounding number of scientific articles on the topic, which account for a substantial majority of current literature on DV prevalence. The CTS provides ample quantitative data about prior-year victimization and perpetration of specific behaviors but is severely limited in offering contextual data that are essential to its applicability and relevance. The next step would be for studies to use mixed-methods approaches and obtain both quantitative and qualitative information about the context in which the violent acts occur, including cultural context. In large-scale studies, a subsample from each ethnic group could also be interviewed to probe more deeply about contextual factors surrounding the violent acts, thus enhancing the quality of the data collected.

The data collection methods in DV research need to be fine-tuned given what is known in the field regarding the limitations of telephone surveys and in-person interviews. For example, the expertise gained by WHO (2005) in the Multi-Country Study of Women's Health and Domestic Violence Against Women could serve as a guide for future studies in the United States. The research team included individuals from research organizations and women in the community who worked with survivors. They used trained community members as interviewers and obtained a response rate over 85% in all but one site. It may well be that prevalence studies on this topic may require this type of academic–community collaboration in the United States as well.

Finally, the study and understanding of DV require that we conceptualize the problem and use methods that take into consideration the complexity of women's lives. As mentioned previously, rather than viewing a survivor as if the occurrence of DV happened in a vacuum, it is essential to consider the intersecting hierarchies (based on age, race/ethnicity, sexual orientation, class, immigration status, etc.) that affect her reality on a daily basis. It is only when we use this type of comprehensive lens in our work that we will be on our way to eradicating DV from our society. The studies that we design and conduct, the services and resources that we offer, and the policies that we enact in the future must all come from this more challenging and complex understanding of domestic violence.

REFERENCES

Aldarondo, E., & Castro-Fernandez, M. C. (2008). Intimate partner violence and recidivism following interventions with men who batter: Cultural and empirical considerations. In R. Carrillo & J. Tello (Eds.), *Family violence and men of color: Healing the wounded male spirit* (pp. 1–35). New York, NY: Springer.

Aldarondo, E., Kaufman Kantor, G., & Jasinski, J. L. (2002). A risk marker analysis of wife assault in Latino families. *Violence Against Women, 8*, 429–454.

American Psychological Association. (1996). *Violence and the family: Report of the American Psychological Association Presidential Task Force on Violence and the Family*. Washington, DC: Author.

Archer, J. (2000). Sex differences in aggression between heterosexual partners: A meta-analytic review. *Psychological Bulletin, 126*, 651–680. doi:10.1037/0033-2909.126.5.651

Bachman, R., & Saltzman, L. (1995). *Violence against women: Estimates from the redesigned National Crime Victimization Survey*. Washington, DC: U.S. Department of Justice, Bureau of Justice Statistics.

Benson, M., Wooldredge, J., Thistlethwaite, A., & Fox, G. (2004). The correlation between race and DV is confounded with community context. *Social Problems, 51*, 326–342. doi:10.1525/sp.2004.51.3.326

Blumberg, S. J., & Luke, J. V. (2007). Coverage bias in traditional telephone surveys of low-income and young adults. *Public Opinion Quarterly, 71*, 734–749. doi:10.1093/poq/nfm047

Brice-Baker, J. R. (1994). Domestic violence in African-American and African-Caribbean families. *Journal of Social Distress and the Homeless, 3*, 23–38. doi:10.1007/BF02087357

Crenshaw, K. (2005). Mapping the margins: Intersectionality, identity politics, and violence against women of color. In R. K. Bergen, J. L Edleson, & C. M. Renzetti (Eds.), *Violence against women: Classic papers* (pp. 282–313). Auckland, New Zealand: Pearson Education.

Dasgupta, S. D. (2002). A framework for understanding women's use of nonlethal violence in intimate heterosexual relationships. *Violence Against Women, 8*, 1364–1389. doi:10.1177/107780102237408

DeKeseredy, W. S., Saunders, D., Schwartz, M. D., & Alvi, S. (1997). The meanings and motives for women's use of violence in Canadian college dating relationships: Results from a national survey. *Sociological Spectrum, 17*, 199–222.

DeKeseredy, W. S., & Schwartz, M. D. (2001). Definitional issues. In C. M. Renzetti, J. L. Edleson, & R. K. Bergen (Eds.), *Sourcebook on violence against women* (pp. 23–34). Thousand Oaks, CA: Sage.

Desai, S., & Saltzman, L. E. (2001). Measurement issues for violence against women. In C. M. Renzetti, J. L. Edleson, & R. K. Bergen (Eds.), *Sourcebook on violence against women* (pp. 35–52). Thousand Oaks, CA: Sage.

Dutton, M. A., Orloff, L., & Hass, G.A. (2000). Characteristics of help-seeking behaviors, resources, and services seeds of battered immigrant Latinas: Legal and policy implications. *Georgetown Journal on Poverty Law and Policy, 7*, 247–305.

Elliott, P. (1996). Shattering illusions: Same-sex domestic violence. In C. M. Renzetti & C. H. Miley (Eds.), *Violence in gay and lesbian domestic partnerships* (pp. 1–8). New York, NY: Haworth Press.

Fairchild, D. G., Fairchild, M. W., & Stoner, S. (1998). Prevalence of adult domestic violence among women seeking routine care in a Native American health care facility. *American Journal of Public Health, 88,* 1515–1517. doi:10.2105/AJPH.88.10.1515

García-Moreno, C., Jansen, H. A., Ellsberg, M., Heise, L., & Watts, C. H. (2006). Prevalence of intimate partner violence: Findings from the WHO multi-country study on women's health and domestic violence. *The Lancet, 368,* 1260–1269. doi:10.1016/S0140-6736(06)69523-8

Gondolf, E. W., & Beeman, A. K. (2003). Women's accounts of domestic violence versus tactics-based outcome categories. *Violence Against Women, 9,* 278–301. doi:10.1177/1077801202250072

Graham-Kevan, N. (2007). Johnson's control-based domestic violence typology: Implications for research and treatment. *Issues in Forensic Psychology, 6,* 109–115.

Green, P. P., Tsai, J., & Floyd, L. (2008, October). *Estimated prevalence for lifetime experience of intimate partner violence among women of childbearing age in eight states and territories, United States, BRFSS, 2006.* Paper presented at the Public Health Without Borders American Public Health Association 136th Annual Meeting and Expo, San Diego, CA.

Heise, L., & García-Moreno, C. (2002). Violence by intimate partners. In E. Krug, L. Dahlberg, J. Mercy, A. B. Zwi, & R. Lozano (Eds.), *World report on violence and health* (pp. 87–121). Geneva, Switzerland: World Health Organization.

Johnson, M. P. (2006). Conflict and control: Gender symmetry and asymmetry in domestic violence. *Violence Against Women, 12,* 1003–1018. doi:10.1177/1077801206293328

Kaufman Kantor, G., Jasinski, J. L., & Aldarondo, E. (1994). Sociocultural status and incidence of marital violence in Hispanic families. *Violence and Victims, 9,* 207–222.

Kimmel, M. S. (2002). "Gender symmetry" in domestic violence: A substantive and methodological research review. *Violence Against Women, 8,* 1332–1363.

Leung, P., & Cheung, M. (2008). A prevalence study on partner abuse in six Asian American ethnic groups in the USA. *International Social Work, 51,* 635–649. doi:10.1177/0020872808093342

Link, M. W., & Kresnow, M. J. (2006). The future of random-digit-dial surveys for injury prevention and violence research. *American Journal of Preventive Medicine, 31,* 444–450. doi:10.1016/j.amepre.2006.07.017

Malley-Morrison, K., & Hines, D. (2004). *Family violence in a cultural perspective: Defining, understanding, and combating abuse.* Thousand Oaks, CA: Sage.

McFarlane, J. M., Groff, J. Y., Watson, O., & Watson, K. (2005). Prevalence of partner violence against 7,443 African American, White, and Hispanic women receiving care at urban public primary care clinics. *Public Health Nursing, 22,* 98–107. doi:10.1111/j.0737-1209.2005.220203.x

Moracco, K. E., Runyan, C. W., Bowling, J. M., & Earp, J. O. L. (2007). Women's experiences with violence: A national study. *Women's Health Issues, 17*, 3–12. doi:10.1016/j.whi.2006.03.007

Oetzel, J., & Duran, B. (2004). Intimate partner violence in American Indian and/or Alaska native communities: A social ecological framework of determinants and interventions. *Journal for the Center of American Indian and Alaska Native Mental Health Research, 11*(4), 49–68.

O'Leary, K. D., Barling, J., Arias, I., Rosenblum, A., Malone, J., & Tyree, A. (1989). Prevalence and stability of physical aggression between spouses: A longitudinal analysis. *Journal of Consulting and Clinical Psychology, 57*, 263–268. doi:10.1037/0022-006X.57.2.263

Perilla, J. L. (1999). Domestic violence as a human rights issue: The case of immigrant Latinos. *Hispanic Journal of Behavioral Sciences, 21*, 107–133. doi:10.1177/0739986399212001

Plichta, S. B., & Falik, M. (2001). Prevalence of violence and its implications for women's health. *Women's Health Issues, 11*, 244–258. doi:10.1016/S1049-3867(01)00085-8

Saltzman, L. E., Fanslow, J. L., McMahon, P. M., & Shelley, G. A. (1999). *Intimate partner violence surveillance: Uniform definitions and recommended data elements.* Atlanta, GA: Centers for Disease Control and Prevention.

Smith, P. H., Tessaro, I., & Earp, J. A. L. (1995). Women's experiences with battering: A conceptualization from qualitative research. *Women's Health Issues, 5*, 173–182. doi:10.1016/1049-3867(95)00615-X

Stets, J. E. (1990). Verbal and physical aggression in marriage. *Journal of Marriage and the Family, 52*, 501–514. doi:10.2307/353043

Straus, M. A. (1979). Measuring intrafamily conflict and violence: The Conflict Tactics (CT) Scales. *Journal of Marriage and the Family, 41*, 75–88. doi:10.2307/351733

Straus, M. A., & Gelles, R. J. (1986). Societal change and change in family violence from 1975 to 1985 as revealed by two national surveys. *Journal of Marriage and the Family, 48*, 465–479. doi:10.2307/352033

Straus, M. A., & Gelles, R. J. (1990). *Physical violence in American families: Risk factors and adaptations to violence in 8,145 families.* New Brunswick, NJ: Transaction.

Straus, M. A., Gelles, R., & Steinmetz, S. (1980). *Behind closed doors: Violence in the American family.* Garden City, NY: Anchor/Doubleday.

Straus, M. A., Hamby, S. L., Boney-McCoy, S., & Sugarman, D. B. (1996). The Revised Conflict Tactics Scales (CTS2): Development and preliminary psychometric data. *Journal of Family Issues, 17*, 283–316. doi:10.1177/019251396017003001

Straus, M. A., & Kaufman Kantor, G. (1994, July). *Change in spouse assault rates from 1975 to 1992: A comparison of three national surveys in the United States.* Paper presented at the 13th World Congress of Sociology, Bielefeld, Germany.

Straus, M., & Sweet, S. (1992). Verbal/symbolic aggression in couples: Incidence rates and relationships to personal characteristics. *Journal of Marriage and the Family, 54*, 346–357. doi:10.2307/353066

Tjaden, P., & Thoennes, N. (2000). *Full report of the prevalence, incidence, and consequences of violence against women*. Washington, DC: National Institute of Justice and the Centers for Disease Control and Prevention. Retrieved from http://www.ncjrs.gov/pdffiles1/nij/183781.pdf

Turell, S. C. (2000). A descriptive analysis of same-sex relationship violence for a diverse sample. *Journal of Family Violence, 15*, 281–293. doi:10.1023/A:1007505619577

West, C. M. (2002). Battered, black, and blue: An overview of violence in the lives of Black women. *Women & Therapy, 25*(3/4), 5–27. doi:10.1300/J015v25n03_02

Williams, O. J., Oliver, W., & Pope, M. (2008). Domestic violence in the African American community. *Journal of Aggression, Maltreatment & Trauma, 16*, 229–237. doi:10.1080/10926770801925486

World Health Organization. (2002). *World report on violence and health: Summary*. Geneva, Switzerland: Author.

World Health Organization. (2005). *Multi-country study on women's health and domestic violence against women: Initial results on prevalence, health outcomes, and women's responses*. Geneva, Switzerland: Author.

Yick, A. G., & Oomen-Early, J. (2008). A 16-year examination of domestic violence among Asians and Asian Americans in the empirical knowledge base. *Journal of Interpersonal Violence, 23*, 1075–1094. doi:10.1177/0886260507313973

Yoshihama, M. (1999). Domestic violence against women of Japanese descent in Los Angeles: Two methods of estimating prevalence. *Violence Against Women, 5*, 869–897. doi:10.1177/10778019922181536

10

RISK AND PROTECTIVE FACTORS FOR DOMESTIC VIOLENCE PERPETRATION

ETIONY ALDARONDO AND MICHELLE CASTRO-FERNANDEZ

> Science is built up with fact as a house is with stone; but a collection of facts is no more a science than a heap of stones is a house.
> —Jules Henri Poincaré (2007, p. 141)

That domestic violence is an important advocacy, legal, clinical, research, and human rights issue can hardly be denied. It is estimated that between 8% and 67% of women around the world are physically assaulted by their intimate partners at some point in their lives, with most countries reporting lifetime prevalence rates of at least 20% (Aldarondo & Fernandez, 2008). National estimates indicate that somewhere between 1.3 million (Tjaden & Thoennes, 2000) and more than 8 million (Straus & Gelles, 1990) women are physically assaulted by male partners each year. Moreover, domestic violence is associated with major depressive episodes, posttraumatic stress disorder, injury, and death in women (Campbell, Glass, Sharps, Laughon, & Bloom, 2007).

Concern about the magnitude of the problem and its effects on women's safety and well-being has shaped public policy and led to both significant developments in the criminal justice response to domestic violence and, of particular importance for the purpose of this chapter, increased calls for the development of a science-based approach to understanding and preventing violence, including the identification of risk factors for domestic violence as one of its main objectives (Crowell & Burgess, 1996; World Health Organization [WHO], 2000). Our aim in this chapter is to contribute to this effort by summarizing what we have learned about risk factors for the perpetration of domestic violence over the past 3 decades, identifying gaps in our knowledge and research priorities in the field, and suggesting an expanded ecological interventionist framework to aid in the realization of a theoretically informed and practice- and policy-oriented domestic violence research agenda.

DEFINITIONAL CONSIDERATIONS

Human service providers, policymakers, researchers, and those seeking to educate themselves about domestic violence can be easily confused by the broad range of definitions that are part of the public conversation about domestic violence. Terms such as *family violence, intimate partner violence, partner aggression, partner violence, battering, intimate terrorism, marital violence, spouse abuse,* and *wife-beating* have all been used by those concerned with the occurrence of violence in adult couple relationships. For advocates and human service providers, the term *domestic violence* is shorthand for relational patterns of coercive control of intimate partners that may be achieved through various behaviors, including intimidation, harassment and persecution, verbal aggression, denial of access to resources, sexual coercion and assault, and physical assault and torture.

Although this broad definition has served well battered women advocates' public education efforts and has been influential in shaping public policy, the operationalization of this multidimensional construct for research purposes has proved to be a major challenge for the field. Alternatively, researchers have tended to focus on specific dimensions of domestic violence and on the occurrence of physical violence in "presumably" heterosexual relationships in particular. We put the word *presumably* in quotation marks because although a growing number of researchers are now focusing on domestic violence in same-gender relationships, most researchers and service agencies do not report sexual orientation data from men and their partners. Thus, this chapter focuses on risk factors for perpetration of physical violence by men against their female partners while recognizing that domestic violence is not an exclusively heterosexual phenomenon and that other forms of violence also have devastating effects on victims.

WHAT DO WE KNOW? A BIRD'S EYE VIEW

Over the years, two main points of consensus have developed among domestic violence researchers: first, that the perpetration of violence is determined by the interplay of individual, relationship, community, and social factors; and second, that domestic violence is not a homogeneous occurrence. Together these factors provide a glimpse of what we may consider to be high-risk men, high-risk relationships, and high-risk communities and societies for domestic violence perpetration.

High-Risk Men

More than half of all risk factors endorsed by domestic violence experts are individual-level variables. These factors touch on issues related to demographic characteristics, history of aggression against female partners, history of violence in the family of origin, psychological functioning and mental health issues, history of violence, substance use, and worldview. Accordingly, the risk for perpetrating physical violence against female partners increases among young adult men and men with low levels of academic achievement (i.e., school dropouts, no high school completion), blue-collar occupational status, and low income (Babcock, Waltz, Jacobson, & Gottman, 1993; Holtzworth-Munroe & Smutzler, 1996). Although most men who experience and witness domestic violence in their families of origin do not go on to abuse their intimate partners, growing up within this context significantly increases the risk of violence perpetration (Delsol & Margolin, 2004; Stith et al., 2000).

The risk also increases among men with somewhat fragile psychological functioning, including men for whom intimate attachments are a source of anxiety (Doumas, Pearson, Elgin, & McKinley, 2008); men who experience higher-than-expected levels of anger (Norlander & Eckhardt, 2005), depression (Boyle & Vivian, 1996; Hastings & Hamberger, 1994), fear (O'Leary & Curley, 1986), jealousy (Dutton, van Ginkel, & Landolt, 1996; Holtzworth-Munroe, Stuart, & Hutchinson, 1997), and stress in their lives (McKenry, Julian, & Gavazzi, 1995; Pan, Neidig, & O'Leary, 1994); men who do not feel good about themselves (Kaufman-Kantor & Jasinski, 1998; Murphy, Meyer, & O'Leary, 1994); men who have rigid and maladaptive cognitive styles (Eckhardt & Kassinove, 1998; Holtzworth-Munroe & Hutchinson, 1993); and men who tend to feel powerless at home (Babcock et al., 1993; Sagrestano, Heavey, & Christensen, 1999). The presence of psychopathology (i.e., emotional dependency, antisocial, and borderline features) also increases the risk of domestic violence perpetration (Dutton, Starzomski, & Ryan, 1996).

In terms of substance use, men who drink heavily and men who use illicit drugs are at a considerably higher risk of perpetrating domestic violence than men who do not (Foran & O'Leary, 2008; Quigley & Leonard, 2000). Moreover, it appears that how men make sense of the world around them also affects this risk. In particular, holding traditional sex role expectations and negative attitudes about women (Dutton, 1995; Hurlbert, Whittaker, & Munoz, 1991), believing that those of perceived lower authority should obey them, being intolerant of others' views (Neidig, Friedman, & Collins, 1986), and approving of the use of physical violence in intimate relationships (Kaufman-Kantor, Jasinski, & Aldarondo, 1994; Stith & Farley, 1993) increase the risk of violence perpetration by men against their female partners. Finally, prior history of violence against intimate partners increases the risk of future violence (Aldarondo, 1996; O'Leary et al., 1989).

High-Risk Relationships

At the relationship level, the risk of domestic violence perpetration increases in relationships characterized by dysfunctional and oppressive dynamics, poor interpersonal skills, and depleted emotional and material resources. Relationships at high risk of domestic violence include those with high levels of conflict (Aldarondo & Sugarman, 1996; Stith, Green, Smith, & Ward, 2008), emotional abuse and verbal aggression (Dutton, 1995; Dutton, Starzomski, & Ryan, 1996), and the presence of male dominance and forced sex (Marshall, 1996; Painter & Farrington, 1998). In addition, domestic violence risk increases when the partners have underdeveloped communication (Berns, Jacobson, & Gottman, 1999) and problem-solving skills (Anglin & Holtzworth-Munroe, 1997) and few other emotional and material resources from which to draw strength.

High-Risk Communities and Societies

A relatively smaller number of community and social correlates are often mentioned by experts in the field as important contributors to the risk of violence perpetration by men. Structurally disadvantaged communities characterized by poverty (Benson, Litton, & Fox, 2004), low levels of trust and human resources to draw from when in need, and where adequate sanctions against domestic violence are not implemented are high-risk communities for violence perpetration. The risk of violence also increases within broader social and cultural contexts in which marked gender and economic inequities exist and use of violence is seen as a legitimate form of conflict resolution between adults.

HOW WE KNOW IT: A CLOSER LOOK AT WHAT WE KNOW

The search for domestic violence risk factors is guided by the belief that such knowledge can be used to develop appropriate violence prevention and intervention strategies, which would ultimately help reduce the incidence and reoccurrence of violence. Within this context, the large number of proposed factors raises important questions for advocates, policymakers, and practitioners attempting to make sense of the literature on risk factors for domestic violence perpetration.

What Are the Strongest or More Powerful Risk Factors for Domestic Violence Perpetration?

Clarity about the relative potency of risk factors is an important consideration for battered women advocates and policymakers. However, not all risk factors are created equal, and methodological differences on issues such as target population (i.e., community volunteers, court-mandated criminal offenders, laboratory research participants), type of data (e.g., qualitative, quantitative), quality of data (i.e., reliability and validity of measures), use of appropriate comparison groups, data collection procedures (e.g., victim and perpetrators reports), design (e.g., cross-sectional, longitudinal), guiding theoretical framework (e.g., feminist perspective, individual psychopathology, relationship dynamics), and data-analytic techniques (e.g., logistic regression, structural equation modeling) all play a role in the empirical validation of risk factors, suggesting prudence in the evaluation of assertions about the potency or strength of risk factors for domestic violence perpetration. Still, the growing application of meta-analytic techniques to examine overall effect sizes and to assess moderators of violence perpetration (e.g., Foran & O'Leary, 2008; Norlander & Eckhardt, 2005; Stith et al., 2008) now adds a small measure of confidence to these assertions.

To date, there is more evidence about the strength of individual and relationship risk factors for violence perpetration than there is for community and social factors. In the most comprehensive meta-analytic reviews of this literature, Schumacher, Feldbau-Kohn, Smith Slep, and Heyman (2001) and Stith, Smith, Penn, Ward, and Tritt (2004) reported small to moderate effect sizes for individual factors, such as low levels of education and income; history of aggression against female partners (both verbal and physical aggression); history of violence in the family of origin (both witnessing and childhood victimization); high levels of reported anger, depression, and jealousy; insecure attachment; perceived need for and lack of power; personality disorders and psychopathology; heavy drinking and drug abuse; and traditional sex role ideology. These teams of researchers also reported small to high effect sizes for relationship risk factors, such as high levels of relationship conflict, low levels of relationship satisfaction, emotional abuse, and forced sexual relations.

How Do Risk Factors for Violence Perpetration Relate to Each Other?

Determining the cumulative effects of risk factors and disentangling their complex relations is a significant challenge for domestic violence researchers and one that has enormous implications for the development of appropriate advocacy, prevention, and intervention strategies. For both pragmatic and theoretical reasons, studies of risk of violence perpetration have typically focused on a selected number of correlates assessed at a given point in time. This strategy favors the in-depth examination of individual variables over overarching, multivariate developmentally sensitive evaluations of potential risk factors. As a result, despite the field's long-stated preference for systemic and ecological accounts of domestic violence (e.g., Dutton, 1985; Edleson & Tolman, 1992; Straus, 1973), relatively little is known about the combined effects of risk factors, about how multiple factors influence each other and affect the risk of violence perpetration, and about how the potency and clustering of risk may vary over time and developmental periods (Aldarondo & Sugarman, 1996).

A closer look at work done in this area shows what appears to be a tangible cumulative effect of risk factors in predicting the occurrence of physical violence by men against their female intimate partners. A 22-item risk factor index for wife-beating first introduced by Straus, Gelles, and Steinmetz in their seminal publication, *Behind Closed Doors* (1980/2006), was created to examine the collective effect of demographic, relationship, and social risk factors and to estimate the probability of violence when intimate relationships had any number of the specific risk factors identified in their work. Straus and colleagues noted that the percentage of men who perpetrated violence against their partners went from under 1% for men with none of the risk factors to over 70% for those who had 14 or more risk factors, supporting the notion that domestic violence must take into account multiple factors. However, as Straus et al.'s data show, as many as 30% of all predictions for wife-beating made through this method turn out to be false positives, suggesting the need for both better ways of combining the specific risk factors and the inclusion of a broader range of risk factors than those in the original list.

In terms of our understanding of the relations between risk factors for violence perpetration, a recent multivariate exploration of 25 theoretically derived and empirically supported individual, relationship, and social risk factors demonstrated that many of these factors are intricately related to each other and not always in ways that are consistent with the literature (O'Leary, Smith Slep, & O'Leary, 2007). For example, whereas the final model of violence perpetration in this study (which accounted for 47% of the variance) included some of the variables in our list of most strongly supported risk factors such as violence in the family of origin, education, jealousy, and depression, it also excluded other widely supported factors such as alcohol abuse, income, and attitudes toward women. Although this study does not allow us to make conclusions about the relative strength of empirically supported risk factors, the fact that the unique contribution of well-established variables to the prediction of violence perpetration was reduced when evaluated in the company of other risk factors raises the possibility that they may affect the risk of violence through their interactions with other factors.

Are Known Risk Factors for Violence Perpetration Applicable Across Ethnic Groups?

Research on risk factors for violence perpetration has focused almost exclusively on what have been called generic risk factors (Aldarondo, Kaufman-Kantor, & Jasinski, 2002), assuming that a core understanding of domestic violence would be applicable across ethnic and cultural groups. However, international, cross-cultural, and national data show considerable variability in domestic violence rates across countries and ethnic groups (Aldarondo & Fernandez, 2008), suggesting in part that there may be important culture-specific variables affecting the risk for violence perpetration. Unfortunately, the accurate assessment of risk factors across ethnic and cultural groups has been hampered by methodological limitations such as language and literacy barriers, lack of demonstrated validity of risk factor and violence measures for specific cultural groups, culturally appropriate definitions of relevant constructs, and the

> grouping together of responses from ethnic groups with different histories of colonization, religious traditions, cultural identity, and gender role expectations into pan-ethnic categories such as Asian/Pacific Islander and Hispanic groups, and when Black people are treated as a homogeneous group with little or no attention paid to differences between African-Americans, African-Caribbeans, and Africans. (Aldarondo & Fernandez, 2008, p. 9)

To date, the National Alcohol and Family Violence Survey is the only study conducted in the United States specifically designed to overcome some of these limitations (Kaufman-Kantor et al., 1994). Using these data, Aldarondo et al. (2002) evaluated the unique and combined contributions of 11 empirically supported individual, relationship, and social factors in the prediction of wife assault among Puerto Rican, Mexican, Mexican American, and Anglo American groups. They found considerable variability both in the extent to which various risk factors were present across ethnic groups and in the combinations of risk factors affecting the risk of violence perpetration for specific ethnic groups. A high level of conflict in the relationship was found to be the strongest and most stable contributor to the risk of violence perpetration across ethnic groups. In terms of differences among ethnic groups, the risk of violence perpetration was higher for Mexican men who had experienced violence in their families of origin, Mexican American men with low economic resources, and Anglo American men who had witnessed domestic violence in their families of origin.

How Useful Are Risk Factors for Domestic Violence Perpetration in Predicting Reabuse?

We know that about 40% of male perpetrators of violence go on to reabuse their partners within a year (Aldarondo, 1996, 2002) and that about 30 assaults occur for each arrest (Bodnarchuk, Kropp, Ogloff, Hart, & Dutton, 1995). Thus, the identification of factors that contribute to reabuse in cases of domestic violence is of critical importance for everyone concerned with how to best intervene to protect women victims of domestic violence and to stop the men's violent behaviors. In a review of 38 individual, interpersonal, and systemic correlates of domestic violence reabuse, Bennett Cattaneo and Goodman (2005) found no conclusive evidence for specific risk factors of domestic violence reabuse and no evidence in support of the predictive utility of known risk factors for domestic violence perpetration such as age, the man's history of violence in the family of origin, and his beliefs about the use of violence against female partners. However, a longitudinal evaluation of participants in the Chicago Women's Health Study found that a high frequency of physical violence and the man's use of power and control tactics significantly increased the risk of reabuse (Sonis & Langer, 2008).

How Useful Are Risk Factors for Violence Perpetration in Predicting Intimate Partner Femicide?

Femicide is both the most severe type of domestic violence and its most feared outcome. Government homicide data indicate that between 30% and 50% of murdered women in the United States are killed by their male intimate partners or ex-partners (Fox, 2005; Langford, Isaac, & Kabat, 1998). Research suggests that close to three quarters of women murdered by their intimate male partners have prior histories of domestic violence (Campbell et al., 2003), thus making domestic violence the most important risk factor for intimate partner femicide. An evaluation of the intimate partner homicide literature (Campbell et al., 2007) shows that although less severe forms of domestic violence perpetration and intimate partner femicide share some risk factors, there are a number of variables specifically related to an increased risk of femicide by their male intimate partners. Consistent with the literature on individual risk factors for violence perpetration, poor, young men with histories of problem drinking, illicit drug use, jealousy, depression, personality disorders, and mental health problems are considered to be at greater risk of murdering their intimate female partners than men without these characteristics (Campbell et al.,

2007). In terms of known relationship risk factors for violence perpetration, instability/estrangement in the form of physical and legal separations, and forced sex (particularly during pregnancy) are also known to significantly increase the risk of murder for women (Dawson & Gartner, 1998). Other important risk factors specific to intimate partner femicide include men's access to guns, being foreign born, the presence of a stepchild in the home, abusive behavior against a pregnant partner, and stalking (Campbell et al., 2007), with the last one more strongly associated with intact marriages and relationships with no history of domestic violence (McFarlane et al., 1999).

WHERE DO WE GO FROM HERE? GAPS AND PRIORITIES IN DOMESTIC VIOLENCE PERPETRATION RESEARCH

We believe that Jules Henri Poincaré's (2007) statement prefacing this chapter rings true when looking at the collection of risk factors for domestic violence perpetration generated after approximately 3 decades of research in this area. As our summary shows, even with a heap of auspicious risk factors in our reach, we remain with a tenuous understanding of domestic violence on issues of theoretical importance for the field and of vital practical significance for the safety and well-being of women. In particular, we have identified significant gaps in our understanding about the relative strength of risk factors, how specific factors relate to each other, how they change over time, their value to predict reabuse, their applicability across ethnic groups, and their utility for prevention and intervention purposes. Within this context, it seems reasonable for domestic violence researchers and policymakers to feel unsure about how to build a better science for the understanding and resolution of domestic violence perpetration.

The Future of Domestic Violence Research Through a Rear-View Mirror

The previously mentioned realization is a somber warning for those of us who believe that science can be used effectively to protect victims and end domestic violence; however, this is not new for domestic violence researchers. Almost 30 years ago, Straus et al. (1980/2006) wrote,

> The truth is, that despite all that has been written about the family and about violence, and the lesser but still considerable writings on violence in the family, our understanding of these aspects of human life remains obscure. Perhaps this is because we are all too close to the problems of the family and of violence to think clearly about what is really involved. (p. xxviii)

Twenty-six years later, in the new preface to their original 1980 publication, Gelles and Straus (1980/2006) wrote,

> There is a painful irony that tempers our pride in having identified the [risk factors] that provide the clues to preventing family violence. Although there are important exceptions . . . almost all the current research on family violence is focused on the treatment or psychopathology of male perpetrators. . . . Research on treatment is crucial. But it does not deal with prevention. . . . Although [our work] may have led the way in defining the underlying causes of family violence, except for the research on gender equity, few social scientists have followed. (pp. xxii–xxiii)

Ameliorative steps, they stated, "will not solve the basic underlying characteristics of the family and of the society that lead to violence and abuse. These are primarily socially created factors. Therefore, they require steps to create a different society and family system" (Gelles & Straus, 1980/2006, p. xxii). Accordingly, Gelles and Straus (1980/2006) invited us to take note of their original recommendations and focus our work on (a) eliminating the norms that legitimize and glorify violence in society and family, (b) reducing the violence-provoking stressors created by society, (c) integrating families into a network of kin and community, (d) changing the sexist character of society and the family, and (e) breaking the cycle of violence in the family.

Almost a decade later, Finkelhor, Hotaling, and Yllö (1988), in their opening remarks in *Stopping Family Violence: Research Priorities for the Coming Decade*, stated that

> after a generation of frenetic social activity to combat family violence, the signs of progress are uncertain. If we simply count programs or publications or services provided, the results look impressive. But if we ask how often family violence has been halted, how much it has decreased, and how many of its negative effects have been mitigated, the answer is unknown . . . the problem lies with limitations of our knowledge. We do not fully understand the sources of family violence. We do not know precisely what to do to stop it. (p. 9)

Moreover, with much conviction in the power of social sciences to help remedy this situation, Finkelhor et al. (1998) went on to highlight an "increasingly wide consensus among policymakers and practitioners that we could be much more optimistic about the problems of family violence if we had more and better research into its causes and effects, and our efforts to deal with them" (p. 9). Among the top 10 research priorities in the area of spouse abuse they outlined, three focused on male perpetrators of domestic violence:

1. identifying the most important individual, relationship, and social factors in stopping domestic violence;

2. using longitudinal designs to study individual characteristics predictive of domestic violence, the development of abusive behaviors over time (i.e., through early dating, later courtship, and early years of marriage), and factors arresting the development of these behaviors; and
3. understanding the social factors accounting for variable rates of domestic violence across countries.

Eight years later, a panel of domestic violence experts was convened by the National Research Council to

synthesize the relevant research literature and develop a framework for clarifying what is known about the nature and scope of violence against women; and identify promising areas of research to improve knowledge of the scope of the problem and interventions for dealing with it. (Crowell & Burgess, 1996, p. 2)

Among other things, Crowell and Burgess (1996) concluded,

In order to significantly reduce the amount of violence against women in the United States the focus must be on prevention. The development of effective preventive interventions will require a better understanding of the causes of violent behavior against women, as well as rigorous evaluations of preventive intervention programs; . . . researchers working on violence against women come from a wide spectrum of disciplines, each of which has its own terms and perspectives. Many studies in the field suffer from methodological weaknesses, including small sample sizes, lack of control groups, and weak instrumentation; . . . there are many gaps in understanding of violence against women. There is relatively little information about violence against women of color, disabled women, lesbians, immigrant women, and institutionalized women; and . . . research on violence against women will be strengthened by a research infrastructure that supports interdisciplinary efforts and helps to integrate those efforts into service programs and institutional policies, especially in the area of preventive intervention. (pp. 2–6)

The following recommendations made by the National Research Council panel are particularly relevant for the purposes of this chapter and remain as important today as they were 15 years ago:

1. Engage in longitudinal research to study the developmental trajectory of violent behavior.
2. Generate clear definitions of terms to be used by researchers and practitioners.
3. Improve the reliability and validity of research instruments with guidance from the targeted populations (e.g., specific ethnic groups).

4. Rely on both qualitative and quantitative research methodologies to study the convergence of factors such as race, ethnicity, socioeconomic status, age, and sexual orientation in shaping the context and experience of violence.
5. Develop a coordinated research strategy by government agencies to support interdisciplinary studies on violence against women, collaboration between researchers and practitioners, and the integration research into practice.

Table 10.1 includes what we consider some of the top gaps, priorities, and recommendations for research on risk factors for violence perpetration, including some past observations and unfulfilled recommendations already noted.

Back to the Future: The Need for Foresight

Make no mistake, researchers in the field know considerably more today about domestic violence perpetration than they did 30 years ago. This is particularly true of the knowledge of psychological correlates of violence. Moreover, welcomed changes in important risk factors over time (e.g., victimization of children, greater gender equality) and ensuing reductions in the rates of domestic violence and intimate homicides (Rennison, 2003; Straus & Gelles, 1986; Straus, Kaufman-Kantor, & Moore, 1997) give us reason to be optimistic about the contribution of risk factor studies to the reduction and prevention of domestic violence. Yet when it comes to the depth of our understanding of risk factors for violence perpetration, we found ourselves in the tempting position of simply echoing many of the same gaps and recommendations voiced by others during the past 30 years. We are afraid, however, that to do so would not accomplish much more than to add our voices to the chorus. Although the current state of affairs is arguably the result of methodological deficiencies, which no doubt will continue to be improved upon by newer generation of researchers, we believe that our limitations are not all technical in nature. Limitations also lie in the failure to expand the aims of our work from a primary focus on understanding the etiology and correlates of domestic violence (Salazar & Cook, 2002) into a broader interventionist focus of working in partnership with advocates, victims, reformed perpetrators, human service providers, and policymakers to protect women, prevent the incidence and recurrence of domestic violence, and, going to back to an earlier quote by Gelles and Straus (1980/2006), "create a different society and family system" that disavows the use of violence and promotes the well-being of its members.

We believe that recasting the purpose of our work within a continuum of intervention ranging from reactive interventions for partners in need of protection, to preventive policies and programs for partners at risk, to proactive program and policy development for the promotion of wellness, would

TABLE 10.1
Knowledge Gaps, Priorities, and Recommendations for Research
on Risk Factors for Domestic Violence Perpetration

Knowledge gaps and priorities	Recommendations for research
Better understand the relative strength of risk factors and their relationship to each other	Conduct multivariate evaluations of empirically supported and theoretically derived individual, relational, and social risk factors
Understand how specific risk factors change over time in response to developmental and situational demands and the conditions arresting the development of abusive behavior in intimate relationships	Conduct longitudinal mixed-methods studies of the developmental trajectory of domestic violence focusing on partners' experiences over time and the multivariate evaluation of empirically supported and theoretically derived potential risk factors and protective factors for violence perpetration
Better understand risk factors associated with reabuse and intimate partner femicide	Conduct mixed-methods multivariate evaluations of empirically supported and theoretically derived individual, relational, and risk factors for reabuse and intimate partner femicide
Assess the applicability of known risk factors across ethnic groups and identify culture-specific factors for violence perpetration	Conduct multivariate evaluations of empirically supported and theoretically derived individual, relational, and social risk factors within specific ethnic and cultural groups, taking into consideration those aspects of ethnicity along which ethnic groups vary, such as histories of immigration and colonization, quality of ethnic identity, spirituality, cultural norms, and cultural adaptation and development
Identify dynamic and malleable risk factors and demonstrate their utility for prevention and treatment purposes	Include the assessment of individual, relational, and social risk factors as standard procedure in the evaluation of prevention and intervention initiatives
Identify individual, relationship, and social factors associated with the cessation of violence and change of abusive behaviors	Conduct retrospective and prospective longitudinal mixed-methods studies focusing on partners' experiences over time and the multivariate evaluation of empirically supported and theoretically derived individual, relational, and social correlates of change in abusive behavior
Understand factors associated with the development of abusive behaviors over time and factors arresting the development of these behaviors	Conduct longitudinal mixed-methods studies focusing on partners' experiences over time and the multivariate evaluation of empirically supported and theoretically derived individual, relational, and social factors associated with the development of abusive behaviors
Improve the reliability and validity of research instruments with guidance of targeted populations	Complete appropriate evaluations of validity and reliability prior to data collection with special populations

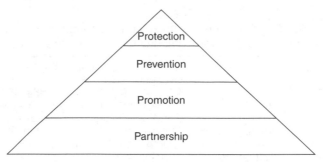

Figure 10.1. The four P's of domestic violence research.

help us generate knowledge with greater practical and theoretical utility to advocates and policymakers. Although some risk factors may have practical utility at each level of intervention, we consider it prudent to assume considerable variability between domains of intervention. Moreover, consistent with previous calls to improve the relevance of domestic violence research for advocacy and policy purposes (e.g., Cook & Koss, 2001; Gondolf, Yllö, & Campbell, 1997), we consider partnerships among researchers, advocates, intimate partners, and policymakers to be the foundation of this effort. For ease of presentation we refer to the proposed continuum of intervention research as the four P's of domestic violence research, as illustrated in Figure 10.1.

The proposed expansion of aims builds on the field's commitment to an ecological view of domestic violence, inclusive of psychological, feminist, and sociological insights about the role of specific factors, relationship dynamics, and larger social structures in shaping behavior. However, unlike the prevailing ecological view for domestic violence perpetration, which assumes low and high levels of risk factors to be casually related to positive (i.e., well-being, nonviolent intimate relationships) and negative (i.e., abusive behaviors) outcomes, respectively, we view the development of positive and negative outcomes in reference to the presence of risk factors in interaction with protective factors (individual, relational, and collective) within specific health- and wellness-promoting contexts. Also, unlike the preference in domestic violence risk studies to focus on effects of generic and static risk factors, we consider it imperative to include a wider range of culture-specific and dynamic factors that may affect the continuity and discontinuity of domestic violence over time.

Within this context, it is reasonable to assume that partners in intimate relationships are affected in uneven ways both by conditions that increase the risk of violence and by countervailing protective and behavioral change factors that neutralize the power of risk factors and promoting their well-being. Thus, drawing from the application of strength-based ecologically oriented approaches to research and practice in the fields of public health and psychology (e.g., DiClemente, Crosby, & Kegler, 2002; Kenny, Horne, Orpinas & Reese, 2009), we believe that the understanding of risk factors for violence perpetration and the prevention of domestic violence can be significantly enhanced by integrating the assessment of specific protective and wellness promotion factors in domestic violence research, evaluating their relations to known risk factors, and determining the extent to which they may reduce the potency of risk factors for domestic violence perpetration.

Figure 10.2 illustrates a combination of risk and protective factors in an expanded ecological interventionist framework for domestic violence perpetration. Included here are known risk factors for violence perpetration and variables noted by psychologists, criminologists, sociologists, community psychologists, and public health researchers to be associated either with wellness or with change of maladaptive or criminal behavior, and which may be thought to prevent the onset of domestic violence and facilitate the elimination of violent behaviors. To be sure, our intent here is not to offer a detailed review of these factors. Instead, by drawing on a wide spectrum of disciplines to generate this list, we hope to draw attention to the practical and heuristic value afforded by an ecological interventionist framework.

A challenge, even for ecologically minded domestic violence risk researchers attempting to link the immediate concerns of a research project to the broader advocacy and policy concerns, is that we do not live with a heightened sense of urgency about issues related to the protection of victims; the scarcity of material resources, programs, and policies for violence prevention; and the efficient coordination of social structures to control and end the violence. Unfettered by these pressing issues, we have the luxury of approaching domestic violence primarily as a research problem to be understood. Moreover, professionally, we are rewarded for our individual achievements as researchers, for attending to individual pathology, and for viewing with suspicion intervention and policy initiatives that may not be fully supported by "basic research evidence." This may not be problematic if domestic violence was primarily a research issue. However, as alluded to in the Definitional Considerations section of this chapter, domestic violence is an advocacy and policy issue that does not neatly comply with our disciplinary preferences. Domestic violence will become purely a research problem when it is no longer a significant social and moral concern. When it comes to the framing of issues in reference to the protection of women, the promotion of wellness, and partnership considerations, our academic and professional life often conspires against our best intentions.

The success of an ecological interventionist framework for domestic violence perpetration research would depend on the commitment, political will, and determination of domestic violence researchers to work in partnership

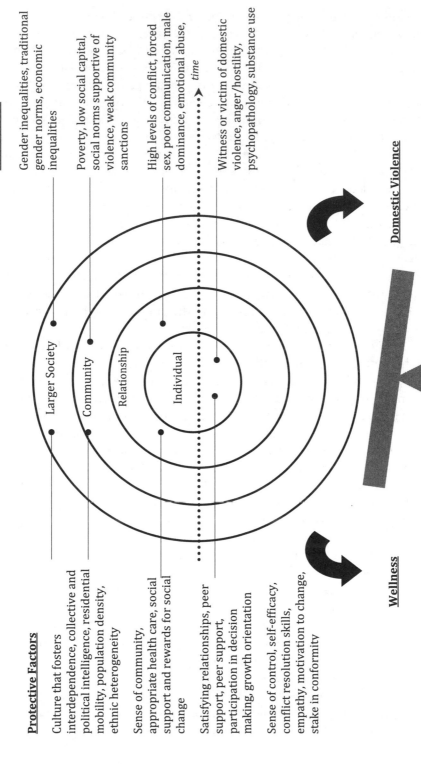

Risk Factors

Gender inequalities, traditional gender norms, economic inequalities

Poverty, low social capital, social norms supportive of violence, weak community sanctions

High levels of conflict, forced sex, poor communication, male dominance, emotional abuse,

Witness or victim of domestic violence, anger/hostility, psychopathology, substance use

Larger Society

Community

Relationship

Individual

time

Domestic Violence

Wellness

Protective Factors

Culture that fosters interdependence, collective and political intelligence, residential mobility, population density, ethnic heterogeneity

Sense of community, appropriate health care, social support and rewards for social change

Satisfying relationships, peer support, peer support, participation in decision making, growth orientation

Sense of control, self-efficacy, conflict resolution skills, empathy, motivation to change, stake in conformity

Figure 10.2. The ecology of risk and protective factors for domestic violence perpetration.

with everyone with a stake in the elimination of domestic violence whether or not they are prepared to take a step in this direction. It will require leadership from researchers to engage other domestic violence stakeholders in the project of building both a better science for domestic violence research and a safer and healthier home for intimate partners. We have argued in this chapter that a renewed sense of foresight from the domestic violence research community is needed to make our skills and knowledge as scientists better fit the needs and aspirations of intimate partners, advocates, and policymakers. The proposed ecological interventionist framework for domestic violence risk research demands that we keep in check our preference to account for the trajectory from risk to psychopathology at the expense of focusing on what needs to be done to protect women, prevent violence, and promote favorable conditions for personal, relational, and community well-being. Without an adequate appreciation of the possibilities that such an expanded framework affords us, we risk arriving 20 years from now at strangely familiar conclusions about research knowledge regarding the perpetration of domestic violence.

REFERENCES

Anglin, K., & Holtzworth-Munroe, A. (1997). Comparing the responses of maritally violent spouses to problematic marital and nonmarital situations: Are skill deficits of physically aggressive husbands and wives global? *Journal of Family Psychology, 11,* 301–313. doi:10.1037/0893-3200.11.3.301

Aldarondo, E. (1996). Cessation and persistence of wife assault: A longitudinal analysis. *American Journal of Orthopsychiatry, 66,* 141–151. doi:10.1037/h0080164

Aldarondo, E. (2002). Evaluating the efficacy of interventions with men who batter. In E. Aldarondo & F. Mederos (Eds.), *Programs for men who batter: Intervention and prevention strategies in a diverse society* (pp. 3-1–3-20). Kingston, NJ: Civic Research Institute.

Aldarondo, E., & Fernandez, M. C. (2008). Intimate partner violence and recidivism following interventions with men who batter: Cultural and empirical considerations. In R. Carillo & J. Tello (Eds.), *Family violence and men of color: Healing the wounded male spirit* (2nd ed., pp. 1–35). New York, NY: Springer.

Aldarondo, E., Kaufman-Kantor, G. K., & Jasinski, J. L. (2002). Risk marker analysis for wife assault in Latino families. *Violence Against Women: An International and Interdisciplinary Journal, 8,* 429–454.

Aldarondo, E., & Sugarman, D. (1996). Risk marker analysis of the cessation and persistence of wife assault. *Journal of Consulting and Clinical Psychology, 64,* 1010–1019. doi:10.1037/0022-006X.64.5.1010

Babcock, J. C., Waltz, J., Jacobson, N., & Gottman, J. (1993). The relation between communication patterns, power discrepancies, and domestic violence. *Journal of Consulting and Clinical Psychology, 61,* 40–50. doi:10.1037/0022-006X.61.1.40

Bennett Cattaneo, L., & Goodman, L. A. (2005). Risk factors for reabuse in intimate partner violence: A cross-disciplinary critical review. *Trauma, Violence & Abuse*, 6, 141–175. doi:10.1177/1524838005275088

Benson, M., Litton, A., & Fox, G. (2004). *When violence hits home: How economics and neighborhood play a role* (Report NCJ 205004). Washington, DC: U.S. Department of Justice, Office of Justice Program.

Berns, S. B., Jacobson, N. S., & Gottman, J. M. (1999). Demand–withdraw interaction in couples with a violent husband. *Journal of Consulting and Clinical Psychology*, 67, 666–674. doi:10.1037/0022-006X.67.5.666

Bodnarchuk, M., Kropp, P., Ogloff, J., Hart, S., & Dutton, D. (1995). *Predicting cessation of intimate assaultiveness after group treatment.* Vancouver, British Columbia, Canada: British Columbia Institute of Family Violence.

Boyle, D., & Vivian, D. (1996). Generalized versus spouse-specific anger/hostility and men's violence against inmates. *Violence and Victims*, 11, 283–317.

Campbell, J. C., Glass, N., Sharps, P., Laughon, K., & Bloom, T. (2007). Intimate partner homicide: Review and implications of research and policy. *Trauma, Violence & Abuse*, 8, 246–269. doi:10.1177/1524838007303505

Campbell, J. C., Webster, D., Koziol-McLain, J., Block, C., Campbell, D., Curry, M., . . . Laughon, K. (2003). Risk factors for femicide in abusive relationships: Results from a multisite case control study. *American Journal of Public Health*, 93, 1089–1097. doi:10.2105/AJPH.93.7.1089

Cook, S., & Koss, M. (2001). Using action-research to inform interventions for male violence against women. In N. Schneiderman, J. Gentry, J. M. Da Silva, M. Speers, & H. Tomes (Eds.), *Integrating behavioral and social sciences with public health* (pp. 115–139). Washington, DC: American Psychological Association. doi:10.1037/10388-006

Crowell, N., & Burgess, A. (1996). *Understanding violence against women.* Washington, DC: National Academy Press. doi:10.1037/10204-000

Dawson, R., & Gartner, R. (1998). Differences in the characteristics of intimate femicides: The role of relationship state and relationship status. *Homicide Studies*, 2, 378–399. doi:10.1177/1088767998002004003

Delsol, C., & Margolin, G. (2004). The role of family-of-origin violence in men's marital violence perpetration. *Clinical Psychology Review*, 24, 99–122. doi:10.1016/j.cpr.2003.12.001

DiClemente, R., Crosby, R., & Kegler, M. (2002). *Emerging theories in health promotion practice and research: Strategies for improving public health.* San Francisco, CA: Jossey-Bass.

Doumas, D. M., Pearson, C. L., Elgin, J. E., & McKinley, L. L. (2008). Adult attachment as a risk factor for intimate partner violence: The "mispairing" of partners attachment styles. *Journal of Interpersonal Violence*, 23, 616–634. doi:10.1177/0886260507313526

Dutton, D. G. (1985). An ecologically nested theory of male violence toward intimates. *International Journal of Women's Studies*, 8, 404–413.

Dutton, D. G. (1995). Trauma symptoms and PTSD-like profiles in perpetrators of intimate abuse. *Journal of Traumatic Stress, 8,* 299–316. doi:10.1002/jts.2490080210

Dutton, D. G., Starzomski, A., & Ryan, L. (1996). Antecedents of abusive behavior in wife assaulters. *Journal of Family Violence, 11,* 113–132. doi:10.1007/BF02336665

Dutton, D. G., van Ginkel, C., & Landolt, M. (1996). Jealousy, intimate abusiveness, and intrusiveness. *Journal of Family Violence, 11,* 411–423. doi:10.1007/BF02333425

Eckhardt, C., & Kassinove, H. (1998). Articulated cognitive distortions and cognitive deficiencies in maritally violent men. *Journal of Cognitive Psychotherapy, 12,* 231–250.

Edleson, J., & Tolman, R. (1992). *Interventions for men who batter: An ecological approach.* Newbury Park, CA: Sage.

Finkelhor, D., Hotaling, G. T., & Yllö, K. (1988). *Stopping family violence: Research priorities for the coming decade.* Thousand Oaks, CA: Sage.

Foran, H., & O'Leary, K. (2008). Alcohol and intimate partner violence: A meta-analytic review. *Clinical Psychology Review, 28,* 1222–1234. doi:10.1016/j.cpr.2008.05.001

Fox, J. (2005). *Uniform crime reports, United States: Supplementary homicide reports, 1976–2002* [Computer file]. Ann Arbor, MI: Inter-University Consortium for Political and Social Research.

Gelles, R., & Straus, M. (2006). Foreword. In M. Straus, R. J. Gelles, & S. K. Steinmetz (Eds.), *Behind closed doors: Violence in the American family* (pp. xxvi–xxviii). New Brunswick, NJ: Transaction. (Original work published 1980)

Gondolf, E., Yllö, K., & Campbell, J. (1997). Collaboration between researchers and advocates. In G. K. Kaufman & J. Jasinski (Eds.), *Out of darkness: Contemporary research perspectives on family violence* (pp. 255–261). Thousand Oaks, CA: Sage.

Hastings, J., & Hamberger, L. (1994). Psychosocial modifiers of psychopathology for domestically violent and nonviolent men. *Psychological Reports, 80,* 667–670.

Holtzworth-Munroe, A., & Hutchinson, G. (1993). Attributing negative intent to wife behavior: The attributions of maritally violent versus nonviolent men. *Journal of Abnormal Psychology, 102,* 206–211. doi:10.1037/0021-843X.102.2.206

Holtzworth-Munroe, A., & Smutzler, N. (1996). Comparing the emotional reactions and behavior intentions of violent and nonviolent husbands to aggressive, distressed and other wife beaters. *Violence and Victims, 11,* 319–339.

Holtzworth-Munroe, A., Stuart, G., & Hutchinson, G. (1997). Violence versus nonviolent husbands: Differences in attachment patterns, dependency and jealousy. *Journal of Family Psychology, 11,* 314–331. doi:10.1037/0893-3200.11.3.314

Hurlbert, D., Whittaker, K., & Munoz, C. (1991). Etiological characteristics of abusive husbands. *Military Medicine, 156,* 670–675.

Kaufman-Kantor, G., & Jasinski, J. (1998). Dynamics and risk factors in partner violence. In J. Jasinski & L. Williams (Eds.), *Partner violence: A comprehensive review of 20 years of research* (pp. 1–43). Thousand Oaks, CA: Sage.

Kaufman-Kantor, G., Jasinski, J., & Aldarondo, E. (1994). Sociocultural status and incidence of marital violence in Hispanic families. *Violence and Victims, 9,* 207–222.

Kenny, M., Horne, A., Orpinas, P., & Reese, L. (2009). *Realizing social justice: The challenges of preventative interventions.* Washington, DC: American Psychological Association. doi:10.1037/11870-000

Langford, L., Isaac, N. E., & Kabat, S. (1998). Homicides related to intimate partner violence in Massachusetts. *Homicide Studies, 2,* 353–377. doi:10.1177/1088767998002004002

Marshall, L. (1996). Psychological abuse of women: Six distinct clusters. *Journal of Family Violence, 11,* 379–409. doi:10.1007/BF02333424

McFarlane, J., Campbell, J. C., Wilt, S., Sachs, C., Ulrich, Y., & Xu, X. (1999). Stalking and intimate partner femicide. *Homicide Studies, 3,* 300–316. doi:10.1177/1088767999003004003

McKenry, P., Julian, T., & Gavazzi, S. (1995). Toward a biopsychosocial model of domestic violence. *Journal of Marriage and the Family, 57,* 307–320. doi:10.2307/353685

Murphy, C. M., Meyer, S. L., & O'Leary, K. D. (1994). Dependency characteristics of partner assaultive men. *Journal of Abnormal Psychology, 103,* 729–735. doi:10.1037/0021-843X.103.4.729

Neidig, P., Friedman, D., & Collins, B. (1986). Attitudinal characteristics of males who have engaged in spouse abuse. *Journal of Family Violence, 1,* 223–233. doi:10.1007/BF00978561

Norlander, B., & Eckhardt, C. (2005). Anger, hostility, and male perpetrators of intimate partner violence: A meta-analytic review. *Clinical Psychology Review, 25,* 119–152. doi:10.1016/j.cpr.2004.10.001

O'Leary, K. D., Barling, J., Arias, I., & Rosenbaum, A., Malone, J. & Tyree, A. (1989). Prevalence and stability of physical aggression between spouses: A longitudinal analysis. *Journal of Consulting and Clinical Psychology, 57,* 263–268. doi:10.1037/0022-006X.57.2.263

O'Leary, K. D., & Curley, A. D. (1986). Assertion and family violence: Correlates of spouse abuse. *Journal of Marital and Family Therapy, 12,* 281–289. doi:10.1111/j.1752-0606.1986.tb00654.x

O'Leary, K. D., Smith Slep, A. M., & O'Leary, S. G. (2007). Multivariate models of men's and women's partner aggression. *Journal of Consulting and Clinical Psychology, 75,* 752–764. doi:10.1037/0022-006X.75.5.752

Painter, K., & Farrington, D. (1998). Marital violence in Great Britain and its relationship to marital and non-marital rap. *International Review of Victimology, 5,* 257–276.

Pan, H., Neidig, P., & O'Leary, K. D. (1994). Predicting mild and severe husband-to-wife physical aggression. *Journal of Consulting and Clinical Psychology, 62,* 975–981. doi:10.1037/0022-006X.62.5.975

Poincaré, J. H. (2007). *Science and hypothesis.* New York, NY: Cosimo.

Quigley, B., & Leonard, K. (2000). Alcohol, drug, and violence. In V. B. Van Hasselt & M. Hersen (Eds.), *Aggression and violence: An introductory text* (pp. 259–283). Boston, MA: Allyn & Bacon.

Rennison, C. M. (2003). *Intimate partner violence, 1993–2001.* Washington, DC: U.S. Department of Justice, Bureau of Justice Statistics.

Sagrestano, L., Heavey, C., & Christensen, A. (1999). Perceived power and physical violence in marital conflict. *Journal of Social Issues, 55,* 65–79. doi:10.1111/0022-4537.00105

Salazar, L., & Cook, S. (2002). Violence against women: Is psychology part of the problem or the solution? A content analysis of psychological research from 1990 to 1999. *Journal of Community & Applied Social Psychology, 12,* 410–421. doi:10.1002/casp.691

Schumacher, J. A., Feldbau-Kohn, S., Smith Slep, A. M., & Heyman, R. E. (2001). Risk factors for male-to-female partner physical abuse. *Aggression and Violent Behavior, 6,* 281–352. doi:10.1016/S1359-1789(00)00027-6

Sonis, J., & Langer, M. (2008). Risk and protective factors for recurrent intimate partner violence in a cohort of low-income inner-city women. *Journal of Family Violence, 23,* 529–538. doi:10.1007/s10896-008-9158-7

Stith, S. M., & Farley, S. C. (1993). A predictive model of male spousal violence. *Journal of Family Violence, 8,* 183–201. doi:10.1007/BF00981767

Stith, S. M., Green, N. M., Smith, D. B., & Ward, D. B. (2008). Marital satisfaction and marital discord as risk markers for intimate partner violence: A meta-analytic review. *Journal of Family Violence, 23,* 149–160. doi:10.1007/s10896-007-9137-4

Stith, S. M., Rosen, K. H., Middleton, K. A., Busch, A. L., Lundeberg, K., & Carlton, R. P. (2000). The intergenerational transmission of spouse abuse: A meta-analysis. *Journal of Marriage and the Family, 62,* 640–654. doi:10.1111/j.1741-3737.2000.00640.x

Stith, S. M., Smith, D. B., Penn, C. E., Ward, D. B., & Tritt, D. (2004). Intimate partner physical abuse perpetration and victimization risk factors: A meta-analytic review. *Aggression and Violent Behavior, 10,* 65–98. doi:10.1016/j.avb.2003.09.001

Straus, M. A. (1973). A general systems theory approach to a theory of violence between family members. *Social Sciences Information, 12,* 105–125. doi:10.1177/053901847301200306

Straus, M. A., & Gelles, R. J. (1986). Societal change and change in family violence from 1975 to 1985 as revealed by two national surveys. *Journal of Marriage and the Family, 48,* 465–479. doi:10.2307/352033

Straus, M. A., & Gelles, R. J. (1990). How violent are American families? Estimates from the National Family Violence Resurvey and other studies. In M. A. Straus

& R. J. Gelles (Eds.), *Physical violence in American families* (pp. 95–112). New Brunswick, NJ: Transaction.

Straus, M. A., Gelles, R. J., & Steinmetz, S. K. (2006). *Behind closed doors: Violence in the American family.* New Brunswick, NJ: Transaction. (Original work published 1980)

Straus, M. A., Kaufman Kantor, G., & Moore, D. W. (1997). Change in cultural norms approving marital violence: From 1968 to 1994. In G. Kaufman Kantor & J. L. Jasinski (Eds.), *Out of the darkness: Contemporary perspectives on family violence* (pp. 3–16). Thousand Oaks: Sage.

Tjaden, P., & Thoennes, N. (2000). *Extent, nature, and consequences of IPV: Findings from the National Violence Against Women Survey.* Washington, DC: National Institute of Justice.

World Health Organization Task Force on Violence and Health. (2000). *Rape and sexual assault and violence in the family.* Geneva, Switzerland: World Health Organization.

11

VULNERABILITY AND PROTECTIVE FACTORS FOR INTIMATE PARTNER VIOLENCE

JACQUELYN C. CAMPBELL, JEANNE ALHUSEN, JESSICA DRAUGHON, JOAN KUB, AND BENITA WALTON-MOSS

Our definition of *intimate partner violence* (IPV) is condensed from that of the IPV consensus panel for the Centers for Disease Control and Prevention (CDC): physical and/or sexual assault or threats of assault against a married, cohabiting, or dating current or estranged intimate partner by the other partner, inclusive of emotional abuse and controlling behaviors in a relationship with history of physical and/or sexual assault (Saltzman, Fanslow, McMahon, & Shelley, 1999). We use *intimate partner abuse* to encompass emotional abuse, controlling behaviors, and other types of psychological abuse (e.g., financial abuse, forced isolation) occurring without violence as well as physical or sexual assault and threats.

In this chapter, we review the major studies of risk and protective factors for IPV over the past decade, building on Stith, Smith, Penn, Ward, and Tritt's (2004) meta-analysis of risk factors for perpetration and victimization, as well as the risk and protective factor analyses using representative databases since 2000, such as Tjaden and Thoennes (2000), Walton-Moss, Manganello, Frye, and Campbell (2005), and Cunradi, Caetano, and Schafer (2002). We also include several reviews of risk and protective factors for various aspects of IPV. Despite many excellent focused reviews, we were unable to find any recent systematic reviews of the overall risk and protective factors for IPV from an interdisciplinary perspective.

We attempted to synthesize evidence from the past decade on risk and protective factors in the United States that used either representative samples or a substantial sample of a particular group generally underrepresented in larger surveys. Other inclusion criteria included risk and protective factors for physical and/or sexual assault or reassault from a current or former intimate partner (current or former spouse; romantic partner, cohabitating or not) of the same or opposite sex. We examined risk and protective factors for victimization only; risk factors for perpetration are covered in Chapter 10, this volume. We also included qualitative analysis or mixed-methods research that elucidates mechanisms by which vulnerability or protective factors help explain increases or decreases in the occurrence, severity, and/or recurrence of IPV.

The chapter first summarizes evidence regarding demographic vulnerabilities and then evidence for other vulnerability factors for IPV victimization, including childhood risk factors (child physical and sexual assault and child witnessing of IPV). Next, we discuss evidence around substance abuse, pregnancy, and disabilities as risk factors for victimization. The next section focuses on protective factors against IPV. A critique of methods follows each major section. Finally, the gaps in research are summarized and recommendations for future research identified.

WHAT DO WE KNOW?

Several demographic vulnerability factors have been consistently associated with IPV victimization in large-scale and population-based studies. Others have been less consistently found because of methodological or sampling differences in studies or a failure to include those variables.

Review of Vulnerability Factors for IPV

We review the evidence on each of the pertinent variables in turn, except for gender, which is thoroughly discussed in Chapter 9, this volume. Most studies of risk for IPV victimization are of women.

Multivariate Analyses

Stith et al.'s (2004) meta-analysis of 94 studies conducted from 1980 to 2000 found several demographic factors predictive of IPV victimization among females but with very small ($< .10$) effect sizes. These included age ($r = -.07$), low income ($r = -.04$), and number/presence of children ($r = .06$). The only moderate or large effect sizes were factors that are more likely consequences of IPV than precursors or vulnerabilities: Female violence toward male partners ($r = .41$), female depression ($r = .28$), and fear of partner violence ($r = .27$). One factor with a small effect size (but $> .10$) that could be interpreted as a true vulnerability factor was female alcohol abuse ($r = .13$), but none of the studies in the analysis were prospective (see fuller discussion below). It is interesting that none of the other vulnerability factors discussed later (e.g., childhood exposure to violence) were measured in enough of the studies considered to include in this only truly relevant meta-analysis.

In a multivariate analysis of Behavioral Risk Factor Surveillance System (BRFSS) data, Vest, Catlin, Chen, and Brownson (2002) found that the following factors differentiated physically abused from nonabused women: educational achievement discordance (woman had greater education than her partner), cohabitating, unmarried, African American, young age, low income, without health insurance or Medicaid insured, cigarette use, history of physical abuse, poor physical and mental health, and children in the home. In a random-sample telephone survey of urban women from 12 geographically diverse U.S. cities, multivariate analysis resulted in only two characteristics of the women (compared with five male partner perpetrator characteristics) independently associated (adjusted odds ratio [AOR] > 2.0) with abuse victimization: younger age and fair or poor mental health (Walton-Moss et al., 2005). In both of these cross-sectional studies, the findings of poor mental health, poor physical health, and cigarette use as risk factors need to be interpreted with caution, given that longitudinal studies have generally interpreted these to be consequences of IPV (e.g., Campbell, 2002). Thus, findings from earlier reviews that there are relatively few factors consistently and confidently identified as precursors (vs. sequelae) to IPV victimization in multivariate analysis continue to be accurate.

Other studies examined risk factors for injury from IPV, a proxy for more severe physical abuse. Thompson, Saltzman, and Johnson (2003) identified risk factors for partner violence injury in multivariate analyses of data from two national surveys: the Canadian Violence Against Women Survey and the U.S. National Violence Against Women Survey. History of prior victimization by the same partner and the woman reporting fear of injury or death, interpretable as a consequence of severe violence, were associated with victim physical injury. Two other vulnerabilities were associated with the partner: his witnessing IPV as a child and alcohol problems. Walton-Moss et al. (2005) had similar findings, with only characteristics of the partner (e.g., fair or poor mental health, prior arrest for IPV) as risk factors for IPV injury.

Age

The most consistent demographic vulnerability for IPV victimization across studies is young age. In every large-scale study, younger women are most at risk of being victimized. AORs for younger age (usually 18–29) range from 2.05 to 3.07 (Bauer Rodríguez, & Pérez-Stable, 2000; Tjaden & Thoennes, 2000; Vest et al., 2002; Walton-Moss et al., 2005). Even higher prevalence is found in investigations among adolescent girls (Glass et al., 2003). Aggressive and violent behavior has long been noted as more common among the young than other age groups, and because young people tend to form intimate relationships with other young people, victims of violent partners will themselves be relatively young.

Marital Status

Some of the major investigations have found being single a vulnerability factor, but the evidence is mixed, and even when found the increased risk is relatively small (Bauer et al., 2000; Stith et al., 2004), with the exception of the BRFSS (Vest et al., 2002). Increased risk associated with separation or divorce is more consistent, but most of these investigations have been cross-sectional (Vest et al., 2002; Walton-Moss et al., 2005). This finding can reflect both abused women leaving the abusive relationship and therefore separated or divorced when responding to surveys and increased violence postseparation.

Sexual Preference

Few studies have examined sexual preference in terms of IPV. Tjaden and Thoennes (2000) found a higher prevalence of IPV among same-sex male couples than same-sex female couples, but there were very few same-sex couples in the national study. In one of the few large-scale studies of same-sex IPV among same-sex male couples, Greenwood et al. (2002) found that younger age (< 40 years), lower education, and positive HIV serostatus were associated with IPV. As has been noted with women in abusive heterosexual relationships, positive HIV serostatus is probably a consequence of IPV, which in turn may increase risk of subsequent abuse (Campbell et al., 2008).

Income and Employment

Income and employment tend to be strongly correlated, and most studies that enter both in multivariate analyses have found some risk attributable to one and/or the other. Generally, low income and unemployment among women have been found to be a vulnerability for IPV, although more so for recent IPV than lifetime (e.g., Tjaden & Thoennes, 2000; Vest et al., 2002). Not all of the large-scale studies found a relation between income and/or unemployment and IPV in multivariate analyses, although they were present in bivariate analyses, suggesting either mediation with other factors or a spurious relation (e.g., Walton-Moss et al., 2005). Again, because most investigations are cross-sectional and more often examining lifetime IPV versus past-year or current IPV, the association with income/employment may indicate a lack of resources interfering with women being able to escape abusive relationships more than a factor making women more vulnerable to IPV starting.

Race or Ethnicity

IPV rates have been shown to vary by race or ethnicity but not in consistent directions. The preponderance of the evidence suggests little relation between race or ethnicity and lifetime IPV victimization when other factors such as income are accounted for. The exception is the BRFSS analysis for 18 states, in which women of multiracial and American Indian/Native Alaskan (AI/NA) background were more likely to report lifetime physical and/or sexual IPV compared with Caucasian women (AOR = 1.74, 95% confidence interval [CI] = 1.35–2.25; Breiding, Black, & Ryan, 2008). The same increased risk for AI/NA women was found by Tjaden and Thoennes (2000), but there has been insufficient representation of both of those groups in most other large-scale analyses. In the BRFSS, Asian women (AOR = 0.28, 95% CI = 0.18–0.43) and Hispanic women (AOR = 0.48, 95% CI = 0.41–0.56) were less likely to report IPV, with no significant differences between African American and Caucasian women. On bivariate analyses, non-White women, primarily African American women, appeared to more often be IPV victims compared with White women (Vest et al., 2002; Walton-Moss et al., 2005), but differences decreased or disappeared when adjusting for other sociodemographic factors, primarily income, or when examined by state (Field & Caetano, 2004; Vest et al., 2002).

Even so, in a review of population-based and longitudinal research on IPV, Field and Caetano (2004) concluded that there is a small increased risk for current IPV for African American women in comparison with White and Hispanic women, even controlling for income and other risk factors. The excess risk for current rather than lifetime risk suggests that although being African American probably does not increase the risk for *ever* being victimized by IPV, the cultural context as well as lack of resources and structural oppression common for African American (and AI/AN) women may contribute to these women having a harder time escaping or changing the violent relationship. Neighborhoods may also matter. In an analysis of a merger of the nationally representative National Survey of Families and Households and the 1990 U.S. Census, Benson and Fox (2004) demonstrated that higher rates among African Americans could be accounted for by their higher levels of economic distress and their greater likelihood of living in disadvantaged neighborhoods. The rate of IPV was virtually identical among African Americans and Whites with high incomes, but African Americans with low and moderate incomes had a significantly higher rate of IPV than Whites in those income categories.

When type of IPV was examined, there were also variations. When women in community-based clinics responded to an anonymous survey, racial and ethnic differences were only observed for physical abuse, not verbal abuse. In this large study, both African American and Mexican American women had elevated rates (Rickert, Wiemann, Harrykissoon, Berenson, & Kolb, 2002). Notably, the sample comprised young women between 14 and 26 years of age, an age group known to have increased rates of IPV in comparison with older women.

Substance Abuse

Women's substance use is associated with IPV victimization in most research. Overall, alcohol misuse has been studied more than other drug use and more consistently related to IPV than other drug use. One meta-analysis of mental health correlates of IPV including 10 studies found a weighted odds ratio of 5.56 for battered women with alcohol abuse or dependence compared with the general population (Golding, 1999). Stith et al.'s (2004) meta-analysis of 11 studies documented that women's alcohol use was a risk factor for victimization, but the effect size was relatively small ($r = .13, p < .001$). Significant relations between women's alcohol use and IPV were also found in 11 studies published since the 2004 meta-analysis. However, almost all studies have been cross-sectional, making it impossible to determine whether the alcohol use is a precursor or sequelae of IPV victimization.

The remaining studies either focused on physical IPV (Cunradi et al., 2002) or examined physical and sexual IPV separately or as a combined variable (e.g., Zablotska et al., 2009). Less frequently, investigations focused on psychological IPV in addition to physical and sexual abuse and were conducted with varied samples, including clinic (Martin, Beaumont, & Kupper, 2003), court (Shannon, Logan, Cole & Walker, 2008), and population-based (Sharps, Campbell, Campbell, Gary, & Webster, 2001; Temple, Weston, Stuart, & Marshall, 2008). Associations were not consistent across IPV types in the group examining all three. Whereas substance abuse was consistently significantly associated with physical IPV, women's alcohol use was unrelated to psychological abuse (Martin et al., 2003; Shannon et al., 2008) and sexual abuse (Temple et al., 2008).

Golding's (1999) meta-analysis of other drug abuse or dependence found a mean odds ratio of 5.62 across four studies comparing battered women and the general population, but there were fewer than the required minimum of four studies on illicit drug use for Stith et al.'s (2004) meta-analysis. However, a meta-analysis specifically examining the relation between drug abuse and IPV was recently published utilizing data from 96 published and unpublished investigations (Moore et al., 2008). Mean effect size (ES) for women's drug use weighted by sample size (d statistic) varied from .33 (seven studies, 19 ESs averaged within the studies) for sexual coercion/abuse to .39 (eight studies, 16 ESs) for psychological aggression and .49 (29 studies, 93 ESs) for physical IPV. Upon examination of specific drugs, female cocaine use had a moderate effect for psychological aggression ($d = .50$, two studies, four ESs), physical abuse ($d = .59$, two studies, six ESs), and sexual coercion ($d = .88$, one study, four ESs). Marijuana had lower effects than cocaine but higher than other drug classes for psychological aggression ($d = .48$, two studies, four ESs) and physical abuse ($d = .18$, three studies, four ESs). Notably, there were significant homogeneous effect sizes only for physical and sexual abuse.

Four studies subsequent to and consistent with Moore et al.'s (2008) meta-analysis also demonstrated significant relations with at least one type of IPV. With one exception (Shannon et al., 2008), women's drug use was related to physical IPV. In that study, women who reported both drug and alcohol use also experienced more sexual assault than with similar levels of alcohol intake and no drug use. The methadone-maintained women in one of the few longitudinal studies, who were frequent users of crack cocaine or marijuana at Wave 2, had 4.4 and 4.5, respectively, greater odds of reporting physical and/or sexual IPV than nondrug (other than methadone) using women (El-Bassel, Gilbert, Wu, Go, & Hill, 2005). Results from the remaining two studies differed according to other contextual factors. Martin et al. (2003) noted an association of drug use and physical and sexual IPV during pregnancy but not the year prior to pregnancy. In the other study, women's drug use was related to victimization after accounting for her partner's drug use but became insignificant after accounting for her mental health and social support (Golinelli, Longshore, & Wenzel, 2009).

Experiencing Violence in Childhood

Many studies consistently show experiencing violence in childhood as a significant vulnerability for IPV victimization. Two of the most persuasive are the Adverse Childhood Experiences (ACE) study, a large retrospective study of 9,367 health maintenance organization patients in San Diego (Whitfield, Anda, Dube, & Felitti, 2003), and the New Zealand prospective birth cohort study (Fergusson et al., 2008). In the ACE study, women who reported one violent childhood experience more than doubled their risk of IPV victimization later in life (AOR = 2.3, 95% CI = 1.6–3.1), and those who experienced physical and sexual abuse and witnessed IPV in childhood were 3.5 times more likely to report IPV victimization (Whitfield et al., 2003). In the New Zealand birth cohort analysis, an overall measure of exposure to abuse in childhood (severity of child physical and sexual abuse and parental violence) was significantly associated with IPV victimization in multivariate analyses. Childhood sexual and physical abuse but not witnessing parental IPV was associated with IPV victimization in females in bivariate analyses.

In most analyses, all types of child maltreatment increased the risk of revictimization; however, Maker, Kemmelmeier, and Peterson (2001) found that victims of childhood sexual abuse were at the highest risk, with a 3 to 5 times greater risk of revictimization than those who did not experience any type of child abuse. Ehrensaft et al. (2003) found childhood physical abuse to increase risk by more than 2 (2.21) and witnessing parental IPV by 3.0.

The large number of studies conducted on large, diverse populations finding this association lends support to the cycle of violence theory. Revictimization is often experienced within the family and is highly associated with low self-esteem as well as dissociation during the revictimization, both resulting from the childhood trauma (Whitfield et al., 2003). The long-term mental health sequelae from childhood trauma, including posttraumatic stress disorder (PTSD) and depression, may make it more difficult for women to escape from abusive adult relationships.

Family Composition

The presence of children in the home increased the risk of IPV victimization in most of the large studies (e.g., Vest et al., 2002) but not all (e.g., Walton-Moss et al., 2005). Having a child in the home not biologically related to the male perpetrator of IPV has been shown to be a risk factor for femicide in several major studies (e.g., Campbell et al., 2003). However, in the analysis of risk factors for IPV, Walton-Moss et al. (2005) did not find a stepchild in the home to be predictive of IPV without a homicide.

Pregnancy

Abuse during pregnancy is recognized as a risk to the health of a woman (depression, smoking), her fetus, and her newborn (e.g., low birth weight, child abuse) in numerous research overviews (e.g., Campbell, Garcia-Moreno, & Sharps, 2004) as well as in a meta-analysis (Murphy, Shei, Myhr, & DuMont, 2001). Between 3% and 19% of pregnant women are abused, with the most common prevalence between 4% and 8.3% across studies in North America (Gazmararian et al., 1996). Studies that measured IPV at some point in all three trimesters found the highest prevalence, whereas other studies typically screened for IPV only once, usually during the first prenatal appointment (Campbell et al., 2004).

Both clinic studies and large-scale population-based studies using Pregnancy Risk Assessment Monitoring System data (Saltzman, Johnson, Gilbert, & Goodwin, 2003; Silverman, Decker, Reed, & Raj, 2006) found that prevalence during pregnancy was lower than the year prior to pregnancy. For some women, however, abuse can start (usually a first pregnancy) or worsen during pregnancy (an indication of a particularly violent man if abuse started, worsened, or continued during pregnancy; Campbell et al., 2004).

Verbal abuse during pregnancy is higher than physical abuse, according to several clinic-based studies (e.g., Yost, Bloom, McIntire, & Leveno, 2005), and can increase even when physical abuse decreases (Castro, Peek-Asa, & Ruiz, 2003). Many of the studies did not measure sexual violence, which also has deleterious health outcomes in nonpregnant women (Campbell et al., 2004). Thus, pregnancy is probably not a risk factor for IPV except for a few women for whom abuse starts during pregnancy and/or who are partnered by a particularly violent man, but it may be a protective factor for physical abuse, if not for psychological abuse. Even if pregnancy does not make women more vulnerable to IPV, the results of this research underscore the importance of health care providers assessing women for IPV in prenatal as well as other health care settings.

Two recent prospective studies suggested that African American and younger women are at increased risk of IPV before, during, and/or after pregnancy (Silverman et al., 2006; Yost et al., 2005). Silverman et al. (2006) also found that American Indian women reported higher rates of IPV at all time points (both prepregnancy and during pregnancy) compared with White women. Torres et al. (2000) found that Puerto Rican women reported the highest levels of abuse during pregnancy, whereas other Latina groups (Mexican, Cuban, and Central American women) reported significantly lower rates than African American and White women.

Women With Disabilities

There is strong evidence that women who have ever experienced IPV are more likely to report a chronic health problem such as heart or circulatory disease, back problems, chronic pain, arthritis, nerve system damage, asthma or other respiratory diseases, depression, or other mental illness as a consequence of abuse (Campbell, 2002; Coker, Smith, & Fadden, 2005). There is also evidence that women with physical or mental disabilities are at increased risk of experiencing violence by an intimate partner (Brownridge, Ristock, & Hiebert-Murphy, 2008). It is thought that women with health and/or strength impairments may be vulnerable to IPV because of inability to fight back, that those with cognitive impairments may be more easily manipulated, or that perpetrators may feel that women with disabilities may be less likely to report the violence for fear that they will have no one to care for them (Martin et al., 2006). Because of the primarily cross-sectional nature of most studies, it is also possible that the disabilities are a result of IPV. There is also evidence that women with physical disabilities are often victimized by multiple perpetrators and that the effects are likely to be severe (Hassouneh-Phillips, 2005). McFarlane et al. (2001) used the Abuse Assessment Screen–Disability with a multiethnic sample of 511 women and found that disability-related abuse was attributed equally to intimate partners, care providers, and health professionals.

Studies investigating the abuse of women with physical disabilities have reported considerable variations in lifetime prevalence of all types of abuse related to methodological problems, including different definitions of abuse or lack of rigorous designs (Nosek, Hughes, Taylor, & Taylor, 2006), such as lack of comparison groups or convenience samples (Martin et al., 2006). Even though three large-scale Canadian surveys have shown women with disabilities reporting a higher prevalence of physical violence than those without disabilities (Brownridge et al., 2008), the statewide analysis of the North Carolina BRFSS (5,694 women) found that women with disabilities were not significantly more likely than women without disabilities to have experienced physical assault alone but were more likely to have experienced sexual assault (Martin et al., 2006).

Nosek et al. (2006) found in a sample of 415 well-educated, predominantly minority women with physical disabilities from private and public specialty clinics that those who were younger, more educated, less mobile, more socially isolated, and had higher levels of depression were more likely to report abuse in the past year. Hassouneh-Phillips (2005) described the abuse pathways model developed from study findings specific to physical disabilities. Identified vulnerability factors were cumulative lifetime trauma and psychosocial factors (poor parental relationships, child abuse, previous intimate partner abuse, and alcohol or drug use) and disability-related factors, including feelings of sexual inadequacy, perceived need of an intimate partner, intimate partners as caregivers, and physical dependency.

Review of Protective Factors for IPV

Compared with vulnerability factors, relatively few protective factors have been specifically studied. For instance, despite frequent mention as potentially important, resilience has seldom been studied as a protective factor against IPV, although work by Humphreys (2003) supported its value as a mediator of physical and psychological distress from IPV.

Education

The one at least relatively consistent demographic protective factor against both initiation and continuation of IPV across studies has been educational level, with completion of a college education or at least some college protective against IPV, both lifetime and current (Rickert et al., 2002; Stith et al., 2004; Vest et al., 2002; Walton-Moss et al., 2005). The meta-analysis by Stith and colleagues also found a very small effect size ($r = .01$) for employment as a protective factor, so small as to be considered negligible.

Social Support

The role of social support has been a factor that has been extensively studied as it relates to stress and health outcomes. Social support has been recognized as a protective factor, a buffer, and enhancer of well-being (Panchanadeswaran, El-Bassel, Gilbert, Wu, & Chang, 2008). This is true for abused women as well as other target populations. Social support for women experiencing abuse may help the abused women reinterpret the abuse as not their fault, help women alter their environments through tangible means (shelter, money), or help women deal with emotions associated with abuse. Sources of social support and help-seeking behaviors in abused women have been studied, as well as the effects of social support, in explaining health outcomes in abused women.

Sources of social support for women experiencing abuse can be informal (family, friends, kin) or formal (health professionals, religious leaders, shelter personnel). In a qualitative study of 31 women, results of the analysis revealed that women used female friends more than family members for support. Relationships with family members, especially parents, were not consistently seen as useful sources of support (Rose, Campbell, & Kub, 2000). Similarly, Coker et al. (2002) found informal sources of emotional support in addition to provision of tangible material resources from parents, friends, and community members as important coping resources.

Goodman, Dutton, Vankos, and Weinfurt (2005) found that women with greater access to resources were better able to keep themselves safe over time than women who did not have access or who lost access to resources over the course of the study. Specifically, strong social support was associated with lower probability of reabuse for women. Similarly, women from homeless shelters and low-income housing in Los Angeles County with higher levels of social support and currently separated from their intimate partner were less likely to have experienced violence during a follow-up period (Wenzel, Tucker, Elliott, Marshall, & Williamson, 2004). Short et al. (2000) found that participants in focus groups felt protective factors from reassault (or incentives for leaving the relationship) were those that fostered social resources, such as family and friends, as well as self-respect.

O'Campo, McDonnell, Gielen, Burke, and Chen (2002), however, in a sample of primarily African American abused women, found that only 4% of the respondents wanted to receive assistance from a family member or friend. In a different study, 15 African American women perceived that their informal networks were willing to offer instrumental support but not emotional support. In addition, these participants felt that the African American community believed that victims of violence were "stupid" for remaining in violent relationships (Morrison, Luchok, Richter, & Parra-Medina, 2006). In a random sample of 416 women on methadone, lower levels of perceived social support were associated with physical aggression, sexual assaults, and injurious attacks. Respondents also perceived highest levels of support from their significant others and lowest levels of support from their friends (Panchanadeswaran et al., 2008).

Studies have also examined the relation of social support in mediating or moderating the relation between abuse and physical and mental health outcomes. A cross-sectional survey of 1,152 women ages 18 to 65 years recruited from family practice settings found that among women experiencing IPV and controlling for IPV frequency, higher social support scores were associated with a significantly reduced risk for impaired physical health and mental health problems (depression, PTSD symptoms, and suicide attempts; Coker et al., 2002). In a sample of 143 economically disadvantaged African American women, social support mediated the relation of IPV and depressive symptoms, anxiety symptoms, and parenting stress and was related to leaving an abusive relationship (Mitchell et al., 2006). This finding was replicated in a prospective nationally representative sample, with leaving the abusive relationship at the 5-year follow-up associated with lower individual income but more social support at Wave 1 (Zlotnick, Johnson, & Kohn, 2006).

It has been posited that supportive communities or communities with strong individual ties are protective against IPV (Benson & Fox, 2004). However, this idea has been challenged with data from impoverished and disadvantaged communities with high rates of IPV that nevertheless are closely knit and insular. The evidence is mixed on whether community collective efficacy or the ability of members of a community to exercise social control is a protective factor against IPV the way it is for general violence (Browning, 2002; Sabol, Coulton, & Korbin, 2004). Thus, social support as a protective factor has been primarily studied and supported as a protective factor from deleterious physical and mental health outcomes from abuse including revictimization rather than as a protective factor from abuse happening at all.

Other Protective Factors

Rickert et al. (2002) found increased use of contraception and older age at first intercourse and/or childbirth to be associated with lower levels of physical and verbal abuse. Theoretically, these findings are hard to explain except either as consequences of lower levels of abuse (because many studies have found unplanned pregnancy to be an outcome of IPV) or as a spurious factor indicating some underlying personal characteristic associated with both IPV and contraceptive use and consequent later age at first birth.

HOW DO WE KNOW IT?

Examining vulnerability factors for IPV remains a challenge for a multitude of reasons. A comprehensive review of risk factors in the past decade of research reveals many of the issues in elucidating how certain vulnerability factors help explain increases in IPV.

Issues in Identifying Demographic Vulnerabilities

As has been mentioned, the lack of longitudinal studies in the field makes the identification and interpretation of demographic vulnerabilities difficult because some, such as divorced or separated marital status, may well be a consequence of the IPV. Furthermore, many studies (e.g., Vest et al., 2002) consider demographic factors in terms of IPV occurring rather than separating risk factors for victimization from those increasing risk of perpetration. Another issue is that few of the analyses have tested for interactions among the demographic variables. For instance, when Vest et al. (2002) stratified for income in one of the states in their 10-state BRFSS analysis, they found that the increased risk conferred by single and separated marital status was only present among low-income women. This kind of complex analysis helps make these vulnerabilities more understandable but unfortunately is seldom undertaken.

Issues in Identifying Race/Ethnicity Vulnerabilities

Much of the discrepancy in evidence seems to center on conceptual definitions of "race" or "ethnic" groups. Focus on Hispanic women as a category reflects a lack of precision in identification of cultural groups; that is, Mexican Americans may have different experiences from Puerto Ricans, Cuban Americans, Central Americans, and other Hispanic origin groups. There are similar issues in clumping together all Asian groups as well as all indigenous groups (e.g., Native Hawaiian and Alaskan Native with other Native American groups). Another issue in determining the extent of vulnerability among Hispanic/Latina women is failure to take into account acculturation in most analyses. In the majority of studies in which it was included, acculturation increased the vulnerability of Hispanic/Latina women to IPV (Klevens, 2007). Less acculturated Spanish-speaking victims are less likely to take part in large population-based studies because of fears of participation or disclosure of IPV leading to deportation or unregistered phone numbers, as well as lack of presence in health care settings and language barriers (Klevens, 2007).

Issues in Determining Vulnerability by Substance Abuse

As previously discussed, in most studies there is a significant albeit relatively small association between women's substance use, especially alcohol abuse and physical IPV victimization, but this is primarily based on cross-sectional studies. Overall, not only was the literature linking women's alcohol use and IPV more consistent, but alcohol use typically was more precisely measured than other drug use with standardized measures such as the Alcohol Use Disorder Identification Test. The two studies that did not observe a relation between alcohol use and increased risk of IPV used a single question to measure IPV with focus on lifetime IPV. Additionally, alcohol use in one of the two studies was combined with other drug use and examined only if the substance use occurred during sexual intercourse (González-Guarda, Peragallo, Urrutia, Vasquez, & Mitrani, 2008). The other study focused on a specific IPV outcome: physical injury (Thompson & Kingree, 2006).

According to the infrequent longitudinal studies completed to date (El-Bassel et al., 2005; Temple et al., 2008), the relation is also bidirectional. However, in one longitudinal study, the New Zealand birth cohort study, alcohol and drug abuse/dependence was well measured (according to *Diagnostic and Statistical Manual of Mental Disorders* criteria; American Psychiatric Association, 2000) and not found to be predictive of victimization in multivariate analysis (Fergusson, Boden, & Horwood, 2008). Certainly more such studies are needed to establish temporality. Perhaps more important, these studies should be incident-based, as the investigations by Sharps et al. (2001) and Thompson and Kingree (2006) were. Only then will it be possible to disentangle women's substance use (or substance withdrawal) that is an additional risk factor precipitating IPV to substance use that is consequent to and used to cope with IPV and its consequent mental health sequelae, especially PTSD. With regard to IPV, many studies used one of the versions of the Conflict Tactics Scale (CTS) or its modifications. Although the CTS is often used, it is well known that the context in which IPV occurs is inadequately captured by this measure. For example, an important factor infrequently accounted for is the woman's partner's substance use, controlled for in six of the 14 studies reviewed (Cunradi et al., 2002; Golinelli et al., 2009; Shannon et al., 2008; Sharps et al., 2001; Temple et al., 2008).

Issues in Childhood Exposure Vulnerabilities

Because of the astronomical investment associated with a prospective cohort study to determine how childhood exposure relates to adult risk for IPV, the majority of studies to date have been retrospective. A potential weakness in studies using retrospective designs is the possibility of difficulty in remembering and reporting childhood experiences. Several longitudinal studies of adults with documented childhood abuse have found that adults are likely to underestimate actual occurrence, thereby underestimating the true relation between experiencing childhood trauma and risk of revictimization (Femina, Yeager, & Lewis, 1990).

Issues in Identifying Vulnerability During Pregnancy

Research comparing prevalence rates of abuse during pregnancy among ethnic groups has found that fewer Hispanic women are abused during pregnancy than non-Hispanic White women and African American women (Campbell et al., 2004). These findings must be interpreted with caution because the majority of studies excluded Cuban American, Puerto Rican, and Central American women. Another limitation is that samples were often working-class and poor women receiving prenatal care in public clinics, thereby failing to assess the influence of social class.

Protective Factors

As previously discussed for vulnerability factors, the majority of research investigating protective factors suffers from a preponderance of cross-sectional work. A few of the studies discussed in the previous section followed women prospectively (e.g., Zlotnick et al., 2006); however, they are by far the minority. Furthermore, there is a dearth of information regarding true protective factors in contrast to protection from the detrimental effects of IPV already experienced.

WHERE DO WE GO FROM HERE?

It is interesting to note that both the vulnerability and protective factors discussed in this chapter are present at every level of the social ecological model. These risk and protective factors pervade every part of society, and any future analysis must take into account the interlocking circles of ecological influence on individuals and their experience of IPV. Although several vulnerability factors have been consistently identified in the population-based or large-scale representative research, the most consistent are demographic (age and separated or divorced marital status), and even the separated or divorced marital status risk factor has the time-ordering issue that makes it difficult to determine which of the vulnerability factors precede IPV and which are consequences. The evidence around other demographic factors such as income, employment, and race/ethnicity increasing vulnerability is less consistent, and these factors are often confounded with or have interacting effects with each other. Increasingly sophisticated analyses of longitudinal data are needed to untangle these relationships.

Prospective studies will also help establish which of the other vulnerability factors are precursors of IPV rather than consequences. These kinds of studies are beginning to illuminate the complicated relations between substance abuse and IPV, but much more is needed. Future research should account for contextual factors such as women's mental health and other problems that may arise as a consequence or antecedent to substance misuse. When drug use is examined, focusing on or separating out cocaine and marijuana, when possible, would also extend knowledge related to IPV. Similarly, studying aspects of type of IPV rather than a global approach would also advance our knowledge.

Further meta-analyses, such as Stith et al.'s (2004) endeavor, are needed, inclusive of protective factors as well as a more complete representation of vulnerabilities. It will also be important to distinguish risk factors for lifetime IPV versus current IPV versus recurrence of IPV. Some of the frequently noted victimization vulnerability factors, such as income and unemployment, may be primarily operative in increasing the risk for current IPV rather than lifetime. In other words, they may increase a woman's risk of being stuck in an abusive relationship (thereby increasing the odds of current IPV) rather than increasing a woman's vulnerability to IPV happening at any time during her lifetime.

It is also important to distinguish risk and protective factors for various forms of IPV; specific physical, psychological, sexual, and stalking aspects may differ. These issues matter not only to researchers but also to those who are trying to prevent IPV at all levels—primary, secondary, and tertiary—because the appropriate strategies at each level may differ. An implication for IPV prevention is to address the effects of childhood exposure to violence in order to prevent IPV as well as to assess all women for both past histories of abuse and current abuse in the health care system.

Finally, far more research is needed that specifically measures potential protective factors, including, but not limited to, various forms of social support. Such research is extremely important in identifying what can be strengthened to help prevent IPV, one of the most important directions for the future.

REFERENCES

American Psychiatric Association. (2000). *Diagnostic and statistical manual of mental disorders* (4th ed., text revision). Washington, DC: Author.

Bauer, H. M., Rodríguez, M. A., & Pérez-Stable, E. J. (2000). Prevalence and determinants of intimate partner abuse among public hospital primary care patients. *Journal of General Internal Medicine, 15*, 811–817.

Benson, M., & Fox, G. (2004). *When violence hits home: How economics and neighborhood play a role* (National Institutes of Justice Research in Brief). Washington, DC: U.S. Department of Justice.

Breiding, M. J., Black, M. C., & Ryan, G. W. (2008). Prevalence and risk factors of intimate partner violence in eighteen U.S. states/territories, 2005. *American Journal of Preventive Medicine, 34,* 112–118. doi:10.1016/j.amepre.2007.10.001

Browning, C. R. (2002). The span of collective efficacy: Extending social disorganization theory to partner violence. *Journal of Marriage and the Family, 64,* 833–850. doi:10.1111/j.1741-3737.2002.00833.x

Brownridge, D. A., Ristock, J., & Hiebert-Murphy, D. (2008). The high risk of IPV against Canadian women with disabilities. *Medical Science Monitor, 14*(5), 27–32.

Campbell, J. C. (2002). Violence against women and health consequences. *The Lancet, 359,* 1331–1336. doi:10.1016/S0140-6736(02)08336-8

Campbell, J. C., Baty, M. L., Ghandour, R. M., Stockman, J., Francisco, L., & Wagman, J. (2008). The intersection of intimate partner violence against women and HIV/AIDS: A review. *International Journal of Injury Control and Safety Promotion, 15,* 221–231. doi:10.1080/17457300802423224

Campbell, J. C., Garcia-Moreno, C., & Sharps, P. (2004). Abuse during pregnancy in industrialized and developing countries. *Violence Against Women, 10,* 770–789. doi:10.1177/1077801204265551

Campbell, J. C., Webster, D., Koziol-McLain, J., Block, L., Campbell, D., Curry, M. A., . . . Laughon, K. (2003). Risk factors for femicide in abuse relationships: Results from a multisite case control study. *American Journal of Public Health, 93,* 1089–1097. doi:10.2105/AJPH.93.7.1089

Castro, R., Peek-Asa, C., & Ruiz, A. (2003). Violence against women in Mexico: A study of abuse before and during pregnancy. *American Journal of Public Health, 93,* 1110–1116. doi:10.2105/AJPH.93.7.1110

Coker, A. L., Smith, P. H., & Fadden, M. (2005). Intimate partner violence and disabilities among women attending family practice clinics. *Journal of Women's Health, 14,* 829–838. doi:10.1089/jwh.2005.14.829

Coker, A. L., Smith, P. H., Thompson, M. P., McKeown, R. E., Bethea, L., & Davis, K. E. (2002). Social support protects against negative effects of partner violence on mental health. *Journal of Women's Health & Gender-Based Medicine, 11,* 465–476. doi:10.1089/15246090260137644

Cunradi, C. B., Caetano, R., & Schafer, J. (2002). Socioeconomic predictors of intimate partner violence among White, Black and Hispanic couples in the United States. *Journal of Family Violence, 17,* 377–389. doi:10.1023/A:1020374617328

Ehrensaft, M. K., Cohen, P., Brown, J., Smailes, E., Chen, H., & Johnson, J. G. (2003). Intergenerational transmission of partner violence: A 20-year prospective study. *Journal of Consulting and Clinical Psychology, 71,* 741–753. doi:10.1037/0022-006X.71.4.741

El-Bassel, N., Gilbert, L., Wu, E., Go, H., & Hill, J. (2005). Relationship between drug abuse and intimate partner violence: A longitudinal study among women receiving methadone. *American Journal of Public Health, 95,* 465–470. doi:10.2105/AJPH.2003.023200

Femina, D. D., Yeager, C. A., & Lewis, D. O. (1990). Child abuse: Adolescent records vs. adult recall. *Child Abuse & Neglect, 14,* 227–231. doi:10.1016/0145-2134(90)90033-P

Fergusson, D. M., Boden, J., & Horwood, L. (2008). Developmental antecedents of interpartner violence in a New Zealand birth cohort. *Journal of Family Violence, 23,* 737–753. http://dx.doi.org/10.1007/s10896-008-9199-y

Field, C. A., & Caetano, R. (2004). Ethnic differences in intimate partner violence in the U.S. general population: The role of alcohol use and socioeconomic status. *Trauma, Violence & Abuse, 5,* 303–317. doi:10.1177/1524838004269488

Gazmararian, J. A., Lazorick, S., Spitz, A. M., Ballard, T. J., Saltzman, L. E., & Marks, J. S. (1996). Prevalence of violence against pregnant women: A review of the literature. *JAMA, 275,* 1915–1920. doi:10.1001/jama.275.24.1915

Glass, N., Fredland, N., Campbell, J. C., Yonas, M., Sharps, P., & Kub, J. (2003). Adolescent dating violence: Prevalence, risk factors, health outcomes, and implications for clinical practice. *Journal of Obstetric, Gynecologic, and Neonatal Nursing, 32*(10), 2–12.

Golding, J. M. (1999). Intimate partner violence as a risk factor for mental disorders: A meta-analysis. *Journal of Family Violence, 14,* 99–132. doi:10.1023/A:1022079418229

Golinelli, D., Longshore, D., & Wenzel, S. L. (2009). Substance use and intimate partner violence: Clarifying the relevance of women's use and partners' use. *Journal of Behavioral Health Services & Research, 36,* 199–211.

González-Guarda, R. M., Peragallo, N., Urrutia, M. T., Vasquez, E. P., & Mitrani, V. B. (2008). HIV risks, substance abuse, and intimate partner violence among Hispanic women and their intimate partners. *Journal of the Association of Nurses in AIDS Care, 19,* 252–266. doi:10.1016/j.jana.2008.04.001

Goodman, L., Dutton, M. A., Vankos, N., & Weinfurt, K. (2005). Women's resources and use of strategies as risk and protective factors for reabuse over time. *Violence Against Women, 11,* 311–336. doi:10.1177/1077801204273297

Greenwood, G. L., Relf, M. V., Huang, B., Pollack, L. M., Canchola, J. A., & Catania, J. A. (2002). Battering victimization among a probability-based sample of men who have sex with men (MSM). *American Journal of Public Health, 92,* 1964–1969. doi:10.2105/AJPH.92.12.1964

Hassouneh-Phillips, D. (2005). Understanding abuse of women with physical disabilities. *Advances in Nursing Science, 28,* 70–80.

Humphreys, J. (2003). Resilience in sheltered battered women. *Issues in Mental Health Nursing, 24,* 137–152. doi:10.1080/01612840305293

Klevens, J. (2007). An overview of intimate partner violence among Latinos. *Violence Against Women, 13*, 111–122. doi:10.1177/1077801206296979

Maker, A. H., Kemmelmeier, M., & Peterson, C. (2001). Child sexual abuse, peer sexual abuse, and sexual assault in adulthood: A multi-risk model of revictimization. *Journal of Traumatic Stress, 14*, 351–368. doi:10.1023/A:1011173103684

Martin, S. L., Beaumont, J. L., & Kupper, L. L. (2003). Substance use before and during pregnancy: Links to intimate partner violence. *American Journal of Drug and Alcohol Abuse, 29*, 599–617. doi:10.1081/ADA-120023461

Martin, S. L., Ray, N., Sotres-Alvarez, D., Kupper, L. L., Moracco, K. E., Dickens, P. A., . . . Gizlice, Z. (2006). Physical and sexual assault of women with disabilities. *Violence Against Women, 12*, 823–837. doi:10.1177/1077801206292672

McFarlane, J., Hughes, R. B., Nosek, M. A., Groff, J. Y., Swedlend, N., & Dolan Mullen, P. (2001). Abuse Assessment Screen–Disability (AAS-D): Measuring frequency, type, and perpetrator of abuse toward women with physical disabilities. *Journal of Women's Health & Gender-Based Medicine, 10*, 861–866. doi:10.1089/152460901753285750

Mitchell, M. D., Hargrove, G. L., Collins, M. H., Thompson, M. P., Reddick, T. L., & Kaslow, N. J. (2006). Coping variables that mediate the relation between intimate partner violence and mental health outcomes among low-income, African American women. *Journal of Clinical Psychology, 62*, 1503–1520. doi:10.1002/jclp.20305

Moore, T. M., Stuart, G. L., Meehan, J. C., Rhatigan, D. L., Hellmuth, J. C., & Keen, S. M. (2008). Drug abuse and aggression between intimate partners: A meta-analytic review. *Clinical Psychology Review, 28*, 247–274. doi:10.1016/j.cpr.2007.05.003

Morrison, K. E., Luchok, K. J., Richter, D. L., & Parra-Medina, D. (2006). Factors influencing help-seeking from informal networks among African American victims of intimate partner violence. *Journal of Interpersonal Violence, 21*, 1493–1511. doi:10.1177/0886260506293484

Murphy, C. C., Shei, B., Myhr, T. L., & DuMont, J. (2001). Abuse: A risk factor for low birth weight? A systematic review and meta-analysis. *Canadian Medical Association Journal, 165*, 1567–1572.

Nosek, M. A., Hughes, R. B., Taylor, H. B., & Taylor, P. (2006). Disability, psychosocial, and demographic characteristics of abused women with physical disabilities. *Violence Against Women, 12*, 838–850. doi:10.1177/1077801206292671

O'Campo, P., McDonnell, K., Gielen, A., Burke, J., & Chen, Y.-H. (2002). Surviving physical and sexual abuse: What helps low-income women? *Patient Education and Counseling, 46*, 205–212. doi:10.1016/S0738-3991(01)00214-2

Panchanadeswaran, S., El-Bassel, N., Gilbert, L., Wu, E., & Chang, M. (2008). An examination of the perceived social support levels of women in methadone maintenance treatment programs who experience various forms of intimate partner violence. *Women's Health Issues, 18*, 35–43. doi:10.1016/j.whi.2007.10.007

Rickert, V. I., Wiemann, C. M., Harrykissoon, S. D., Berenson, A. B., & Kolb, E. (2002). The relationship among demographics, reproductive characteristics, and intimate partner violence. *American Journal of Obstetrics and Gynecology, 187*, 1002–1007. doi:10.1067/mob.2002.126649

Rose, L. E., Campbell, J., & Kub, J. (2000). The role of social support and family relationships in women's responses to battering. *Health Care for Women International, 21*, 27–39. doi:10.1080/073993300245384

Sabol, W. J., Coulton, C. J., & Korbin, J. E. (2004). Building community capacity for violence prevention. *Journal of Interpersonal Violence, 19*, 322–340. doi:10.1177/0886260503261155

Saltzman, L. E., Fanslow, J. F., McMahon, P. M., & Shelley, G. A. (1999). *Intimate partner violence surveillance: Uniform definitions and recommended data elements, Version 1.0.* Atlanta, GA: National Center for Injury Prevention and Control, Centers for Disease Control and Prevention.

Saltzman, L. E., Johnson, C. H., Gilbert, B. C., & Goodwin, F. (2003). Physical abuse around the time of pregnancy: An examination of prevalence and risk factors in 16 states. *Maternal and Child Health Journal, 7*, 31–43. doi:10.1023/A:1022589501039

Shannon, L., Logan, T. K., Cole, J., & Walker, R. (2008). An examination of women's alcohol use and partner victimization experiences among women with protective orders. *Substance Use & Misuse, 43*, 1110–1128. doi:10.1080/10826080801918155

Sharps, P. W., Campbell, J., Campbell, D., Gary, F., & Webster, D. (2001). The role of alcohol use in intimate partner femicide. *American Journal on Addictions, 10*, 122–135. doi:10.1080/105504901750227787

Short, L. M., McMahon, P. M., Chervin, D. D., Shelley, G. A., Lezin, N., Sloop, K. S., & Dawkins, N. (2000). Survivors' identification of protective factors and early warning signs for intimate partner violence. *Violence Against Women, 6*, 272–285. doi:10.1177/10778010022181840

Silverman, J. G., Decker, M. R., Reed, E., & Raj, A. (2006). Intimate partner violence victimization prior to and during pregnancy among women residing in 26 U.S. states: Associations with maternal and neonatal health. *American Journal of Obstetrics and Gynecology, 195*, 140–148. doi:10.1016/j.ajog.2005.12.052

Stith, S. M., Smith, D. B., Penn, C. E., Ward, D. B., & Tritt, D. (2004). Intimate partner physical abuse perpetration and victimization risk factors: A meta-analytic review. *Aggression and Violent Behavior, 10*, 65–98. doi:10.1016/j.avb.2003.09.001

Temple, J. R., Weston, R., Stuart, G. L., & Marshall, L. L. (2008). The longitudinal association between alcohol use and intimate partner violence among ethnically diverse community women. *Addictive Behaviors, 33*, 1244–1248. doi:10.1016/j.addbeh.2008.05.005

Thompson, M. P., & Kingree, J. B. (2006). The roles of victim and perpetrator alcohol use in intimate partner violence outcomes. *Journal of Interpersonal Violence, 21*, 163–177. doi:10.1177/0886260505282283

Thompson, M. P., Saltzman, L. E., & Johnson, H. (2003). A comparison of risk factors for intimate partner violence-related injury across two national surveys on violence against women. *Violence Against Women, 9,* 438–457. doi:10.1177/1077801202250955

Tjaden, P., & Thoennes, N. (2000). *Extent, nature and consequences of intimate partner violence: Findings from the National Violence Against Women Survey* (NCJ 181867). Washington, DC: U.S. Department of Justice.

Torres, S., Campbell, J. C., Campbell, D., Ryan, J., King, C., Price, P., . . . Laude, M. (2000). Abuse during and before pregnancy: Prevalence and cultural correlates. *Violence and Victims, 15,* 303–321.

Vest, J. R., Catlin, T. K., Chen, J. J., & Brownson, R. C. (2002). Multistate analysis of factors associated with intimate partner violence. *American Journal of Preventive Medicine, 22,* 156–164. doi:10.1016/S0749-3797(01)00431-7

Walton-Moss, B. J., Manganello, J., Frye, V., & Campbell, J. C. (2005). Risk factors for intimate partner violence and associated injury. *Journal of Community Health, 30,* 377–389. doi:10.1007/s10900-005-5518-x

Wenzel, S. L., Tucker, J. S., Elliott, M. N., Marshall, G. N., & Williamson, S. L. (2004). Physical violence against impoverished women: A longitudinal analysis of risk and protective factors. *Women's Health Issues, 14,* 144–154. doi:10.1016/j.whi.2004.06.001

Whitfield, C., Anda, R., Dube, S., & Felitti, V. (2003). Violent childhood experiences and the risk of intimate partner violence in adults. *Journal of Interpersonal Violence, 18,* 166–185. doi:10.1177/0886260502238733

Yost, N. P., Bloom, S. L., McIntire, D. D., & Leveno, K. J. (2005). A prospective observational study of domestic violence during pregnancy. *Obstetrics and Gynecology, 106,* 61–65.

Zablotska, I. B., Gray, R. H., Koenig, M. A., Serwadda, D., Nalugoda, F., Kigozi, G., . . . Wawer, M. (2009). Alcohol use, intimate partner violence, sexual coercion and HIV among women aged 15–24 in Rakai, Uganda. *AIDS and Behavior, 13,* 225–233.

Zlotnick, C., Johnson, D. M., & Kohn, R. (2006). Intimate partner violence and long-term psychosocial functioning in a national sample of American women. *Journal of Interpersonal Violence, 21,* 262–275. doi:10.1177/0886260505282564

12

PSYCHOLOGICAL, REPRODUCTIVE AND MATERNAL HEALTH, BEHAVIORAL, AND ECONOMIC IMPACT OF INTIMATE PARTNER VIOLENCE

ANN L. COKER, CORRINE M. WILLIAMS, DIANE R. FOLLINGSTAD, AND CAROL E. JORDAN

For our review in this chapter, we define *intimate partner violence* (IPV) as physical, sexual, or psychological abuse by an intimate partner who may be a current or former spouse, boyfriend, or dating partner. We also include studies that address interpersonal violence (e.g., physical or sexual assaults) in which the partner was the perpetrator for the majority of these assaults. Figure 12.1 provides a schematic to orient the reader as to what is covered in our literature review. Although not intended to be a theoretical model, it does guide our organization of the literature and highlights certain assumptions. For example, rates of IPV vary internationally (Garcia-Moreno, Jansen, Ellsberg, Heise, & Watts, 2006), providing evidence for the influence of social, cultural, and economic factors, and perhaps the impact of IPV on health and wellness. As the arrows in the figure indicate, IPV may directly or indirectly influence a range of mental and physical health conditions.

We begin with a review of studies addressing IPV and mental health because the majority of research has been conducted in this area. IPV may influence mental and physical health indirectly by changing risk-taking behaviors such as substance use or contraceptive control. IPV may also directly affect rates of adverse pregnancy outcomes through repeated physical assaults or indirectly through the chronic stress of psychological, physical, or sexual

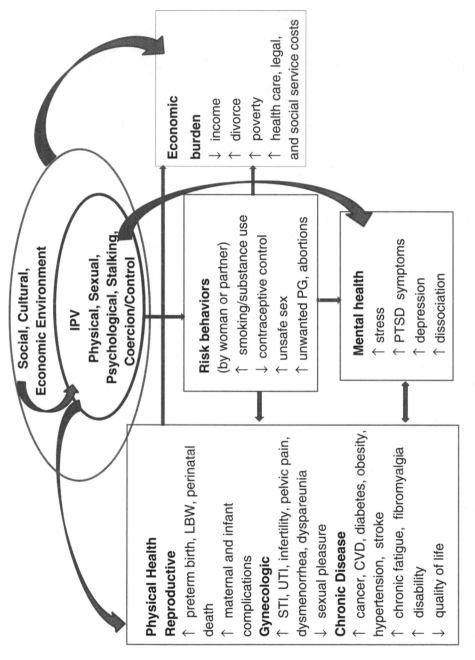

Figure 12.1. Conceptual model for health effect of intimate partner violence (IPV). Arrows indicate the potential direction by which violence and intermediate factors may affect health outcomes. LBW = low birth weight; STI = sexually transmitted infection; UTI = urinary tract infection; CVD = cardiovascular disease; PG = pregnancy; PTSD = posttraumatic stress disorder.

IPV during pregnancy. Other reproductive and gynecologic health outcomes may be directly or indirectly influenced by either current or lifetime IPV experienced. Little research has investigated the association between IPV and chronic diseases. IPV may influence chronic disease such as hypertension or stroke through chronic stress and associated chronic inflammation or the association may be mediated by substance use or lack of access to routine health care. Finally, IPV may result in an increased economic burden for individual women experiencing this violence. IPV also has economic consequences for society in terms of increased health care costs and more women and children needing governmental assistance for survival.

WHAT DO WE KNOW?

For this literature review covering a wide range of health outcomes, we used PubMed and PsycINFO from 1980 to 2008 to identify abstracts, which we then reviewed. For the purpose of brevity, these findings were summarized, and selective examples of published research are provided. IPV was defined using the search term *spouse abuse, intimate partner violence,* or *interpersonal violence*. The following search terms (in parentheses) were used to describe the health indicators for (a) risk behaviors (postcoital contraception, barrier contraception, immunologic contraception, contraception behavior, abortion, sex or unsafe sex, substance use, illegal drug, smoking, or binge drinking), (b) reproductive health (pregnancy complications, low birth weight, preterm or postpartum depression), (c) gynecologic health (papillomavirus infections or human papillomavirus, chlamydia infections or sexually transmitted diseases or gonorrhea or hepatitis B, infertility, female genital diseases, hysterectomy, pelvic pain or endometriosis, leiomyoma, amenorrhea or menstrual cycle or menstruation disturbances or polycystic ovary syndrome or anovulation, dysmenorrhea, dyspareunia, or urinary tract infections), (d) chronic disease (neoplasms, cancer, carcinoma, squamous cell or cervical intraepithelial neoplasia or carcinoma in situ or uterine cervical neoplasms, cardiovascular disease, heart disease, obesity, hypertension, diabetes, arthritis, chronic fatigue syndrome, fibromyalgia, or chronic disease), (e) mental health (depression, anxiety, posttraumatic stress disorder, mental health, or suicide), and (f) economic impact (costs or economic). Only original quantitative research studies with at least 500 participants were included. At least 100 articles met these inclusion criteria. Note that because several meta-analyses have been conducted for the mental health outcomes associated with IPV, these reviews were also used to evaluate the association between IPV and mental health.

IPV and Mental Health

Although the literature attends primarily to the sequelae that are associated with or that follow violence exposure, any analysis of the association of mental health and victimization must note that women with preexisting major mental illnesses are at significant risk of victimization. The National Violence Against Women Survey found, for example, that women with severe mental disorders are 16 times more likely to experience violent victimization than are women in general community samples (Goodman et al., 2001).

Effects of Physical Violence on Mental Health

With respect to the aftermath of violence, much of the existing research literature has concentrated on the impact of physical abuse on women in their intimate relationships (whether or not other abuse forms were assessed); therefore, the most reliable information about mental health effects is available in this sphere. Because physical assaults are highly likely to produce anxiety and fears of pain, injury, and even death, posttraumatic stress disorder (PTSD) has been frequently assessed in battered women. This diagnosis seems to be solidly established, with high rates (63.8%) of mean prevalence (Kessler, Sonnega, Bromet, Hughes, & Nelson, 1995), odds ratios of 2.87 (Kemp, Green, Hovanitz, & Rawlings, 1995), and consistency of the diagnosis. Although predicting the likelihood of PTSD may be initially useful for planning treatment, Briere and Jordan (2004) argued convincingly for a broader conceptualization of the effects of physical IPV. They suggested that the ongoing nature of the violence and the challenges of negotiating an ongoing relationship with the abuser create a complexity of psychological symptoms, beyond those variously defined as PTSD, that need to be addressed.

A significant number of articles have also assessed the occurrence of depression in women who have been physically abused, with a mean prevalence of 47.6% (Golding, 1999) and an odds ratio of 3.8 (McCauley et al., 1995). Golding's (1999) meta-analysis was not able to provide a model that accurately accounted for the highly inconsistent prevalence rates of depression across studies. Some associations found in the literature that may have influenced the variability indicate that higher rates of depression were found in studies that assessed battered women in shelters, measured physical violence by means other than the Conflict Tactics Scale (Straus, 2007), had larger numbers of battered women, and were conducted by female investigators. Battered women coming to emergency rooms for services had the highest odds ratios for exhibiting depression. Several authors' works appear to have established a temporal link between battering and depression (Orava, McLeod, & Sharpe, 1996), thus strengthening the causal connection between physical IPV and depression. In one study that followed women over 2 years, for example, 91% of the sample had clear patterns of decreased depression following the end of the abusive relationship (Campbell, Sullivan, & Davidson, 1995).

Suicidality (including both ideation and attempts) seems well established as linked to IPV, with a weighted mean odds ratio of 3.55 (Vitanza, Vogel, & Marshall, 1995), although the prevalence rate of 17.9% is lower than that of PTSD or depression. The inconsistent reporting of suicidality across studies has not been adequately explained (Golding, 1999), although the highest rates were found among battered women who were also psychiatric patients, with shelter residents demonstrating the next highest rating. The populations of battered women with the highest rates of suicidality appear to be women needing significant resources, such as hospitalization or physical shelter, suggesting that the effects of physical IPV were quite devastating for them. This interpretation seems to be supported by Bergman and Brismar's (1991) finding that the highest odds ratio for suicidality occurred among IPV victims who were emergency room patients. Although deliberate self-injury or mutilation has been more strongly associated with child sexual abuse, women experiencing IPV may also be at increased risk of this behavior, particularly during adolescence (Klonsky & Moyer, 2008).

Effects of Partner Sexual Abuse on Mental Health

Sexual abuse within intimate relationships has been infrequently assessed as an independent factor in IPV studies, and even when this form of IPV shows a relation with a diagnosis or discrete symptom, it is often difficult to understand its unique contribution. Marshall (2001), for example, found sexual aggression and certain forms of psychological aggression to be related to severe depression and suicidality in her sample. Vitanza et al. (1995) found sexual abuse to partially explain cognitive failure in contrast with physical and psychological aggression. Coker et al. (2002) provided one of the stronger comparisons of the relative effects of physical and sexual abuse on mental health and determined that, in general, effects were stronger for women experiencing sexual IPV alone than for physical IPV alone. Coggins and Bullock (2003) theorized that sexual abuse in violent relationships is motivated by coercion, control, and power (sounding both more physical and psychological in nature), reinforcing the idea that conceptualizing and measuring forms of IPV as discrete experiences may be difficult. Currently, sexual abuse within long-term intimate relationships is studied more often as to its implications for women's physical health but certainly deserves more investigation as to its effect on their mental health.

Effects of Psychological Aggression on Mental Health

Of the various forms of IPV, the impact of psychological aggression on women's mental well-being is likely to be the most difficult to investigate adequately. The more subjective nature of the experience in comparison with sexual or physical abuse, the interactional nature of interpersonal communication, and the need to understand the context in which psychological actions occur all contribute to difficulties in conceptualization and measurement of this phenomenon. Although it is highly likely that serious forms of psychological aggression (e.g., high frequency, particular types) certainly would affect women's mental health, major conceptualization and measurement difficulties hinder the development of this field of inquiry (for a detailed critique, see Follingstad, 2007).

In summary, a critique of the existing literature on the deleterious mental health effects of psychological aggression determined that conclusions about this relation cannot be formed at this time (Follingstad, 2009). The relatively small number of studies that exist typically rely on samples with co-occurring physical and/or sexual abuse. In addition, even the symptoms that have been investigated most frequently have produced contradictory findings across studies, and typically, studies have not required a threshold level for symptoms to meet diagnostic or impairment criteria for reporting significance.

IPV and Risky Behaviors

Although studies have examined the issue of smoking and IPV in different populations and with different measures of IPV, adult women who experienced psychological, physical, or sexual abuse are consistently more likely to smoke than nonabused women (Black & Breiding, 2008) and to be current smokers (Gerber, Ganz, Lichter, Williams, & McCloskey, 2005). Pregnant women who experienced IPV prior to or during the pregnancy were more likely to have smoked during the pregnancy (Silverman, Decker, Reed, & Raj, 2006). However, the association between smoking and IPV is not consistent among adolescent victims of physical dating violence (Silverman, Raj, Mucci, & Hathaway, 2001).

Alcohol abuse or dependence has shown a mean prevalence rate of 18.5% among IPV victims, with a weighted mean odds ratio of 5.56; however, across studies, rates are fairly variable (Golding, 1999). Women who experienced recent or lifetime IPV are more likely to report problem drinking or drinking every day (Carbone-López, Kruttschnitt, & MacMillan, 2006). In a study of women attending internal medicine outpatient clinics in Mexico, current or prior alcohol or drug use by both the woman and her partner was associated with current IPV (Díaz-Olavarrieta, Ellertson, Paz, Ponce de Leon, & Alarcon-Segovia, 2002). Pregnant women who experienced IPV before the pregnancy only were more likely to have used alcohol or other drugs during the pregnancy (Silverman et al., 2006). Adolescent female victims of physical dating violence were more likely to report binge drinking (Silverman et al., 2001).

A limitation of many of these studies is the lack of prospective data to show that IPV produces problematic drinking. Warburton and Abel (2006) focused on the existence of, rather than the reason for, substance problems in battered women and opined that even if substance abuse in battered women predated IPV, their abuse of substances might increase their risk of IPV, and substance dependence might hinder women's ability to leave the abuser or make important changes in their lives.

Drug abuse/dependence has a lower mean prevalence rate (8.9%) among women experiencing IPV than that for alcohol problems. Mean odds ratios were homogeneous across studies (McCauley et al., 1995). Specifically, higher rates of drug abuse were found with shelter residents and studies with smaller numbers of participants. Not only are substance use and IPV frequently associated, but when they do coexist, the coupling often changes the nature of the victimization experience as studies find abuse severity, weapon use, and homicide risk associated with cases involving substance-using offenders (Campbell et al., 2003).

IPV also influences sexual risk-taking behaviors. Among women attending a public sexually transmitted disease clinic, experiencing IPV in the last 12 months was associated with alcohol or other drug use before last intercourse and a nonmonogamous main sex partner (Bauer et al., 2002). In a study of women with domestic violence protective orders, 97.6% engaged in at least one risky sexual behavior with the partner against whom they had the protective order (Cole, Logan, & Shannon, 2007). Adolescent victims of physical or sexual dating violence were more likely to have first intercourse before age 15, to have three or more sex partners in the past 90 days, and not to have used a condom at last intercourse (Roberts, Auinger, & Klein, 2005).

IPV and Physical Health

IPV has been shown to be significantly associated with unintended pregnancies (Coker, 2007). Physical abuse during pregnancy was associated with an increased risk of both unwanted and mistimed pregnancies (D'Angelo, Gilbert, Rochat, Santelli, & Herold, 2004). Adolescent victims of physical or sexual dating violence were more likely to ever have been pregnant (Roberts et al., 2005). Although pregnancies among adolescents may not be unintended from an individual perspective, the topic warrants consideration because of the public health consequences of adolescent pregnancies.

Women seeking abortions show elevated rates of IPV violence compared with the general population (Woo, Fine, & Goetzl, 2005). Women who were either physically or sexually abused were more likely to report a legally terminated pregnancy (Garcia-Moreno et al., 2006), although one study conducted in England did not find a significant association (John, Johnson, Kukreja, Found, & Lindow, 2004). Women experiencing recent physical abuse were less likely to disclose an induced abortion to their partners, with a significant subset of abused women reporting fear of personal harm as the primary reason for nondisclosure (Woo et al., 2005). A history of physical abuse by a male partner and a history of sexual abuse or sexual violence were found to be associated with repeat abortion among Canadian women (Fisher et al., 2005).

Despite the literature linking IPV and both unintended pregnancies and induced abortion, little quantitative data are available on differences in contraceptive use other than condoms between abused and nonabused women. Young women attending a family planning clinic who were in a violent relationship were less likely to have used hormonal contraceptives at last intercourse (Rickert, Wiemann, Harrykissoon, Berenson, & Kolb, 2002). Women in New Zealand who experienced IPV were more likely to report ever having used contraception than nonabused women but were also more likely to report that a partner had refused to use or tried to stop them from using contraception (Fanslow, Whitehead, Silva, & Robinson, 2008). One study of adolescent dating violence did not find an association between contraception use at last intercourse and either current or past involvement in an abusive relationship (Roberts et al., 2005). However, consistent use of contraception is less likely among abused adolescents (Manlove, Ryan, & Franzetta, 2004).

Most published studies that address IPV as the primary exposure noted a significant association with perinatal death (Taft & Watson, 2008). Similarly, numerous studies noted a significant increase in low-birth-weight risk associated with IPV exposure yet not with an increase in preterm labor or delivery (Silverman et al., 2006). The majority of studies to address IPV and maternal complications in the antenatal or postnatal periods noted an association (Taft & Watson, 2008). Postpartum depressive symptoms were associated with IPV in most studies (Tiwari et al., 2008). Hospitalization during pregnancy was correlated with IPV in the majority of studies (Lipsky, Holt, Easterling, & Critchlow, 2004). Bleeding during pregnancy was noted to be associated with IPV in four studies (Janssen et al., 2003). Pregnancy complications associated with IPV experienced during pregnancy include antenatal infection (Curry, Perrin, & Wall, 1998) and pregnancy-induced hypertension and hyperemesis (Kearney, Haggerty, Munro, & Hawkins, 2003). One (Silverman et al., 2006) of two studies (Yost, Bloom, McIntire, & Leveno, 2005) to address IPV and infant neonatal intensive care unit stays noted an association. One (Kearney et al., 2003) of two studies (Yost et al., 2005) to address IPV and lower Apgar scores noted a significant association. Whereas IPV appears to be associated with perinatal mortality, low birth weight, and several maternal and infant complications, there is insufficient evidence that IPV is consistently associated with preterm labor or delivery.

Sexually Transmitted Infections

The majority of peer-reviewed studies found IPV to be associated with having a sexually transmitted infection (STI; Garcia-Moreno et al., 2006). Parish, Wang, Laumann, Pan, and Luo (2004) reported that although physical IPV was associated with having ever had an STI among men, this association was not statistically significant for women. Tubman, Montgomery, Gil, and Wagner (2004) found that for men and women increasing numbers of abuse experiences were associated with ever having had an STI. Three studies reported that sexual IPV was more strongly associated with a history of an STI than was physical or psychological abuse (Campbell et al., 2002). The majority of studies were cross-sectional, and thus the temporal sequence associating IPV and STI cannot be established. However, five studies did address both lifetime and current STI status to better time-frame exposure and outcomes sequencing. From these studies, IPV was more strongly associated with having a history of an STI than with current STI (Champion, Piper, Holden, Korte, & Shain, 2004). Few studies were able to conduct biological testing of relevant samples to confirm current STI status (Champion et al., 2004). In summary, these is consistent evidence that IPV is associated with an increased prevalence of ever having an STI, yet the relation between currently experiencing IPV and incident STI cannot be confirmed with existing data.

Gynecologic Outcomes

IPV has consistently been associated with an increased risk of chronic pelvic or abdominal pain (Pikarinen, Saisto, Schei, Swahnberg, & Halmesmäki, 2007). IPV and particularly sexual IPV have consistently been associated with painful intercourse or dyspareunia (Champion et al., 2004). Campbell et al. (2002) noted that sexual abuse was more strongly associated with painful intercourse than was physical abuse. IPV was associated with painful menses or dysmenorrhea in the majority of studies to address this association (Loxton, Schofield, Hussain, & Mishra, 2006). Similarly, IPV was also consistently associated with menstrual irregularity, including excessive bleeding and/or endometriosis (Champion et al., 2004). Both of the studies to evaluate IPV and hysterectomies noted an association (Coker, Smith, Bethea, King, & McKeown, 2000; Loxton et al., 2006). Only one study (Campbell et al., 2002) addressed IPV and uterine fibroids and found no association. All three studies to address IPV and having an abnormal pap test (John et al., 2004; Vos et al., 2006) or cervical dysplasia (Coker, Bond, Madeleine, Luchok, & Pirisi, 2003) noted a significant association. The majority of studies to explore associations between IPV and lack of sexual pleasure or sexual dysfunction noted that IPV increased the risk of this outcome (Pikarinen et al., 2007).

In summary, IPV is consistently associated with chronic pelvic pain, menstrual irregularity/excessive menstrual flow, and ever having an abnormal Pap test. However, a causal relation cannot be inferred given the relatively small numbers of replicate studies, the lack of temporal sequence based on cross-sectional studies without time-frame exposure and outcome data, and the lack of diagnostic confirmation of gynecologic conditions in larger population-based studies.

IPV and Hypertension, High Cholesterol, Diabetes, Heart Disease, and Obesity

IPV was associated with hypertension in one study (Lown & Vega, 2001). IPV has not been consistently associated with diabetes (Black & Breiding, 2008). Black and Breiding noted an increased prevalence of high cholesterol associated with IPV among women but not men, yet IPV was not associated with obesity. IPV has consistently been associated with heart disease (Díaz-Olavarrieta et al., 2002), except in the largest study (Loxton et al., 2006). IPV has also been associated with ever having a stroke or symptoms consistent with a stroke in women and men (Black & Breiding, 2008).

The majority of studies addressing rates of chronic disease (Ruiz-Pérez, Plazaola-Castaño, & Del Río-Lozano, 2007) or generic physical symptoms (Díaz-Olavarrieta et al., 2002) have found that IPV was associated with an increase in the number of symptoms. IPV has consistently been associated with gastrointestinal disorders, including irritable bowel syndrome (Loxton et al., 2006), chronic fatigue syndrome (Patel et al., 2005), and arthritis (Black & Breiding, 2008). Few studies have explored an association between IPV and specific cancers. IPV was associated with an increased risk of invasive cervical cancer (Loxton et al., 2006). In summary, there is insufficient evidence to confirm that IPV is consistently associated with hypertension, diabetes, obesity, or heart disease because of the small number of studies ($N = 5$), the lack of diagnostically confirmed disease status, and the lack of information to appropriately time-frame IPV exposure and cardiovascular disease incidence.

IPV and Disabilities

IPV has been associated with a increase in physical and mental disabilities for men and women victims (Black & Breiding, 2008; Carbone-López et al., 2006).

IPV and Poorer Quality of Life

IPV appears to be consistently associated with poorer quality of life in multiple domains (Tiwari et al., 2008). The finding that lifetime IPV (not necessarily current) remains a strong correlate of poorer current quality of life indicates the persistent effect of IPV in many cases long after women have left an abusive relationship. Understanding how IPV influences quality of life and what factors mediate or moderate this relation may be important in efforts to improve mental and physical health.

Economic Impact of IPV

Women who experience IPV are more likely to live in economically vulnerable households and in disadvantaged neighborhoods (Fox & Benson, 2006). These women are more likely to be unemployed (Weinbaum et al., 2001) and to miss more days from work (National Center for Injury Prevention and Control, 2003). Participation in services directed at low-income women is higher among women experiencing IPV. Adult women who were victims of IPV in the past 12 months were more likely to have enrolled in the Women, Infants and Children program in the past 2 years (Weinbaum et al., 2001). Among women attending prenatal care clinics, 10.6% of women with public insurance were physically abused, compared with 2.3% of women with private insurance (Kearney et al., 2003). Women seeking welfare who reported violence in the past year were also more likely to report recent homelessness and divorce or separation (Lown, Schmidt, & Wiley, 2006).

Women who experience IPV have more annual health care visits and higher annual health care costs (Ulrich et al., 2003). Estimates of the annual costs of IPV range from $2.3 to $7.0 billion for direct health care costs; the indirect costs of lost of productivity are approximately $1.8 billion (Brown, Finkelstein, & Mercy, 2008).

Health care costs for women who experience IPV remain elevated even after the violence stopped (Rivara et al., 2007). Women who were ever abused used mental health and alcohol/drug services more than nonabused women and had more hospital outpatient and emergency department visits; inpatient admission was the only type of service that did not differ by abuse status (Rivara et al., 2007).

HOW DO WE KNOW IT? GAPS AND WEAKNESSES IN EXISTING KNOWLEDGE

Much of the research summarized here has arisen from a range of relatively small cross-sectional studies that are often either unfunded or underfunded. Based on existing literature, we cannot address directionality; we do not have data to establish causality or even temporal sequence. The majority of studies addressing the health impact of IPV have relied on self-report of both health outcomes and IPV experienced. To empirically determine the short- and long-term health consequences of IPV, large well-funded cohort studies are needed. The following are gaps noted when reviewing existing research on IPV and either the mental or physical health, risk behaviors, or economic impact of IPV.

- Few studies have had the resources to comprehensively measure IPV. Women frequently experience overlapping types (e.g., physical, sexual, psychological, stalking, coercive control), and the combined effects of the range of IPV experiences are difficult to measure and evaluate (Dutton, Goodman, & Bennett, 1999). Further, few studies have measured the duration and intensity of women's experience with IPV or the perceived impact of IPV on women's lives (Bonomi, Allen, & Holt, 2006) and correlated these measures of dose–response on health outcomes.
- The majority of large population-based studies of IPV and mental or physical health effects have used cross-sectional designs. Without knowledge of the dates of IPV experienced and dates of specific diagnoses or behavior initiation, it is difficult to make causal inferences. In the case of many mental disorders, dates of diagnoses may be less informative because symptoms may be present years before a diagnosis is obtained.
- With a few exceptions, the majority of studies have not addressed factors that may mediate or moderate the effect of IPV on health.
- For the majority of large population-based studies, it is not logistically feasible to obtain medical records data to confirm self-reported health outcomes. However, the lack of ability to confirm diagnoses will continue to hamper efforts to establish causal relation because misclassification of health outcomes remains a possible bias.
- With the possible exception of STIs, there have not been enough large studies to make the case for a consistent association between IPV and health outcomes.
- Generally, studies of the impact of IPV on reproductive health lack the context of reproductive decision making. Quantitative studies of abused women's contraceptive use are needed to understand how to reduce unintended pregnancies and induced abortions among this population. In particular, studies of the barriers to consistent use of contraception are needed.
- To include the health care costs of children whose mothers were abused, more information is needed on co-occurring child abuse, which may help to explain increased utilization. Understanding why children have increased utilization of mental health services

and higher primary care costs even if the violence stopped before their birth is critical (Rivara et al., 2007). However, if children of abused women who were never themselves abused or exposed to IPV in the household also have increased costs, interventions should be directed toward this population, which may currently be neglected.

- Estimates of the costs of IPV have focused primarily on health care costs. National estimates of the costs of IPV for legal services, law enforcement, and social services provided to abused women, including shelter, support groups, and batterer treatment, are needed.

WHERE DO WE GO FROM HERE?

The following are recommendations to improve the quality of the research and to address current gaps.

- More comprehensive assessments of the nature of the IPV experienced are needed. Further, the mix of different IPV types and the duration, frequency, and impact of IPV need to be described. Examples of measures of impact include the Women's Experience With Battering (Smith, Tessaro, & Earp, 1995) and questions about the degree to which IPV may be perceived as a problem in the relationship, as well as measures of women's self-identifying as experiencing IPV by type. Methodological research is needed to develop valid and reliable measures of IPV by type. Although the Conflict Tactics Scale (Straus, 2007) is the most commonly used measure of partner violence, there is considerable disagreement whether this or any single measure captures the impact of IPV on women (Rathus & Feindler, 2004). Additional research is needed to quantitatively define and measure psychological abuse, whether concurrent with other forms of IPV or not.

- Briere and Jordan's (2004) recommendation that a broader conceptualization of mental health outcomes be applied to assessment and research can also apply to physical health. A comprehensive conceptual model hypothesizing the interactive role of IPV types on the range of health behaviors and health outcomes may be an important guide for future research. Specifically, for mental health, a broader focus that includes other feeling states, functional impairments, shifts in personality traits, and behavioral responses might illuminate our understanding of IPV's influence on women's mental functioning and provide more direction for intervention and prevention. For physical health, the interactive role of mental health and health behaviors also needs to be evaluated. Understanding elements of resiliency and increased risk is crucial to health care professionals' ability to support and care for women who have ever been in an abusive relationship. Examples of specific mediators and moderators for the IPV and health association may include forms of social and emotional support, smoking and other substance use, and family and individual history of child abuse or neglect or past partner violence. Evaluating interactions between multiple levels of influence (e.g., individual, couple, family, community, larger social cultural environment) to include the influence of ethnicity, socioeconomic status, and sexual orientation (Sokoloff & Dupont, 2005), although complicated, will provide further evidence for a causal role of IPV in health outcomes. Multilevel structural equation modeling using prospectively collected data could greatly future research in this area.

- To establish causality and begin to develop effective interventions to reduce the risk of adverse health outcomes associated with IPV, studies are needed to determine the biological mechanisms by which IPV causes specific health outcomes. Prospective cohort studies would be ideal because of the temporal sequencing issue and the ability to address more than one mental or physical outcome.

- Because the majority of existing studies are cross-sectional and not appropriately time-framed to ensure that IPV precedes health outcomes, cohort studies are needed. Cohort studies will additionally reduce the potential for disease misclassification if medical records or other diagnostic confirmation can additionally be obtained to validate the health outcome when feasible.

- Defining the scope of what costs should be attributed to IPV is difficult. Studies to date have used a variety of methods of defining and measuring costs associated with IPV. The health care costs of IPV could include not only the direct costs for treatment of injuries sustained but also the increased cost of health care overall due to the exacerbation of chronic diseases and the increased prevalence of reproductive health conditions and adverse pregnancy outcomes. For example, the costs of IPV could also include costs associated with delivery and care of a low-birth-weight infant.

Research reveals that at least 25% of women in the United States have been physically assaulted by a partner. These numbers find their way into criminal justice files and prevalence studies, but as explored in this review, they are also dramatically revealed in medical and mental health records and on the bodies of women for whom this is a life experience. The physical and mental health effects of violence are now well documented: IPV exposure is associated with an increased risk of a range of adverse reproductive and gynecologic conditions as well as several stress-associated chronic diseases. There is also a well-documented association with symptoms of PTSD and depression. The toll of violence is not only apparent at the individual level; studies find that the annual direct and indirect costs of IPV in the United States are estimated at $9.8 billion. The costs of IPV are significant, and although some effects are easily documented, the actual suffering of women who face abuse, and that of their children who witness it, is immeasurable. Within the pages of this review, within the lines that describe research studies and abuse effects, is a robust call to action. The lives of women and children depend on that call being heard.

REFERENCES

Bauer, H. M., Gibson, P., Hernandez, M., Kent, C., Klausner, J., & Bolan, G. (2002). Intimate partner violence and high-risk sexual behaviors among female patients with sexually transmitted diseases. *Sexually Transmitted Diseases, 29*, 411–416. doi:10.1097/00007435-200207000-00009

Bergman, B., & Brismar, B. (1991). Suicide attempts by battered wives. *Acta Psychiatrica Scandinavica, 83*, 380–384. doi:10.1111/j.1600-0447.1991.tb05560.x

Black, M. C., & Breiding, M. J. (2008). Adverse health conditions and health risk behaviors associated with intimate partner violence, United States 2005. *Morbidity and Mortality Weekly Report, 57*, 113–117.

Bonomi, A. E., Allen, D. G., & Holt, V. L. (2006). Conversational silence, coercion, equality: The role of language in influencing who gets identified as abused. *Social Science & Medicine, 62*, 2258–2266. doi:10.1016/j.socscimed.2005.10.022

Briere, J., & Jordan, C. E. (2004). Violence against women: Outcome complexity and implications for treatment. *Journal of Interpersonal Violence, 19*, 1252–1276. doi:10.1177/0886260504269682

Brown, D. S., Finkelstein, E. A., & Mercy, J. A. (2008). Methods for estimating medical expenditures attributable to intimate partner violence. *Journal of Interpersonal Violence, 23*, 1747–1766.

Campbell, J. C., Jones, A. S., Dienemann, J., Kub, J., Schollenberger, J., & O'Campo, P. (2002). Intimate partner violence and physical health consequences. *Archives of Internal Medicine, 162*, 1157–1163. doi:10.1001/archinte.162.10.1157

Campbell, J. C., Sullivan, C. M., & Davidson, W. S. (1995). Depression in women who use domestic violence shelters: A longitudinal analysis. *Psychology of Women Quarterly, 19,* 237–255. doi:10.1111/j.1471-6402.1995.tb00290.x

Campbell, J. C., Webster, D., Koziol-McLain, J., Block, C., Campbell, D., Curry, M. A., . . . Xu, X. (2003). Risk factors for femicide in abusive relationships: Results from a multisite case control study. *American Journal of Public Health, 93,* 1089–1097. doi:10.2105/AJPH.93.7.1089

Carbone-López, K., Kruttschnitt, C., & MacMillan, R. (2006). Patterns of intimate partner violence and their associations with physical health, psychological distress, and substance use. *Public Health Reports, 121,* 382–392.

Champion, J. D., Piper, J., Holden, A., Korte, J., & Shain, R. N. (2004). Abused women and risk for pelvic inflammatory disease. *Western Journal of Nursing Research, 26,* 176–191. doi:10.1177/0193945903256402

Coggins, M., & Bullock, L. F. (2003). The wavering line in the sand: The effects of domestic violence and sexual coercion. *Issues in Mental Health Nursing, 24,* 723–738. doi:10.1080/01612840305322

Coker, A. L. (2007). Does physical intimate partner violence affect sexual health? A systematic review. *Trauma, Violence & Abuse, 8,* 149–177. doi:10.1177/1524838007301162

Coker, A. L., Bond, S. M., Madeleine, M. M., Luchok, K., & Pirisi, L. (2003). Psychosocial stress and cervical neoplasia risk. *Psychosomatic Medicine, 65,* 644–651. doi:10.1097/01.PSY.0000041471.57895.08

Coker, A. L., Smith, P. H., Bethea, L., King, M. R., & McKeown, R. E. (2000). Physical health consequences of physical and psychological intimate partner violence. *Archives of Family Medicine, 9,* 451–457. doi:10.1001/archfami.9.5.451

Coker, A. L., Smith, P. H., Thompson, M. P., McKeown, R. E., Bethea, L., & Davis, K. E. (2002). Social support protects against the negative effects of partner violence on mental health. *Journal of Women's Health, 11,* 465–476.

Cole, J., Logan, T. K., & Shannon, L. (2007). Risky sexual behavior among women with protective orders against violent male partners. *AIDS and Behavior, 11,* 103–112. doi:10.1007/s10461-006-9085-7

Curry, M. A., Perrin, N., & Wall, E. (1998). Effects of abuse on maternal complications and birth weight in adult and adolescent women. *Obstetrics and Gynecology, 92,* 530–534. doi:10.1016/S0029-7844(98)00258-0

D'Angelo, D. V., Gilbert, B. C., Rochat, R. W., Santelli, J. S., & Herold, J. M. (2004). Differences between mistimed and unwanted pregnancies among women who have live births. *Perspectives on Sexual and Reproductive Health, 36,* 192–197. doi:10.1363/3619204

Díaz-Olavarrieta, C., Ellertson, C., Paz, F., Ponce de Leon, S., & Alarcon-Segovia, D. (2002). Prevalence of battering among 1780 outpatients at an internal medicine institution in Mexico. *Social Science & Medicine, 55,* 1589–1602. doi:10.1016/S0277-9536(01)00293-3

Dutton, M. A., Goodman, L. A., & Bennett, L. (1999). Court-involved battered women's responses to violence: The role of psychological, physical, and sexual abuse. *Violence and Victims, 14*, 89–104.

Fanslow, J., Whitehead, A., Silva, M., & Robinson, E. (2008). Contraceptive use and associations with intimate partner violence among a population-based sample of New Zealand women. *Australian and New Zealand Journal of Obstetrics and Gynaecology, 48*, 83–89. doi:10.1111/j.1479-828X.2007.00805.x

Fisher, W. A., Singh, S. S., Shuper, P. A., Carey, M., Otchet, F., MacLean-Brine, D., . . . Gunter, J. (2005). Characteristics of women undergoing repeat induced abortion. *Canadian Medical Association Journal, 172*, 637–641. doi:10.1503/cmaj.1040341

Follingstad, D. R. (2007). Rethinking current approaches to psychological abuse: Conceptual and methodological issues. *Aggression and Violent Behavior, 12*, 439–458. doi:10.1016/j.avb.2006.07.004

Follingstad, D. R. (2009). Psychological aggression and women's mental health: The status of the field. *Trauma, Violence & Abuse, 10*, 271–289.

Fox, G. L., & Benson, M. L. (2006). Household and neighborhood contexts of intimate partner violence. *Public Health Reports, 121*, 419–427.

Garcia-Moreno, C., Jansen, H. A. F. M., Ellsberg, M., Heise, L., & Watts, C. (2006). *WHO multi-country study on women's health and domestic violence against women.* Geneva, Switzerland: World Health Organization.

Gerber, M. R., Ganz, M. L., Lichter, E., Williams, C. M., & McCloskey, L. A. (2005). Adverse health behaviors and the detection of partner violence by clinicians. *Archives of Internal Medicine, 165*, 1016–1021. doi:10.1001/archinte.165.9.1016

Golding, J. M. (1999). Intimate partner violence as a risk factor for mental disorders: A meta-analysis. *Journal of Family Violence, 14*, 99–132. doi:10.1023/A:1022079418229

Goodman, L. A., Salyers, M. P., Mueser, K. T., Rosenberg, S. D., Swartz, M., Essock, S. M., . . . Swanson, J. (2001). Recent victimization in women and men with severe mental illness: Prevalence and correlates. *Journal of Traumatic Stress, 14*, 615–632. doi:10.1023/A:1013026318450

Janssen, P. A., Holt, V. L., Sugg, N. K., Emanuel, I., Critchlow, C. M., & Henderson, A. D. (2003). Intimate partner violence and adverse pregnancy outcomes: A population-based study. *American Journal of Obstetrics and Gynecology, 188*, 1341–1347. doi:10.1067/mob.2003.274

John, R., Johnson, J. K., Kukreja, S., Found, M., & Lindow, S. W. (2004). Domestic violence: Prevalence and association with gynaecological symptoms. *British Journal of Obstetrics and Gynaecology, 111*, 1128–1132.

Kearney, M. H., Haggerty, L. A., Munro, B. H., & Hawkins, J. W. (2003). Birth outcomes and maternal morbidity in abused pregnant women with public versus private health insurance. *Journal of Nursing Scholarship, 35*, 345–349. doi:10.1111/j.1547-5069.2003.00345.x

Kemp, A., Green, B. L., Hovanitz, C., & Rawlings, E. I. (1995). Incidence and correlates of post-traumatic stress disorder in battered women: Shelter and community samples. *Journal of Interpersonal Violence, 10*, 43–55. doi:10.1177/088626095010001003

Kessler, R. C., Sonnega, A., Bromet, E., Hughes, M., & Nelson, C. B. (1995). Post-traumatic stress disorder in the National Comorbidity Survey. *Archives of General Psychiatry, 52*, 1048–1060.

Klonsky, E. D., & Moyer, A. (2008). Childhood sexual abuse and non-suicidal self-injury: Meta analysis. *British Journal of Psychiatry, 192*, 166–170. doi:10.1192/bjp.bp.106.030650

Lipsky, S., Holt, V. L., Easterling, T. R., & Critchlow, C. M. (2004). Police-reported intimate partner violence during pregnancy and the risk of antenatal hospitalization. *Maternal and Child Health Journal, 8*, 55–63. doi:10.1023/B:MACI.0000025727.68281.aa

Lown, E. A., Schmidt, L. A., & Wiley, J. (2006). Interpersonal violence among women seeking welfare: Unraveling lives. *American Journal of Public Health, 96*, 1409–1415. doi:10.2105/AJPH.2004.057786

Lown, E. A., & Vega, W. A. (2001). Intimate partner violence and health: Self-assessed health, chronic health, and somatic symptoms among Mexican American women. *Psychosomatic Medicine, 63*, 352–360.

Loxton, D., Schofield, M., Hussain, R., & Mishra, G. (2006). History of domestic violence and physical health in midlife. *Violence Against Women, 12*, 715–731. doi:10.1177/1077801206291483

Manlove, J., Ryan, S., & Franzetta, K. (2004). Contraceptive use and consistency in U.S. teenagers' most recent sexual relationships. *Perspectives on Sexual and Reproductive Health, 36*, 265–275. doi:10.1363/3626504

Marshall, L. L. (2001). Effects of men's subtle and overt psychological abuse on low-income women. In K. D. O'Leary & R. D. Maiuro (Eds.), *Psychological abuse in violent domestic relations* (pp. 153–175). New York, NY: Springer.

McCauley, J., Kern, D. E., Kolodner, K., Dill, L., Schroeder, A. F., DeChant, H. K., Derogatis, L. R. (1995). The "battering syndrome": Prevalence and clinical characteristics of domestic violence in primary care internal medicine practices. *Annals of Internal Medicine, 123*, 737–746.

National Center for Injury Prevention and Control. (2003). *Costs of intimate partner violence against women in the United States*. Atlanta, GA: Centers for Disease Control and Prevention.

Orava, T. A., McLeod, P. J., & Sharpe, D. (1996). Perception of control, depressive symptomatology, and self-esteem in women in transition from abusive relationships. *Journal of Family Violence, 11*, 167–186. doi:10.1007/BF02336668

Parish, W. L., Wang, T., Laumann, E. O., Pan, S., & Luo, Y. (2004). Intimate partner violence in China: National prevalence, risk factors and associated health problems. *International Family Planning Perspectives, 30*, 174–181.

Patel, V., Kirkwood, B. R., Weiss, H., Pednekar, S., Fernandes, J., Pereira, B., . . . Mabey, D. (2005). Chronic fatigue in developing countries: Population based survey of women in India. *British Medical Journal, 330,* 1190–1193. doi:10.1136/bmj. 38442.636181.E0

Pikarinen, U., Saisto, T., Schei, B., Swahnberg, K., & Halmesmäki, E. (2007). Experiences of physical and sexual abuse and their implications for current health. *Obstetrics and Gynecology, 109,* 1116–1122.

Rathus, J. H., & Feindler, E. L. (2004). *Assessment of partner violence: A handbook for researchers and practitioners.* Washington, DC: American Psychological Association. doi:10.1037/10685-005

Rickert, V. I., Wiemann, C. M., Harrykissoon, S. D., Berenson, A. B., & Kolb, E. (2002). The relationship among demographics, reproductive characteristics and intimate partner violence. *American Journal of Obstetrics and Gynecology, 187,* 1002–1007. doi:10.1067/mob.2002.126649

Rivara, F. P., Anderson, M. L., Fishman, P., Bonomi, A. E., Reid, R. J., Carrell, D., & Thompson, R. S. (2007). Intimate partner violence and health care costs and utilization for children living in the home. *Pediatrics, 120,* 1270–1277. doi:10.1542/peds.2007-1148

Roberts, T. A., Auinger, P., & Klein, J. D. (2005). Intimate partner abuse and the reproductive health of sexually active female adolescents. *Journal of Adolescent Health, 36,* 380–385. doi:10.1016/j.jadohealth.2004.06.005

Ruiz-Pérez, I., Plazaola-Castaño, J., & Del Río-Lozano, M. (2007). Physical health consequences of intimate partner violence in Spanish women. *European Journal of Public Health, 17,* 437–443. doi:10.1093/eurpub/ckl280

Silverman, J. G., Decker, M. R., Reed, E., & Raj, A. (2006). Intimate partner violence victimization prior to and during pregnancy among women residing in 26 U.S. states: Associations with maternal and neonatal health. *American Journal of Obstetrics and Gynecology, 195,* 140–148. doi:10.1016/j.ajog.2005.12.052

Silverman, J. G., Raj, A., Mucci, L. A., & Hathaway, J. E. (2001). Dating violence against adolescent girls and associated substance use, unhealthy weight control, sexual risk behavior, pregnancy, and suicidality. *JAMA, 286,* 572–579. doi:10.1001/jama.286.5.572

Smith, P. H., Tessaro, I., & Earp, J. A. (1995). Women's experience with battering: A conceptualization from qualitative research. *Women's Health Issues, 5,* 173–182. doi:10.1016/1049-3867(95)00615-X

Sokoloff, N. J., & Dupont, I. (2005). Domestic violence: Examining the intersections of race, class, and gender. In N. J. Sokoloff & C. Pratt (Eds.), *Domestic violence at the margins: Readings on race, class, gender, and culture* (pp. 1–13). New Brunswick, NJ: Rutgers University Press.

Straus, M. A. (2007). Conflict Tactics Scales. In N. A. Jackson (Ed.), *Encyclopedia of domestic violence* (pp. 190–197). New York, NY: Routledge, Taylor & Francis Group.

Taft, A. J., & Watson, L. F. (2008). Depression and termination of pregnancy (induced abortion) in a national cohort of young Australian women: The confounding effect of women's experience of violence. *BMC Public Health, 8,* 75–82. doi:10.1186/1471-2458-8-75

Tiwari, A., Chan, K. L., Fong, D., Leung, W. C., Brownridge, D. A., Lam, H., . . . Ho, P. C. (2008). The impact of psychological abuse by an intimate partner on the mental health of pregnant women. *British Journal of Obstetrics and Gynaecology, 115,* 377–384.

Tubman, J. G., Montgomery, M. J., Gil, A. G., & Wagner, E. F. (2004). Abuse experiences in a community sample of young adults: Relations with psychiatric disorders, sexual risk behaviors, and sexually transmitted diseases. *American Journal of Community Psychology, 34,* 147–162. doi:10.1023/B:AJCP.0000040152.49163.58

Ulrich, Y. C., Cain, K. C., Sugg, N. K., Rivara, F. P., Rubanowice, D. M., & Thompson, R. S. (2003). Medical care utilization patterns in women with diagnosed domestic violence. *American Journal of Preventive Medicine, 24,* 9–15. doi:10.1016/S0749-3797(02)00577-9

Vitanza, S., Vogel, L. C. M., & Marshall, L. L. (1995). Distress and symptoms of PTSD in abused women. *Violence and Victims, 10,* 23–34.

Vos, T., Astbury, J., Piers, L. S., Magnus, A., Heenan, M., Stanley, L., . . . Webster, K. (2006). Measuring the impact of intimate partner violence on the health of women in Victoria, Australia. *Bulletin of the World Health Organization, 84,* 739–744. doi:10.2471/BLT.06.030411

Warburton, A. L., & Abel, K. M. (2006). Domestic violence and its impact on mood disorder in women: Implications for mental health workers. In D. J. Castle, J. Kulkarni, & K. M. Abel (Eds.), *Mood and anxiety disorders in women* (pp. 92–115). New York, NY: Cambridge University Press. doi:10.1017/CBO9780511543647.008

Weinbaum, Z., Stratton, T. L., Chavez, G., Motylewski-Link, C., Barrera, N., & Courtney, J. G. (2001). Female victims of intimate partner physical domestic violence (IPP-DV), California. *American Journal of Preventive Medicine, 21,* 313–319. doi:10.1016/S0749-3797(01)00363-4

Woo, J., Fine, P., & Goetzl, L. (2005). Abortion disclosure and the association with domestic violence. *Obstetrics and Gynecology, 105,* 1329–1334.

Yost, N. P., Bloom, S. L., McIntire, D. D., & Leveno, K. J. (2005). A prospective observational study of domestic violence during pregnancy. *Obstetrics and Gynecology, 106,* 61–65.

IV

CONCLUSIONS AND NEXT STEPS

13

CONCLUSIONS AND NEXT STEPS

JACQUELYN W. WHITE, MARY P. KOSS, AND ALAN E. KAZDIN

The closing chapter for this volume is a first step toward realizing the lofty goal of integration. We include concise summaries of each author's views on established knowledge and its limitations, accompanied by a table that identifies methodological issues repeatedly identified throughout the chapters. The reviews offered by the authors in this volume present a strong case that the field of violence against women and children is splintered, often in some counterproductive ways. Across the forms of violence is evidence of grappling with the same definitional, design, measurement, risk, impact, treatment, and prevention issues. It is also clear from these chapters that a vibrant field of violence scholarship has emerged and is poised to go to the next level. The recommendations emerging from these chapters offer a platform for a transformation to occur.

The cogent analyses and conclusions drawn by the authors in this volume suggest that the scope of child abuse, sexual assault, and domestic violence is immense, with numerous short-term and long-term consequences. Some chapters reviewed and critiqued definitions of child abuse, sexual violence, and domestic violence. Other chapters identified where consensus exists regarding the scope and consequences of these problems and identified limitations of the available information and the methods used to collect it.

Other chapters focused on factors that are associated with high risks of violence or even directly cause it, as well as the factors that protect against violence through moderating the risks, particularly those that could be modified via public health interventions. The reviews make it clear that the overwhelming number of perpetrators of violence against women and children are related to or known to the victim. The literature on risk and protective factors unfortunately all too often is weighted in the direction of stranger assaults rather than those that occur in the home, suggesting a need for a major shift in emphasis, especially in terms of communicating to the public and to policymakers and increasing preventive efforts. The repeated use of ecological models of analysis to both organize the extant literature and develop theories also suggests the need for its greater emphasis in future research, practice, and policy. Research has identified numerous risk and protective factors at each level of the social ecology. Authors across all areas have issued a call for improvement in definitions (for legal and for research purposes), assessment strategies, and models that focus on mechanisms that account for etiology as well as those that have implications for prevention, intervention, and treatment.

Table 13.1 presents a synthesis of the major findings regarding incidence and prevalence, risk and protective factors for victimization and perpetration, and consequences for victims.

WHAT DO WE KNOW?

The evidence documenting violence against women and children is compelling. The contributors to *Violence Against Women and Children, Volume 1: Mapping the Terrain* support what many experts have suggested: Nations worldwide are experiencing an epidemic (World Health Organization, 2009). In the United States, the Violence Against Women Act, originally enacted by Congress in 1994 and reauthorized in 2000 and 2008, attests to the significance of the problem. Taken together, it is not surprising that violence against women has been identified as a priority in a report establishing a national mental health agenda for women in the United States (Russo, 1985) and in a September 1995 report of the Fourth World Conference on Women, the Beijing Declaration and Platform for Action, reaffirming women's rights internationally, conclusions supported by the Koss and White (2008) analysis. Likewise, high priority has been given to the prevention of child abuse (American Psychological Association, 2009; National Center for Injury Prevention and Control, 2009; Whitaker, Lutzker, & Shelley, 2005). According to the World Report on Violence Against Children (United Nations, 2006), infants and preschool children are at greater risk of abuse than older children. Furthermore, violence against children is gendered.

TABLE 13.1
Summary of Conclusions

Area	What do we know?
	Prevalence
Child abuse	• Estimates reflect incidence, prevalence, both for a child's lifetime and for a more limited period, and vary greatly depending on source.
	• Information comes from community surveys, agency tabulations, self-report, retrospective, or official reporting sources, often in a context of crime; various inclusion/exclusion criteria, types of samples, and recruitment methods are used.
	• Most data are cross-sectional and retrospective in nature.
	• Rates range, for a 1-year period, from a low of 0.02/1,000 for homicide to a high of 810/1,000 for sexual harassment; two thirds of victimized children experience more than one type.
	• Data across time indicate a downward trend in all forms except child abuse fatalities.
	• Data based on ethnic and cultural group membership are not readily available.
Sexual violence	• Estimates may be for incidence, prevalence, either for lifetime or for a more limited period, and vary greatly depending on source and range from estimates of rapes to other forms of sexual assault.
	• Information comes from large-scale national surveys such as the National Crime Victimization Survey, surveys of college students using the Sexual Experiences Survey, health studies, and adolescent studies.
	• Most are cross-sectional in design and are based on non-representative samples.
	• Units of analysis may be the individual, aggregated data from agency reports, or data extracted from medical records.
	• Past-year incidence range from 60/100,000 to 18% for lifetime; 1.4 rapes/sexual assaults per 1,000; college women and adolescent females report sexual assaults in the range of 11% to 30%, if Internet-based assaults are included.
	• Data based on ethnic and cultural group membership are not readily available.
Domestic violence	• Estimates include a range of experiences from verbal and psychological abuse, to physical and sexual abuse and stalking, and may be episodic or ongoing.
	• Data may come from national data sets, such as the National Crime Victimization Survey and the Centers for Disease Control and Prevention's Behavioral Risk Factor Surveillance Survey; the Conflict Tactics Scales has been used in a number of large-scale national surveys.
	• Estimates depend on target population, type of data, type of comparison groups, data collection procedures, design, theoretical framework, and data-analytic techniques.

(continues)

TABLE 13.1
Summary of Conclusions *(Continued)*

Area	What do we know?
	• Estimates range from 4% (stalking, lifetime) to 75% (verbal abuse, prior year) with little information on rates of cooccurrence; less is known about verbal abuse than other forms, although it is the most frequent.
	• Data based on ethnic and cultural group membership are not readily available, and what is available rarely addresses within group; immigrants and sexual minorities are not adequately studied.
	Risk and protective factors for perpetration
Child abuse	• Individual level: personal characteristics of the child and abuser (adjustment, coping skills, temperament, disabilities, stigmas, etc.), parents' cognitive social-informational processes that explain distorted beliefs and attributions
	• Family level: disruption, adversity, social status, income, quality of parent–child interactions, how parents learn to deal with frustration, etc.
	• Community level: neighborhood dangerousness
	• Sociocultural level: power differential between adult and child; lack of systemic provision of support and alternative solutions or clear-cut restraints on parents nor consideration of looking at child abuse in the context of exposure to domestic violence or date rape within context of sexual assault more generally
Sexual violence	Individual-level factors:
	• Hypersexuality (impersonal sexuality, sexual preoccupation, sexual conservatism); antisocial/impulsive tendencies (alcohol use)
	• Unemotionality/callousness (behavioral control, facets of psychopathology), with higher anger and aggression, lack of empathy, guilt, dominance/narcissism, emotional restriction
	• Attitudes (cognitive perceptional distortions that erroneously suggest apparent sexual interest on the part of the victim, mistrust/perceptual proclivities that justify violence against women, negative masculinity, women's communications, acceptance of rape myths, acceptance of violence, hostility toward women)
	• Genetic factors
	Relational-level factors:
	• Adverse childhood experiences
	• Deviant peers
	Societal-level factors:
	• Rape myths
	• Media (pornography)
	• Cultural construction of masculinity

TABLE 13.1
Summary of Conclusions *(Continued)*

Area	What do we know?
Domestic violence	• Individual level: low level of education, low income, history of aggression, childhood victimization, fragile psychological functioning and mental health issues, substance use, a restricted worldview • Interpersonal level: high-risk relationships marked by dysfunctional dynamics, an oppressive relational context, underdeveloped interpersonal skills, and resource depletion • Community level: residence in high-risk communities; structural disadvantage • Societal level: structural inequality and ideological norms supportive of violence against women; issues of power and control • Complex interactions between risk and protective factors at each level of the social ecology may vary across ethnic and cultural groups

Vulnerability and protective factors

Area	
Child abuse	• Individual level: gender, age, disability status, sexual orientation, and exposure to violence • Social network level: family and parental contexts, poverty • Societal level: environmental factors and cultural identity affect what happens in families, neighborhoods, and societies
Sexual violence	• Individual level: being female, history of assault, mental health, risk-taking behaviors, attitudes, demographics, avoidance of high-risk behaviors, risk perception, sexual assertiveness, resistance and self-defense training, and coping strategies • Situational level: location, use of alcohol, presence and role of bystanders, and social support • Family dynamics • Societal level: attitudes about gender inequality that lead to women's lower absolute lower status; economic and educational opportunities
Domestic violence	• Individual level: cohabitating, being unmarried, being African American, young age (under age 26), low income, without health insurance or Medicaid insured, cigarette use, having a history of physical abuse, self-perceptions of poor physical and mental health, and children in the home • Relationship level: educational achievement discordance, specifically when the woman had a higher education than her partner; divorced or separated marital status • Societal level: vulnerability and protective factors occur and interact at each level of the social ecology model

(continues)

TABLE 13.1
Summary of Conclusions   (Continued)

Area	What do we know?
	Psychological, health, behavioral, and economic impact
Child abuse	• The consequences of child abuse are extraordinarily complex and variable, both in the short and long term.
	• Psychological and emotional functioning—including depression, suicidal thoughts and attempts, lowered self-esteem, substance use, anxiety, separation anxiety, and posttraumatic stress disorder—are likely, as are externalizing behaviors.
	• Physical health, both the acute and direct to the more long term, is compromised.
	• Interpersonal relationships are impaired.
	• School performance is likely to also be disrupted.
	• Economic cost is estimated conservatively to be $103.8 billion/year, a figure that reflects expenditures for mental health services, hospitalizations, child welfare services, law enforcement, special education, juvenile delinquency, criminal justice, health care, and lost productivity; intangibles, such as a compromised quality of life, are difficult to estimate.
Sexual violence	• Psychological problems include posttraumatic stress disorder, anxiety, depression, and suicide ideation and attempts, coping, self-blaming, cognitive processing.
	• Social reactions of formal systems and informal social networks
	• Physical health consequences range from violent death, to injury, gynecologic and reproductive health problems, unintended pregnancy, gastrointestinal problems, headaches, sleep, functional limitations, and disabilities.
	• Risky behaviors may include alcohol and drug use, tobacco use, and unsafe sex behaviors.
	• Economic costs have been estimated at $992 per intimate partner rape ($\times$ 322,230) = $319.7 million; when including all types of sexual violence, as well as tangible and intangible costs, the estimate rises to $127 billion—the highest annual victim costs of all crimes studied.
Domestic violence	• Psychological health, including posttraumatic stress disorder, depression, suicidality
	• Risky behaviors, including smoking, drug abuse/dependency
	• Physical health, including unintended pregnancies, abortions, perinatal death, low birth weight, sexually transmitted infections, gynecological outcomes, hypertension, high cholesterol, diabetes, coronary heart disease, obesity, disabilities, poorer quality of life
	• Economic impact: $8.8 billion for direct health care costs, lost productivity

Prevalence

Across all forms of interpersonal violence reviewed, authors noted great variability, depending on the breadth of definitions used, time frame examined, and reporting source. Despite such variability, estimates are discernible. For child abuse, for example, rates range, for a 1-year period, from a low of 0.02/1,000 for homicide to a high of 810/1,000 for sexual harassment. Of great importance is the finding that of children who experience any kind of victimization, two thirds experience more than one type (i.e., poly-victims). Data across time indicate a downward trend in all forms except child abuse fatalities. Similarly, for sexual assault, estimates may be for incidence and prevalence, either for lifetime or for a more limited period. However, as with child abuse, estimates are possible. Past-year incidence ranges from 60/100,000 to 18% for lifetime, depending on source. Whereas the Uniform Crime Report estimates 60.9 offenses per 100,000 female inhabitants, the National Crime Victimization Survey estimates 1.4 rapes/sexual assaults per 1,000. College women and adolescent girls report sexual assaults in the range of 11% to 30%, if Internet-based assaults are included. Similar issues regarding definition and sources of data emerge for domestic violence, which are compounded because various forms of domestic violence often cooccur, but this is usually not addressed in the literature. As a result, estimates range from 4% (stalking, lifetime) to 75% (verbal abuse, prior year) with little information on rates of cooccurrence. For each of these areas, data based on ethnic and cultural group membership are not readily available, and what is available rarely addresses within-group differences.

Risk and Protective Factors for Victimization and Perpetration

The remarkable similarity across descriptions of risk and protective factors for victimization and perpetration must be highlighted. In all cases factors were identified at all levels of the social ecology, from structural inequalities to biological mechanisms. In all cases authors noted how the burden of poverty and lack of resources that support effective parenting create a context of risk for child abuse and risky environments for adolescents, with early negative childhood experiences increasing the risk of further victimization as an adolescent and adult, as well as the likelihood of becoming a perpetrator.

Of course, structural inequalities are not the only identified risk factor. At the structural level, racism and sexism were identified by authors as well. At the interpersonal level, dysfunctional dynamics and traditions within social networks and parent–child and partner dyads also contribute to increased risk. Related to, and most likely a consequence of, structural and interpersonal dynamics, various attitudinal and personality attributes, along with engagement in a host of risky behaviors (i.e., alcohol and drug use), are also identified risk factors. Child abuse is embedded in myriad family problems associated with multiple intersecting adversities that create pathways to child abuse. These pathways may work through the family environment, family disruption and adversity, dangerous neighborhoods, and personal characteristics of the child (e.g., temperament, disabilities, stigmas), as well as of the abuser. In contrast to the research on risk factors, all authors noted that much less work has been done on protective factors and they recognize that a protective factor is not simply the absence of a risk factor. Protective factors are factors that reduce the risk of victimization or perpetration in the presence of a risk factor. For example, it is known that resources for parents living in poverty can mitigate the stress associated with poverty. Many children reared in poverty thrive because of good parenting and other community support, such as the faith community.

Scope of the Consequences of Victimization

One of the most, if not the most, profound themes that emerges from the analyses in this volume is the devastating consequences of power differentials between adults and children, as well as gender inequality, in violence toward women and children. Women and children are all too often victimized by some form of intimate violence (i.e., child physical and sexual abuse and neglect, sexual assault, and domestic violence). For many reasons, the risk of intimate, but not nonintimate, victimization is significantly greater for women and children than for men. In all analyses of violence against women and children, a disturbing conclusion is unavoidable: We live in a society that tolerates and even sanctions men's authority and entitlement to subdue and control women and children against their will.

Consequences for both women and children are remarkably similar, in impact on psychological and physical health, risk-taking behaviors, and both the short term and long term. Across all areas, impaired psychological and emotional functioning, including depression, suicidal thoughts and attempts, lowered self-esteem, substance use, anxiety, and posttraumatic stress disorder, is likely, as are externalizing behaviors. Physical health, both the acute and direct to the more long term, is compromised. Physical health consequences range from violent death to injury, gynecologic and reproductive health problems, unintended pregnancy, gastrointestinal problems, headaches, sleep, functional limitations, and disabilities. Increased engagement in risk behaviors is another consequence and may include alcohol and drug use, tobacco use, and unsafe sex behaviors. For women, consequences of domestic violence and sexual assault may include abortions, perinatal death, low birth weight, sexually transmitted infections, gynecological outcomes, hypertension, high cholesterol, diabetes, coronary heart disease, obesity, disabilities, and an overall poorer quality of life. For maltreated children, school performance is likely to be disrupted, whereas for adults work performance is likely to be negatively affected. For children and adults alike, interpersonal relationships, with family members, with friends, and with intimate partners, are likely to be impaired. Efforts to understand the cognitive and biological pathways from abuse to long-term health problems, however, are difficult to determine. Also affected are strategies of coping, self-blaming, and cognitive processing. The social reactions of formal systems and informal social networks, such as family and friends, also affect psychological symptoms and coping.

Economic costs are substantial as well. For child abuse, economic cost is estimated conservatively to be $103.8 billion per year, a figure that reflects expenditures for mental health services, hospitalizations, child welfare services, law enforcement, special education, juvenile delinquency, criminal justice, health care, and lost productivity. Economic costs associated with sexual assault have been estimate at $992 per intimate partner rape ($\times$ 322,230) = $319.7 million. When including all types of sexual violence, as well as tangible and intangible costs, the estimate rises to $127 billion—the highest annual victim costs of all crimes studied. The economic impact of domestic violence has been estimated to be $8.8 billion for direct health care costs and lost productivity alone. Intangibles, such as a compromised quality of life, are difficult to estimate. These numbers are staggering and likely to be underestimates. All told, however, it is clear that the costs of all forms of violence against women and children reviewed in the present volume top $110 billion per year.

Course of Violence: Life-Span and Longitudinal Perspectives

We have learned across all the areas that the possibility of a long-term life course exists. A young girl abused early in life is at increased risk of abuse by an intimate partner later in life. Adult victims are at risk for revictimization. A young boy abused early in life is at increased risk of becoming an aggressor later in life. Perpetrators are at risk of reoffending. Abused children are at increased risk of victimization by their peers. It is clear that understanding the causes and course of violence requires a life-span or longitudinal perspective. Violence can occur at any point over the course of development, although abuse during childhood is often the most consequential, particularly insofar as it heightens vulnerability to stress reactions from future trauma. There is value in understanding how a discrete or initial act of violence occurred, but there are likely to be multiple episodes of victimization and perpetration of violence. Violence is about people's lives over time and not isolated events that can be studied in a circumscribed fashion.

Role of Risk in Understanding Causality and Change

A common concern across areas is the need for further conceptual and empirical work to understand how risk factors operate and whether they play a causal role in being a victim or perpetrator. Too often risk factors are assumed to be causal; however, risk factors may be a proxy for some other influence and not causal in and of themselves (Kraemer et al., 1999). Some risk factors do not necessarily cause the onset of a problem, and thus altering or reducing them would not necessarily produce the desired prevention or treatment outcome. The conceptual basis of prevention interventions need to address not only empirically supported risk factors that are malleable but also, most important, those that are causal.

Risk factors are useful for identifying situations, contexts, and individuals most likely to engage in the violence we wish to prevent. However, identifying those at risk carries a danger of error. When screening for risk, sensitivity and specificity data are essential to note how many true and false-positive cases we are identifying. These concepts involve answering two questions: What is the proportion of individuals missed by screening who later become victims or perpetrators of violence? Conversely, what proportion of individuals may be targeted and potentially stigmatized as at risk when in fact they never commit a violent act? Some statistics, such as odds ratios, that show increased chances of an outcome depending on the presence of various risk factors are intuitively appealing but in reality are readily misunderstood. A risk factor can produce high odds ratios and be impressive on other measures but still not capture many of the cases that are likely to be victims or perpetrators.

Certain assumptions about risk and protective factors are deeply embedded. One is that theories of causation and theories of change are very similar or indeed identical. For example, in the area of sexual violence, we know that alcohol consumption is a risk factor for victimization. Changing that risk by telling women to not drink may reduce the likelihood of individual women being assaulted, although it will do little or nothing to alter perpetrator behavior; a woman's drinking may affect some of the perpetrator's actions, but it is not a cause of the perpetrator's behavior.

HOW DO WE KNOW IT?

The authors in this volume provided descriptions of the major methods used to assess incidence and prevalence as well as those used to assess risk and protective factors for victimization and perpetration. Table 13.2 provides a distillation of the various issues they noted along with suggested solutions. In

TABLE 13.2
Methodological Issues

Issue	Specific problems and dilemmas
Knowledge gaps	• Inadequate attention is given to connecting laboratory research, intervention testing in controlled settings within universities, and community-engaged action research. • Not enough communication occurs between stakeholders during planning phases of research or evaluation studies. • Researchers often have little understanding of what is going on in the community and do not appreciate the constraints on ideal designs. • Service providers often do not appreciate the need for evaluation and good design to generate new knowledge.
Challenges on the front line	• "Standard" operating procedures do not work; standard experimental methods do not work for community-based projects. • There is little recognition of dilemmas associating with work on interpersonal violence that distinguish the field from all others. • Dilemma of overreliance on self-report when it may be the only method of assessment
Definitions	• Lack of consensus on standardized and accepted definitions • Lack of criteria for when to use narrow to broad definitions
Types of data	• Need clarity on what is being measured: incidence or prevalence, for lifetime or shorter periods, an experience or event? • Inconsistent annual national and state-level data • Discrepancies between data sources need further analysis: large-scale surveys, convenience samples, criminal justice statistics, health care statistics, other agency sources.
Measurement/instrumentation	• Many cases of victimization and perpetration often cannot be substantiated, as they go unreported or undetected; must rely on self-report. • Overreliance on self-report, interviews, or random-digit dialing procedures, but sometimes the only option • No standardized measures based on agreed-upon definitions • Little reliability/validity data exist. • Measures vary in length and specificity; purpose is not always clear. • Qualitative data are insufficient to get at nuanced questions. • Proxy measures are not always clearly distinguished from the actual outcome of interest.

(*continues*)

TABLE 13.2
Methodological Issues   (Continued)

Issue	Specific problems and dilemmas
	• Training for those who extract data from criminal and health records is inadequate. • Measures of the economic costs, including tangible and intangible, are too variable from study to study. • Methods for assessment of contextual factors surrounding victimization are inadequate. • Assessment methods may interfere with workforce duties in community settings.
Sampling	• Not clear on who is selected and why: random, representative, or convenience samples? • Arbitrary age ranges are used. • Inclusion/exclusion criteria vary across studies. • Comparison groups may be missing or inappropriate. • Little effort to get input from consumers of service (patients, clients) about their ideas and reactions to proposed studies or their input into how to recruit and get out messages
Theoretical models	• Not always clear on what is the question being asked, which drives the method and interpretation • Most work is descriptive. • Etiology and causal mechanisms too often inferred from correlations. • Too few multilevel models that include mediators and moderators, which address roles of multiple systems • Little work on pathways to victimization and perpetration, as well as to outcomes • Lack of clear implication of etiologic models for treatment/intervention • More work has been done on risk factors than protective factors (these are more than the opposite of absence of risk). • More theorizing at the individual level than system level • Lack of recognition of the interconnectedness of various types of abuse, their interactions, and the interactions among outcomes
Designs	• Designs do not always match question: basic, theory-driven, or evaluation? • The pros of cross-sectional studies are not always identified. • Too few multilevel, longitudinal designs to separate out cause and effect • Too few innovative designs, such as quasi-experimental, mixed methods • Randomized clinical trials are not always possible, appropriate, or ethical. • Too few evidence-based evaluations

TABLE 13.2
Methodological Issues   *(Continued)*

Issue	Specific problems and dilemmas
Analyses	• Statistics used are often not robust enough to deal with available data. • Confidence intervals are often not reported but are necessary with small sample sizes. • Inadequate use of sophisticated analytic techniques that can handle longitudinal and missing data • Inadequate evaluation of programs • Too many racial biases
Cultural appropriateness	• Various ethnic and cultural groups are under-represented. • Inadequate information for cultural appropriateness of assessment method • Language barriers to understanding and reporting are not always acknowledged. • Too much focus on individual-level variables and analyses
Collaboration	• Not enough interaction among those with different types of expertise • Lack mechanisms and support for large-scale, interdisciplinary work
Funding	• Inadequate funding for the level of research and evaluation that needs to be done
Dissemination	• Inadequate attention to making research findings accessible and useful • Inadequate use of the Internet for stories, descriptive data, user-friendly synopses of studies

Note. Assumptions: All parties (researchers, service providers, policymakers, advocates) recognize the value of research-generated knowledge for moving the field forward, including continuous quality improvement in interventions, prevention programs, and to advocate for policy change. Each problem has various responses/solutions that depend on context. Responses to a problem may include improving current practice or developing new practices.

this section, we focus primarily on various definitional, design, and statistical solutions that have been offered. Recommendations that deal with translating research to practice and policy, and a call for interdisciplinary collaboration, funding, and dissemination, are offered in the concluding chapter of *Violence Against Women and Children, Volume 2: Navigating Solutions* (Koss, White, & Kazdin, 2011).

Knowledge Gaps and Challenges on the Front Line

Throughout the chapters, contributors acknowledged the existence of "silos." They expressed concern that inadequate attention was paid to connecting laboratory research, intervention testing in controlled settings within universities, and community-engaged action research. They also noted that traditional structures for funding and publication for researchers and real-world demands and limitations on practitioners and service providers interfered with communication between stakeholders during planning phases of research or evaluation studies. Researchers, as well as grant reviewers, often have little understanding of what is going on in the community and do not appreciate the constraints on ideal designs. "Standard" operating procedures often do not work for victimized populations, nor for perpetrators, nor do they work for community-based projects. Conversely, there was a sense that service providers often do not appreciate the need for evaluation and good design to generate new knowledge and to demonstrate effectiveness. Overall, the dilemmas associating with work on interpersonal violence distinguish the field from all others and require both improvement in methods currently used along with new and creative solutions.

Definitional Issues

Across all areas, authors noted a lack of consensus on standardized and accepted definitions, as well as a lack of criteria for when to use narrow to broad definitions and what timeframe to use. Multiple definitions of a given type of violence are in place. Some of these are by statute and are not easily changed or brought into uniformity. Yet, contributors agree that researchers could do more to provide consistent definitions. Consistent findings are not very likely if the phenomenon itself is a moving target. More could be done to develop instruments that lend themselves to more consistent but also more refined operational definitions.

One thing becomes apparent: There is no one definition or set of criteria or time frame that will work for all situations. Researchers, practitioners, members of the criminal justice system, and health care providers must determine why they need to know something about incidence or prevalence and then clearly communicate the rationale for choices made. The field would also benefit from a compendium of operational definitions and guidelines for when to use which definition and time frame. In any given study, the rationale for reporting incidence or prevalence, as well as lifetime or shorter periods, should be provided. Also, there is a need to distinguish an event (i.e., a rape) from an ongoing experience (i.e., battering). Such information would provide a context for understanding the numbers presented and allow for more adequate comparison across studies.

There is a way in which the definition of violence can be made on a consensus approach based on a priori considerations or another that is empirically determined. A consensus definition might be based on identifying extremes of a problem that could help decide where one must absolutely intervene. In contrast, an empirically based definition is one that determines where deleterious effects begin as a result of certain actions based on evidence. For example, consider child abuse. Child abuse is defined by most states as an extreme variation of corporal punishment (e.g., using an object, leaving a mark on a child); this is a consensus approach. However, from years of psychological research we have learned that the deleterious effects of corporal punishment do not require abuse at the level usually defined by the statutes (e.g., Gershoff, 2002). That is, the state consensus definition has the bar very high for intervening, but empirical evidence now tells us that considerable negative health and psychological outcomes do not require an abuse level of violence. The scope of violence and the continuum of degrees need to be studied. There is a spectrum of violence, and knowing more about that spectrum and the scope of effects is essential. This has implications for definitions insofar as type of definition affects the likelihood of finer-grained analyses.

Authors also noted inconsistencies among data at the national, state, and regional levels, as well as data from samples of convenience. Such inconsistencies could be addressed in part by considering issues of race, ethnicity, class, region, and cultural factors in the definitions of child abuse, sexual assault, and domestic violence. Discrepancies between data sources, such as large-scale surveys, convenience samples, criminal justice statistics, health care statistics, and other agency sources, need further analysis.

Assessment Issues

Standard measures could readily be developed that permit evaluation of a given type of violence on dimensional and categorical scales along with characteristics (e.g., number of episodes, onset, and other characteristics that describe the violence, duration, severity, and other facets). Such instruments could include a definition of violence, but even more useful would be inclusion of critical descriptive information that would allow evaluation of different definitions. Modularization could be an approach in which more questions relevant to public health or criminal justice could be moved in or out of a particular survey given its research goals, but with a core of items remaining that would eventually permit accumulation of knowledge. Such an approach would allow more recognition of commonalities and differences across disciplines and accommodate each in an integrated approach. For example, commonly used instruments such as the Child Trauma Questionnaire for child abuse, the Sexual Experiences Survey for sexual assault, and the Conflict Tactics Scale for physical partner violence could be enhanced with questions related to the social context of the assault or health outcomes, depending on the purpose of the study. It is well established that behaviorally specific questions that avoid labeling and value judgments constitute good assessment practice in the field of violence, so it is not a huge leap to ask policymakers to initiate funding of projects to develop a portfolio of standard assessments. For example, we need very short approaches that can be embedded in studies on other health or justice topics, as well as behaviorally specific screening when the setting and research goals permit the time and the tolerance of frank language. In contrast, less behaviorally specific language may be necessary when community norms or the goals of the study suggest finding a balance between ideal specificity and community norms. Furthermore, more attention to the cooccurrence of various types of violence should be considered. For example, psychological abuse, a seriously understudied problem, is a frequent precursor of other forms of abuse, and physical and sexual violence often cooccur in abusive relationships.

Interviews might be developed along the lines of structured and semistructured psychiatric diagnostic interviews that cover a range of characteristics of a problem. This could be improved on by including the parameter of violence and perhaps key moderators or contextual factors as well. A more elaborate description of a given type of violence can help determine whether there are critical cut points in defining violence. For example, the extremes of sexual assault might be agreed on, but a measure that permits evaluation of a broad range of assaults, threats to assault, and approximation of assault would contribute greatly to research. The goal is not to expand definitions so that anything is called *assault*, but rather to ensure that assault can be evaluated from the standpoint of a spectrum rather than present or absent and to permit evaluation of various definitions and cut points.

We need tools to assess violence comprehensively across the life span. We need funding for measurement development and psychometric study. Consensus on definitions and measurement is foundational to any future efforts to grow our knowledge base and to move to more collaborative approaches that span disciplines and systems, similar to advancement in other fields within mental health or the physical sciences that have come to agreement on definitions and measurement. What we know depends on how we know it. Common terminology will lead to better assessment tools that will give us better databases. Better databases in turn will help us further refine our definitions and tools. Such a synergistic relation between these three elements will truly advance the field.

Types of Data, Proxies, and Validity

Many of the contributors in this volume raised concerns about assessment, especially the use of self-report and retrospective assessment. Self-report allows the person who completes the measure to distort, deny, or express events that normal memory processes imperfectly record. Any single method of assessment has its liabilities, but self-report seems especially subject to bias. However, self-report is not invariably suspect or even a barely tolerable fallback option when "better" methods of assessment are unavailable. For example, for juvenile delinquency and criminal behavior, self-report is arguably better than institutional records in light of the amount of crime detected and consistency of findings with other reports (e.g., of victims). Institutional records omit a significant amount of crime. Similarly, in these chapters, we have learned that institutional and agency records can yield massive underreporting of abuse and violence. Parent self-report of child abuse can be 40 times greater than the rates obtained from records or agency reports, and sexual abuse up to 15 times greater by self-report than these other records. Data such as these do not lend themselves to comparing self-report with "actual" or "true" abuse, but they do convey that self-report provides data that are less likely to underestimate rates of violence than do institutional records. For our purposes, we note the limitations of self-report and lobby for more than one modality of assessment when possible. However, self-report is not inherently limiting in the assessment of interpersonal violence and clearly in many instances is the only avenue to obtain information. Well-established measures are needed that examine many samples and become part of the accruing database. Success stories abound in psychological measurement (e.g., Minnesota Multiphasic Personality Inventory, Beck Depression Inventory) in which self-report has been well validated and accepted by research and nonresearch communities after decades of use and empirical evaluation.

Contributors also noted debate about the most appropriate assessment method (e.g., in-person or telephone surveys, interviews, third-party reports). Issues of reliability and validity abound in an area in which self-report, as noted earlier, often provides the only access to the information and independent substantiation of a claim is often impossible. The need to develop reliable and valid measures of violence and its many characteristics was a common topic that emerged.

Retrospective assessment too was discussed as a concern. Retrospective assessment raises the issues of self-report and adds to that the limitations of memory. As one might well expect, prospective and retrospective reports covering the same time period for the same sample can reveal different information. People often deny or forget what they had stated in the past (e.g., Henry, Moffitt, Caspi, Langley, & Silva, 1994; Kazemian & Farrington, 2005; Rosenbaum, 2009). All the cautions about retrospective reporting are well placed. Yet, retrospective assessment has its place and is not invariably flawed. An excellent example can be seen in the results of the National Comorbidity Study in which the long-term course of psychiatric disorders are assessed, mostly retrospectively (Kessler & Merikangas, 2004). In-depth and detailed interviews provide the data. The study affords the opportunity to study critical questions about onset, comorbidity, life course, and paths leading to dysfunction that would not be feasible in long-term prospective studies. Moreover, retrospective studies can serve as a screen to sift through many hypotheses to help prioritize what ought to be studied prospectively.

Although there is no substitute for the direct data of interest, there are pretty good to very good approximations. We can use interim measures that relate to long-term outcomes. However, the connection must be demonstrated. Typically a measure is assumed to have that connection without the proper data to support it. For example, if a set of risk factors related to perpetration of violence is shown to be reduced by a prevention program, an assumption is made that the reduced scores translate to reduced rates of violence later. It is often assumed also that these risk factors were causal. Data are needed to move beyond such assumptions. Are scores on a more easily obtained measure now correlated strongly with the later outcome in which we are really interested? Also, a significant and even moderate-to-high correlation between an interim proxy measure and longer term outcome is not sufficient. We need to know how the score translates to a particular level of outcome, that is, elimination of spouse abuse or reduction by one half (see Blanton & Jaccard, 2006). Better assessment of interim markers of long-term change can enhance research. Here both prospective and retrospective designs can be used to develop the needed assessments. For example, retrospective studies could identify who to recontact later as a way of assessing the connection between interim and longer term outcomes.

The various definitional and assessment issues raised by the contributors to this volume suggest that the development of better measurement in the violence field and psychometric studies should be of the highest priority. The most sophisticated approaches available should be used to maximize the quality of self-report in a field that hinges heavily on it. We need to advocate for the field, editorial boards, grant review committees, and others to coalesce around a certain group of assessments and insist they be included, whatever else investigators decide to adopt or create for themselves.

Research Design and Data Analyses

Three separate themes identified in Table 13.2 are concerns about theoretical models, research designs, and data analyses. They unite nicely and call attention to an overarching theme: the interdependence of each with the other. Although theory drives design and data analysis, design and data analysis inform theory. A weakness or flaw in one jeopardizes the quality of the others. A concern related to the models is the overemphasis on correlational data rather than causal models and more attention to description rather than explanation. Theories can be improved, to be sure, but the restricted range of research designs that are used and the statistical analyses partially confine the theories that are generated and tested. Within the past generation, various statistical analyses (e.g., meta-analysis, structural equation modeling, hierarchical linear modeling, growth models) did not merely improve evaluation but also changed some of the questions that could be asked in research. Also, with many sophisticated data analyses now available, description can be much more in-depth and multileveled and even help blur the distinction of description and explanations.

Among the commonalities across the areas of violence was reliance on a very restricted range of research designs, that is, how conditions are arranged to test the hypotheses. As noted in Table 13.2, key concerns were raised about the limits of cross-sectional studies to address longitudinal questions, especially in efforts to sort out causes, correlates, and consequences. Because of the need for longitudinal data that span years to fully understand the relations among variables, and an impatience as well as inability to wait, cross-sectional and longitudinal designs can be combined with a multicohort or accelerated multicohort longitudinal design that samples different groups for overlapping durations (see Kazdin, 2003). The challenge is to use multiple designs (e.g., cross-sectional, longitudinal, retrospective, and accelerated longitudinal) to find convergent evidence or more options to address questions that might otherwise be neglected.

There was consensus on the difficulties of conducting randomized controlled trials (RCTs) to test models of causality. Although RCTs are recognized as the gold standard for intervention research, they may not be ideal for studies of causes and consequences in the area of violence (for a discussion of RCTs in intervention and prevention research, see the concluding chapter in *Violence Against Women and Children, Volume 2: Navigating Solutions*; Koss et al., 2011). They need to be supplemented with other strategies that can answer many questions where RCTs are not feasible. For example, there cannot be randomly comprised control groups (e.g., for rape victims, battered women) for ethical and feasibility reasons.

In studies of violence, it is difficult to have large numbers to permit allocation of individuals to different conditions, whether random or not. Within the quantitative tradition, there is increased recognition that small samples are often the rule and statistical power is an inherent problem. Examples include the study of samples with unique experiences (e.g., multiple types of abuse). There are many design alternatives that have been articulated for such situations to extract causal relations and to clarify the relations among multiple variables of interest (e.g., sequential designs, decision analysis-based designs, risk allocation designs, and others; see Evans & Ildstad, 2001). Apart from the quantitative tradition, single-case experimental research designs represent another viable strategy to address concerns raised in the prior chapters. The designs permit valid inferences to be drawn about causal relations with an individual, a single group, and multiple groups (Kazdin, 2010). Finally, qualitative research is a third strategy to expand designs across areas of violence. The methodology provides in-depth description and evaluation of an individual's experience (Berg, 2001; Denzin & Lincoln, 2005). How individuals subjectively view, perceive, and react to situations and contexts are the central foci. For example, qualitative research can look at the experience of individuals who have been assaulted and the ways in which their lives are influenced. The in-depth focus moves well beyond questionnaires and standardized interviews.

A common theme among contributors is the need to look at multiple levels of analyses, something qualitative research can do by evaluating individuals in extensive detail, and to elaborate the situations and contexts in which they are functioning. Worth noting is that qualitative research can generate as well as test hypotheses. Such research is a useful place to begin to generate theory by elaborating themes that emerge and how they interrelate to the experience of violence.

Statistical Analyses

A common concern across the areas is the need to study violence in novel ways to address multiple levels of influence. Advances in statistics could greatly augment knowledge about violence. Some of the advances are not new, but they are slow to enter areas of research and rarely addressed in graduate education. We can only highlight these briefly.

Among the themes to emerge is that violence involves multiple variables, levels of analyses, and a longitudinal perspective. Growth curve modeling looks at multiple variables over time and within-person models of variables and their interrelations (Duncan, Duncan, & Strycker, 2006). Although several individuals are evaluated, the analyses take into account individual differences and how they affect moderators over time. The analyses provide tools to address both multilevel variables and longitudinal perspectives.

We mention quasi-experiments as a viable design strategy and an alternative when RCTs cannot be used. Statistical methods for matching across different treatment groups when random assignment cannot be done (e.g., propensity scores, full matching) have greatly increased the quality of inferences from quasi-experiments.

Within the different areas of violence, a common concern was the importance of identifying mechanisms through which variables operate and moving from correlational to causal analyses. Statistical methods to address these questions (e.g., instrumental variable techniques, group-based trajectory modeling, configural frequency analyses, latent transition models) all provide options to move from associations to mechanisms of action or deeper explanations among relations involving several variables and variables at multiple levels (for descriptions and illustrations, see Foster & Kalil, 2008).

Statistical analyses are not a matter of testing for significance and strength of relations. They can play a critical conceptual role by developing mathematically based models with functions that describe and account for real-world problems such as violence. It is not that anything we do in conceptualizing violence should be replaced with more sophisticated statistical and mathematical modeling techniques; however, these latter techniques should not be ruled out by virtue of training or lack of training opportunities. The complexity of violence in etiologies, multiple levels of influence, and multiple outcomes call for the most sophisticated methods of data analyses available. Among the many arguments for collaboration in the areas of violence is the need to involve colleagues from disciplines that specialize in the analyses of complex, dynamic, and multilevel influences.

Cultural Appropriateness

One of the emergent themes in the chapters was the insufficient work on the different types of violence among diverse ethnic and cultural groups. Some of this might be neglect among the studies when it was quite possible to attend to different populations. Yet, sometimes it is difficult to accrue a sufficient sample for traditional designs to permit careful analyses of multiple ethnicities, especially to capture the vast differences within pan-ethnic groups. Also, designs that merely compare different ethnic and cultural groups can have inherent cultural biases based on the measures that were used and how those measures were constructed. As a rule, "standardized" scales are standardized with an ethnic group rather than with multiple groups. Here is a case in which qualitative research shines. Individuals from different groups could be evaluated in depth to identify themes that are unique to groups as well as common among groups. There could be an understanding from qualitative research both to better describe the experience of violence and disparities entering services or other programs and to better generate theories that may explain why some groups react differently from others. Greater attention to diversity would also contribute to the development of culturally appropriate definitions and assessment tools. Qualitative studies would also permit a more nuanced study of how the intersection of identities (i.e., race, ethnicity, gender, age, sexual orientation, disability status, etc.) affects the experience of abuse.

NEXT STEPS

The contributors to *Violence Against Women and Children, Volume 1: Mapping the Terrain* have provided an unquestionably strong foundation for concluding that violence against women and children is a huge and costly problem. They have identified common risk and protective factors at multiple levels of the social ecology. In showing the field where it is in terms of knowledge and methods, they have revealed many gaps in our knowledge and provided a rich set of suggestions for next steps.

This chapter has focused on various steps that could enhance movement toward common definitions and better assessment techniques. We have noted multiple methodologies to address a common theme of the need for expanded research. The limited range of designs in use impedes the information yield and the questions that can be asked. The multiple methods available provide complementary information. For example, qualitative analysis is an excellent basis for identifying themes and commonalities that emerge in the experience of violence. In-depth analyses of qualitative data would be an excellent basis for developing the content of measures used in quantitative research. Occasionally, studies combine qualitative and quantitative research and provide an unusually rich yield because the same sample is evaluated from different levels and perspectives (e.g., Yoshikawa, Weisner, Kalil, & Way, 2008).

The reader is invited to use the information provided in this volume as a foundation for reading *Violence Against Women and Children, Volume 2: Navigating Solutions* (Koss et al., 2011). Volume 2 examines how service sectors respond to violence against women and children, including victim responses, offender responses, justice responses, and prevention. Within each of these topics, Volume 2 contains contributions from experts in child abuse, domestic violence, and sexual violence. The volume represents the stages of the public health model that use scientific information to raise awareness to support change, identify modifiable risk factors and groups at risk, and design, evaluate, and scale up programs across the country. Prevention efforts may occur at several levels, including initiatives designed to eradicate the problem (primary), reduce it among those at risk (secondary), or ameliorate negative impacts and stabilize health (tertiary).

REFERENCES

American Psychological Association. (2009). *Effective strategies to support positive parenting in community health centers: Report of the Working Group on Child Maltreatment Prevention in Community Health Centers.* Washington, DC: Author.

Berg, B. L. (2001). *Qualitative research methods for the social sciences* (4th ed.). Needham Heights, MA: Allyn & Bacon.

Blanton, H., & Jaccard, J. (2006). Arbitrary metrics in psychology. *American Psychologist, 61,* 27–41. doi:10.1037/0003-066X.61.1.27

Denzin, N. K., & Lincoln, Y. S. (Eds.). (2005). *The Sage handbook of qualitative research* (3rd ed.). Thousand Oaks, CA: Sage.

Duncan, T. E., Duncan, S. C., & Strycker, L. A. (2006). *An introduction to latent variable growth curve modeling: Concepts, issues, and applications* (2nd ed.). Mahwah, NJ: Erlbaum.

Evans, C. H., & Ildstad, S. T. (2001). *Small clinical trials: Issues and challenges*. Washington, DC: National Academy Press.

Foster, E. M., & Kalil, A. (2008). New methods for new questions in developmental psychology. *Developmental Psychology, 44*, 201–304.

Fourth World Conference on Women (1995, September). *Beijing declaration and platform for action*. Beijing, China: Author. Retrieved from http://www.un.org/womenwatch/daw/beijing/platform/

Gershoff, E. T. (2002). Corporal punishment by parents associated with child behaviors and experiences: A meta-analytic and theoretical review. *Psychological Bulletin, 128*, 539–579. doi:10.1037/0033-2909.128.4.539

Henry, B., Moffitt, T. E., Caspi, A., Langley, J., & Silva, P. A. (1994). On the "remembrance of things past": A longitudinal evaluation of the retrospective method. *Psychological Assessment, 6*, 92–101. doi:10.1037/1040-3590.6.2.92

Kazdin, A. E. (2003). *Research design in clinical psychology* (4th ed.). Needham Heights, MA: Allyn & Bacon.

Kazdin, A.E. (2010). *Single-case research designs: Methods for clinical and applied settings* (2nd ed.). New York, NY: Oxford University Press.

Kazemian, L., & Farrington, D. P. (2005). Comparing the validity of prospective, retrospective, and official onset for different offending categories. *Journal of Quantitative Criminology, 21*, 127–147. doi:10.1007/s10940-005-2489-0

Kessler, R. C., & Merikangas, K. R. (2004). The National Comorbidity Survey Replication (NCS-R): Background and aims. *International Journal of Methods in Psychiatric Research, 13*, 60–68. doi:10.1002/mpr.166

Koss, M. P., & White, J. W. (2008). National and global agendas on violence against women: Historical perspective and consensus. *American Journal of Orthopsychiatry, 78*, 386–393. doi:10.1037/a0014347

Koss, M. P., White, J. W., & Kazdin, A. E. (Eds.). (2011). *Violence against women and children, Vol. 2: Navigating solutions*. Washington, DC: American Psychological Association.

Kraemer, H. C., Kazdin, A. E., Offord, D. R., Kessler, R. C., Jensen, P. S., & Kupfer, D. J. (1999). Measuring the potency of a risk factor for clinical or policy significance. *Psychological Methods, 4*, 257–271.

National Center for Injury Prevention and Control. (2009). *CDC injury research agenda, 2009–2018*. Atlanta, GA: U.S. Department of Health and Human Services, Centers for Disease Control and Prevention.

Rosenbaum, J. E. (2009). Patient teenagers? A comparison of the sexual behavior of virginity pledgers and matched nonpledgers. *Pediatrics, 123*, e110–e120. doi:10.1542/peds.2008-0407

Russo, N. F. (1985). *A women's mental health agenda*. Washington, DC: American Psychological Association.

United Nations. (2006). *World report on violence against children*. New York, NY: Author.

Whitaker, D. J., Lutzker, J. R., & Shelley, G. A. (2005). Child maltreatment prevention priorities at the Centers for Disease Control and Prevention. *Child Maltreatment, 10*, 245–259. doi:10.1177/1077559505274674

World Health Organization. (2009). *Violence prevention: The evidence*. Geneva, Switzerland: Author.

Yoshikawa, H., Weisner, T. S., Kalil, A., & Way, N. (2008). Mixing qualitative and quantitative research in developmental science: Uses and methodological choices. *Developmental Psychology, 44*, 344–354. doi:10.1037/0012-1649.44.2.344

INDEX

Antidepressants, 138
Antisocial behavior
    and ADHD, 137
    in maltreated children, 82
    prevention of, 141
    and sexually coercive behavior,
        130–131, 133
Antiviolence agendas, xvii–xviii
Anxiety
    in maltreated children, 81
    and sexual violence, 174
APA. *See* American Psychological
    Association
Archer, J., 212
Arousal, of abusive parents, 36–37
Asian women, domestic violence/IPV
    risk for, 205, 206, 247
Assault
    and alcohol/drug use, 183
    of children, 15, 19, 24
    sexual. *See* Sexual assault
    and vulnerability to sexual assault, 154
Assertiveness, sexual, 162
Assessments
    of child maltreatment, 87–89
    of sexually coercive behavior risk
        factors, 142–143
    of sexual violence, 185–186, 189
    of violence against women and
        children, 301–304
Attention-deficit/hyperactivity disorder
    (ADHD), 136, 137
Attitudes
    rape-supportive, 127
    of sexual assault perpetrators, 153
    of sexual assault victims, 155–156
    of sexually coercive men, 140
Attributes
    of perpetrators of violence. *See*
        Individual-level factors
    of sexually coercive men, 130–134
Attributions, of abusive mothers, 62
Avoidance, and sexual violence, 181

Bachman, R., 113
Back, S. E., 102
"Backlash" hypothesis of sexual assault,
    153
Banyard, V. L., 160, 161
Basile, K. C., 102, 111–112

Battering, 199, 268–269. *See also*
    Domestic violence
Beaver, K. M., 137
Becker-Blease, K. A., 68
Behavioral equivalence, 11
Behavioral health
    of maltreated children, 81–82
    and sexual violence, 181–184
    and violence against women and
        children, 292
Behavioral impulsivity, 131
Behavioral inhibition, 137
Behavioral Risk Factor Surveillance
    System, 202, 210, 245–247, 252
Behind Closed Doors (M. Straus, R.
    Gelles, & S. K. Steinmetz), 226
Beliefs, masculine ideological, 127
Bennett Cattaneo, L., 228
Benson, M., 206, 247
Bergman, B., 269
Berliner, L., 92
Betrayal trauma theory, 58, 60
Biases
    in child maltreatment reporting,
        88–89
    in Conflict Tactics Scale, 211
    cultural, 307
    positivity, 128
    in sexual assault reporting, 167
Biological antecedents, of sexually
    coercive behavior, 134–138
Biological functioning, of maltreated
    children, 83
Bishop, S. J., 39
BJS. *See* Bureau of Justice Statistics
Black, M. C., 274
Blended families, 64
Bowling, J. M., 117
Breiding, M. J., 274
Briere, J., 268, 277
Brismar, B., 269
Brodsky, S. L., 133
Brown, A. L., 162
Brownson, R. C., 245
Buck, P., 129
Bullock, L. F., 269
Bullying, 17, 19
Bureau of Justice Statistics (BJS),
    203, 210
Burgess, A., 231

Burke, J., 253
Bursik, R., 155
Bystander intervention, 160–161

Caetano, R., 247
Callousness–unemotionality (CU)
        scale, 131, 133–134, 140
Campbell, J. C., 228, 273
Canadian Violence Against Women
        Survey, 245
Cancer, 274
Caputo, A. A., 133
Caspi, A., 136, 137
Castro-Fernandez, M. C., 205, 206
Catlin, T. K., 245
Causality
    in sexually coercive behavior
            research, 138–139, 142–143
    in violence research, 296
Centers for Disease Control and Pre-
        vention (CDC), 102, 119, 199,
        202, 203, 209, 243
Cerce, D. D., 132–133
Chadwick Center, 92
Chaffin, M., 81
Change, theories of, 296
Chart review methods, 113–114
Chau, M., 162–163
Chen, J., 111–112, 245
Chen, Y.-H., 253
Cheung, M., 206
Chicago Child–Parent Centers
        program, 142
Chicago Women's Health Study, 228
Child abuse. *See also* Child victimiza-
        tion; Violence against women
        and children
    defined, 10, 31–32, 56, 61, 79
    impact of, 292
    and intimate partner violence,
            276–277
    prevalence of, 289
    prevention of, 36, 43–46, 70–72, 166
    protective factors for. *See* Protective
            factors for child abuse
    risk factors for. *See* Risk factors for
            child abuse perpetration
    scope of, 31–32
    tracking perpetrators of, 42
    vulnerability factors for. *See* Vulner-
            ability factors for child abuse

Child Behavior Checklist, 25
Child-care burden, 37
Childhood experience of violence,
        249–250, 256–257
Child maltreatment
    assessment of, 87–89
    criminality of, 11
    defined, 10, 11, 32, 56, 77–78
    economic costs of, 83–84
    outcomes of. *See* Child maltreatment
            outcomes
    and physical/psychological health of
            perpetrator, 38
    prevention of, 43–46
Child maltreatment outcomes, 77–92
    and assessment of maltreatment,
            87–89
    behavioral, 81–82
    in context of abuse and neglect,
            84–86
    definition and classification, 77–80
    economic costs in, 83–84
    mediators and moderators of, 86
    physical health, 82–83
    psychological, 80–81
    research on, 89–92
Child molesters, 133
Child neglect, 78–79. *See also* Neglect
Child physical abuse. *See also* Physical
        abuse
    defined, 78
    and intimate partner violence, 250
    and rape prevention, 142
    of sexually coercive men, 135
Child Physical and Sexual Abuse (B. E.
        Saunders, L. Berliner, & R. F.
        Hanson), 92
Child protection services (child
        protective services)
    assessments by, 87
    effectiveness of, 42
    reports from, 67–68
    treatment of racial/ethnic minorities
            by, 88–89
Child-rearing practices, child abuse and,
        39, 42–43
Children
    criminal offenses against, 10, 11
    desire for, of sexual violence
            survivors, 179

Children, *continued*
exposure to violence of, 89
perceptions of, by abusive parents, 40–41
poly-victimization and personal characteristics of, 23
presence of, and intimate partner violence, 250
resilience of, 46, 55, 68, 86
role of, in child abuse, 40
victimization of adults vs., 13, 19
violence by, 10–11
Child sexual abuse (CSA). *See also* Sexual abuse
defined, 78
and intimate partner violence, 250
and rape prevention, 142
of sexually coercive men, 134–135
and violent delinquency, 137
and vulnerability to sexual assault, 154, 156
Child victimization, 9–27
defined, 9–13
fragmentation in, 12–13
historical trends in, 23–26
poly-victims, 20–23
research on, 26–27
scope of, 14–20
Child welfare, 25–26, 42
Chronic disease, 274
Chronic violence victimization, 188. *See also* Revictimization
Cicchetti, D., 61
Clinton-Sherrod, A. M., 129
Closing the Quality Chasm in Child Abuse Treatment (Chadwick Center), 92
Cocaine, 249
Coding, in health care studies of sexual violence, 113–114
Coercion, sexual violence and, 102, 103. *See also* Risk factors for sexually coercive behavior
Coggins, M., 269
Cognitive functioning, of maltreated children, 81
Cognitive processing
by sexual assault victims, 176
by sexual violence survivors, 181, 188
Cohen, J., 114

Cohort studies, of intimate partner violence, 278
Coker, A. L., 253, 269
Collaboration, in violence research, 299
College students
in domestic violence studies, 212
interventions for sexually coercive, 142, 143
in sexual assault research, 165
in sexual violence studies, 109–110, 114–115
Commonwealth Fund Survey of Women's Health, 202, 207
Communities
child abuse prevention in, 46, 71
child abuse risk factors in, 34–36, 42, 48–49
and child maltreatment outcomes, 84–86
domestic violence risk factors in, 224
IPV risk factors in, 254
and poly-victimization condition, 22–23
Community-residing women, sexual assault research with, 165, 167
Community surveys, on child victimization, 26
Community violence, in neighborhood structure, 37
Comparison groups, in sexual violence research, 186
Compulsivity, of sexually coercive men, 133
COMT gene, 137
Concentration of risk, in child victimization, 21
Condition, victimization as, 22
Conflict, child abuse and, 41–42
Conflict Tactics Scale (CTS), 210, 211, 216, 256, 277
Consensus definition of violence, 300, 301
Consequences of sexual violence, 173–190
on behavioral health, 181–184
economic cost, 184–185
knowledge gaps on, 187–188
on physical health, 177–181
on psychological health, 174–177
research on, 185–190

Consequences of violence against
women and children, 294–295
Context, in sexual violence assessments,
186
Contraceptive use, IPV and, 254, 272,
276
Convenience samples, in sexual violence research, 186
Coordination of services, child abuse
and, 42
Coping resources and strategies
of child abuse perpetrators, 37–43
of sexual assault victims, 163, 176
Corporal punishment, 11–12, 17, 23,
43, 63. See also Discipline, child
abuse and
Crime
and child victimization, 10,
14–20, 24
reporting vs. occurrence of, 112
and vulnerability to sexual assault,
155
Criminal activity level, child maltreatment and, 86
Criminality
of behavior in sexual violence
studies, 116
of child victimization, 11
Criminal justice studies of sexual violence, 107–108, 112–113
Criminal offenses against children, 10, 11
Cross-sectional research
on effects of sexual violence, 186
on intimate partner violence, 257,
275, 276
on sexual assault, 164
Crowell, N., 231
CSA. See Child sexual abuse
CTS. See Conflict Tactics Scale
CTS2 (Revised Conflict Tactics Scale),
210–211
Cultural spillover theory, 152
Culture
and child abuse prevention, 45
and child abuse risk, 34, 42–43, 49,
66–67
and child maltreatment assessment/
intervention, 88–89
and definition of sexual violence,
116–118

and domestic violence risk, 204–207,
213–214, 227–228
and effects of child maltreatment, 78
and sexual assault risk, 152, 160
in violence research, 299, 307
CU scale. See Callousness–
unemotionality scale
Custodial interference, 15
Cycle of violence, 37, 61–62, 250

DAFR/IR. See Drug-Facilitated, Incapacitated, and Forcible Rape
National Study
Danielson, C. K., 110
Data analysis
in sexual violence research, 111–115
in violence research, 297, 299, 301,
304–306
Data collection
in domestic violence research,
213–214, 216
in sexual violence research, 117–120
DAT gene, 137
Death
as result of domestic violence/child
victimization. See Homicide
sexual assault-related, 177–178, 187
Definitional issues
with child maltreatment, 56–57,
77–80
with child victimization, 9–13
with domestic violence, 209–210
with violence against women and
children, 297, 300–301
Delinquency, violent, 137
Demographic factors
in domestic violence perpetration,
223
in domestic violence risk, 206, 213
in effects of sexual violence, 177,
181, 184, 188
in vulnerability to IPV, 244–245, 255
in vulnerability to sexual assault,
158–159
Dependency, of children, 13
Depression
and intimate partner violence,
268–269
and serotonin transporter gene in
boys, 137
and sexual violence, 174

McDonnell, K., 253
McFall, R. M., 128
McFarlane, J., 205, 251–252
Measurements, in violence research,
    297–298
Measure of impact, for intimate partner
    violence, 277
Mediators, of child maltreatment
    outcomes, 86
Medical records, in sexual violence
    studies, 114
Men, high-risk, 223–224
Mental health
    of domestic violence perpetrators,
        223
    and effects of IPV, 268–270,
        277–278
    of maltreated children, 83
    and risk of child abuse, 45, 85
    and risk of IPV, 254
    and vulnerability to sexual assault,
        156–157
Messman-Moore, T. L., 162
Meta-analyses
    in domestic violence research, 225
    in IPV research, 258
    in sexual violence research, 118
Methadone use, IPV risk and, 249
Methodological issues, with violence
    research, 296–299
Mexican Americans, domestic violence/
    IPV risk for, 227–228, 248
Mexicans, domestic violence perpetra-
    tion by, 227
MIDSA. See Multidimensional Inven-
    tory of Development, Sex, and
    Aggression
Military veterans, sexual violence
    research on, 174, 179, 180, 182
Miller, A. G., 162
Milner, J. S., 62
Minnesota Longitudinal Study, 87–88
Minority groups, domestic violence
    research for, 204–207, 213
Moderators
    of child maltreatment outcomes, 86
    of domestic violence, 225
Modularization, in violence research,
    301
Monoamine neurotransmitters, 136, 137

Montgomery, M J., 273
Moore, T. M., 249
Moracco, K. E., 117
Mosher, D. L., 127
Mothers, abusive, 37–39, 41, 62
Moves, frequency of, 35
Moynihan, M. M., 160
Multi-Country Study on Women's
    Health and Domestic Violence
    Against Women, 200, 216
Multidimensional Inventory of Devel-
    opment, Sex, and Aggression
    (MIDSA), 127, 129–130, 132
Multilevel rape prevention strategies,
    141
Multivariate analyses, of intimate
    partner violence, 244–245
Murnen, S. K., 127

NAFVS. See National Alcohol and
    Family Violence Survey
Najdowski, C. J., 158, 163
National agenda, for violence against
    women and children, 288
National Alcohol and Family Violence
    Survey (NAFVS), 201, 203, 207,
    213, 227
National Child Abuse and Neglect Data
    System (NCANDS), 26, 59–61,
    78, 79
National Child Traumatic Stress
    Network (NCTSN), 90–92
National Committee for Prevention of
    Child Abuse, 62
National Comorbidity Study, 303–304
National Crime Survey, 108
National Crime Victimization Survey
    (NCVS), 293
    child victimization data in, 14–20, 26
    domestic violence data in, 201, 203,
        210
    sexual assault data in, 158
    sexual violence data in, 105, 107,
        108, 112–113
National Data Archive on Child Abuse
    and Neglect, 90
National Electronic Injury Surveillance
    System–All Injury Program
    (NEISS-AIP), 106, 108–109,
    113, 114

National Family Violence Survey, 201, 203, 207
National health surveillance systems, 189
National Hospital Ambulatory Medical Care Survey (NHAMCS), 106, 108, 113–114
National Institute of Child Abuse and Neglect, 71
National Partnership to End Interpersonal Violence, xix
National Research Council, 231–232
National Survey of Adolescents (NSA), 110
National Survey of Children Exposed to Violence (NatSCEV), 14, 18, 19
National Survey of Families and Households, 247
National surveys, on domestic violence, 200–204, 209–210, 213, 215
National Violence Against Women Survey (NVAWS)
    domestic violence data in, 201, 204, 210, 213
    IPV data in, 245, 268
    sexual assault data in, 158
    sexual violence data in, 113, 178, 182
National Violent Death Reporting System, 178
National Women's Study, 178, 179, 183
Native Alaskan women, domestic violence risk for, 207, 247
NCANDS. See National Child Abuse and Neglect Data System
NCTSN (National Child Traumative Stress Network), 90–92
NCVS. See National Crime Victimization Survey
Negative masculinity, 140
Neglect
    age as moderator of, 59–60
    child victimization rates for, 15
    defined, 61, 78–79
    gender as moderator of, 57
    and stress, 31, 32, 63
    and substance abuse, 38
Neighborhood cohesion, child maltreatment and, 86
Neighborhoods
    child abuse risk factors in, 34
    child abuse vulnerability factors in, 64–65

IPV risk factors in, 247
    poly-victimization risk factors in, 22–23
Neighborhood structure, child abuse and, 36–37
Neighbors, C., 158
NEISS-AIP. See National Electronic Injury Surveillance System–All Injury Program
Neurotransmitters, monoamine, 136, 137
New Zealand prospective birth cohort study, 249, 256
NHAMCS. See National Hospital Ambulatory Medical Care Survey
Nigoff, A., 162–163
Noncrime victimizations, 10–11
Noncriminal juvenile crime equivalents, 10–11
Nosek, M. A., 252
NSA (National Survey of Adolescents), 110
NVAWS. See National Violence Against Women Survey

Obesity, 273
O'Campo, P., 253
O'Leary, K. D., 226–227
O'Leary, S. G., 226–227
Online victimization, 17
Orme, T. C., 63
Outcomes
    of child maltreatment victims. See Child maltreatment outcomes
    of intimate partner violence victims. See Health outcomes of intimate partner violence
    of poly-victims, 21–22
    of sexual violence victims, 129. See also Consequences of sexual violence
Overperception of sexual intent, 128

Pan, S., 273
Pandemic victimizations, 19
Parental monitoring, sexual assault and, 159
Parent management training, 142
Parent reports, of child abuse, 68
Parents, vulnerability factors for child abuse by, 61–64

Parish, W. L., 273
Parks, K. A., 157
Part I crimes, 112
Part II crimes, 112
Past-year prevalence measures, 117
Path confluence model of sexual
        aggression, 131–132
PCL-R. *see* Psychopathy Checklist—
        Revised
Penn, C. E., 225, 243
Perceived support, child abuse and, 35
Perceptions
        of sexual assault victims, 155
        of sexually coercive men, 128, 140
Perinatal death, IPV and, 272–273
Period prevalence, lifetime vs., 103
Perpetration
        of child abuse, 63–64. *See also*
                Risk factors for child abuse
                perpetration
        of domestic violence. *See* Risk
                factors for domestic violence
                perpetration
        of sexual assault, 164–166
        of sexually coercive behavior. *See*
                Risk factors for sexually
                coercive behavior
        of violence against women and chil-
                dren, 293–294
Perpetrator–victim relationship
        and child maltreatment, 57–58, 60
        and sexual violence, 175–176
Personal adjustment of child abuse
        perpetrators, 37–43
        community level, 42
        as determinant of health, 48
        family level, 41–42
        individual level, 37–41
        societal/cultural level, 42–43
Personality factors, sexual assault and,
        166
Perspective taking, by abusive parents, 40
Peterson, C., 250
Physical abuse
        adult risk factors for, 248–249
        childhood risk factors for, 31–32, 57
        in child victimization rates, 15, 23–24
        defined, 32
        and domestic violence, 200, 203
        and vulnerability to sexual assault, 154

Physical assault, of children, 15, 19, 24
Physical disabilities
        and child abuse, 60–61
        and intimate partner violence,
                251–252
Physical environment
        and child abuse perpetration, 36–37
        as determinant of health, 47
Physical health
        of abusive parents, 38–39
        and effects of IPV, 271–274, 278
        and effects of sexual violence,
                177–181
        and effects of violence, 294–295
        of maltreated children, 82–83
        and risk of IPV, 254
Physical violence
        and mental health, 268–269
        risk factors for, 226
Pincus, J. H., 135
Plante, E. G., 160
Poincaré, Jules Henri, 221, 229
Policies
        on child abuse, 67–71
        on sexual assault, 166–168
Poly-victims, 20–23
Pornography use
        and sexual assault, 152
        and sexually coercive behavior,
                129–130, 140
Positive distancing coping strategies,
        176
Positivity bias, 128
Posttraumatic stress disorder (PTSD)
        and child maltreatment, 81
        and intimate partner violence, 268
        and sexual assault, 177
        and sexual violence, 174–176, 181
        and victimization, 22
Potency, of domestic violence risk
        factors, 225
Poverty, child abuse/maltreatment and,
        33, 64–65, 67–68
Power differentials, 294
Pregnancy
        and intimate partner violence,
                250–251, 257, 271–273
        and sexual violence, 179, 188
Pregnancy Risk Assessment Monitoring
        System, 250

Prentky, R. A., 132
Presidential Summit on Violence and
Abuse in Relationships, xviii–xix
Prevalence, period vs. lifetime, 103
Prevalence of child victimization. *See*
Child victimization
Prevalence of domestic violence,
199–216, 289–290
national surveys on, 200–204
research on, 209–216
in specific communities, 204–208
and theoretical/philosophical
stances, 208–209
Prevalence of sexual violence,
101–120, 289
analysis of data on, 111–115
contemporary findings, 104–110
data collection recommendations,
117–120
definitions associated with, 102–104
incidence vs., 103
knowledge gaps about, 115–117
Prevalence of violence against women
and children, 289–290, 293
Prevent Child Abuse in America 2007, 84
Prevention
of antisocial behavior, 141
of child abuse, 36, 43–46, 70–72, 166
of domestic violence, 230, 231,
234–235
of rape, 141–143
of sexual assault, 160–161, 166–167
of violence, xv
Prior victimization, sexual assault and,
154, 156, 157, 167
Problem drinking. *See also* Alcohol
abuse/use
and intimate partner violence,
270–271
and sexual assault, 158
Probst, D. R., 162–163
Prospective studies of intimate partner
violence, 258
Protective factors for child abuse, 46,
55–72, 86
analysis of literature on, 67–68
definitions of, 56–57
environment and social factors,
64–67
research and policies on, 69–71

Protective factors for domestic violence,
234–236
Protective factors for intimate partner
violence
education, 252
research on, 257–258
social support, 253–254
Protective factors for sexual assault,
159–168
funding and policies for, 166–168
macro level, 160
meso level, 160–161
micro level, 161–163
research on, 164–166
Protective factors for violence against
women and children, 290–291,
294, 296
Proxy measures, 304
Psychiatric medications, child welfare
and, 25
Psychological abuse (psychological
maltreatment), 15, 79
Psychological aggression, 248, 249,
269–270
Psychological functioning, of domestic
violence perpetrators, 223
Psychological growth, sexual violence
and, 177
Psychological health
of abusive parents, 38–39
of maltreated children, 80–81
of sexual violence survivors,
174–177
of women and children, 292, 294,
295
Psychology of Violence, xix
Psychopathy, sexually coercive behavior
and, 130–131
Psychopathy Checklist—Revised
(PCL-R), 131, 133–134
Psychopathy Screening Device, 133
PsycINFO, 267
PTSD. *See* Posttraumatic stress disorder
Public health
and child abuse prevention, 43, 44
and child victimization, 26–27
and violence against women and
children, xiii–xv
PubMed, 267
Puerto Ricans, IPV risk for, 251

Risk factors for child abuse perpetration, 31–49, 290
  and determinants of health, 47–48
  education, 36
  income and social status, 33–34
  levels of action, 48–49
  and personal adjustment/coping resources, 37–43
  physical environment, 36–37
  prevention and interventions for, 45–46
  research on, 44
  scope and definition of child abuse, 31–32
  social support networks, 35
Risk factors for domestic violence perpetration, 221–237, 291
  communities/societies, high-risk, 224
  and definition of domestic violence, 222
  ethnic and cultural variability, 227–228
  interrelatedness of, 225–227
  interventionist framework for, 232, 234–237
  men, high-risk, 223–224
  potency of, 225
  and prediction of reabuse/femicide, 228–229
  relationships, high-risk, 224
  research on, 229–233
Risk factors for rape, 126–130
Risk factors for sexually coercive behavior, 125–143, 249
  attributes and dispositional characteristics, 130–134
  defined, 126
  developmental and biological antecedents, 134–138
  and rape prevention, 141–143
  research on, 138–140
  and risk factors for rape, 126–130
Risk factors for violence perpetration, 290–291, 293–294, 296
Risk perception, sexual assault and, 156, 157, 162
Risk-taking behaviors (risky behaviors)
  and effects of intimate partner violence, 270–271
  of sexual violence survivors, 115, 183–184

of victims of violence, 294
and vulnerability to sexual assault, 156
Robbery, child victims of, 15, 19
Rogosch, F. A., 61
Ronis, S. T., 132
Runyan, C. W., 117
Rural areas, sexual assault in, 152

Safety, home, 36
Saltzman, L. E., 245
Same-gender (same-sex) relationships. See also Sexual orientation (sexual preference)
  domestic violence in, 208, 222
  intimate partner violence in, 246
Sampling
  in domestic violence research, 212, 215
  in sexual violence research, 118, 119, 186, 189
  in violence research, 298, 305–306
Sanday, P. R., 160
Saunders, B. E., 92
Schemas, of maltreated children, 86
Schumacher, J. A., 225
Second Injury Control and Risk Survey (ICARIS-2), 104, 105, 111
Self-blame, sexual assault and, 176
Self-defense, and sexual assault, 162–163
Self-destructive behavior, of maltreated children, 81, 82
Self-protection, and sexual assault, 161
Self-report(s)
  of child maltreatment, 87–88
  of effects of sexual violence, 185, 186
  in intimate partner violence research, 276
  of psychopathy and sexuality, 138
  in violence research, 302–303
Serotonin transporter gene, 136–137
Severity of sexual violence, psychological effect and, 175
Sex, forced, 111–112
Sex offenders, 131–135
Sexual abuse
  adult risk factors for, 248, 249
  childhood risk factors for, 57, 58, 60, 66
  in child victimization rates, 15, 18

Thompson, M. P., 245
Tjaden, P., 205, 246, 247
Tobacco use, by sexual violence
 survivors, 183
Torres, S., 251
Trauma history, sexual assault and, 155
Trauma theory, 89
Treat, T. A., 128
Tritt, D., 225, 243
Tubman, J. G., 273
Turchik, J. A., 162–163
Two-path confluence model of sexual
 aggression, 131–132, 135

UCR Program. *See* Uniform Crime
 Reporting Program
Ullman, S. E., 158, 163
Unemployment, child abuse and, 34.
 See also Employment
Uniform Crime Reporting (UCR)
 Program, 105, 107, 112, 293
Unintended pregnancies, 271–272
University of New Hampshire National
 Research Laboratory, 203, 210
Unsafe sex behaviors, 183–184. *See also*
 Risk-taking behaviors (risky
 behaviors)
Urban areas, sexual assault in, 152
Urquiza, A., 66
U.S. Census, 247
U.S. Children's Bureau, 26
U.S. Consumer Product Safety
 Commission, 108

Validity
 of domestic violence research,
  212–213
 of sexual violence research, 114–116
 of violence research, 303
Vankos, N., 253
Verbal abuse
 defined, 79
 as domestic violence, 203, 209–210
 during pregnancy, 251
 risk factors for, 248
 of sexually coercive men, 135
Vest, J. R., 245, 255
Victimization. *See also* Child
 victimization
 of adults vs. children, 13, 19

corporal punishment as, 11–12
defined, 10–11
as event vs. condition, 22
multiple/poly-victimization, 20–23
pandemic, acute, and extraordinary,
 19
sexual assault and prior, 154, 156,
 157, 167
of women and children, 293–295
Victimization surveys, 119
Victimology, developmental, 10, 13. *See
 also* Child victimization
Victim surveys, of sexual violence,
 112–113
Vilken, R. J., 128
Violence
 child abuse as predictor of future, 45
 childhood experience of, 249–250,
  256–257
 community, 37
 corporal punishment as, 11–12
 cycle of, 37, 61–62, 250
 defined, 9
 history of, 223, 224
 life-span and longitudinal perspectives on, 295
 prevention of, xv
 as public health problem, xiv–xv
 repeated exposure to, 61
 research on, xvii–xix
 risk factors for perpetration of,
  226–227
 socioecological model of, xiv–xv
 women as perpetrators of, 209
Violence Against Women Act, 101, 288
Violence against women and children,
 287–308
 assessment issues, 301–304
 conclusions about, 288–292
 consequences of, 294–295
 cultural issues, 307
 definitional issues, 300–301
 knowledge gaps, 299–300
 life-span and longitudinal
  perspective on, 295
 methodological issues, 296–299
 prevalence, 293
 as public health problem, xiii–xv
 research on, 304–308
 risk and protective factors, 293–294,
  296

ABOUT THE EDITORS

Jacquelyn W. White, PhD, is a professor of psychology and associate for research in the College of Arts and Sciences at the University of North Carolina at Greensboro. Her research focuses on gender issues, aggression, and intimate partner violence. Dr. White has conducted research in the area of aggression and violence for more than 30 years. She is a past editor of the *Psychology of Women Quarterly* and is on the board of editors for the journal *Aggressive Behavior*. She was the 2008 recipient of the Carolyn Wood Sherif Award, given by the Society for the Psychology of Women. She currently cochairs the National Partnership to End Interpersonal Violence.

Mary P. Koss, PhD, is a Regents' professor in the Mel and Enid Zuckerman Arizona College of Public Health at the University of Arizona, Tucson. She has served on the National Academy of Sciences Panel on Violence Against Women and currently sits on the Coordinating Committee of the Sexual Violence Research Initiative, funded by the Global Forum and the Ford Foundation, based in Johannesburg, South Africa. She is a member of the Department of Defense Rapid Research Response Team on children, youth, and families. She consults nationally with the Gallup Organization on sexual assault prevalence and response in the military justice system. She recently served as *rapporteur* on gender-based violence at the fourth Milestones of a Global Campaign for Violence Prevention in Geneva, Switzerland. She received the Award for Distinguished Contributions to Research in Public Policy in 2000, the Committee on Women in Psychology Leadership Award in 2003, and a presidential citation in 2008 from the American Psychological Association. In 2010, she was the eighth recipient of the Visionary Award from Ending Violence Against Women International (Vice President Joe Biden was the first).

Alan E. Kazdin, PhD, is the John M. Musser Professor of Psychology and Child Psychiatry at Yale University, New Haven, Connecticut, and Director of the Yale Parenting Center and Child Conduct Clinic, an outpatient treatment service for children and families. Before coming to Yale, he was on the faculty of The Pennsylvania State University, State College, and the University of Pittsburgh School of Medicine, Pittsburgh, Pennsylvania. At Yale, he has been chairman of the Psychology Department, director of the Yale Child Study Center at the School of Medicine, and director of Child Psychiatric Services, Yale–New Haven Hospital. In 2008, he was President of the American Psychological Association. He has authored or edited more than 650 articles, chapters, and books. His 45 books focus on child and adolescent psychotherapy, parenting, and aggressive and antisocial behavior. His work has been featured on television (e.g., *Good Morning America*, *Primetime*, *20/20*, and PBS) as well as in articles on parenting challenges in *Slate.com*.